Discovering Christ In Acts

Discovering Christ

In

The Acts Of The Apostles

Donald S. Fortner

Go *publications*

Go Publications
Gibb Hill Farm, Ponsonby, Cumbria, CA20 1BX, ENGLAND

© Go Publications 2017 New Edition
First Published 1995 Life After Pentecost (Evangelical Press)

British Library Cataloguing in Publication Data available

ISBN 978-1-908475-06-0

*Printed and bound in Great Britain
By Lightning Source UK Ltd.*

Dedicated to:

Faithful preachers of the gospel
who follow in the Apostles' footsteps
as they followed their Lord

Contents

Foreword

On the day of Pentecost the apostle Peter made certain everyone knew that even though Christ's apostles were preaching, it was the exalted Lord Jesus Christ who "hath shed forth this, which ye now see and hear". We know Luke's inspired writing as "The Acts Of The Apostles". But as Peter declared, it is truly the acts of our resurrected sovereign King working through His apostles.

Therefore, when I heard the second edition of Pastor Don Fortner's commentary on Acts would be re-titled "Discovering Christ In The Acts Of The Apostles" my first thought was it could not have a more appropriate title. The reader will find that whether dealing with the ascension, the pouring out of the Holy Spirit on the day of Pentecost or subjects such as, *What Happens When A Church Member Falls?*, Christ and Him crucified is the message proclaimed in every passage.

Unlike many commentaries on Acts, this commentary was written as Pastor Fortner preached through the book. It was purposely written simply and clearly so that anyone can read it. Every person taught of God will benefit from using this commentary as they carefully look up the scriptural references. For the preacher there are chapters such as *A Lesson In Preaching The Gospel, Preachers And Their Hearers, The Message Of The Gospel* and *A Sermon That Cost A Preacher His Life*. Believers will be instructed on subjects of prayer, persecution, Christian graces, and faithfulness. Whether it is a sinner God is drawing to Christ for the first time or a child of grace whom God has preserved in faith for years, whatever the subject, the reader will discover who Christ is, why He came, what He accomplished, where He is and what He is doing now.

It has been thirty years since God first made the path of the author of this commentary to cross with mine. Since that time every sermon I have heard him preach and every word I have read from his pen has faithfully exalted Christ, giving the Triune God all the glory in the salvation of chosen sinners. This commentary is no exception. May God be pleased to make it as beneficial to the reader who now holds it in their hands as He has to me.

Clay Curtis
Pastor of Sovereign Grace Baptist Church
Princeton, New Jersey

Acts 1:1 The former treatise have I made, O Theophilus, of all that Jesus began both to do and teach,

Acts 1:2 Until the day in which he was taken up, after that he through the Holy Ghost had given commandments unto the apostles whom he had chosen:

Acts 1:3 To whom also he shewed himself alive after his passion by many infallible proofs, being seen of them forty days, and speaking of the things pertaining to the kingdom of God:

Acts 1:4 And, being assembled together with them, commanded them that they should not depart from Jerusalem, but wait for the promise of the Father, which, saith he, ye have heard of me.

Acts 1:5 For John truly baptized with water; but ye shall be baptized with the Holy Ghost not many days hence.

Acts 1:6 When they therefore were come together, they asked of him, saying, Lord, wilt thou at this time restore again the kingdom to Israel?

Acts 1:7 And he said unto them, It is not for you to know the times or the seasons, which the Father hath put in his own power.

Acts 1:8 But ye shall receive power, after that the Holy Ghost is come upon you: and ye shall be witnesses unto me both in Jerusalem, and in all Judaea, and in Samaria, and unto the uttermost part of the earth.

Chapter 1

'Ye shall be witnesses unto me'

Acts 1:1-8

The book of Acts is an inspired history of the apostolic ministry of the early church, covering a period of thirty to thirty-five years. The central theme throughout the book is the ascension and lordship of Jesus Christ. It was written by Luke, who was also the author of the gospel narrative bearing his name. Acts begins where the Gospel of Luke ends, with the ascension of Christ. It is a history of the church of Christ in its infancy, showing God's constant care and special providence for it. In these first verses five important lessons are set before us.

1. The Lord Jesus Christ is the only lawgiver in his church (1:1, 2)

Luke makes a connection between his Gospel and the book of Acts. Both were written specifically for a man named Theophilus (Luke 1:3), a man of rank and honour. Not many noble are called (1 Corinthians 1:26), but some are. God has chosen some of all ranks. Theophilus means either 'lover of God' or 'loved of God'.

Luke describes his Gospel as 'a treatise ... of all that Jesus began both to do and teach, until the day in which he was taken up'. Though they did not record every word and deed of Christ (John 21:25), Luke and the other Gospel writers did record all that the Holy Spirit inspired, all that we need to know — particularly all that Christ did and said relating to the salvation of his people: his obedience to God, his conformity to the law, and his death as our substitute, by which he brought in everlasting righteousness and obtained eternal redemption for us.

Christ gave his commandments by the Holy Spirit to chosen apostles, and by them to his church. All the doctrines and ordinances, faith and practice of the church are, by the commandment of Christ, laid down in the Word of God (2 Timothy 3:16).

13

2. Our Lord Jesus gave many infallible proofs of his resurrection from the dead (1:3)

Our Saviour appeared to his disciples many times, publicly and privately, giving irrefutable proof of his resurrection (1 Corinthians 15:1-8). He spent forty days on the earth after his resurrection, eating and drinking, walking and talking with his disciples, showing them his hands and side and teaching them things concerning the kingdom of God. The testimony of those honest men and women who saw the risen Christ cannot be rejected except by those who are wilfully ignorant.

3. The gift of the Holy Spirit is the promise of the Father (1:4, 5)

There are thousands of promises in the Bible, but only the promise of the Spirit is called 'the promise of the Father'. God the Father promised that he would pour out his Spirit upon all flesh in the last day (Joel 2:28), and Christ promised his disciples the gift of the Spirit from the Father (John 14:16; 15:26; 16:7; 7:37-39; Galatians 3:13, 14).

4. Even the most gifted and useful men in the world are only fallible men and are sometimes confused (1:6, 7)

The apostles asked, 'Lord, wilt thou at this time restore again the kingdom to Israel?' They were curious about the fulfilment of prophecy. They did not yet understand the spiritual nature of Christ's kingdom. These were faithful, believing men, loyal to Christ; but they were only men. Being men, they were confused about the kingdom of Christ. We learn two things from verse 6.

First, there are no infallible men in this world! The apostles themselves were not infallible. They wrote the Holy Scriptures by the infallible direction of God the Holy Spirit (2 Peter 1:21). What they wrote is the infallible, inerrant Word of God. But the apostles themselves were just men, sinners saved by grace!

Secondly, we ought to be patient and forbearing with one another's faults, weaknesses and failures. Our Lord did not show the least bit of anger towards his erring disciples. Certainly we should be as kind to one another (Ephesians 4:32).

The lesson of verse 7 is one we need often to be reminded of; there are some things God does not intend us to know! No one on earth knows when Christ will come again, or when the end of the world will be. Indeed, there are many things known only to God. We must never pry into that which God has not revealed (Deuteronomy 29:29). We are to search the Scriptures, studying the Word of God, that we might know those things he has revealed concerning himself, us, his Son and his salvation.

5. Our Lord plainly tells us what is the lifelong work and responsibility of every believer (1:8)

'Ye shall be witnesses unto me' (Isaiah 43:10, 12; 44:8; Luke 24:48). Notice two things in this eighth verse:

'Ye shall receive power after that the Holy Ghost is come upon you.' Without question, this refers to the special, apostolic power that came upon those men chosen to be our Lord's apostles. Yet it certainly has meaning for us today. No one can ever be saved, serve God, or lay down his life in the cause of Christ as his witness until the life-giving power of the Holy Spirit comes upon him in regeneration. 'Salvation is of the Lord!' It is by God's grace alone (Romans 11:6; Ephesians 2:8, 9).

When the life-giving power of the Holy Spirit comes upon you, the Son of God says, 'Ye shall be witnesses unto me.' A witness is one who accurately and honestly relates to others that which he has heard with his own ears, seen with his own eyes, and felt and experienced in his own heart. He does not relate second-hand information. He declares only what he himself knows to be true (1 John 1:1-3). It is the privilege, responsibility and honour of every believer to be a witness for Christ in his generation. This is every believer's calling and vocation in this world. Every true Christian is a missionary. Every true believer is an evangelist. Every true follower of Christ is a preacher. Every true child of God is his witness. The Greek word for 'witness' is the one from which we get the word 'martyr'. Christ's witnesses are his martyrs, people who lay down their lives in the cause of Christ! Go ahead and work at your job, so that you can pay the expenses of life; but do not forget that your calling, your life's work, is to be his witness. Let nothing interfere with that!

Acts 1:9 And when he had spoken these things, while they beheld, he was taken up; and a cloud received him out of their sight.

Acts 1:10 And while they looked stedfastly toward heaven as he went up, behold, two men stood by them in white apparel;

Acts 1:11 Which also said, Ye men of Galilee, why stand ye gazing up into heaven? this same Jesus, which is taken up from you into heaven, shall so come in like manner as ye have seen him go into heaven.

Chapter 2

'This same Jesus'

Acts 1:9-11

These three verses of Holy Scripture are both solemn and delightful, instructive and practical. They speak of the glorious ascension and second advent of our Lord Jesus Christ. Having finished his work upon the earth (John 19:30), our Lord Jesus, the God-man, ascended into heaven and assumed his rightful place upon the throne of God, as King of kings and Lord of lords (John 17:1-5; Romans 14:9; Philippians 2:5-11; Hebrews 1:3; 10:12-14). In the same way, when he has finished his work in heaven, our Saviour will come again to this earth in power and great glory (Revelation 1:7; 19:11-17; 1 Thessalonians 4:13-18; 2 Thessalonians 1:8-10; John 14:1-3). Here are four things that are of paramount importance.

1. The Lord Jesus Christ has ascended into heaven

'And when he had spoken these things, while they beheld, he was taken up; and a cloud received him out of their sight' (1:9; Luke 24:50-52). What is the meaning of the ascension? Why was the Lord Jesus taken up into heaven? What happened to the Son of God when he went back to glory clothed in human flesh? What is he doing in heaven? All these questions are plainly answered in the Word of God. Read the answers for yourself (Psalm 2:6-8; 68:17-20; 110:1-4; Isaiah 53:10-12; John 16:7; Acts 2:25-36; 4:11, 12; 5:30-32; Ephesians 4:8-12; Philippians 2:5-11; Hebrews 10:12-14).

Christ Jesus ascended back into heaven to claim his rightful place as King of the universe (Daniel 7:13, 14). The Father's reward to the Son for his mediatorial obedience as our substitute is dominion over all things (Psalm 2:8). God the Father has put all things into the hands of, and under the rule of, Jesus Christ, the God-man. In heaven the Son of God is carrying on his great intercessory work as our Advocate and High Priest. Entering into heaven with his own blood, he sat down upon the throne of God, having

17

obtained eternal redemption for us (Hebrews 9:12). By virtue of that blood he offers continual intercession for his redeemed people (Romans 8:34; 1 John 2:1, 2). And through the virtue of his blood all the blessings of grace are bestowed upon God's elect (Ephesians 1:3-6).

The exalted Christ has claimed and taken possession of heaven as the forerunner of his people (Hebrews 6:14, 16-20). He has claimed all the inheritance of heaven's glory for all God's elect, for all for whom his blood was shed, for all who will believe on him.

Our Saviour took his place upon the throne of glory to secure the everlasting salvation of all his redeemed ones. He reigns in life to save those he purchased in death (Romans 5:10). He rules all things for the salvation of his people (John 17:2; Romans 8:28). In a word, Christ has gone to prepare a place in the Father's house for all his adopted sons and daughters, and he will bring them there.

2. The Lord Jesus Christ is coming again

'And while they looked stedfastly toward heaven as he went up, behold two men stood by them in white apparel; which also said, Ye men of Galilee, why stand ye gazing up into heaven? This same Jesus, which is taken up from you into heaven, shall so come in like manner as ye have seen him go into heaven' (1:10, 11). God sent two angels with this word of promise to his beloved children upon the earth, so that we might constantly live in anticipation of it — Christ is coming again! This promise ought to cheer our hearts, enliven our souls and encourage our hope. God has not told us when Christ is coming. He does not intend us to know the time of our Lord's appearing. But the second advent of Christ is a matter of certainty. It should be, to every believer, a matter of imminent expectancy (Hebrews 9:26-28; Zechariah 14:4, 5, 9; Matthew 16:27; 24:27; John 14:1-3; Philippians 3:20; 1 Thessalonians 4:16; 2 Timothy 4:8; Titus 2:13; James 5:7, 8; Jude 14; Revelation 1:7; 22:20). Here are four things revealed in the Scriptures about the Lord's coming:

1. It will be a personal, bodily advent (Revelation 1:7).
2. It will be a glorious appearing (2 Thessalonians 1:7-10).
3. It will be the consummation of our salvation (Romans 13:11; Ephesians 1:14).
4. Our Lord will appear suddenly, without warning, as a thief in the night (1 Thessalonians 5:1-6).

18

3. Our Lord's second advent will be the climactic consummation of God's eternal purpose (3:19-21; 1 Corinthians 15:24-28)

From a careful reading of the Scriptures it appears that once our Lord Jesus appears in his second advent everything after that will happen with great speed. With great swiftness, the Lord God will wrap up his work among men. The resurrection of the dead, the judgment, the conflagration of the earth and the new creation, the final separation of the righteous and the wicked — all seem to take place in a matter of moments!

There will be a general resurrection (John 5:28, 29). The dead will be raised. The living saints will be changed, translated in a moment and gathered out of the earth. All men will stand before God and be judged by him. According to the strict standards of inflexible justice, everyone will receive exactly what is his due. The righteous, made righteous by grace, will inherit glory. The wicked will be cast into hell.

There will be a great regeneration (2 Peter 3:9-14). Our God will indeed make all things new! There will be a new heavens and a new earth where nothing dwells but righteousness!

There will be a global reconciliation (Revelation 5:13). The Lord God will demonstrate to all creation how that all creation has served his purpose and brought glory to him.

Then there will be a glorious rest (Hebrews 4:9). The triune God and all the countless multitude of his elect will enter into an eternal sabbath. In heaven's glory we shall rest from all our troubles and from all our works. There we shall worship our God perfectly, serve him without labour and love him completely!

4. The one who is coming for us is 'this same Jesus'!

The angelic messengers assure us that our Lord will never forget his people. The one coming to bring us home to glory is the very same Jesus who died to redeem us. 'This same Jesus', who is full of love and sympathy, who brought in everlasting righteousness, who has gone into heaven for us, who now appears in the presence of God for us, who sits upon the throne of universal dominion, ruling all things for us, 'This same Jesus' is coming again!

Acts 1:12 Then returned they unto Jerusalem from the mount called Olivet, which is from Jerusalem a sabbath day's journey.

Acts 1:13 And when they were come in, they went up into an upper room, where abode both Peter, and James, and John, and Andrew, Philip, and Thomas, Bartholomew, and Matthew, James the son of Alphaeus, and Simon Zelotes, and Judas the brother of James.

Acts 1:14 These all continued with one accord in prayer and supplication, with the women, and Mary the mother of Jesus, and with his brethren.

Acts 1:15 And in those days Peter stood up in the midst of the disciples, and said, (the number of names together were about an hundred and twenty,)

Acts 1:16 Men and brethren, this scripture must needs have been fulfilled, which the Holy Ghost by the mouth of David spake before concerning Judas, which was guide to them that took Jesus.

Acts 1:17 For he was numbered with us, and had obtained part of this ministry.

Acts 1:18 Now this man purchased a field with the reward of iniquity; and falling headlong, he burst asunder in the midst, and all his bowels gushed out.

Acts 1:19 And it was known unto all the dwellers at Jerusalem; insomuch as that field is called in their proper tongue, Aceldama, that is to say, The field of blood.

Acts 1:20 For it is written in the book of Psalms, Let his habitation be desolate, and let no man dwell therein: and his bishoprick let another take.

Acts 1:21 Wherefore of these men which have companied with us all the time that the Lord Jesus went in and out among us,

Acts 1:22 Beginning from the baptism of John, unto that same day that he was taken up from us, must one be ordained to be a witness with us of his resurrection.

Acts 1:23 And they appointed two, Joseph called Barsabas, who was surnamed Justus, and Matthias.

Acts 1:24 And they prayed, and said, Thou, Lord, which knowest the hearts of all men, shew whether of these two thou hast chosen,

Acts 1:25 That he may take part of this ministry and apostleship, from which Judas by transgression fell, that he might go to his own place.

Acts 1:26 And they gave forth their lots; and the lot fell upon Matthias; and he was numbered with the eleven apostles.

Chapter 3

Faithful But Fallible Leaders

Acts 1:12-26

Acts 1:12-26 covers a brief waiting period (of about ten days) between the ascension of Christ and the outpouring of the Holy Spirit on the Day of Pentecost. The things that are recorded here were written by Luke, by divine inspiration, for our learning and admonition. If we are wise, we will lay them to heart.

1. The Lord Jesus Christ fulfilled every prophecy of the Old Testament Scriptures relating to his incarnation, life, earthly ministry, crucifixion, resurrection and ascension (1:12)

When Luke tells us that the disciples returned from the mount called Olivet to Jerusalem, he is, almost casually, telling us that Christ stood upon Mount Olivet when he ascended to heaven, just as the prophet Zechariah had said he would (Zechariah 14:4; Ezekiel 11:23). The mount had been divided into two parts by a great earthquake in the days of Uzziah. Our Lord ascended from that part of it which was near Bethany (Luke 24:50). It was there that he began his sufferings (Luke 22:39). It was most fitting therefore that he should cast off the reproach of his sufferings there by his glorious ascension.

2. The path of blessedness and usefulness is the path of obedience (1:12-14)

The disciples returned to Jerusalem because the Lord commanded them to do so (1:4). There their enemies awaited them. There they were most likely to suffer and be persecuted. But the Lord's commandment was clear. So they returned (Proverbs 3:5, 6). There, in a large upper room, they met together in prayer, united in heart, waiting for the promise of the Holy Spirit. Much needed to be done. They had a message to proclaim. Sinners were perishing.

21

But the Lord had commanded them to wait. So they waited. They were waiting upon the Lord, waiting for God to move, waiting for God to come upon them, waiting for God to open the door before them (Psalm 27:14; 62:5-7; 1 Chronicles 15:13). We must obey his word and wait for his direction. In all things, the point of our responsibility is the commandment of God. We must obey him. Obeying his word, the disciples were filled with the Spirit and greatly used of God for much good.

3. Even the best of men are only men at best (1:15-26)

So long as we are in this world we shall be prone to error and sin. We stray in many ways and err in many things. Even true, faithful servants of God are weak, fallible men of flesh and blood. This is manifest in the fact that Peter led the disciples to choose an apostle God had not chosen.

Without question, Peter was a faithful man. He had the heart of a true pastor. On other occasions he acted rashly from bad motives, but not here. His motives were good. He wanted what was best for the glory of God, the people of God and the gospel of God. The sin of Judas had made a vacancy in the apostolic office. Twelve apostles were originally chosen and ordained. As there were twelve tribes in Israel, descended from the twelve patriarchs, so there were twelve apostles. They are the twelve stars which make up the church's crown (Revelation 12:1). For them, twelve thrones were reserved (Matthew 19:28). Peter read Psalm 69:25 and concluded that it was the responsibility of the church to fill the vacancy left by Judas' apostasy. His error was an error of judgment, not of motive or principle.

He humbly recognized the sovereignty of God in all that had happened (1:16). He understood that the death of Christ was the work of God for the redemption of his people (Acts 2:23; 4:27, 28). He realised that God had sovereignly overruled the evil deeds of Judas to accomplish his own eternal purpose (Psalm 41:9).

Peter sorrowfully remembered the fall of his former friend and companion (1:17-19). He said no more about the subject than was necessary. Though he and Judas had been close friends, he bowed to the will of God and honoured the judgment of God upon his friend. Peter knew that the only difference between him and Judas was the grace of God (1 Corinthians 4:7).

He reverenced and honoured the word of God (1:20). Peter sincerely wanted to obey the Scriptures. He thought he was doing what God would have him do. He was motivated by an earnest desire for the glory of God. With genuine reverence, he sought the will of God (1:21-25).

Peter should have sought the Lord before he appointed Justus and Matthias. Never say to God, 'Lord, I am going to do this or that; you choose which you want me to do.' Rather, go to God and say, 'What will you have me to do?'

When the lots were cast, Peter led the church to ordain an apostle God had not chosen (1:26). It was true, the Lord's intention was for his church to have twelve apostles — twelve and only twelve. David's prophecy must be fulfilled. Another apostle must take Judas' place. But, like the others, he must be personally chosen and ordained to the office by Christ himself. The Lord had not chosen Justus or Matthias for this office. He had chosen Paul (1 Corinthians 15:8).

How could Peter have made such a mistake? He sought to determine the will of God by casting lots. Like David, he made the mistake of seeking to determine the will of God by seeking the will of the people (1 Chronicles 13:1-4). He tried to accomplish the will and work of God by the wisdom and energy of the flesh! As a result, Matthias was chosen to do what God had not gifted him to do. So far as we know, he never preached a sermon or wrote an epistle. We can only speculate about what became of him. But his name is never mentioned again. Where God ordained twelve apostles there was neither room nor need for thirteen!

Still, Peter was God's appointed leader for that early church. In spite of his many errors, faults and falls, Peter was God's man, and the people of God rightfully submitted to his rule as their pastor (Hebrews 13:7, 17). Though he was a fallible man, he was a faithful man. He preached the gospel of Christ, sought the will of God, lived for the glory of God and served the people of God. Blessed is that congregation who has been given such a pastor after God's own heart (Jeremiah 3:15). Faithful pastors do sin. Faithful pastors do err in judgment. Faithful pastors do even err in doctrine. Faithful pastors do make mistakes. Faithful pastors need the prayers and the love of God's people (1 Thessalonians 5:12, 13, 25; Hebrews 13:18).

Acts 2:1 And when the day of Pentecost was fully come, they were all with one accord in one place.

Acts 2:2 And suddenly there came a sound from heaven as of a rushing mighty wind, and it filled all the house where they were sitting.

Acts 2:3 And there appeared unto them cloven tongues like as of fire, and it sat upon each of them.

Acts 2:4 And they were all filled with the Holy Ghost, and began to speak with other tongues, as the Spirit gave them utterance.

Acts 2:5 And there were dwelling at Jerusalem Jews, devout men, out of every nation under heaven.

Acts 2:6 Now when this was noised abroad, the multitude came together, and were confounded, because that every man heard them speak in his own language.

Acts 2:7 And they were all amazed and marvelled, saying one to another, Behold, are not all these which speak Galilaeans?

Acts 2:8 And how hear we every man in our own tongue, wherein we were born?

Acts 2:9 Parthians, and Medes, and Elamites, and the dwellers in Mesopotamia, and in Judaea, and Cappadocia, in Pontus, and Asia,

Acts 2:10 Phrygia, and Pamphylia, in Egypt, and in the parts of Libya about Cyrene, and strangers of Rome, Jews and proselytes,

Acts 2:11 Cretes and Arabians, we do hear them speak in our tongues the wonderful works of God.

Acts 2:12 And they were all amazed, and were in doubt, saying one to another, What meaneth this?

Acts 2:13 Others mocking said, These men are full of new wine.

Chapter 4

'What meaneth this?'

Acts 2:1-13

The events of Pentecost recorded in Acts 2 rightfully claim the attention of the church of God. Here Luke records for us the great outpouring of God the Holy Spirit upon his church. Let us carefully and prayerfully study what happened on that great day. Some try to fabricate a re-enactment of Pentecost, while others simply ignore it as an event in history which has no relevance to the church today. Both are in error. While we recognize that the miraculous gifts of the Spirit were temporary signs, given for specific purposes, we also realise that the events of that great day have an application to God's church today. What the Holy Spirit was then, he is now. He is God who changes not. Whatever he did for the church of God at Pentecost, he is able to do for the church of God today. His power has not diminished. God the Holy Spirit is still with the church of Christ in this world. We should expect his divine work among us!

1. What was Pentecost?

Pentecost was one of three great feasts given by the commandment of God (Leviticus 23:4-21). The others were the feast of Passover which included the feast of Firstfruits and the feast of Tabernacles or Booths. The reason why there was such a great crowd at Jerusalem was the fact that God required every male Israelite to attend these feasts every year.

The feast of Passover (Leviticus 23:4-8) originated in Egypt (Exodus 12:1-13). When the judgment of God fell upon Egypt the Passover lamb was sacrificed. The blood of the lamb was put on the door of every house in Israel. When judgment fell, God looked on the blood and passed over every house where blood was on the door. The Passover lamb represented Christ, the Lamb of God, who was sacrificed for us (1 Corinthians 5:7), by whose blood we are saved. Our Lord kept the Passover feast with his disciples just before he was crucified. It was then that he instituted the Lord's Supper (Matthew 26:17-30).

The feast of Firstfruits (Leviticus 23:9-11) was on the Sunday after the Passover sabbath. On this feast Israel brought a handful of the firstfruits of harvest and waved it before the Lord. This signified that every product of the soil, every result of man's labour and toil, is from God. It was on this day that our Lord arose from the grave and became the firstfruits of the resurrection (1 Corinthians 15:20-23). All the results of his work on the cross, our redemption and resurrection, are of God.

The feast of Pentecost (Leviticus 23:15-21) was held seven weeks after the Passover. Here the Jews renewed their vows and dedicated themselves anew to the Lord God. It was on this day that the Holy Spirit was given, as our Saviour had promised.

The feast of Tabernacles commemorated Israel's forty-year wandering in the wilderness.

2. When did the Holy Spirit come upon the apostles? (2:1)

He came at the divinely appointed time, 'when the day of Pentecost was fully come'. Once Christ ascended back to heaven and was exalted, the Spirit was given (Psalm 68:18, 19; Ephesians 4:7-12; Galatians 3:13, 14). It was Sunday morning. The disciples were gathered for worship in the appointed place. They were all with one accord, in prayer and expectation (Acts 1:14), waiting for the promise of the Spirit. The blessings of God always attend such unity and obedience (Psalm 133:1-3; Matthew 18:20). But strife and division grieve the Spirit and drive him away (Ephesians 4:30).

3. What were the symbols of the Holy Spirit's presence? (2:2, 3)

The wind is a symbol of deity and, therefore, a proper emblem of the Spirit. In fact, in both Hebrew and Greek the words for wind and the Spirit are the same. Wind is frequently used to represent the power and presence of God (Ezekiel 37:9; Job 38:1). The sound of rushing, mighty wind symbolizes the irresistible power of grace which comes by the Spirit of God (John 3:8; Psalm 65:4; 110:3). Like the wind, God is uncontrolled by man; sovereign, almighty and irresistible in all his works!

The fire is also an emblem of divinity. God appeared to Abraham as a burning lamp (Genesis 15:17) and to Moses in the burning bush (Exodus 3:1-6). The symbol of his presence with Israel was a pillar of fire (Exodus 13:21, 22). He showed himself for Elijah as a devouring fire (1 Kings 18:38). Isaiah's lips were cleansed by a live coal of fire (Isaiah 6:1-8). 'Our God is a consuming fire' (Hebrews 12:29). Like fire, the Spirit of God illuminates the people of God (John 16:13, 14; 1 Corinthians 2:11-14). Like fire, he gives power to energize and invigorate the church of God and the servants of God. Without him we can do nothing. With him there is nothing we cannot do!

4. What were the immediate effects of the Spirit's presence? (2:4-11)

First, 'They were all filled with the Holy Ghost.' Oh, that we might each be filled with the Spirit! To be filled with the Spirit is to be controlled by him (Ephesians 5:18-20). It is to be filled with his grace (Galatians 5:22, 23), filled with his comfort (John 14:16-18) and filled with his influence (Romans 8:14).

Second, they 'began to speak with other tongues (or languages), as the Spirit gave them utterance'. The gift of tongues was the ability to speak a language that had not been learned (2:6-11). It was not the meaningless repetition of unintelligible sounds! This gift was a temporary gift bestowed upon the apostles, identifying them as God's inspired messengers and confirming their writings as the Word of God (Hebrews 2:3, 4). Because we have the complete revelation of God in Holy Scripture, there is no need for supernatural gifts (miracles, tongues, etc.) to confirm God's revelation (1 Corinthians 13:10; 2 Peter 1:19). The Spirit is the same today as he was then, but he does not manifest himself in the same way. Yet three things always give evidence of the Holy Spirit's presence and power in the church.

1. He enables God's servants to preach with power (2:4).

2. He enables chosen sinners to hear, understand and believe the gospel of Christ (2:6; 1 Thessalonians 1:5).

3. He makes the gospel a savour of life to some and death to others (2:11-13; 2 Corinthians 2:14-16).

5. What was the subject preached by the apostles?

They all declared 'the wonderful works of God' (2:11). Just read Peter's sermon and you will see what those wonderful works of God are. On that day, as on all other occasions in the book of Acts, and on any day when a man preaches by the power of God the Holy Spirit, the subject matter was Christ and him crucified (1 Corinthians 2:2). The words 'preach', 'preaching' and 'preached' appear thirty-seven times in the book of Acts. Every time they have reference to the preaching of Christ. We shall look at it in more detail in the next chapter, but notice what Peter preached on the Day of Pentecost.

1. Free salvation through the merits of Christ (2:21).
2. The glorious sovereignty of God (2:23).
3. The desperate wickedness and depravity of man (2:23).
4. The crucifixion and death of Christ (2:23).
5. The exaltation and glory of Christ (2:32-36).
6. Repentance and the remission of sins by the gift of God (2:38-40).

Let us pray for the presence and power of God the Holy Spirit to attend the assemblies of God's church today (Isaiah 64:1, 2).

Spirit divine! Attend our prayers,
And make God's house thy home;
Descend with all thy gracious powers,
Oh come, great Spirit, come!

Andrew Reed, 1829

'What meaneth this?'

Acts 2:14 But Peter, standing up with the eleven, lifted up his voice, and said unto them, Ye men of Judaea, and all ye that dwell at Jerusalem, be this known unto you, and hearken to my words:

Acts 2:15 For these are not drunken, as ye suppose, seeing it is but the third hour of the day.

Acts 2:16 But this is that which was spoken by the prophet Joel;

Acts 2:17 And it shall come to pass in the last days, saith God, I will pour out of my Spirit upon all flesh: and your sons and your daughters shall prophesy, and your young men shall see visions, and your old men shall dream dreams:

Acts 2:18 And on my servants and on my handmaidens I will pour out in those days of my Spirit; and they shall prophesy:

Acts 2:19 And I will shew wonders in heaven above, and signs in the earth beneath; blood, and fire, and vapour of smoke:

Acts 2:20 The sun shall be turned into darkness, and the moon into blood, before that great and notable day of the Lord come:

Acts 2:21 And it shall come to pass, that whosoever shall call on the name of the Lord shall be saved.

Acts 2:22 Ye men of Israel, hear these words; Jesus of Nazareth, a man approved of God among you by miracles and wonders and signs, which God did by him in the midst of you, as ye yourselves also know:

Acts 2:23 Him, being delivered by the determinate counsel and foreknowledge of God, ye have taken, and by wicked hands have crucified and slain:

Acts 2:24 Whom God hath raised up, having loosed the pains of death: because it was not possible that he should be holden of it.

Acts 2:25 For David speaketh concerning him, I foresaw the Lord always before my face, for he is on my right hand, that I should not be moved:

Acts 2:26 Therefore did my heart rejoice, and my tongue was glad; moreover also my flesh shall rest in hope:

Acts 2:27 Because thou wilt not leave my soul in hell, neither wilt thou suffer thine Holy One to see corruption.

Acts 2:28 Thou hast made known to me the ways of life; thou shalt make me full of joy with thy countenance.

Acts 2:29 Men and brethren, let me freely speak unto you of the patriarch David, that he is both dead and buried, and his sepulchre is with us unto this day.

Acts 2:30 Therefore being a prophet, and knowing that God had sworn with an oath to him, that of the fruit of his loins, according to the flesh, he would raise up Christ to sit on his throne;

Acts 2:31 He seeing this before spake of the resurrection of Christ, that his soul was not left in hell, neither his flesh did see corruption.

Acts 2:32 This Jesus hath God raised up, whereof we all are witnesses.

Acts 2:33 Therefore being by the right hand of God exalted, and having received of the Father the promise of the Holy Ghost, he hath shed forth this, which ye now see and hear.

Acts 2:34 For David is not ascended into the heavens: but he saith himself, The LORD said unto my Lord, Sit thou on my right hand,

Acts 2:35 Until I make thy foes thy footstool.

Acts 2:36 Therefore let all the house of Israel know assuredly, that God hath made that same Jesus, whom ye have crucified, both Lord and Christ.

Chapter 5

Pentecost: Revelation Of The Sovereign Christ

Acts 2:14-36

We have before us the sermon which Peter preached on the Day of Pentecost. It is remarkably simple. It displays no great learning. It contains no heights of oratory. It contains no thrilling stories or illustrations. It is a simple declaration of divine truth, delivered to the hearts of men by the power of God. There is nothing in it to impress the flesh. But there is much here to prick the heart! The one object of Peter's sermon at Pentecost, and the one object of the Holy Spirit who inspired it, was to set forth before fallen, guilty, needy sinners the redemptive accomplishments and resurrection glory of the Lord Jesus Christ.

1. Peter explained the significance of what happened on the Day of Pentecost (2:14-21)

Peter met these men where they were. They were mocking the apostles upon whom the Holy Spirit had fallen. They attempted to explain away the work of the Spirit which they could not understand (1 Corinthians 2:14) by saying that those men who spoke by the Spirit of God were drunk (2:13). Peter stood, lifted up his voice with confidence and boldness and said, 'Listen to me. I will explain to you from the Word of God, which you profess to believe, what is happening in your midst. This marvellous outpouring of the Holy Spirit is the fulfilment of Joel's prophecy' (Joel 2:28-32). Joel identified the Messiah positively by giving a fourfold proof of his enthronement and the establishment of his kingdom. These things point to the Lord Jesus Christ and say, 'This is the Messiah!'

31

First, 'the last days' began with the coming of the Messiah (1 John 2:18). 'The last days' encompass the whole space of time from the first advent to the second advent of Christ.

Secondly, the Spirit of God has been poured out upon all flesh, Jews and Gentiles, men and women, rich and poor (2:17, 18; Galatians 3:13, 14; Colossians 3:11). Though men in the Old Testament were from time to time filled with the Spirit (1 Peter 1:11; Nehemiah 9:20), this great outpouring of the Spirit was reserved as a signal that Christ has come and his kingdom has been established. People in the Old Testament were regenerated by the Spirit of God just as they are today (John 3:3-8). Yet the works of God's grace were primarily limited to the nation of Israel. Now his grace is scattered throughout the nations of the world.

As we noted in the previous chapter, the miraculous gifts of tongues, prophecy, visions, etc. were temporary. They were given to announce the enthronement of Christ. It should also be noted that as early as Paul's first letter to the Corinthians God forbade any kind of public ministry by women (1 Corinthians 14:26, 34).

Thirdly, the judgment of God has fallen upon the nation of Israel for their rejection and crucifixion of Christ (3:19, 20; Matthew 22:7). Joel described God's judgment of Israel in figurative symbols. Because of their contempt of the gospel, God destroyed the civil government of Israel as a nation and turned the light he had given them into darkness (Luke 19:41-44; 23:28, 29; Romans 11:7-11, 25). Blinded Israel stands as a beacon to warn all who trifle with the things of God (Romans 1:21; Proverbs 1:23-33).

Fourthly, the gospel of the grace of God is now proclaimed to all the nations of the world (2:21). God now gathers his elect from among the Gentiles by the preaching of the gospel according to his wise and sovereign purpose of grace (Psalm 2:7, 8; Romans 10:10-13). This is the meaning of Pentecost. The outpouring of the Holy Spirit declares that Christ has come, redeemed his people and established his kingdom. At last, God's promise to Abraham is fulfilled (Galatians 3:13, 14).

2. Peter proclaimed the person and work of Christ (2:22-24)

Peter seems to have anticipated a question which the Jews, whose hands were freshly stained with the blood of Christ, might ask: 'If this Jesus of Nazareth is the Christ of God, if he has established his kingdom, how do you explain the fact that we have nailed him to the cross?'

'Jesus of Nazareth' was 'a man approved of God' as the God-man (2:22). His claims to divinity (John 8:56; 14:9; Romans 9:5; 1 Timothy 3:16) were proved by his miracles. Those miracles performed by Christ were facts of indisputable public record. They could not be denied even by his murderers. That man who turned water to wine, calmed the raging sea, gave sight to the blind, fed the multitudes, cleansed lepers and raised the dead is God!

How did Christ, the God-man, come to die the painful, shameful death of the cross? Verse 23 gives us the answer. The death of Christ was an act of God (Romans 5:8; 8:32; 2 Corinthians 5:21; Isaiah 53:10). He was foreordained and predestinated to be our substitutionary sacrifice (1 Peter 1:18-20; Revelation 13:8; Hebrews 13:20). The only way sinners could be saved is by the satisfaction of justice. The only one who could satisfy justice is the Son of God. And the only way he could do it was by death (Hebrews 9:22), the death of the cross (Galatians 3:13). Yet Christ died by the hands of wicked men, acting according to their own free will. If nothing else convinces men of the abhorrence of free-will doctrine, this should — free will crucified the Lord of glory!

By his resurrection from the dead our Saviour abolished death (2:24). He abolished the penal aspect of death for his people. He abolished its power, its terror and its fears for all who believe (Hebrews 2:15). The resurrection of Christ was God's public declaration that justice has been satisfied for his people's sins (Romans 4:25-5:1).

3. Peter gives proof from the Old Testament Scriptures that the Messiah must both suffer death and be resurrected by the power of God (2:25-31)

Quoting Psalm 16:8-11, the apostle shows that David's words were a prophecy of Christ's death, resurrection and exaltation. In all that he did, our Redeemer sought the glory of God, doing his Father's will. He said, 'I foresaw the Lord always before my face' (John 12:28-32; 17:4, 5). He was, as a man, sustained and strengthened in his work by the assurance of his Father's presence. He said, 'He is on my right hand, that I should not be moved' (Isaiah 50:5-7).

Our Saviour faced his greatest trial with joyful confidence that he would, by his obedience unto death, both obtain the place of highest glory and save his people (2:26-28; Philippians 2:5-11; Hebrews 12:1-3). In all these things, the person spoken of was not David, but David's Lord, Jesus Christ (2:29-31).

May God give us grace ever to follow our Redeemer's example, doing the will of God for the glory of God, being sustained by the awareness that God is with us, rejoicing always in the hope of everlasting glory.

4. Peter declares that Jesus Christ, the Son of God, has been given dominion as Lord over all God's creation (2:32-36)

We shall study these verses more fully in the next chapter, but here are two facts that all men must face.

First, the Christ whom we have crucified is now the exalted King of heaven and earth (2:32, 33, 36).

Second, sooner or later we must all bow to and acknowledge the rightful dominion and lordship of Jesus Christ (2:34, 35).

Acts 2:32 This Jesus hath God raised up, whereof we all are witnesses.

Acts 2:33 Therefore being by the right hand of God exalted, and having received of the Father the promise of the Holy Ghost, he hath shed forth this, which ye now see and hear.

Acts 2:34 For David is not ascended into the heavens: but he saith himself, The LORD said unto my Lord, Sit thou on my right hand,

Acts 2:35 Until I make thy foes thy footstool.

Acts 2:36 Therefore let all the house of Israel know assuredly, that God hath made that same Jesus, whom ye have crucified, both Lord and Christ.

Chapter 6

'Both Lord and Christ'

Acts 2:32-36

The subject before us in these verses is the exaltation and glory of Jesus Christ as Lord. This was the issue Peter pressed upon his hearers on the Day of Pentecost. He did not ask them to raise their hands, walk down the aisle, come to the altar, or say the sinner's prayer. Peter demanded as God's ambassador that those who heard him bow to, trust and acknowledge Jesus Christ as their Lord.

Peter shows us in this part of his sermon that the singular purpose for the outpouring of the Holy Spirit on the Day of Pentecost was to announce the exaltation of Christ as Lord. The outpouring of the Spirit was not in any way a change in God's plan. It did not alter God's method of grace in salvation. The outpouring of the Holy Spirit was not the beginning of 'the church age', or a new 'dispensational age'. This mighty outpouring announced the exaltation of Christ. The exaltation and glory of Christ as Lord over all things is the theme of all gospel preaching, the acknowledgement of all true faith and the ground of the believer's hope.

We must understand this: the one issue between God and man is the lordship of Jesus Christ. God demands that all men bow to and acknowledge the rightful dominion of his Son over all things. All men will bow to Christ, either in this life in repentance and faith, or in the Day of Judgment, but all will bow to Christ (Philippians 2:9-11).

1. What is the significance of our Saviour's exaltation?

Peter tells us that Christ is indeed exalted. The baby of Bethlehem is now the King of glory. The man we nailed to the cursed tree now sits upon the throne of universal dominion. The King of glory has come into his kingdom and taken possession of his throne (Psalm 24:7-10). What does that mean? What is the significance of Christ's exaltation?

First, Christ upon the throne means that his work is finished and complete (Hebrews 1:1-3; 10:10-14). Our great High Priest is pictured as a priest seated in the holy of holies, in heaven itself. In the Old Testament there was no chair in the holy place. Those priests could never sit down, because their work was never finished. Their sacrifices could never take away sin (Hebrews 10:1-4). But our High Priest is seated in heaven, in a posture of rest, because his work is finished! All that was agreed upon in the covenant of grace he has done (John 17:4). He came to do his Father's will, and he has done it. He brought in, by his obedience in life, perfect righteousness for God's elect. By his death he satisfied all the demands of God's law and justice as our substitute (Isaiah 59:16; 63:1-5; John 19:30).

Secondly, Christ's exaltation upon the throne of glory means that God the Father has accepted the sacrifice of his Son for the salvation of his people (Romans 8:34). The believer's assurance that sin is pardoned is the ascension and exaltation of Christ. If Christ, who was made to be sin for us, is now exalted with everlasting glory upon the throne of God, then our sins that were imputed to him are gone forever! His blood has indeed put away our sins!

Thirdly, the exaltation of Christ proclaims reconciliation between God and man (Colossians 1:18-22). There is a man in glory whose righteousness has been accepted, whose death has satisfied the very justice of God. The debt for sin has been fully paid. Godhood and manhood are in perfect harmony in Christ, the God-man. Therefore, there is hope for men.

Fourthly, the exalted Christ is able to save fallen men (Hebrews 7:25). Christ on the throne is able to save all who come to God by him. Christ on the throne is touched with the feeling of our infirmities. Christ on the throne is able to keep you from falling and to present you holy, unblameable and unreproveable before the presence of his glory! (Jude 24: Colossians 1:22).

2. What is the exalted Son of God doing in heaven?

He is enjoying the honour and dignity he won as our mediator. In his divinity, as God, our Saviour has always enjoyed the bliss and glory of total sovereignty. Though he humbled himself as a man, even unto the death of the cross, he never ceased to be God over all! But as a man the Lord Jesus Christ earned the right to rule the entire universe (Romans 14:9; Philippians 2:9-11). He enjoys the highest honour that heaven affords. He is King of kings and Lord of lords. And the honour he receives is well deserved (Revelation 5:9, 10).

The exalted Christ is ruling this world in total sovereignty (John 17:1-4; 1 Peter 3:22). He is the only Potentate (1 Timothy 6:15). He rules all things according to the eternal purpose and pleasure of God for the salvation and eternal, spiritual good of God's elect. And he rules all things well (Romans 8:28).

Christ, exalted in heaven, is making intercession for chosen sinners according to the will of God (Hebrews 7:25; 1 John 2:1, 2). On the basis of his perfect righteousness and blood atonement, he pleads with the Father for the salvation of his redeemed ones, the non-imputation of sin to them and their presence with him in glory at last (John 17:24), and he always prevails!

The exaltation of Christ is a representative exaltation. That is to say, he was exalted as the representative of God's elect and we are already exalted with him (Ephesians 2:5, 6). So certain is the salvation of God's elect, so certain is it that Christ's redeemed ones will possess the glory of an eternal inheritance in heaven, that we are already possessors of it in Christ!

3. What has the exalted Redeemer been promised?

When he was exalted to the right hand of the majesty on high, God the Father promised his Son that he would make all his foes his footstool (Hebrews 1:5, 8-13). It is virtually done now and it will be carried out in all the universe. As he promised to make all Christ's enemies his footstool, the Father also promised the Son that he would save all his ransomed people (Isaiah 53:10-12; Hebrews 2:13). As I said before, all men and women will bow to Christ. You will either bow to him in faith, surrendering to his rule now, or you will bow to him in fear and trembling, acknowledging his sovereign justice in the Day of Judgment, but bow to him you will (Isaiah 45:23-25).

4. 'What shall we do?' (2:37)

The people who heard Peter's message had sense enough to realise that there is only one way to deal with an absolute sovereign. We must bow to his claims, acknowledging his lordship over all things (Romans 10:9, 10; 1 Corinthians 12:3). True faith involves surrender to the rule and dominion of Christ as a willing servant to him (Luke 14:25-33). Where there is no surrender there is no faith!

Let every believer rejoice. Christ is exalted. Christ is Lord. That means all is well! Let us trust him in all things, rejoice in him in all circumstances, walk before him in submissive faith and wait for him with hope and expectation (1 John 3:2).

Acts 2:37 Now when they heard this, they were pricked in their heart, and said unto Peter and to the rest of the apostles, Men and brethren, what shall we do?

Acts 2:38 Then Peter said unto them, Repent, and be baptized every one of you in the name of Jesus Christ for the remission of sins, and ye shall receive the gift of the Holy Ghost.

Acts 2:39 For the promise is unto you, and to your children, and to all that are afar off, even as many as the Lord our God shall call.

Acts 2:40 And with many other words did he testify and exhort, saying, Save yourselves from this untoward generation.

Acts 2:41 Then they that gladly received his word were baptized: and the same day there were added unto them about three thousand souls.

Acts 2:42 And they continued stedfastly in the apostles' doctrine and fellowship, and in breaking of bread, and in prayers.

Acts 2:43 And fear came upon every soul: and many wonders and signs were done by the apostles.

Acts 2:44 And all that believed were together, and had all things common;

Acts 2:45 And sold their possessions and goods, and parted them to all men, as every man had need.

Acts 2:46 And they, continuing daily with one accord in the temple, and breaking bread from house to house, did eat their meat with gladness and singleness of heart,

Acts 2:47 Praising God, and having favour with all the people. And the Lord added to the church daily such as should be saved.

Chapter 7

'The Lord added to the church'

Acts 2:37-47

As we noted earlier, Peter's sermon was exceedingly simple. There were no illustrations, no stirring stories, no marvellous points of logic, no soaring heights of oratory. The apostle simply declared the truth of God, boldly exposing the sin of his hearers and explaining the meaning of Christ's death and resurrection. But every word he spoke was carried to the hearts of chosen sinners by the effectual power and grace of God the Holy Spirit. When the day was over three thousand men and women had been converted by the power of God, saved and added to the church. Here two lessons are clearly taught and illustrated that every preacher, teacher, church leader and church member should learn and lay to heart.

1. Salvation is the work of God alone (2:37-41)

When Peter had finished preaching, those whose hearts had been pricked by the Word of God cried, 'What shall we do?' Like all men, once they were awakened to a sense of their sin and of God's just wrath against them, these men hoped to do something by which they could be saved. We are all legalists by nature! These men wanted to know what they could do to atone for their sins, to set things right with God, to appease his wrath and win his favour. 'What shall we do?' What a foolish question! Salvation does not come by something man does. Salvation is the result of what God does (Romans 3:28; 11:6; Ephesians 2:8, 9; 2 Timothy 1:9; Titus 3:5). In verses 37-41 the Holy Spirit gives us a beautiful, clear picture of God's method of grace.

41

When God intends to save a sinner, he causes that sinner to hear the gospel preached in the power of the Holy Spirit (2:37). 'When they heard this,' the gospel of God's sovereign purpose of grace in the redemptive work of Christ (2:23) and the exaltation and glory of Christ as Lord (2:32-36), 'they were pricked in their heart'. God saves sinners through the preaching of the gospel (Romans 10:13-17; 1 Corinthians 1:21; James 1:18; 1 Peter 1:23-25). In his wise and sovereign providence God brings that sinner to whom he will be gracious under the sound of a gospel preacher's voice. As he brought Philip to the Ethiopian eunuch, brought Peter to Cornelius, brought Paul to Lydia, the Philippian jailor and 'the barbarous people' of Malta, and brought Onesimus to Paul, so God always finds a way to bring chosen sinners under the sound of the gospel. Blessed indeed are those men and women to whom God sends his messengers of grace (Jeremiah 3:15; Ephesians 4:8-16).

When God has purposed to save a sinner, he sends his Spirit into that sinner's heart and produces in him a real, heart conviction of sin (2:37). 'They were pricked in their heart.' Holy Spirit conviction is a painful, but necessary work of grace. Without it no sinner can be saved (John 16:7, 8). He strips that he may clothe, empties that he may fill, wounds that he may heal and kills that he may make alive. Conviction of sin, righteousness and judgment is the work of God the Holy Spirit upon the heart, by which our pride and self-righteousness are made to wither (Isaiah 6:1-8). It arises from the revelation of Christ's substitutionary sacrifice (Zechariah 12:10). It acknowledges the justice of God in punishing sin. And true Holy Spirit conviction always results in repentance and faith in Christ (John 6:44, 45).

When God comes to a sinner in saving grace he commands the sinner to repent (2:38). Peter, speaking by the Spirit, gave a command from God. They must obey or perish (Matthew 10:11-15, 40). Repentance is more than sorrow for sin. It is a change, a change of mind, a change of motives, a change of masters! It is a change of heart and a change of life that is continuous.

The word 'for' in verse 38 has caused much confusion. It would be better translated 'because of'. Baptism is not the cause of, or the means of, the remission of sins. Baptism is a symbolic confession of faith in the sacrificial death, burial and resurrection of Christ. Being immersed in the watery grave, the believer professes his faith in the substitutionary work of Christ by which his sins have been purged away. Coming up out of the grave, he professes his allegiance to Christ, to walk in newness of life (Romans 6:4-6). 'The gift of the Holy Ghost' here promised to those who obey God's command in the gospel is everlasting salvation in Christ.

When God comes to sinners in saving grace, he calls them by the irresistible grace and power of his Spirit (2:39). The promise of God is, 'Whosoever shall call upon the name of the Lord shall be saved' (Romans

10:13). It is given to 'as many as the Lord our God shall call'. Not all men are called. God sends the gospel to some and hides it from others (Matthew 11:20-26). There is a general call issued to all who hear the gospel, which all who hear are responsible to obey (Proverbs 1:25-33; Romans 10:18-21). But there is an effectual, irresistible call by God the Holy Spirit which is given to God's elect alone and graciously causes them to come to Christ (1 Thessalonians 1:4, 5; Psalm 65:4). 'He calleth his own sheep by name, and leadeth them out' (John 10:3).

When God comes to sinners in saving power he causes them to obey his voice in the gospel (2:40, 41). These people, whose hands were yet dripping with the blood of Christ, were now made willing in the day of his power to trust him and surrender to him as their Lord and Saviour (Psalm 110:3). Grace made them willing!

2. The building of the church is the work of God alone (2:41-47)

The church of God cannot be built by human ingenuity. It is built by the power of God alone through the preaching of the gospel of Christ. Every effort of men to build the church, other than the preaching of the gospel, is wood, hay and stubble. God will never honour it (1 Corinthians 3:11-15). 'The Lord added to the church daily such as should be saved,' and he still does!

In these last verses of chapter 2, Luke gives us an example of what every local church should be. It is a blessed fellowship of believers in Christ, a fellowship created and maintained by the Spirit of God (Ephesians 2:19-22).

1. It is a doctrinal fellowship. 'They continued stedfastly in the apostles' doctrine.' All true Christian fellowship is built upon the doctrines of the gospel of Christ.

2. It is a fraternal fellowship. Believers are men and women united in Christ. They truly have 'all things common'. Each uses what he has for the good of all. They are of 'one accord', built up in love, with 'singleness of heart', seeking the glory of God.

3. It is a spiritual fellowship of worship. When the local church is what it ought to be the people gladly receive the Word of God, obey the ordinances of Christ and assemble together with one accord in the worship of God.

Acts 3:1 Now Peter and John went up together into the temple at the hour of prayer, being the ninth hour.

Acts 3:2 And a certain man lame from his mother's womb was carried, whom they laid daily at the gate of the temple which is called Beautiful, to ask alms of them that entered into the temple;

Acts 3:3 Who seeing Peter and John about to go into the temple asked an alms.

Acts 3:4 And Peter, fastening his eyes upon him with John, said, Look on us.

Acts 3:5 And he gave heed unto them, expecting to receive something of them.

Acts 3:6 Then Peter said, Silver and gold have I none; but such as I have give I thee: In the name of Jesus Christ of Nazareth rise up and walk.

Acts 3:7 And he took him by the right hand, and lifted him up: and immediately his feet and ankle bones received strength.

Acts 3:8 And he leaping up stood, and walked, and entered with them into the temple, walking, and leaping, and praising God.

Acts 3:9 And all the people saw him walking and praising God:

Acts 3:10 And they knew that it was he which sat for alms at the Beautiful gate of the temple: and they were filled with wonder and amazement at that which had happened unto him.

Acts 3:11 And as the lame man which was healed held Peter and John, all the people ran together unto them in the porch that is called Solomon's, greatly wondering.

Chapter 8

'Such as I have give I thee'

Acts 3:1-11

The healing of this lame man at the Beautiful Gate of the temple is a very instructive event. It is recorded here for our learning and our admonition.

Certainly, the events of this day show us the blessedness of public worship. At the appointed hour of prayer Peter and John came to the appointed place of public worship to worship God. Though the lame man came only for carnal reasons, still he came to the place where his needs were most likely to be met — the house of God. There God made himself known, both to his servants and to 'a certain man lame from his mother's womb'. Let every needy soul cherish the house of God, attend the assembly of worship and give thanks to God for the privilege of doing so (Psalm 122:1; Hebrews 10:25). It is in the assembly of God's saints that needy sinners have hope of meeting the mighty Saviour (Matthew 18:20).

This passage also shows us an example of Christian charity and kindness. Though Peter and John had no money in their pockets, they did not ignore this man's miserable plight and condition. We ought always to do what we can to relieve the suffering of others (Matthew 6:3; 10:42; Luke 10:25-37).

But, primarily, the purpose of this miracle is to demonstrate the power of the risen, exalted Christ to save sinners. This is the interpretation Peter himself gave of the miracle (Acts 4:10-12). The healing of this crippled beggar is a beautiful picture of God's sovereign power and effectual, saving grace in Christ. In these eleven verses the Spirit of God teaches us five important lessons.

1. All men are spiritually impotent by nature (3:2)

This man's impotence was not the result of an accident or a disease. It was a defect of birth. He was born in this helpless condition. This is our condition by nature, not physically, but spiritually. Our hearts are plagued with the incurable disease of sin. Spiritually, our legs are broken, our hands are withered, our eyes are blind, our ears are deaf. All men by nature are 'dead in

45

trespasses and sins' (Ephesians 2:1-4). So thorough is the natural man's spiritual impotence that he is altogether without ability to help himself. All the children of Adam are born totally depraved (Jeremiah 17:9; Matthew 15:19). Because his heart is evil, no man can or will come to Christ and be saved (John 5:40; 6:44). He has neither the desire nor the ability to do so (Jeremiah 13:23). God must do a work of grace in the heart before any sinner will ever come to Christ in faith. And if God does a work of grace in his heart, the sinner will come to Christ (John 6:45; Psalm 65:4; 110:3).

Because he was a cripple, he was unable to work for a living. He spent his days begging. That is our condition too! Before God we are poor, helpless beggars. We have no ability to earn anything from God, except death. We have no claim upon his mercy. All we can do is fall before him and beg for grace (Luke 18:13). As Matthew Henry said, 'Those that need, and cannot work, must not be ashamed to beg!'

This beggar was a chosen object of divine mercy. He was both poor and helpless, but there were many others in that condition around the temple. Luke speaks of this man as 'a certain man'. God had chosen him and was determined to be gracious to him (2 Thessalonians 2:13, 14). Providence had made him poor and helpless and put him in the place where grace would be found.

2. Religion without Christ is a mockery to the souls of men

There stood the temple in all its breathtaking splendour. Josephus tells us that it was made of solid white, polished marble. This Beautiful Gate was made of fine Corinthian gold. With the midday sun shining upon it, its brilliance was almost blinding. The Jews were very proud of their temple, but it was an empty, desolate place. God had left it! The glory of God had departed. There was nothing and no one connected with that temple that could be of any real benefit to that poor, helpless beggar. Its splendour, riches and beauty only mocked him! What a sad picture of modern religion! There is in religion much to impress the flesh: wealth, influence, talent, entertainment, and rituals and ceremonies to soothe the conscience — a form of godliness, but no power, no gospel, no grace, no Christ, no life! It is a mockery to God and to the souls of men!

3. When God intends to save a sinner he uses certain means (3:1-5)

Were he pleased to do so, the sovereign, almighty God could perform his works of mercy without the use of means. But that is not his pleasure. God condescends to honour us by allowing us to be instruments in his hands by which he performs his works of mercy towards his chosen. He who raised the dead Lazarus could easily have removed the stone from the tomb; but he allowed and commanded men to do what they could do, saying, 'Take ye away the stone' (John 11:39). In the same way, this poor, lame beggar was healed by the power of God alone. Peter makes that abundantly clear (3:12-16). But three things had to be done by men before he could be healed.

First, Peter and John came to the temple to preach the gospel of Christ (Romans 1:16, 17; 10:17; 1 Corinthians 1:21; James 1:18; 1 Peter 1:23).

Secondly, this man's friends brought him to the temple, the place where he was most hopeful of finding mercy (cf. Luke 5:18-20).

Thirdly, this man did what God's servants told him to do (3:4-6). We know that God's purpose will never fail. This man had to be healed on this occasion. God had purposed it. Yet, if Peter and John had not obeyed their Lord and gone to preach the gospel, if this man's friends had not brought him to the temple, or if the man himself had refused to obey the voice of God's servants, he would never have been healed.

4. The Lord Jesus Christ is an almighty, all-sufficient Saviour (3:6-8)

This is a picture of true conversion. Charles Simeon commented on this passage: 'You have seen how this man's body has been healed, even by faith in the Lord Jesus Christ; and it is in this way that your soul must be saved, for there is no other power that can effect such a change within you, a change from weakness to strength, from death to life.' Christ is able to save! By the mere exercise of his sovereign will sin is subdued, guilt is removed, the dead live, bloodthirsty lions are made to be lambs and wretched sinners are made new creatures in him. Christ on the tree has put away sin (Hebrews 9:26). Christ on the throne is able to save (Hebrews 7:25).

5. The gospel of Christ is always effectual (3:8-11)

The gospel always accomplishes its intended purpose (Isaiah 55:10, 11). It opens salvation and eternal life to all who come to Christ (Isaiah 45:22). The gospel is the means by which God the Holy Spirit brings chosen sinners to Christ (Psalm 65:4). And it gives praise, honour and glory to God for his saving goodness (1 Corinthians 1:26-31).

Acts 3:11 And as the lame man which was healed held Peter and John, all the people ran together unto them in the porch that is called Solomon's, greatly wondering.

Acts 3:12 And when Peter saw it, he answered unto the people, Ye men of Israel, why marvel ye at this? or why look ye so earnestly on us, as though by our own power or holiness we had made this man to walk?

Acts 3:13 The God of Abraham, and of Isaac, and of Jacob, the God of our fathers, hath glorified his Son Jesus; whom ye delivered up, and denied him in the presence of Pilate, when he was determined to let him go.

Acts 3:14 But ye denied the Holy One and the Just, and desired a murderer to be granted unto you;

Acts 3:15 And killed the Prince of life, whom God hath raised from the dead; whereof we are witnesses.

Acts 3:16 And his name through faith in his name hath made this man strong, whom ye see and know: yea, the faith which is by him hath given him this perfect soundness in the presence of you all.

Acts 3:17 And now, brethren, I wot that through ignorance ye did it, as did also your rulers.

Acts 3:18 But those things, which God before had shewed by the mouth of all his prophets, that Christ should suffer, he hath so fulfilled.

Acts 3:19 Repent ye therefore, and be converted, that your sins may be blotted out, when the times of refreshing shall come from the presence of the Lord;

Acts 3:20 And he shall send Jesus Christ, which before was preached unto you:

Acts 3:21 Whom the heaven must receive until the times of restitution of all things, which God hath spoken by the mouth of all his holy prophets since the world began.

Acts 3:22 For Moses truly said unto the fathers, A prophet shall the Lord your God raise up unto you of your brethren, like unto me; him shall ye hear in all things whatsoever he shall say unto you.

Acts 3:23 And it shall come to pass, that every soul, which will not hear that prophet, shall be destroyed from among the people.

Acts 3:24 Yea, and all the prophets from Samuel and those that follow after, as many as have spoken, have likewise foretold of these days.

Acts 3:25 Ye are the children of the prophets, and of the covenant which God made with our fathers, saying unto Abraham, And in thy seed shall all the kindreds of the earth be blessed.

Acts 3:26 Unto you first God, having raised up his Son Jesus, sent him to bless you, in turning away every one of you from his iniquities.

Chapter 9

A Lesson In Preaching The Gospel

Acts 3:11-26

Preachers and churches would be wise to study carefully the preaching and the sermons of God's servants which are recorded for us in the Word of God, especially those found in the book of Acts. If we would be of any spiritual, eternal benefit to the souls of men, serve the interests of Christ's kingdom and honour God, there must be a return to the apostolic preaching of the cross.

Peter and John went to the temple at the hour of prayer to preach the gospel of Christ as the Lord had commanded them. As they were going into the temple, they met a poor, crippled beggar who was healed by Christ. This man, as soon as he was healed, went into the temple leaping and praising God. Of course, this miracle caused a great commotion and aroused the interest of many. In the passage now before us Peter met this crowd of people at the point of their curiosity and preached the gospel to them. This was his second sermon after the outpouring of the Holy Spirit on the Day of Pentecost. There is no substantial difference between this message and the one preached on that day. Like the other apostles and like Paul, who was yet to be converted, Peter constantly preached Christ to men (1 Corinthians 2:1, 2). In this sermon at the temple Peter shows us how the gospel is to be preached.

1. Peter's first concern was to get the attention of his hearers focused on Christ (3:11, 12)

These people were excited and curious about the healing of the lame man. They were amazed at the mighty work performed (as they thought) by Peter

49

and John. Therefore, Peter's first concern was to turn their attention away from the man healed, away from John and away from himself. The matter of first concern was to get people to think not about the healed man, or the act of healing, but about Christ the Healer! They were in Solomon's porch and filled with wonder. Seizing the opportunity, Peter stepped forward and said, 'Behold, one greater than Solomon has done this!' He met these people where they were, at their point of interest, but immediately endeavoured to turn their attention to Christ.

There was no reason for amazement. 'Why marvel ye at this?' True, a lame man had been healed, but just a few weeks prior to this the Lord Jesus had raised a dead man! (John 11:43-45). Christ had repeatedly displayed his power over life and death as God. We should never be surprised to see him display that power. We ought to expect it!

Peter would allow no honour, credit, praise, or applause to be given to himself and John. They were only instruments in the hands of Christ. Certainly, those who are the instruments of God's favour to us should be loved, honoured, respected and highly esteemed by us for their work's sake (1 Thessalonians 5:12, 13). But God's servants must not be idolized. True gospel preachers carefully shun recognition, desiring that Christ only be exalted and honoured (1 Corinthians 3:5-7; 4:1; 2 Corinthians 4:5, 7).

2. Peter preached Christ to this multitude (3:13-16)

This is the one thing preachers today have in common with the apostles. None today has apostolic gifts of inspiration, miracles, or tongues. But every gospel preacher is called and gifted of God to preach Christ (1 Corinthians 1:17-23; 2 Corinthians 4:5). In preaching Christ to this crowd of men who were guilty of murdering the Lord of glory Peter did four things.

First, he told them who Christ is (3:13). He is the true and living God, the God of Abraham, Isaac and Jacob. He is the promised Messiah, the Son of David, the King of Israel. Essentially, Peter said, 'This Jesus, whom you crucified, is God over all, blessed forever. He is the God-man, the only Lord and Saviour. That one whom you crucified, God has glorified!' (See Isaiah 55:5; John 17:1-5; Romans 14:9; Philippians 2:9-11).

Secondly, Peter exposed their sin (3:13-15). Looking them squarely in the eye, planting his feet firmly, with great boldness, the apostle flatly and plainly charged these men with murdering the Son of God! That is what preachers are supposed to do. Faithful gospel preachers probe and probe and probe until they find your point of rebellion. They expose the enmity of your heart to God. They know that they must. Until sinners are made to see and confess their sin, they will not trust Christ and be reconciled to God.

Thirdly, God's servant declared what Christ has done (3:15). Though he died the painful, shameful, ignominious death of the cross, Jesus Christ was raised from the dead by the power of God. That resurrection removed all reproach from him, ratified his claims (Romans 1:1-4), confirmed his doctrine and is the basis of all faith and hope in him (Romans 4:25-5:1; 8:33, 34).

Fourthly, the apostle proclaimed the power of the risen Christ (3:16). This miracle was performed in the name of Christ, by virtue of his power. It was a miracle done by 'the faith which is by him', by the faith which he gave. Every miracle of grace is performed by the name of Christ (4:12), through faith in him, a faith that he gives (Ephesians 1:19; 2:8; Colossians 2:12).

3. Peter gave a reason for hope (3:17, 18)

Once he had wounded them, he hoped to see them healed. They were guilty; but there is hope for the guilty because Christ died to save sinners (1 Timothy 1:15). Though they had indeed crucified the Lord of glory, the death of Christ was according to the wise and gracious purpose of God (Isaiah 53:10, 11; Acts 2:23). When Joseph's brothers realised who he was and what power he had, they remembered their sin and feared. But Joseph said, 'Fear not, for am I in the place of God? But God meant it unto good ... to save much people alive' (Genesis 50:19, 20). The Lord Jesus Christ, our Joseph, says to guilty sinners, 'Fear not, for I am in the place of God to save much people alive.' The Lord Jesus Christ died, arose and ascended to glory to save sinners according to the will of God (Acts 5:30, 31).

4. Peter pressed upon his hearers the claims of the sovereign Christ (3:19-26)

Peter urged them to repent, holding before them the promise of grace, forgiveness and reconciliation now and forever (3:19-21). He urged them to repentance by showing them the certain destruction of all who refuse to obey Christ (3:22, 23). At last, Peter urged these men to repent by pointing out the fulfilment of all God's covenant blessings in Christ (3:24-26).

Acts 3:14 But ye denied the Holy One and the Just, and desired a murderer to be granted unto you;

Acts 3:15 And killed the Prince of life, whom God hath raised from the dead; whereof we are witnesses.

Chapter 10

'The Prince of life'

Acts 3:14, 15

In this passage Peter is preaching to the Jews and their religious leaders in the temple. He who once quivered before a maid now speaks with boldness. He glories in the cross of Christ and plainly exposes the hideous sin of the people to whom he preaches, saying, 'Ye ... killed the Prince of life!' Here the apostle gives an example to all who preach the gospel. The subject of our preaching must always be the cross of our Lord Jesus Christ, and in preaching the cross we must expose the enmity of man's heart towards God, calling the wicked to repentance and faith.

This text of Holy Scripture is full of gospel doctrine: 'Ye denied the Holy One and the Just, and desired a murderer to be granted unto you; and killed the Prince of life, whom God hath raised from the dead; whereof we are witnesses.'

1. The depravity of man

The astonishing hideousness of human sin is glaringly evident in the murder of our Lord Jesus Christ. Jeremiah tells us, 'The heart is deceitful above all things, and desperately wicked' (Jeremiah 17:9). Paul declares, 'The carnal mind is enmity against God' (Romans 8:7). But the infamous measure of human sin is discovered only in the crucifixion of God's dear Son by the hands of men, men who were acting as representatives of all men. The cold-blooded murder of Jesus Christ is a glaring proof of man's hatred of God! That is the essence of the doctrine of total depravity.

53

2. The holiness and justice of God

When God made his own Son to be sin for us, he forsook the darling of heaven, poured out the vials of his unmitigated wrath upon him, punished him to the full satisfaction of his infinite justice and killed him! The death of Christ upon the cross declares that our God is a just God and a Saviour (Isaiah 45:21), both just and the justifier of all who trust him (Romans 3:24-26).

3. The condescension of Christ

Wonder of wonders! He who is the Prince of life stooped to die! He who is Lord of all humbled himself to die by the hands of wicked men. He who gives and sustains all life was killed by men who live upon his goodness. The nails in his hands and feet could never have held the Son of God to the cursed tree. It was his zeal for the glory of God and his love for his people that held him there (Philippians 2:5-11; 2 Corinthians 8:9). Because he saved others, he would not and could not save himself.

4. The folly of rebellion

All rebellion against the Lord Jesus Christ is madness (Psalm 2:1-12). It is true, these men killed the Prince of life. They rebelled against his claims. They would not have him to reign over them. So they killed him. But he is the Prince of life! Now that very Christ whom man has crucified is risen, exalted and given power over all flesh. One day, either in repentance or in judgment, every sinner will bow to him and acknowledge him as Lord (Isaiah 45:22-25; Philippians 2:10, 11).

5. The glorious triumph of Christ

He is 'the Prince of life, whom God hath raised from the dead'! His own Godhead raised him. God the Father raised him. God the Spirit raised him. He resumed his life triumphantly. By his resurrection from the dead, Jesus Christ was declared to be the Son of God with power (Romans 1:1-4). His resurrection declares that Satan is vanquished (John 12:31; Revelation 20:1-3), the sins of God's elect have been put away (Colossians 2:12-15), his people are justified (Romans 4:25), God's justice is satisfied (Isaiah 53:10-12) and all his redeemed will also be raised from the dead (John 11:25; 1 Corinthians 15:23).

6. The credibility of the gospel

The credibility of the gospel is the fact that it is the revelation of God. Yet, so gracious is the Almighty that he gives men undeniable proof that the gospel of Christ (the message of his death, burial and resurrection as the sinners' substitute) is true. Peter says, with regard to these things, 'whereof we are witnesses'.

There stood Peter and John, two evidently honest men. They had nothing to gain by their testimony, and much to lose. They might have called upon the other apostles. They might even have called upon more than 500 brethren who had seen the risen Lord at one time to confirm their testimony (1 Corinthians 15:4-7). The witness of such men is unquestionably true. Jesus Christ the Lord overcame the powers of death. His body rose from the tomb three days after he died. His victorious resurrection is a matter of fact, as certain and credible as any fact recorded upon the pages of human history. Jesus Christ of Nazareth, though he died upon the cross, lives today as the Prince of life!

7. The Lord Jesus Christ is the Prince of life

This is one of those famous titles by which the Son of God reveals himself to mankind. He will be gloriously known by this name in the day of his appearing, when he will raise the dead. But it is a title which rightfully belonged to him before he was crucified, for his murderers 'killed the Prince of life'. This title belonged to him even when he was in the tomb. Though his body was dead, Christ was still the Prince of life. Now that he is risen from the dead and ever lives to make intercession for us, the Lord Jesus fully possesses all that is implied in this title. He shares it with no one, and no one can take it away from him. The Lord Jesus Christ, our Saviour, is the Prince of life. What does this title imply?

He is the Author of life. All life proceeds from Jesus Christ, God our Creator, by whom all things consist. This is especially true of spiritual, eternal life. The gift of life is entirely the prerogative of the Prince of life (John 5:21; 17:2; 1 John 5:11, 12).

Christ possesses life supremely. Life is in him emphatically and superlatively. He is the life (John 14:6; 1 John 1:2). Apart from him there is no life. Christ is life self-existent, life essential and life eternal. Life dwells in him in all its fulness, force, perfection and independence (John 5:26). Everything else is passing away, but Jesus Christ lives and gives eternal life to all who trust him.

He won for his people the right to live. Christ has 'abolished death, and brought life and immortality to light through the gospel' (2 Timothy 1:10). He delivered us from death (spiritual and eternal) by his obedience to God as our substitute and the power of his grace. He delivered us from the fear of death (physical) by granting us faith in him (Hebrews 2:14, 15).

Jesus Christ freely gives life to dead sinners (Psalm 68:18-20). While in this world, whenever our Saviour came into contact with death it fled from his presence. He always triumphed over it (Mark 5:35-42; Luke 7:11-15; John 11:43, 44). The same is true today.

Wherever the Prince of life comes in saving power, spiritual death flees (John 5:25). So it will be when he comes again (John 5:28, 29). Christ marvellously sustains life. By the power of his grace (John 10:28, 29), by keeping us in union with himself (John 15:5) and by feeding our souls upon the Bread of life (John 6:47, 48, 51, 53-56), our Saviour keeps us in life!

The Prince of life is the Ruler of life. Where Christ lives, he reigns! All true, spiritual life gladly yields obedience to him (Luke 14:33). He wears no empty titles. All to whom he gives life willingly bow to him as 'the Prince of life'.

'The Prince of life'

Acts 4:1 And as they spake unto the people, the priests, and the captain of the temple, and the Sadducees, came upon them,

Acts 4:2 Being grieved that they taught the people, and preached through Jesus the resurrection from the dead.

Acts 4:3 And they laid hands on them, and put them in hold unto the next day: for it was now eventide.

Acts 4:4 Howbeit many of them which heard the word believed; and the number of the men was about five thousand.

Acts 4:5 And it came to pass on the morrow, that their rulers, and elders, and scribes,

Acts 4:6 And Annas the high priest, and Caiaphas, and John, and Alexander, and as many as were of the kindred of the high priest, were gathered together at Jerusalem.

Acts 4:7 And when they had set them in the midst, they asked, By what power, or by what name, have ye done this?

Acts 4:8 Then Peter, filled with the Holy Ghost, said unto them, Ye rulers of the people, and elders of Israel,

Acts 4:9 If we this day be examined of the good deed done to the impotent man, by what means he is made whole;

Acts 4:10 Be it known unto you all, and to all the people of Israel, that by the name of Jesus Christ of Nazareth, whom ye crucified, whom God raised from the dead, even by him doth this man stand here before you whole.

Acts 4:11 This is the stone which was set at nought of you builders, which is become the head of the corner.

Acts 4:12 Neither is there salvation in any other: for there is none other name under heaven given among men, whereby we must be saved.

Chapter 11

Name Above All Names

Acts 4:1-12

The religious leaders at Jerusalem seem to have been stunned and confounded by the great outpouring of the Holy Spirit on the Day of Pentecost and by the conversion of so many to Christ. But they quickly rallied their forces against the apostles, as they had against Christ, and attempted to silence the gospel. Their efforts were futile. As always, the powers of darkness were confounded by the Prince of light. Study this record of the first persecution of God's servants and be assured that the cause of Christ cannot fail. The God and King whose cause we serve rules this world in absolute sovereignty. He must prevail! It is written, 'He must reign, till he hath put all his enemies under his feet' (1 Corinthians 15:25).

1. Peter and John were arrested for preaching the gospel (4:1-4)

The powers of darkness were against Peter and John. They had invaded the very domain of Satan. They were in the temple at Jerusalem preaching the gospel of Christ! They could not do otherwise. This is what the Lord had sent them to do. After healing the lame man, while they had the attention of the crowd, they preached Christ to them.

With great boldness these two men bore faithful witness to Christ in the midst of his enemies (4:1, 2). The principal point of their doctrine on this occasion was the resurrection of the dead. 'They preached through Jesus the resurrection of the dead.' Peter and John knew their business. They did not meddle in the affairs of the state. They did not seek, or become involved with social reform. They did not even attempt to shut down the dens of vice in Jerusalem. These men were preachers so they preached. They pointed sinners to Christ and proclaimed him as the resurrection and the life (John 11:25). Declaring only what they had seen and heard, they preached the fact of Christ's resurrection from the dead. To preach the resurrection by Christ is to preach these five things:

59

1. The death of Christ as the substitute for sinners (2 Corinthians 5:21; Galatians 3:13; Acts 3:13-15).

2. The resurrection of Christ as the representative of God's elect (Hebrews 6:20; Ephesians 2:5, 6; Acts 3:13).

3. The exaltation of Christ as Lord over all (John 17:2; Romans 14:9; Acts 2:32-36).

4. The Second Coming of Christ (1 Thessalonians 4:13-18; Acts 3:19-21).

5. Salvation and eternal life to all who trust Christ (John 11:25; Romans 10:9-13; Acts 3:19, 26).

The gospel which Peter and John preached was made effectual to many by the Holy Spirit (4:4). Though the preachers were persecuted, the Word of God grew and prevailed. A few days earlier 3,000 souls had been converted by the grace of God (Acts 2:41). Now faith had been granted to 5,000 more. Two sermons were preached in the power of the Holy Spirit, and the church grew from 120 to more than 8,000 believers in Jerusalem!

Yet, to the religious leaders of the city the gospel of Christ was an offence (4:2, 3). The doctrines of substitutionary atonement, resurrection glory and free salvation by Jesus Christ were offensive to the pride, religious works and self-righteousness of these men. They were grieved by that which should have made them rejoice. They were grieved by the glory of Christ! Not only were they offended by the message of salvation by grace through the merits of the crucified substitute, they were also fearful of losing their hold on the people. So they arrested Peter and John. For the present, these faithful servants of God only had to suffer imprisonment. Later, Peter and others would be put to death for preaching the gospel. The Lord wisely trains his people for suffering by degrees. He sends lesser trials to prepare them for the greater. From the very beginning, the history of God's church has been one of suffering at the hands of persecutors. It is a history written in blood. The cause of the persecution is the preaching of the gospel of the free grace of God flowing to sinners through the merits of Christ's precious blood. This message is an offence to self-righteous, religious people (Galatians 5:11).

2. The religious leaders of the nation tried to intimidate Peter and John into silence (4:5-7)

These 'rulers, and elders, and scribes' were the men of greatest respect, power and influence in the nation of Israel, the Sanhedrin. They asked Peter and John, 'By what power, or by what name have ye done this?' Had they replied, 'Jehovah, the only true and living God, did this,' their answer would have been true, but it would have been a denial of Christ! The Sanhedrin would have said, 'Bless his name,' and the affair would have ended. But Peter knew that the object of their hatred was not God as they conceived him to be, but God in the flesh, the Lord Jesus Christ. He had faced those men before and wilted (Luke 22:54-62). He would never deny his Lord again! Picture Peter standing in the midst of this ecclesiastical court. He braced himself, planted his feet firmly, not knowing what they might do to him but, being fully aware of his own responsibility, he spoke as a faithful servant of God.

3. Boldly, with defiant conviction, Peter preached Christ to his persecutors, without compromise (4:8-10)

Peter was filled with the Holy Spirit, who taught him what to say and gave him the courage to say it (Luke 12:11, 12). He was altogether innocent of any evil in the matter at hand. He had done exactly what the Lord had commanded him to do. Yet he knew he was in the place where God had put him. So he seized the opportunity and boldly confessed Christ in the very teeth of his enemies (read his confession in verses 10-12). In this confession Peter places great emphasis upon the name of the Lord Jesus Christ, as do all the Scriptures (Isaiah 9:6, 7; Matthew 1:21). 'God ... hath highly exalted him, and given him a name which is above every name' (Philippians 2:9).

The name of the Lord Jesus Christ is precious (Song of Solomon 1:3; 1 Peter 2:7). Power is associated with his name (Philippians 2:9-11). His name is the source and cause of the believer's pardon (1 John 2:12). We are saved by faith in his name (John 1:12, 13; Romans 10:13). All that God does for sinners in grace he does for Christ's sake (Ephesians 4:32). All true prayer is offered to God in the name of Christ, our representative and substitute. To call upon his name is to trust him as our Saviour. We come to God only in his name (John 14:13, 14). The believer has peace through the name of Christ (John 14:27; 16:33). The name of the Lord is our protection at all times (Proverbs 18:10; 2 Samuel 22:1-4). The preservation of God's elect, our eternal security, is in his name (John 17:11). What would become of his name, if one of his believing ones was lost? His name is the theme of all true preaching (Luke 24:47). In the Word of God, the name of the Lord Jesus Christ is always associated with prosperity (Jeremiah 23:5; Revelation 19:11-16). 'The pleasure of the Lord shall prosper in his hand' (Isaiah 53:10). 'He shall not fail!' (Isaiah 42:4). The Lion of the tribe of Judah will prevail. The Lamb of God will be satisfied. His people will be saved. His cause will be triumphant. His enemies will bow before his feet. His name will be glorified (Revelation 5:5, 9-14).

Acts 4:13 Now when they saw the boldness of Peter and John, and perceived that they were unlearned and ignorant men, they marvelled; and they took knowledge of them, that they had been with Jesus.

Acts 4:14 And beholding the man which was healed standing with them, they could say nothing against it.

Acts 4:15 But when they had commanded them to go aside out of the council, they conferred among themselves,

Acts 4:16 Saying, What shall we do to these men? for that indeed a notable miracle hath been done by them is manifest to all them that dwell in Jerusalem; and we cannot deny it.

Acts 4:17 But that it spread no further among the people, let us straitly threaten them, that they speak henceforth to no man in this name.

Acts 4:18 And they called them, and commanded them not to speak at all nor teach in the name of Jesus.

Acts 4:19 But Peter and John answered and said unto them, Whether it be right in the sight of God to hearken unto you more than unto God, judge ye.

Acts 4:20 For we cannot but speak the things which we have seen and heard.

Acts 4:21 So when they had further threatened them, they let them go, finding nothing how they might punish them, because of the people: for all men glorified God for that which was done.

Acts 4:22 For the man was above forty years old, on whom this miracle of healing was shewed.

Chapter 12

What Does My Life Say About Christ?

Acts 4:13-22

Several things in this paragraph need to be carefully observed. Each is a matter worthy of more detailed study than can be given here.

1. Neither the gospel that Peter and John preached nor the miracle they performed could be denied.

The evidence was undeniable (4:13-16). These men had honoured God. They faithfully confessed Christ, bearing witness to him before his enemies, and God honoured their faithfulness. Though they were now prisoners before the Sanhedrin, the Lord was with them. As he had promised, the Holy Spirit gave them the wisdom and the words they needed (Matthew 10:19). God always honours those who honour him (1 Samuel 2:30).

2. When there is a conflict between the will of God and the laws of men, the believer must obey God, regardless of cost (4:17-20)

In all things regarding civil life and government, believers are to be subject to the power and authority of civil rulers (Romans 13:1-4). However, if we are required by law to do that which is in direct violation of the Word of God, we are bound to obey God.

3. All who serve the cause of God in this world will be protected by God and the cause they serve will succeed (4:21, 22)

God will be glorified! In his wise and adorable providence God makes all things work together for the spiritual, eternal good of his elect and the glory of his own great name (Psalm 76:10; Romans 8:28; Revelation 4:11). He always does what is best. At this time, it was best for Peter and John to be released. Later, it was best for them to be beaten and imprisoned. Still later, it was best for Peter to be brutally killed for the testimony of Christ.

4. It was evident that they had been with Christ

However, the thing that seems most significant in this paragraph is recorded in verse 13. 'Now when they saw the boldness of Peter and John, and perceived that they were unlearned and ignorant men, they marvelled; and they took knowledge of them, that they had been with Jesus.' Those men, who had no reverence for God, no regard for Christ, and no interest in the gospel, took notice of Peter and John as being men whose lives were manifestly under the influence and control of the Lord Jesus Christ. Their communion and conversation with Christ so influenced their lives, their speech and their conduct that even their enemies acknowledged them to be followers of Christ.

Here is a question that ought to pierce every believer's heart: 'What does my life say about Christ? What does my behaviour say to the people among whom I work and live about the Christ I profess to trust, love and serve?' This much is certain: if a person truly knows Christ, if a person lives in communion with Jesus Christ by faith, Christ will be manifest in his or her life. Paul knew the Thessalonians were elect of God because Christ was manifest in them (1 Thessalonians 1:3-10). Give thoughtful consideration to the following questions ...

1. What is a Christian?

A Christian is all of these things: a person who has been chosen by God in eternal election as an object of his love and grace (Ephesians 1:4; 2 Thessalonians 2:13); a person who has been redeemed from the curse of the law by the blood of Christ shed for the satisfaction of divine justice for God's elect (Galatians 3:13; 1 Peter 3:18); a person who has been regenerated by the Holy Spirit through the preaching of the gospel (1 Peter 1:23; James 1:18), a person who by the irresistible influence of God the Holy Spirit freely acknowledges his or her sin and believes on the Lord Jesus Christ, confessing him as Lord (Romans 10:9-13; 1 John 1:9). A Christian is a person in whom Christ dwells (Colossians 1:27; 2 Peter 1:4).

The new birth is nothing less than Christ coming into a sinner's heart, taking possession of him, ruling him and causing him to become a follower of himself (Matthew 12:29; Luke 14:26, 27). Anything less than this is not Christianity. A Christian, a true believer, is a man or a woman who desires and seeks the perfection of Christ's character in himself or herself

(Philippians 3:10; Colossians 3:1-3; Hebrews 12:14). Perfect conformity to Christ cannot be attained in this life, but that fact does not hinder the pursuit of it. The believer longs to be like Christ, to walk in his steps, to follow his example (John 13:15). Here are four things that characterized our Saviour's life. These four things will, to one degree or another, characterize all who know and follow him:

1. Unflinching boldness for the honour of God (Matthew 21:12, 13);
2. Gentleness and love (John 8:1-12; 1 Corinthians 13:1-8; Ephesians 4:32-5:1);
3. Self-abasing humility (Philippians 2:5-8);
4. Righteousness (Luke 2:49-52; Ephesians 4:17-32).

Find a person whose life truly exemplifies these characteristics and you have found one who has evidently 'been with Jesus'. Those who bear the fruit of the Spirit are born of the Spirit (Galatians 5:22, 23). Good works have nothing to do with salvation. We are saved by grace alone. But grace always produces good works (Ephesians 2:8-10).

2. When should believers strive to be like Christ?

I hope this question appears to be redundant to you. Yet there are many who seem to think that Christianity is for Sundays and for church, but should not greatly interfere with a person's life. If your religion does not interfere with your life your religion is a sham (2 Corinthians 5:17). That person who knows Christ strives to be like him at all times, in all places, in all circumstances: in the house of God (1 Timothy 3:15, 16); in the daily affairs of life (Matthew 5:14-16); in the home (Ephesians 5:22-6:4); in heart and attitude (Psalm 139:23, 24).

3. Why should those who love Christ strive to be like him?

The believer's life is not motivated by law, but by grace. God's people do not serve him for fear of punishment or in hope of reward. And they certainly do not do what they do to be seen of men (Matthew 6:1-18), but they do seek to imitate Christ in all things.

Earnestly strive to be like Christ in all things for your own sake. Your happiness in this world greatly depends upon your obedience to Christ. Your spiritual health, in great measure, depends upon your willingness to follow your Saviour. Imitate Christ in all things for the gospel's sake (Titus 2:10). The gospel you profess to believe will gain or lose credibility in the eyes of men by the way you live. Strive to conform your life to Christ for Christ's sake. Loving gratitude demands it (2 Corinthians 5:14). Child of God, never forget who you are and whose you are (1 Corinthians 6:20; 7:23).

4. How can a person be like Christ?

Many who admire the love and purity of Christ's life try to follow his example. But they are building without a foundation. The house they build will soon crumble around them. It will do you no good to mould your behaviour to the example of Christ until your heart is renewed by grace. 'Ye must be born again!' (John 3:7). Only Christ can make men and women to be like Christ. He does this by four mighty works of grace:

1. Blood atonement (1 Peter 3:18);
2. Imputed righteousness (2 Corinthians 5:21);
3. Regenerating, sanctifying grace (2 Peter 1:4);
4. Resurrection glory (Philippians 3:21).

What Does My Life Say About Christ?

Acts 4:23 And being let go, they went to their own company, and reported all that the chief priests and elders had said unto them.

Acts 4:24 And when they heard that, they lifted up their voice to God with one accord, and said, Lord, thou art God, which hast made heaven, and earth, and the sea, and all that in them is:

Acts 4:25 Who by the mouth of thy servant David hast said, Why did the heathen rage, and the people imagine vain things?

Acts 4:26 The kings of the earth stood up, and the rulers were gathered together against the Lord, and against his Christ.

Acts 4:27 For of a truth against thy holy child Jesus, whom thou hast anointed, both Herod, and Pontius Pilate, with the Gentiles, and the people of Israel, were gathered together,

Acts 4:28 For to do whatsoever thy hand and thy counsel determined before to be done.

Acts 4:29 And now, Lord, behold their threatenings: and grant unto thy servants, that with all boldness they may speak thy word,

Acts 4:30 By stretching forth thine hand to heal; and that signs and wonders may be done by the name of thy holy child Jesus.

Acts 4:31 And when they had prayed, the place was shaken where they were assembled together; and they were all filled with the Holy Ghost, and they spake the word of God with boldness.

Chapter 13

The Church In Prayer

Acts 4:23-31

After their arrest and trial for preaching the gospel of Christ, Peter and John were released, but were given strict command by the Jewish Sanhedrin 'not to speak at all nor teach in the name of Jesus' (4:18). As soon as they were released Peter and John went to the place where God's saints were gathered for worship and told their brethren what had happened to them. Then the saints 'lifted up their voice to God with one accord'. They had a prayer meeting. What a weapon! Nothing strengthens the hands of God's church and his servants in the work of the gospel like prayer. I want to draw attention to three things in this passage.

1. The comfort and joy of a real church family (4:23)

When Peter and John were released from bondage, they did not go home. They did not go to the courts to file a lawsuit. They did not do any of the things that many today do in the name of God when they feel that they have been wronged (see 2 Corinthians 10:3, 4). Peter and John went to their family, the church of God, and told them what had happened. The Holy Spirit describes it in simple, tender terms. 'They went to their own company, and reported all that the chief priests and elders had said unto them.'

The saints of God were meeting together at the appointed place in the hour of worship. Peter and John went directly to the meeting place because that is where they wanted and needed to be. There is no joy that can compare to the fellowship of God's saints in the house of worship. There is no comfort like the comfort of believing men and women as they sit together in fellowship in the house of God, singing his praise, calling upon him in prayer and hearing the gospel of Christ preached in the power of the Spirit, worshipping the triune God. When David was driven from his throne and forced to live in the wilderness for fear of his life, above all else, he longed to go once more with his brethren into the house of God to worship the Lord (Psalm 84:1-4, 10). The man after God's own heart said, 'I was glad when they said unto me, let us go into the house of the Lord' (Psalm 122:1).

Nothing is more important and beneficial in the life of a believer than the assembly of God's saints in public worship. Every true local church is the temple of the Holy Spirit (1 Corinthians 3:16). Christ has promised to meet with every assembly of men and women gathered in his name (Matthew 18:20). You are most likely to hear from God in that place where men and women gather to hear the gospel preached (Romans 10:17; Ephesians 4:11-16). In the house of God the people of God gather to worship at the throne of God. In our songs of praise, in our observance of the ordinances, in our prayers and in our preaching, our object is the worship of God. The assembly of the saints is the meeting of God's family. What can be more delightful and beneficial than a family gathering? When I am sick, in trouble, sorrowful, depressed, or rejoicing, I want to be with my family (Psalm 133:1).

The writer of the epistle to the Hebrews gives us wise counsel when he admonishes us not to despise and neglect the assembly of God's saints. That is the first step to total apostasy (Hebrews 10:24-26). We need those things God has provided for his children in his house more than we need anything else in this world: the ministry of the Word, the fellowship of God's saints, the communion of Christ and the worship of God. After spending two days and nights among the Lord's enemies, Peter and John wanted, above anything else, to spend a little time in the house of God with the family of God.

2. The matters of great concern in prayer (4:24-30)

After the apostles told the church what had happened to them, with one accord they began to pray. They did not take up arms. They did not try to rally the nation behind the cause of religious freedom. They did not try to form a ministerial association so that the Jewish leaders and the apostles of Christ might learn to work together. They did not turn on Peter and John and ask them to resign because they could not fit into the community. And they did not take a vote to form a committee to investigate the social impact of Christianity upon the Jewish world. They prayed!

Obviously, one man led the congregation in prayer. Perhaps several led them at successive times. But they did not all audibly pray at once. In the house of God all things are 'done decently and in order' (1 Corinthians 14:40). No aspect of public worship is more important than public prayer. When a man leads the congregation in prayer, as he lifts his voice to God, the whole congregation ought to lift their hearts with his, ascribing praise to God, acknowledging his good providence and the blessings of his grace, seeking the power of his Spirit to attend the ministry of the Word for the glory of Christ. This is exactly what happened in verses 24-30.

They adored the supremacy and greatness of the Lord God (4:24). Nothing encourages people to do God's work or to suffer for his name's sake like the realization of his greatness. Our God is great! We may reasonably expect great things from him. He who made all things and rules all things has all things at his disposal (Psalm 135:6). Get hold of that and you will get hold of both courage and peace.

The saints of God here acknowledged and bowed to the sovereign purpose of God revealed in the accomplishment of his providence (4:24-28). These men and women confidently believed that both they and their enemies were completely, totally, absolutely in the hands of God. That fact secured their hearts in peace. They believed his Word (4:25, 26), submitted to his providence (4:27) and acknowledged his purpose (4:28). Nothing thwarts the purpose of God. Nothing escapes his absolute rule (Isaiah 14:24-27; Daniel 4:34, 35). The purpose of God is the salvation of his people by the death of his Son. He sovereignly controls even the rage of ungodly, reprobate men to accomplish that great purpose!

Then these saints of God asked the Lord to grant to his servants grace and strength to preach the Word (4:29, 30). They made three simple, submissive requests of faith to God, whose cause they served, whose glory they sought.

1. They asked God to watch over them: 'Now, Lord, behold their threatenings' (cf. Zechariah 2:8).

2. They asked him to grant his servants boldness to preach the gospel.

3. They asked him to stretch forth his hand, to reveal his power, his grace and his glory in their midst (4:30).

They asked these things in the name of Christ and for the glory of Christ.

3. The Lord's gracious answer to the cry of his people (4:31)

In response to their prayer, God made himself known in the midst of his people. The church was filled with the Spirit. The apostles preached the Word of God with boldness. God was honoured. Let every congregation imitate this congregation and God will be honoured in his church today!

Acts 4:32 And the multitude of them that believed were of one heart and of one soul: neither said any of them that ought of the things which he possessed was his own; but they had all things common.

Acts 4:33 And with great power gave the apostles witness of the resurrection of the Lord Jesus: and great grace was upon them all.

Acts 4:34 Neither was there any among them that lacked: for as many as were possessors of lands or houses sold them, and brought the prices of the things that were sold,

Acts 4:35 And laid them down at the apostles' feet: and distribution was made unto every man according as he had need.

Acts 4:36 And Joses, who by the apostles was surnamed Barnabas, (which is, being interpreted, The son of consolation,) a Levite, and of the country of Cyprus,

Acts 4:37 Having land, sold it, and brought the money, and laid it at the apostles' feet.

Acts 5:1 But a certain man named Ananias, with Sapphira his wife, sold a possession,

Acts 5:2 And kept back part of the price, his wife also being privy to it, and brought a certain part, and laid it at the apostles' feet.

Acts 5:3 But Peter said, Ananias, why hath Satan filled thine heart to lie to the Holy Ghost, and to keep back part of the price of the land?

Acts 5:4 Whiles it remained, was it not thine own? and after it was sold, was it not in thine own power? why hast thou conceived this thing in thine heart? thou hast not lied unto men, but unto God.

Acts 5:5 And Ananias hearing these words fell down, and gave up the ghost: and great fear came on all them that heard these things.

Acts 5:6 And the young men arose, wound him up, and carried him out, and buried him.

Acts 5:7 And it was about the space of three hours after, when his wife, not knowing what was done, came in.

Acts 5:8 And Peter answered unto her, Tell me whether ye sold the land for so much? And she said, Yea, for so much.

Acts 5:9 Then Peter said unto her, How is it that ye have agreed together to tempt the Spirit of the Lord? behold, the feet of them which have buried thy husband are at the door, and shall carry thee out.

Acts 5:10 Then fell she down straightway at his feet, and yielded up the ghost: and the young men came in, and found her dead, and, carrying her forth, buried her by her husband.

Acts 5:11 And great fear came upon all the church, and upon as many as heard these things.

Chapter 14

'Such as I have give I thee'

Acts 4:32-5:11

In the book of Acts the Holy Spirit gives us a detailed picture of the early church. Like the church today, it was a mixed multitude. Tares grew with the wheat. Goats were mingled with the Lord's sheep. Among the people of God there were, even in those early days, covetous, idolatrous hypocrites. Every Sunday School child has heard about Ananias and his wife Sapphira. Their story begins in Acts 4:32 and continues through to chapter 5:11. In this story the Spirit of God gives us a striking contrast between true faith in Christ and a mere hypocritical profession of faith. True faith surrenders all to Christ. Religious hypocrisy merely pretends to surrender all to Christ. If you will carefully read these few verses of the inspired record, three things will catch your attention.

1. An attitude of grace

The first thing the Holy Spirit directs our attention to in this passage is an attitude of grace among the people of God (4:32-35). Believing hearts are gracious hearts. True faith really converts sinners. The person who is born again by the Spirit of God is no longer a selfish, self-centred, self-seeking, self-serving person; but a grateful, thoughtful, generous, serving person. All who live unto God die unto the world. The person who finds his life in Christ loses his life to Christ (Matthew 10:39). These early disciples show by their example that faith lives not for material gain, but for spiritual good. Faith does not seek temporal riches. Faith loves, not the things of this world, which are passing away, but the things of that world which is to come, which are eternal (2 Corinthians 4:18). Faith seeks the kingdom of God and his righteousness, not the mammon of unrighteousness (Matthew 6:24, 31-33). Faith in Christ produces an attitude of grace in the heart. Those who have experienced the grace of God are gracious. Is not this the teaching of these four verses?

Faith unites the people of God. Luke tells us that 'The multitude of them that believed were of one heart and of one soul' (4:32). All of God's people truly are one in Christ. We are one family (Ephesians 3:14, 15), a family of

73

sinners saved by grace. Our hearts love one person supremely, the Lord Jesus Christ (1 Peter 1:8; 1 John 4:19). We are devoted to one cause, the kingdom of God. We seek one thing above all other things, the will of God (Matthew 6:10, 33). We have one dominating, ultimate goal, the glory of God (John 12:28). These things are true of all believers! Many other things, regrettably, may divide us while we live in this body of flesh and sin. But here we are one. Let every child of God endeavour, therefore, to keep 'the unity of the Spirit in the bond of peace' (Ephesians 4:1-6).

Faith in Christ makes men and women generous with their possessions: 'Neither said any of them that ought of the things which he possessed was his own; but they had all things common' (4:32). These men and women were so taken up with the cause of Christ and with their love for one another that they placed no value upon personal property, personal wealth, or personal advantages. These believers were truly indifferent to such things. They did not even look upon their own possessions as their own. In their hearts' affection they had forsaken all to follow Christ. They recognized that all earthly, material things are only temporary. They were so thoroughly united to one another in love that they each looked upon their own property as the common property of God's people.

These men and women had learned what every child of God in this world must learn: all that we have in this world belongs to God. God has entrusted each of us with certain of this world's goods to use as stewards in his house. We are responsible to use them wisely for the advancement of his kingdom, the furtherance of his gospel, the comfort of his people and the glory of his name. These men and women were willing to rob themselves of comfort, convenience and personal satisfaction for one another's good. Is it any wonder that the apostles preached with such power when such 'great grace was upon them all'? (4:33).

True faith actually causes God's saints to prefer each other above themselves. This is manifest in verses 34 and 35. These men and women sold their possessions, their houses and their lands rather than allow their brothers and sisters in Christ to be in need of the necessities of life! The grace of God still produces this kind of graciousness, mercifulness and love (Philippians 2:1-8; James 2:14-17; 1 John 3:16-18).

Their gifts were free, voluntary sacrifices of love. No one told them to give. No one told them how to give. No one told them how much to give. In the church of God giving is not regulated by law, but by love (2 Corinthians 9:7). The only constraint these people felt was the constraint of love (2 Corinthians 5:14). They saw what the needs of the church were and willingly met those needs, without the least pressure to do so. Notice also that the people of God trusted the servants of God to distribute their gifts under the direction of the Spirit of God (4:35). Where the Spirit of God rules the hearts of men there is trust and trustworthiness! The apostles of Christ were not (and his servants are not) greedy men. They took only what they needed to sustain themselves. Everything else was distributed as needs demanded.

2. An act of generosity

The Spirit of God inspired Luke to tell us about one man specifically, who was an example of the rest. Barnabas performed a great deed, an act of generosity (4:36, 37). As one who was ordained of God to be a preacher of the gospel, Barnabas disentangled himself from the affairs of this world (2 Timothy 2:4; 1 Corinthians 9:6-14). Perhaps Barnabas did not know it at this time, but God was preparing him for the work of preaching the gospel. Indeed, all who are called of God to preach the gospel are prepared, equipped and qualified by him to do so (1 Timothy 3:1-7; Titus 1:6-9). Barnabas was just the kind of man God uses in the work of the ministry. God had made him such a man by his Spirit and by his grace. He was a peaceful man, one who comforted and encouraged the saints. He was a generous man, an example of Christian charity. He was willingly submissive to the apostles, the servants of Christ (Hebrews 13:7, 17). Barnabas was a man of good report, who in the providence of God gained the love and respect of God's people. Then, after God prepared him for it, he was made a preacher of the gospel (Acts 13:2).

3. An act of greed

There was a wicked, hypocritical couple in the church, Ananias and Sapphira. When Ananias saw how greatly Barnabas was admired by God's people, he was filled with envy. So he and his wife agreed to lie to God. Hypocrisy is lying to God! They made a great gift to the church, but their gift was an act of greed. They gave because they wanted recognition. At first glance they appear to have done a great thing. They sold a piece of property to help the church. They gave a handsome amount of money, perhaps much more than Barnabas had given. But God looks on the heart (1 Samuel 16:7). The gift Ananias and Sapphira brought revealed graceless, greedy hearts. They pretended to give all, when in fact they had given nothing. No one asked them to give anything. Theirs was an unwilling sacrifice, given only in a hypocritical pretence, a sham, a show, a mockery. Their gift was an act of covetousness and greed, not of grace and love. They hoped to gain by giving, to gain the applause of men! Their gift was an abomination to God (Luke 16:15). Beware of covetousness and hypocrisy!

Acts 5:3 But Peter said, Ananias, why hath Satan filled thine heart to lie to the Holy Ghost, and to keep back part of the price of the land? ...

... Acts 5:12 And by the hands of the apostles were many signs and wonders wrought among the people; (and they were all with one accord in Solomon's porch.

Acts 5:13 And of the rest durst no man join himself to them: but the people magnified them.

Acts 5:14 And believers were the more added to the Lord, multitudes both of men and women.)

Acts 5:15 Insomuch that they brought forth the sick into the streets, and laid them on beds and couches, that at the least the shadow of Peter passing by might overshadow some of them.

Acts 5:16 There came also a multitude out of the cities round about unto Jerusalem, bringing sick folks, and them which were vexed with unclean spirits: and they were healed every one.

Chapter 15

When A Church Member Falls

Acts 5:3, 12-16

Everything was going well for the church at Jerusalem. The gospel was being preached in the power of the Holy Spirit. The saints of God were united in heart, committed to Christ, committed to the gospel and committed to one another. God was doing great things among his people. The little band of believers had grown from 120 to well over 8,000 in number. The church of God, which had been a joke in the minds of men, was gaining respect and influence. But there were some traitors within; hypocrites, who were of the seed of the serpent. Two of them committed a terrible act of hypocrisy by which their evil hearts were exposed, and judgment began at the house of God. Ananias and Sapphira were both killed by the hand of God for lying to the Holy Spirit. The news of what happened that day in the house of God spread like wildfire through the streets of Jerusalem. One of the despised band, along with his wife, had proved himself to be a hypocrite! You can imagine the talk, the sniggers, the gossip, the finger-pointing.

Church members, professed followers of Christ, do often fall, just like this wicked pair. Some who, by their actions, appear to be pillars in the church do forsake Christ and his gospel. Pastors, elders and deacons, evangelists and missionaries, respected men and women in the church fall into sin, forsake Christ, forsake the gospel, forsake the worship of God and prove to be hypocrites by wilfully abandoning all that they know to be right and true. From time to time many who profess to be our Lord's disciples go back and walk no more with him (John 6:66). Every time we see that happen, we ask ourselves and one another, 'What is happening? Why have they left us? What effect will this have on the cause of Christ? How is this going to affect the church of God?'

What happens when a church member falls? Our natural tendency is to be full of doubt and fear. We fear what might happen to the church of God. We fear that the gospel might somehow lose its power and influence because

77

some religious hypocrite has shown himself for what he really is. But our fears are without foundation. The honour of God, the purpose of God and the church of God are safe and secure! Even when reprobate men and women fall from our ranks, our God is graciously accomplishing his purpose in his wise and adorable providence, performing what is best for his church and making himself a great and glorious name (Romans 8:28; Psalm 76:10; Isaiah 63:10-14).

Here are five comforting answers given in the Word of God to the question under consideration in this chapter: 'What happens when a church member falls?'

1. God is separating the precious from the vile

From the very beginning local churches have been a mixed multitude of real believers and mere professors. In every field where our Lord sows his wheat Satan plants his tares. Goats, and even some wolves, have always been found among the Lord's sheep. In every band of true, sincere believers some hypocrites will be found. The names of Judas, Demas, Alexander, Simon Magus, Hymenaeus, Philetus, Diotrephes, Ananias and Sapphira stand upon the pages of Holy Scripture to warn us of the presence of false professors among the people of God. But God separates the tares from the wheat, the goats from the sheep and the hypocrite from the true believer (Matthew 13:30, 41-43; 1 John 2:19, 20).

This separation is the work of God. He plainly commands us to let the tares grow with the wheat, lest we uproot the wheat while trying to get rid of the tares. God knows how to weed his garden. He uses many things to do it. Earthly trials, the preaching of the Word, the temptations of Satan, acts of judgment, even the apostasy of reprobate men, are instruments in God's hands by which he separates the precious from the vile (1 Corinthians 11:19).

2. God reminds us by the fall of others that salvation is by his grace alone (1 Corinthians 4:7)

Were it not for the grace of God none would persevere in faith (John 6:66-68). Let us never be proud, boastful, or presumptuous. Our only hope before God is the righteousness and blood of Christ our substitute. Were it not for the fact that Christ holds our hearts we would soon cease to hold him (1 Corinthians 10:11-13). Yet we rejoice in the comforting assurance that his grace is sufficient, even for us (2 Corinthians 12:9). 'Greater is he that is in you, than he that is in the world' (1 John 4:4). Without Christ I am nothing and I can do nothing. But in Christ, by the grace of God, I can go on believing. I can persevere even to my final day in faith. I can do all things through Christ who strengthens me! His grace is sufficient! He can and will preserve his own. In spite of the weakness, infirmity and sinfulness of their flesh, 'They shall never perish' (John 10:28).

3. Whenever one is taken in the snare of the devil God graciously draws his saints closer to Christ and confirms them in the faith of the gospel (Hebrews 6:1-12; 10:38, 39)

The sight of 'mighty men around us falling' reminds us of our own weakness. And every reminder of our weakness in the flesh and of the danger of Satan's devices drives believing hearts to Christ for refuge (Proverbs 18:10). Often we see our companions fall. Our only comfort, security and rest are in the immutability of God's grace (Malachi 3:6; Lamentations 3:24-26; 2 Timothy 2:15-19).

4. Though many do forsake Christ, God sovereignly accomplishes his purpose of grace (5:14)

No real harm has been done. Christ has not lost one of his ransomed ones. The Good Shepherd has not lost one of his sheep. The Son of God has not been defeated by the powers of darkness. Ananias and Sapphira fell and God's judgment fell on them, but their apostasy and God's retribution only caused the people of God to be more fully united to one another. Like a loving family, huddled together in their house for fear of danger, the saints of God were 'all with one accord in Solomon's porch', and the Word of God flourished (Acts 5:12-16).

5. Though many who profess faith in Christ do fall along the way and depart from him, yet our God still preserves his church and maintains his cause in this world (Matthew 16:18; Acts 5:38, 39)

God's covenant cannot be nullified. His purpose cannot be thwarted. His power cannot be defeated. The church of God is safe. The honour of God is secure. Our God will yet be universally honoured in all the fulness of his triune glory and saving grace (Revelation 5:9-14). All is well, for the ark of God is safe! Though many do fall, all who truly trust Christ on this earth are as safe and secure as the saints of God in heaven (1 John 2:1, 2; Romans 8:29-39).

When any turn from Zion's way,
(Alas, what numbers do!)
Methinks I hear my Saviour say,
'Wilt thou forsake me too?'

Ah, Lord, with such a heart as mine,
Unless Thou hold me fast,
I feel I must, I shall decline,
And prove like them at last.

Yet Thou alone hast power, I know,
To save a wretch like me:
To whom or whither could I go,
If I should turn from Thee?

Beyond a doubt I rest assured
Thou art the Christ of God;
Who hast eternal life secured
By promise and by blood.

The help of men and angels joined,
Could never reach my case;
Nor can I hope relief to find,
But in Thy boundless grace.

No voice but Thine can give me rest,
And bid my fears depart;
No love but Thine can make me blest,
And satisfy my heart.

What anguish has that question stirred,
If I will also go;
Yet, Lord, relying on Thy word,
I answer humbly, 'No.'

John Newton, 1779

When A Church Member Falls

Acts 5:17 Then the high priest rose up, and all they that were with him, (which is the sect of the Sadducees,) and were filled with indignation,

Acts 5:18 And laid their hands on the apostles, and put them in the common prison.

Acts 5:19 But the angel of the Lord by night opened the prison doors, and brought them forth, and said,

Acts 5:20 Go, stand and speak in the temple to the people all the words of this life.

Acts 5:21 And when they heard that, they entered into the temple early in the morning, and taught. But the high priest came, and they that were with him, and called the council together, and all the senate of the children of Israel, and sent to the prison to have them brought.

Acts 5:22 But when the officers came, and found them not in the prison, they returned, and told,

Acts 5:23 Saying, The prison truly found we shut with all safety, and the keepers standing without before the doors: but when we had opened, we found no man within.

Acts 5:24 Now when the high priest and the captain of the temple and the chief priests heard these things, they doubted of them whereunto this would grow.

Acts 5:25 Then came one and told them, saying, Behold, the men whom ye put in prison are standing in the temple, and teaching the people.

Acts 5:26 Then went the captain with the officers, and brought them without violence: for they feared the people, lest they should have been stoned.

Acts 5:27 And when they had brought them, they set them before the council: and the high priest asked them,

Acts 5:28 Saying, Did not we straitly command you that ye should not teach in this name? and, behold, ye have filled Jerusalem with your doctrine, and intend to bring this man's blood upon us.

Acts 5:29 Then Peter and the other apostles answered and said, We ought to obey God rather than men.

Acts 5:30 The God of our fathers raised up Jesus, whom ye slew and hanged on a tree.

Acts 5:31 Him hath God exalted with his right hand to be a Prince and a Saviour, for to give repentance to Israel, and forgiveness of sins.

Acts 5:32 And we are his witnesses of these things; and so is also the Holy Ghost, whom God hath given to them that obey him.

Acts 5:33 When they heard that, they were cut to the heart, and took counsel to slay them.

Acts 5:34 Then stood there up one in the council, a Pharisee, named Gamaliel, a doctor of the law, had in reputation among all the people, and commanded to put the apostles forth a little space;

Acts 5:35 And said unto them, Ye men of Israel, take heed to yourselves what ye intend to do as touching these men.

Acts 5:36 For before these days rose up Theudas, boasting himself to be somebody; to whom a number of men, about four hundred, joined themselves: who was slain; and all, as many as obeyed him, were scattered, and brought to nought.

Acts 5:37 After this man rose up Judas of Galilee in the days of the taxing, and drew away much people after him: he also perished; and all, even as many as obeyed him, were dispersed.

Acts 5:38 And now I say unto you, Refrain from these men, and let them alone: for if this counsel or this work be of men, it will come to nought:

Acts 5:39 But if it be of God, ye cannot overthrow it; lest haply ye be found even to fight against God.

Acts 5:40 And to him they agreed: and when they had called the apostles, and beaten them, they commanded that they should not speak in the name of Jesus, and let them go.

Acts 5:41 And they departed from the presence of the council, rejoicing that they were counted worthy to suffer shame for his name.

Acts 5:42 And daily in the temple, and in every house, they ceased not to teach and preach Jesus Christ.

Chapter 16

The Persecution Of God's Church

Acts 5:17-42

The church of God has always had to endure persecution. Her history is written in the blood of faithful martyrs. Sometimes the persecution is fierce, sometimes more subtle, but it is always there. Usually the persecution comes not from profligate, base men, but from devout, religious men. The bloodiest persecutions in history have been executed in the name of God! Until Christ comes again, the persecution will not cease (John 15:18, 20; Matthew 10:22).

In Acts 5:17-42 the Holy Spirit gives us a brief description of the second persecution of the church after the resurrection of Christ. The first was in Acts 4:1-22. Why were these men of God thrown into prison? Why did the religious leaders of their nation want to murder them? The apostles had not held any political rallies, trying to overthrow the liberal Roman government. They had broken no laws. They were not raising a social protest. They were not even crusading against pornography, prostitution and homosexuality, the common social ills of their day. They were being persecuted for only one reason — preaching the gospel of Christ! That is all. They plainly exposed the evil of man's depraved heart, declared the necessity of a substitute, proclaimed the forgiveness of sins by the grace of God through the blood of the Lord Jesus Christ and pressed upon all men the claims of Christ, the risen, sovereign Lord. They had also committed the terrible evils of improving their society by healing the sick and teaching their followers to live in righteousness and peace! For these things, and these things alone, they were persecuted, imprisoned, beaten and threatened with death!

Here are six lessons which the Holy Spirit intends us to learn from this brief history of the church's second persecution at Jerusalem.

1. The cross of Christ is an offence to men (5:17, 18)

This persecution was primarily instigated and carried out by the sect of the Sadducees. They were the liberal, freethinking, broad-minded, religious gentlemen of the day. They did not agree with the fanatical Pharisees. They disapproved of the philosophical pagans. Yet, they were tolerant of both. However, when the apostles came preaching the gospel of Christ, these supposedly tolerant religious men were filled with rage and ready to kill! The fact is, those who claim to be broad-minded and tolerant in matters of religion are broad-minded enough to accept any form of religion that leaves salvation in the hands of man, but the message of salvation by grace alone through the merits of Christ, the sinners' crucified substitute, is an offence to them (Galatians 5:11). The gospel of Christ is offensive to all, except those who are saved by it (1 Corinthians 1:23, 24; Romans 1:15-17).

2. God takes care of his own (5:19-26)

It is written in the Scriptures: 'Them that honour me I will honour' (1 Samuel 2:30). If we belong to God, if we serve the interests of his kingdom, if we are seeking his will and his glory, we have no reason to fear any man. 'If God be for us, who can be against us? (Romans 8:31).

Until a believer's work on earth is done, so long as he can be useful in the cause of Christ, until his appointed days are fulfilled and the Lord calls him home, he can be assured of these three things:

1. God will direct his path (Proverbs 3:5, 6).
2. God will protect his life (Hebrews 13:5, 6).
3. God will supply his needs (Psalm 34:10).

3. It is the responsibility of believers in this world to obey God (5:27-32)

The proof of faith in Christ is obedience to him. The fruit of God-given faith is obedience to God (1 John 5:1-3). Hebrews 11 is faith's hall of fame. It records the great deeds of faith performed by men and women in obedience to God. The apostles followed their example. When they were commanded not to preach the gospel of Christ, they not only said they must continue to do so, but they preached Christ to their persecutors. And they did it publicly! They did not consider the consequences of their actions. They knew their duty and they did it. That is faith in action. Our lives, our course of action at any given point in life, must be determined by four things:

1. What does the Word of God require of me?
2. What is the will of God in my present situation?
3. What will best serve the glory of God?
4. What is in the best interests of God's people?

4. God's truth cannot be silenced, God's cause cannot be defeated and God's kingdom cannot be overthrown (5:33-40)

What an encouraging lesson this is! The truth of God, the cause of God and the kingdom of God are not in any way dependent upon men and circumstances! If God is in a thing, if it is of God, it will be successful. Nothing can stop it. God will even use the counsel of Gamaliel to preserve his work!

There is much in these verses of Holy Scripture for the comfort and encouragement of every preacher and every congregation of believers. God's man in God's place doing God's work will be maintained by God's hand. There is no need for compromise, fear, or even hesitation. God will promote the gospel we preach by the power of his Spirit. He will provide for the needs of his church by the hand of his providence (Ezra 4:2, 3; Genesis 14:22, 23). God will protect his cause in this world (Ezra 8:22, 23).

5. It is an honour for anyone to serve the cause of Christ in this world, even if your service is to suffer for the honour of his name (5:41)

Shortly after I was converted, I was asked to serve as caretaker at our church. I counted it an honour to keep the house of God clean and comfortable as a place where sinners could hear the gospel and worship Christ. It is a great mercy and honour that now I am called to preach the gospel of Christ. If I am counted worthy of suffering abuse, reproach and scorn for doing so, that too is my honour. I am astonished that God is pleased to use me in any way for his honour!

6. Our one business and responsibility in this world is to preach the gospel of Christ

These apostles were given an angelic commission (5:19, 20) and they were obedient to it (5:42). You and I have the same commission. Every man and woman who is born of God is a missionary sent by God into the world to preach the gospel. Not all are called and gifted to be public preachers. (No woman is allowed to do that, 1 Timothy 2:11, 12). But all who have seen Christ are his witnesses. All who know him are to proclaim him (Matthew 28:18-20; Acts 1:8).

God has chosen to save sinners by using saved sinners to tell them of his great grace in Christ (Matthew 22:8, 9; Luke 14:21-23; John 1:35-45). 'Go ... and speak ... to the people all the words of this life!'

Acts 5:31 Him hath God exalted with his right hand to be a Prince and a Saviour, for to give repentance to Israel, and forgiveness of sins.

Chapter 17

'A Prince and a Saviour'

Acts 5:31

When Peter and the rest of the apostles stood before the high priest and the Sadducees, they were commanded not to teach or preach in the name of the Lord Jesus. 'Then Peter and the other apostles answered and said, We ought to obey God rather than men' (5:29). They gave three specific reasons why they had to go on preaching Christ and him crucified to all who would hear them.

1. Jesus Christ is the exalted Lord of glory

'The God of our fathers hath raised up Jesus, whom ye slew and hanged on a tree. Him hath God exalted with his right hand to be a Prince and a Saviour' (5:30, 31). If Jesus Christ is indeed our only Lord, we must obey him!

2. This Prince and Saviour, the Lord Jesus Christ, is the sinner's only hope

God has exalted him 'to be a Prince and a Saviour, for to give repentance to Israel, and forgiveness of sins' (5:31). Sinners have no hope without Christ. He alone can give life to dead sinners. Christ alone can change the heart. Only Christ can forgive sin. If we do not tell perishing sinners about him, they will perish for ever under the wrath of God.

3. 'And we are his witnesses' (5:32)

The apostles were the representatives of Messiah, the Prince. They were, by the power of God the Holy Spirit, acting by the authority of God himself. They asserted that their teaching and preaching could not be set aside by any earthly, human authority, civil or ecclesiastical. Are we his witnesses? If so, we are under the constraint of love and allegiance to Christ our almighty, sovereign King, to proclaim him to men, insofar as we are able to fill the world with his doctrine.

87

Our mission as his witnesses is twofold. First and foremost, we seek to exalt, magnify and glorify the name of God our Saviour. Above all else, let us seek the glory of God (1 Kings 18:36, 37). Second, we seek the salvation of God's elect, realizing that it is not possible for sinners to be saved until they know Christ and that they cannot know him unless someone tells them who he is and what he has done (Romans 1:16, 17; 10:13-17; 1 Corinthians 1:21-24; Matthew 28:18-20).

Who is the Lord Jesus Christ?

We know that Jesus Christ is God (John 1:1-3). We also know that Christ Jesus is a real man, God incarnate (1 Timothy 3:16; Isaiah 9:6). He is the God-man, as much God as though he were not man, and as much man as though he were not God. But in the text under consideration, the Holy Spirit describes the Lord Jesus Christ in his saving character as 'a Prince [King] and a Saviour'. Those who are so taught of God that in their hearts they know Christ as both 'a Prince and a Saviour' are saved persons. They bow to Christ as their Prince and trust him as their Saviour. Some see Christ only as a Prince to regulate their lives. So they have a lifeless religion of laws and works. Others see Christ only as a Saviour to keep them out of hell. Because they do not recognize Christ's lordship, they live as licentious antinomians. Their religion, having no real effect upon their hearts and lives, is a useless religion. Only those who see the Lord Jesus Christ as both 'a Prince and a Saviour' are true believers. True believers resign themselves to Christ's will and subject the passions of their souls to Christ, their glorious Prince. They yield themselves to his will, direction and control as their Lord. At the same time they trust Christ as their Saviour, realizing the infinite sufficiency of his righteousness and the infinite merit of his blood as the sinners' substitute for the pardon of sin and everlasting acceptance with God.

No one is saved until he bows to Christ the Prince, acknowledging him as his Lord (Romans 10:9, 10; 1 Corinthians 12:3; Luke 14:25-33). As C.H. Spurgeon says, 'No man has truly given himself to Christ until he has said, "My Lord, I give thee this day my body, my soul, my power, my talents, my goods, my house, my children, and all that I have. Henceforth, I hold them at thy will, as a steward under thee. Thine they are. As for me, I have nothing. I have surrendered all to thee!"' If we would have Christ as our Saviour, we must have him as our Prince, our Lord and King. If he is not our Ruler and Commander, he is not our Saviour. One of the first instincts of a newborn soul is to fall at the Saviour's feet in adoring, worshipful submission, crying, 'Lord, what wilt thou have me to do?' (Acts 9:6). A person saved by the grace of God does not need to be told that he is under solemn obligations to serve Christ. The new life within tells him that! It is no burden to the believing heart to be under Christ's yoke. It is our delight! He who believes gladly surrenders to Christ as his Master (1 John 5:2). As soon as a sinner sees the glory and grace of God in Christ by faith, he willingly bows before his throne crying: All to Jesus I surrender. All to him I freely give!

Christ must be acknowledged as our rightful Prince and trusted as our only Saviour. He is a Prince with sovereign authority and power. He is a Saviour with infinite merit and grace. Jesus Christ, the God-man, has established the grounds of salvation — righteousness! He has paid the price for salvation — his own blood! And he possesses the power to save all who come to God by him (Hebrews 7:25; John 17:2).

What are the conditions of salvation?

That may appear to be a strange question to some, but Acts 5:31 sets before us two things required by God, two conditions that must be met before a holy, righteous and just God can save any sinner. They are 'repentance ... and forgiveness of sins'.

Repentance is the work and gift of God's goodness and grace (Romans 2:4; Zechariah 12:10). It is a change of character, a change of heart brought about by the regenerating power and grace of God the Holy Spirit. Without genuine repentance there is no faith in the heart, no salvation wrought in the soul, no true hope of life to come (Isaiah 55:6, 7; Matthew 9:13; Mark 6:12; Luke 13:3; 24:47; Acts 2:38; 20:21; 2 Timothy 2:25; Revelation 2:5). Repentance is constant. Like faith, it is a lifelong grace. Yet repentance is no grounds for salvation. Repentance cannot satisfy justice and atone for sin.

Forgiveness must be granted by God our Saviour. In order for a holy, just God to forgive sin four things must be done. First, the sinner must be punished. Second, justice must be satisfied. Third, the sin must be removed, put away, annihilated from record. And, fourthly, the sinner must be made righteous. This can be accomplished only by the substitutionary sacrifice of the Lord Jesus Christ and the free imputation of his righteousness to us by the grace of God (2 Corinthians 5:21; Romans 3:24-26).

This repentance and forgiveness of sins are the gift of Christ to all the Israel of God, to all who look to him in faith. Every sinner who looks to Christ is forgiven of all sin forever and is saved (Isaiah 45:22). Once a sinner knows that he is forgiven, he truly repents of his sins (Psalm 32:1-5; 51:1-17; Zechariah 12:10).

Acts 5:17 Then the high priest rose up, and all they that were with him, (which is the sect of the Sadducees,) and were filled with indignation,

Acts 5:18 And laid their hands on the apostles, and put them in the common prison ...

... Acts 5:26 Then went the captain with the officers, and brought them without violence: for they feared the people, lest they should have been stoned.

Acts 5:27 And when they had brought them, they set them before the council: and the high priest asked them,

Acts 5:28 Saying, Did not we straitly command you that ye should not teach in this name? and, behold, ye have filled Jerusalem with your doctrine, and intend to bring this man's blood upon us.

Acts 5:29 Then Peter and the other apostles answered and said, We ought to obey God rather than men.

Acts 5:30 The God of our fathers raised up Jesus, whom ye slew and hanged on a tree.

Acts 5:31 Him hath God exalted with his right hand to be a Prince and a Saviour, for to give repentance to Israel, and forgiveness of sins.

Acts 5:32 And we are his witnesses of these things; and so is also the Holy Ghost, whom God hath given to them that obey him.

Acts 5:33 When they heard that, they were cut to the heart, and took counsel to slay them.

Acts 5:34 Then stood there up one in the council, a Pharisee, named Gamaliel, a doctor of the law, had in reputation among all the people, and commanded to put the apostles forth a little space;

Acts 5:35 And said unto them, Ye men of Israel, take heed to yourselves what ye intend to do as touching these men.

Acts 5:36 For before these days rose up Theudas, boasting himself to be somebody; to whom a number of men, about four hundred, joined themselves: who was slain; and all, as many as obeyed him, were scattered, and brought to nought.

Acts 5:37 After this man rose up Judas of Galilee in the days of the taxing, and drew away much people after him: he also perished; and all, even as many as obeyed him, were dispersed.

Acts 5:38 And now I say unto you, Refrain from these men, and let them alone: for if this counsel or this work be of men, it will come to nought:

Acts 5:39 But if it be of God, ye cannot overthrow it; lest haply ye be found even to fight against God.

Acts 5:40 And to him they agreed: and when they had called the apostles, and beaten them, they commanded that they should not speak in the name of Jesus, and let them go.

Acts 5:41 And they departed from the presence of the council, rejoicing that they were counted worthy to suffer shame for his name.

Chapter 18

'Counted worthy to suffer'

Acts 5:17, 18, 26-41

The apostles of Christ were called into court by the Jewish Sanhedrin. The members of the Sanhedrin were the seventy top men in Israel. They were the most highly respected, most influential, and were thought to be the most spiritual, godly men of the religious world. Normally they were very tolerant. But the apostles were publicly proclaiming Christ as the only Lord and Saviour of men, and they were doing it in the temple! The Sanhedrin thought the temple belonged to them, but it was God's temple. The angel of the Lord expressly commanded these men to go to the temple, the place where God's name was profaned, and preach the gospel there, even though the people who worshipped there despised the God they claimed to worship (5:20).

The leaders of the Jewish church, these guardians of the temple, would have killed God's preachers on the spot, but they feared that such action would stir up the wrath of the people. Therefore, because it was politically expedient to do so, they spared the lives of God's servants, but only just. The word 'beaten' in verse 40 means 'skinned'. It is the same word that would be used to describe the skinning of an animal. These men were brutally scourged with a whip — a whip designed to rip the skin from the body! It was not uncommon for men to die from such beatings. In the very next verse we read, 'And they departed from the presence of the council, rejoicing that they were counted worthy to suffer shame for his name' (5:41).

Their bodies were full of pain, but their hearts were full of joy, 'rejoicing that they were counted worthy to suffer shame for Christ'. They considered it a high honour bestowed upon them that God would allow such worthless, sinful creatures as they were to suffer for the honour of Christ. They rejoiced in his faithfulness to them, knowing that 'God is faithful, who will not suffer you to be tempted above that ye are able; but will with the temptation also make a way to escape, that ye may be able to bear it' (1 Corinthians 10:13). It is truly an honour to suffer patiently as a Christian for the honour of Christ (1 Peter 4:16).

What is the cause of our suffering?

Everyone knows something about suffering. Some suffer more than others and some less, but all suffer. Basically, all that we suffer in this world is either physical pain or spiritual distress. We suffer physically, in the flesh; and we suffer spiritually in the heart, the soul and the mind. Like Job, we recognize that all we suffer must ultimately be traced to the hand of our God (Job 2:10; Romans 8:28; 11:36). We rejoice to know that 'All things are of God' (2 Corinthians 5:18). Realizing that all suffering is ordered, like all other things, by the providential rule of our God, we may trace the sufferings of God's children in this world to four subordinate causes.

1. Cosmic suffering. There are some things men and women suffer simply because we live in this world. These are common to all since the fall of our father Adam. Sin has made this world a place of sorrow, pain and suffering. All people, believers and unbelievers, suffer from satanic oppression (Job 1:12; 2:7, 8; Matthew 8:28-34; 15:22; 2 Corinthians 12:7). Satan is not only God's enemy, he is the subtle, crafty, powerful enemy of all mankind. Though governed by the hand of God's providence, Satan causes people to suffer both mentally and physically. We also suffer because of sin. Because all are sinners, all are sufferers. Were it not for sin there would be no thorns of sorrow, thistles of suffering, sweat of fever, or death in the world. Moreover, by acts of sin men and women bring certain evils upon themselves. Because of sin we are all suffering, mortal, dying creatures.

2. Circumstantial sufferings. From time to time people suffer simply because of their circumstances. In times of famine, plague and war both the righteous and the wicked suffer together, though even then the children of God are under his special care (Psalm 91:1-16).

3. Conscientious sufferings. Frequently, the saints of God choose to suffer for Christ as a matter of conscience (Acts 4:18-20; 5:29-32; Hebrews 11:24-26). They willingly take up their cross and follow Christ. They willingly choose pain and sorrow, even persecution and death, rather than disobey the will of God, violate the Word of God, or compromise the truth of God. Men and women of faith and conviction make great personal sacrifices, deliberately, for the honour of Christ (Matthew 10:34-38; Mark 8:34-38; Luke 14:25-33).

4. Corrective sufferings. Like a loving, caring Father, our God chastens his children for their eternal, spiritual good (Hebrews 12:5-11). God does not punish his elect for sin! He punished us for our sins in Christ when he suffered the wrath of God as our substitute (Romans 3:24-26; Galatians 3:13; 2 Corinthians 5:21; 1 Peter 3:18). A.M. Toplady wrote: 'Payment God cannot twice demand, First at my bleeding Surety's hand And then again at mine!'

God will not punish sin where he will not impute sin; and God will not impute sin to his elect, whose sins were imputed to Christ (Romans 4:8; 8:33, 34). The only place where God deals with the sins of his elect in a penal way is Calvary! When God chastens us it is not to punish us, but to correct us (Psalm 119:65-71).

When can it be said that a person is suffering for Christ?

A person is not suffering for Christ when his sufferings are the result of his own evil actions or attitude. Neither is someone suffering for Christ when he wallows in self-pity, murmuring and complaining against God. But there are some living martyrs in this world, men and women who hazard their lives for the name of Christ (Acts 15:26).

To suffer for Christ is to suffer patiently, trusting God's providence and believing his promise (1 Peter 2:20-24). Job, Eli, Moses and Paul were all examples of such suffering (Job 2:10; Hebrews 11:24-26; 1 Samuel 3:18; 2 Corinthians 12:9). We ought to follow their examples.

Those who willingly expose themselves to pain, affliction and heartache for the honour of Christ suffer for his name's sake. The apostles knew what the consequences of their actions would be. They had been forewarned (Acts 4:21). Many pay a high price for confessing Christ, worshipping him and obeying him, and consider it a high honour to do so. The martyrs who were burned at the stake in England in the sixteenth century died simply because they refused to say that the bread and wine of the Lord's Table are the body and blood of Christ! John Bunyan spent twelve years in jail because he would not agree not to preach in the town of Bedford!

To suffer for Christ is to be a true believer. It is to lose your life for him. It is to obey him, follow him, submit to him and trust him, regardless of cost or consequence. To refuse to suffer for Christ is to deny him (Matthew 10:16, 22, 24, 28, 31-39).

Every believer will, as long as he or she lives in this world, be called to suffer for his Saviour's name. But you have these promises: you will not be forsaken (Isaiah 41:10; 43:1-5); you will never suffer more than you can bear (1 Corinthians 10:13); Christ will keep you (John 10:28); God will honour you (1 Peter 1:7). If you would learn how to suffer for Christ look to Christ (Hebrews 12:1-5).

Acts 6:1 And in those days, when the number of the disciples was multiplied, there arose a murmuring of the Grecians against the Hebrews, because their widows were neglected in the daily ministration.

Acts 6:2 Then the twelve called the multitude of the disciples unto them, and said, It is not reason that we should leave the word of God, and serve tables.

Acts 6:3 Wherefore, brethren, look ye out among you seven men of honest report, full of the Holy Ghost and wisdom, whom we may appoint over this business.

Acts 6:4 But we will give ourselves continually to prayer, and to the ministry of the word.

Acts 6:5 And the saying pleased the whole multitude: and they chose Stephen, a man full of faith and of the Holy Ghost, and Philip, and Prochorus, and Nicanor, and Timon, and Parmenas, and Nicolas a proselyte of Antioch:

Acts 6:6 Whom they set before the apostles: and when they had prayed, they laid their hands on them.

Acts 6:7 And the word of God increased; and the number of the disciples multiplied in Jerusalem greatly; and a great company of the priests were obedient to the faith.

Chapter 19

The First Seven Deacons

Acts 6:1-7

As we have already seen, the church at Jerusalem grew in a very short time from 120 to several thousand members. This early church, though a great multitude, was a community of love and care. They had all things in common. Many sold their estates and gave the money to the church. There were also many in the congregation who were poor. These poor ones, particularly the fatherless and the widows, were clothed, fed and housed from church funds. But a problem arose. Some of the Grecian widows were being neglected (or at least thought they were), not receiving an equal share of financial support with those widows from Judea (6:1). Several things in this passage deserve our attention.

First, though the church suffered much persecution, it continued, by the grace of God, to grow. Like Israel in Egypt, the more it was afflicted, the more it multiplied. The work of God, the cause of Christ and the success of the gospel cannot be hindered by man, or even by hell itself (Matthew 16:18).

Secondly, when the church increased, strife and discord arose from within. Until now they had been of one accord (Acts 1:14; 2:1, 46; 4:24; 5:12). They had been one in heart, mind and purpose, serving the interests of Christ and one another. But when they began to multiply, their unity was marred. They increased in numbers, but not in joy. Like Abraham and Lot, when the family increased, there was strife. 'There arose a murmuring,' not an open falling out, but a petty strife, nurtured by selfishness and pride (Proverbs 16:28; 17:14, 19; 26:21; 28:25).

Thirdly, of all things, the complaint was about money! It is a great pity that the insignificant things of this world should ever cause strife between those who profess to be taken up with the far greater things of the world to come. Yet this evil is so often repeated that it must not be ignored. 'The love of money is the root of all evil' (1 Timothy 6:10). It blinds the eye and perverts the judgment of men (Exodus 23:8). Husbands and wives quarrel more often about money than anything else. When family members fall out with one another it usually has something to do with money or other earthly possessions. Most church splits begin with strife about money. How sad!

Fourth, no church has ever been pure and perfect, and no church in this world ever will be. Any congregation of believers will, from time to time, have problems to face, deal with and overcome. Never forsake the church of God, or the local church to which you belong, because a problem arises. Instead, work together with God's saints to overcome the problem. Husbands and wives do not break up the family because of a quarrel over some trivial matter. Neither should we allow petty differences to break up the household of faith. Let us rather yield to one another and serve one another (Philippians 2:1-5; Ephesians 4:1-6).

In order to solve the problem and to prevent such problems in the future, the apostles, under the direction of the Holy Spirit, established a new office in the church, the office of deacon. Acts 6:1-7 records the establishment of this office.

We should note that the apostles did not simply invent an office in the church as a matter of expediency. They did what they did under the direction and influence of the Holy Spirit. Unlike the choosing of Matthias to be an apostle, this was an act inspired of God. We know that it was, because it is confirmed in the epistles. We have no authority to invent offices in the church and appoint people to fill them.

These first seven deacons were chosen to meet a specific need in the church. Seven were chosen because seven were needed, but that certainly does not imply that every church needs seven deacons.

Why was the deacon's office established?

God ordained this office in his church for one specific and noble reason: deacons are to relieve their pastors of all secular, worldly concerns, so that those who preach the gospel may give themselves entirely to the ministry of the Word (1 Timothy 4:12-16; 2 Timothy 2:4; 4:1-5; Acts 6:2, 3). No man can properly give himself to more than one weighty employment. Therefore the churches of God have deacons whose responsibility it is to see that their pastors have no need to concern themselves with mundane affairs. Deacons must take care to see that the material needs of the pastor and his family are met. Deacons are to make certain that the church property and church members are cared for properly. Deacons are to distribute the church's funds for the ministry of the Word and the care of the poor (1 Corinthians 16:2). Deacons are servants. They serve tables, the Lord's table, the pastor's table, the tables of God's saints.

How were the first deacons chosen?

Without doubt, the church at Jerusalem met in several congregations scattered throughout the area. The apostles called together the preachers from these congregations and instructed them to choose from among the saints of God 'seven men of good report'. Then those men were ordained to the work. This much is certain: the deacons were all men; they were chosen in compliance with the apostles' instructions; they were chosen from among the members of the church; and they were permanently ordained in the office, not installed for a short term.

What kind of men were the deacons to be?

The Word of God clearly describes the character of those men who may properly be ordained to the office of deacon. They are not to be chosen upon the basis of friendship, but of faithfulness. Carefully read Acts 6:3 and 1 Timothy 3:8-12. These two passages tell us what the qualifications of a deacon are. No man should ever be placed in this high office who does not meet the qualifications given in the Word of God.

What is the work for which deacons are ordained?

The word 'deacon' means 'servant'. A deacon is a man who serves Christ's church, the interests of the gospel and the pastor who proclaims the gospel to him. As the first seven deacons were chosen to relieve the apostles of the burden of caring for the poor, so it is the work of deacons to do whatever they can to relieve their pastor of any burden or care that would in any way distract him from the preaching of the gospel.

What effect did the service of these seven deacons have upon the church of Christ and the ministry of the gospel?

Because of the quiet, unassuming, faithful service of these first seven deacons, the Word of God increased and many of God's elect were converted (6:7). The gospel was preached where it could not have been preached, if these men had not relieved the apostles. And the church of God grew. Faithful deacons are an asset to any congregation and to any pastor's labours. Pastors, elders and deacons, together with the membership of the local church, work together in the cause of Christ. Deacons who serve faithfully in this office earn the respect and esteem of their pastor and of the church (1 Timothy 3:13).

Acts 6:8 And Stephen, full of faith and power, did great wonders and miracles among the people.

Acts 6:9 Then there arose certain of the synagogue, which is called the synagogue of the Libertines, and Cyrenians, and Alexandrians, and of them of Cilicia and of Asia, disputing with Stephen.

Acts 6:10 And they were not able to resist the wisdom and the spirit by which he spake.

Acts 6:11 Then they suborned men, which said, We have heard him speak blasphemous words against Moses, and against God.

Acts 6:12 And they stirred up the people, and the elders, and the scribes, and came upon him, and caught him, and brought him to the council,

Acts 6:13 And set up false witnesses, which said, This man ceaseth not to speak blasphemous words against this holy place, and the law:

Acts 6:14 For we have heard him say, that this Jesus of Nazareth shall destroy this place, and shall change the customs which Moses delivered us.

Acts 6:15 And all that sat in the council, looking stedfastly on him, saw his face as it had been the face of an angel.

Chapter 20

Stephen: A Faithful Servant

Acts 6:8-15

Stephen was a Hellenistic Jew, a Jew by birth, but one born in Greece. The apostles were all Galileans. They were, in the eyes of men, a crude, uneducated rabble of fishermen and tax collectors. When Peter and John stood before the Sanhedrin in Acts 4, they were perceived to be 'unlearned and ignorant men'. But Stephen was a preacher of a different kind. He was from another culture. He was a man of learning, education and refinement. He was a man of rank and reputation. Some of the historians tell us that, like Saul of Tarsus (before whom he boldly defended the gospel of Christ, Acts 7:58), Stephen was trained at the feet of Gamaliel. As we study the history of his death, we learn the dominant character of his life. Stephen was a faithful man, faithful to the gospel, faithful to the church of God, faithful to Christ, faithful unto death. He is an example of faithfulness, held up for all who would honour God to follow (Hebrews 13:7). Here are four lessons set before us by God the Holy Spirit in this portion of his Word.

1. Faithfulness is the one thing God requires of his servants and the one thing God honours in his servants (6:8)

Stephen served God first as a member of his church, then as a deacon, then as a gospel preacher. As he had been faithful and diligent in serving tables, he was faithful in preaching the gospel. He was a man with uncommon gifts, talents and abilities. Yet he thought it was an honour to serve as a deacon in God's church, an honour to distribute food to the poor. Stephen used the office of a deacon well and thereby purchased to himself a good degree and great boldness in the faith which is in Christ Jesus (1 Timothy 3:13).

God's people are his servants in this world. It does not matter what our service is, where our service is, or who is aware of our service. The only thing that matters is that we faithfully serve our God (1 Corinthians 4:2). Be

99

faithful in the place of your calling (1 Corinthians 7:20-23), in the work God has given you to do and with the possessions God has entrusted to your hands (Proverbs 3:9, 10). Honour God in all things and with all things, and he will honour you (1 Samuel 2:30). There is much that you cannot do but, by the grace of God, you can be faithful (Matthew 13:12; Luke 16:10).

Stephen was a man 'full of faith'. That is what the word 'faithful' means — 'full of faith'. He believed God. He knew and believed the Word of God, trusted the Son of God, obeyed the will of God and found contentment with the providence of God. Because he was full of faith, he was 'full ... of power'. He preached the gospel, taught the people and defended the truth of God with power, boldness and courage. Faith makes naturally timid men courageous and bold. And the confidence of faith makes gospel preachers powerful. The man who believes what he preaches is a powerful preacher. Being full of faith and power, Stephen 'did great wonders and miracles among the people'. In this way God confirmed his work. You can be certain that if God sends a man to preach the gospel, he will confirm that man as his messenger and confirm his word from that man in the hearts of his people.

2. Every word spoken for God and every work done for God accomplishes its purpose (6:9, 10)

Saul of Tarsus was probably the chief spokesman of those with whom Stephen was disputing. Tarsus was in Cilicia. And Saul was present at this time (Acts 7:58). Though Stephen convinced none, though none was converted at the time, though none believed the gospel, though the preacher himself was stoned to death, this faithful servant of God had successfully accomplished what God sent him to do. Only eternity will tell, but I suspect that Stephen's sermon never stopped ringing in Saul's ears, until he found himself in the dust crying, 'What wilt thou have me to do, Lord?'

Two things, and two things alone, determine the success of any man's or any church's labours for the glory of God and the souls of men: the purpose of God and the power of God (Isaiah 55:11; 2 Corinthians 2:15, 16; 3:5, 6; 4:7). We are entirely dependent upon God! If we are God's servants, doing God's service, failure is an impossibility. No one serves God in vain (1 Corinthians 15:58). Sometimes a man preaches one sermon in the power of the Spirit and thousands are saved, as on the Day of Pentecost. Sometimes a man preaches thousands of sermons in the power of the Spirit before one sinner is saved, as was the case with the missionary Adoniram Judson in Burma. Sometimes the preacher is killed and the one God saves turns out to have been one of his murderers, as was the case here. God does his will, even when he obscures it from sight (Proverbs 16:33).

3. The gospel of Christ is offensive to men (6:11-14)

When these religious men were convinced that Stephen's doctrine was the truth of God revealed in Holy Scripture, when they could not resist his arguments, they still would not yield to the claims of Christ. Instead, they hired false witnesses to twist and pervert Stephen's words.

Nothing has changed. Until a sinner's heart is changed by the regenerating grace of God, he will not receive the gospel of the grace of God. Salvation by grace, through the merits of a crucified substitute, received by faith alone, without works, is both foolishness (1 Corinthians 1:22-25) and offensive to him (Galatians 5:11). It offends his pride, his religious notions, his love of self and his self-righteousness. Any man who boldly declares the gospel of Christ to lost, unbelieving followers of religion will be marked by them as a hard man and a bitter enemy (Galatians 4:16). When the pearls of the gospel (free forgiveness, effectual atonement, imputed righteousness and infallible, irresistible grace) are cast before swine, they will trample the pearls in the mud to get at the one who preaches God's free grace in Christ, and will destroy him if they can.

4. God is faithful to his faithful servants (6:15)

Stephen's conscience was pure and free from guilt with regard to the charges made against him. Therefore, he had nothing to fear. What he had said and done had been for the glory of God. He knew he had done nothing but serve the honour of God, the will of God, the interests of his kingdom, his gospel and his people. Therefore, in the face of death, he was calm and courageous — so much so that his face looked as bright, happy and radiant as the face of an angel. In the hour of his greatest trial he did not forsake his God and his God did not forsake him (Hebrews 13:5, 6).

What an example Stephen is! Let us be faithful servants to Christ, our God and Saviour. If we willingly serve him in all things, he will use us as he sees fit for his glory. He will give us grace to do his will. He will crown us with life everlasting (Revelation 2:10).

Acts 7:1 Then said the high priest, Are these things so?

Acts 7:2 And he said, Men, brethren, and fathers, hearken; The God of glory appeared unto our father Abraham, when he was in Mesopotamia, before he dwelt in Charran,

Acts 7:3 And said unto him, Get thee out of thy country, and from thy kindred, and come into the land which I shall shew thee.

Acts 7:4 Then came he out of the land of the Chaldaeans, and dwelt in Charran: and from thence, when his father was dead, he removed him into this land, wherein ye now dwell.

Acts 7:5 And he gave him none inheritance in it, no, not so much as to set his foot on: yet he promised that he would give it to him for a possession, and to his seed after him, when as yet he had no child.

Acts 7:6 And God spake on this wise, That his seed should sojourn in a strange land; and that they should bring them into bondage, and entreat them evil four hundred years.

Acts 7:7 And the nation to whom they shall be in bondage will I judge, said God: and after that shall they come forth, and serve me in this place.

Acts 7:8 And he gave him the covenant of circumcision: and so Abraham begat Isaac, and circumcised him the eighth day; and Isaac begat Jacob; and Jacob begat the twelve patriarchs.

Acts 7:9 And the patriarchs, moved with envy, sold Joseph into Egypt: but God was with him,

Acts 7:10 And delivered him out of all his afflictions, and gave him favour and wisdom in the sight of Pharaoh king of Egypt; and he made him governor over Egypt and all his house.

Acts 7:11 Now there came a dearth over all the land of Egypt and Chanaan, and great affliction: and our fathers found no sustenance.

Acts 7:12 But when Jacob heard that there was corn in Egypt, he sent out our fathers first.

Acts 7:13 And at the second time Joseph was made known to his brethren; and Joseph's kindred was made known unto Pharaoh.

Acts 7:14 Then sent Joseph, and called his father Jacob to him, and all his kindred, threescore and fifteen souls.

Acts 7:15 So Jacob went down into Egypt, and died, he, and our fathers,

Acts 7:16 And were carried over into Sychem, and laid in the sepulchre that Abraham bought for a sum of money of the sons of Emmor the father of Sychem.

Acts 7:17 But when the time of the promise drew nigh, which God had sworn to Abraham, the people grew and multiplied in Egypt,

Acts 7:18 Till another king arose, which knew not Joseph.

Acts 7:19 The same dealt subtilly with our kindred, and evil entreated our fathers, so that they cast out their young children, to the end they might not live.

Acts 7:20 In which time Moses was born, and was exceeding fair, and nourished up in his father's house three months:

Acts 7:21 And when he was cast out, Pharaoh's daughter took him up, and nourished him for her own son.

Acts 7:22 And Moses was learned in all the wisdom of the Egyptians, and was mighty in words and in deeds.

Acts 7:23 And when he was full forty years old, it came into his heart to visit his brethren the children of Israel.

Acts 7:24 And seeing one of them suffer wrong, he defended him, and avenged him that was oppressed, and smote the Egyptian:

Acts 7:25 For he supposed his brethren would have understood how that God by his hand would deliver them: but they understood not.

Acts 7:26 And the next day he shewed himself unto them as they strove, and would have set them at one again, saying, Sirs, ye are brethren; why do ye wrong one to another?

Acts 7:27 But he that did his neighbour wrong thrust him away, saying, Who made thee a ruler and a judge over us?

Acts 7:28 Wilt thou kill me, as thou diddest the Egyptian yesterday?

Acts 7:29 Then fled Moses at this saying, and was a stranger in the land of Madian, where he begat two sons.

Acts 7:30 And when forty years were expired, there appeared to him in the wilderness of mount Sina an angel of the Lord in a flame of fire in a bush.

Acts 7:31 When Moses saw it, he wondered at the sight: and as he drew near to behold it, the voice of the Lord came unto him,

Acts 7:32 Saying, I am the God of thy fathers, the God of Abraham, and the God of Isaac, and the God of Jacob. Then Moses trembled, and durst not behold.

Acts 7:33 Then said the Lord to him, Put off thy shoes from thy feet: for the place where thou standest is holy ground.

Acts 7:34 I have seen, I have seen the affliction of my people which is in Egypt, and I have heard their groaning, and am come down to deliver them. And now come, I will send thee into Egypt.

Acts 7:35 This Moses whom they refused, saying, Who made thee a ruler and a judge? the same did God send to be a ruler and a deliverer by the hand of the angel which appeared to him in the bush.

Acts 7:36 He brought them out, after that he had shewed wonders and signs in the land of Egypt, and in the Red sea, and in the wilderness forty years.

Acts 7:37 This is that Moses, which said unto the children of Israel, A prophet shall the Lord your God raise up unto you of your brethren, like unto me; him shall ye hear.

Acts 7:38 This is he, that was in the church in the wilderness with the angel which spake to him in the mount Sina, and with our fathers: who received the lively oracles to give unto us:

Acts 7:39 To whom our fathers would not obey, but thrust him from them, and in their hearts turned back again into Egypt,

Acts 7:40 Saying unto Aaron, Make us gods to go before us: for as for this Moses, which brought us out of the land of Egypt, we wot not what is become of him.

Acts 7:41 And they made a calf in those days, and offered sacrifice unto the idol, and rejoiced in the works of their own hands.

Acts 7:42 Then God turned, and gave them up to worship the host of heaven; as it is written in the book of the prophets, O ye house of Israel, have ye offered to me slain beasts and sacrifices by the space of forty years in the wilderness?

Acts 7:43 Yea, ye took up the tabernacle of Moloch, and the star of your god Remphan, figures which ye made to worship them: and I will carry you away beyond Babylon.

Acts 7:44 Our fathers had the tabernacle of witness in the wilderness, as he had appointed, speaking unto Moses, that he should make it according to the fashion that he had seen.

Acts 7:45 Which also our fathers that came after brought in with Jesus into the possession of the Gentiles, whom God drave out before the face of our fathers, unto the days of David;

Acts 7:46 Who found favour before God, and desired to find a tabernacle for the God of Jacob.

Acts 7:47 But Solomon built him an house.

Acts 7:48 Howbeit the most High dwelleth not in temples made with hands; as saith the prophet,

Acts 7:49 Heaven is my throne, and earth is my footstool: what house will ye build me? saith the Lord: or what is the place of my rest?

Acts 7:50 Hath not my hand made all these things?

Acts 7:51 Ye stiffnecked and uncircumcised in heart and ears, ye do always resist the Holy Ghost: as your fathers did, so do ye.

Acts 7:52 Which of the prophets have not your fathers persecuted? and they have slain them which shewed before of the coming of the Just One; of whom ye have been now the betrayers and murderers:

Acts 7:53 Who have received the law by the disposition of angels, and have not kept it.

Acts 7:54 When they heard these things, they were cut to the heart, and they gnashed on him with their teeth.

Acts 7:55 But he, being full of the Holy Ghost, looked up stedfastly into heaven, and saw the glory of God, and Jesus standing on the right hand of God,

Acts 7:56 And said, Behold, I see the heavens opened, and the Son of man standing on the right hand of God.

Acts 7:57 Then they cried out with a loud voice, and stopped their ears, and ran upon him with one accord,

Acts 7:58 And cast him out of the city, and stoned him: and the witnesses laid down their clothes at a young man's feet, whose name was Saul.

Acts 7:59 And they stoned Stephen, calling upon God, and saying, Lord Jesus, receive my spirit.

Acts 7:60 And he kneeled down, and cried with a loud voice, Lord, lay not this sin to their charge. And when he had said this, he fell asleep.

Chapter 21

A Sermon That Cost A Preacher His Life

Acts 7:1-60

Stephen had been accused of speaking blasphemy against the law and the temple because he told the Jews that the Lord Jesus Christ had fulfilled all the types of the law and satisfied all its demands, and that all forms of carnal worship must be obliterated (Acts 6:8-15; John 4:23, 24; Colossians 2:8-23). In Acts 7 the Holy Spirit has preserved a transcript of Stephen's last sermon, the sermon preached to the Sanhedrin that cost him his life. What did Stephen preach that so enraged these religious leaders? These men were known to be tolerant and compromising with one another. That is how they held their 'denomination' together. But when Stephen had finished his sermon they stoned him to death! Why? What did he say to infuriate them so?

1. Stephen preached the doctrine of God's sovereignty in providence

Beginning with the call of Abraham, Stephen showed how everything in the history of the Old Testament pointed to Christ and was fulfilled by him. He demonstrated how that God gradually unfolds and accomplishes his sovereign purpose of redemption and grace in providence.

2. The Lord our God is a God of purpose

God's purpose is good, wise and full of grace. It includes all things (Isaiah 14:26; Romans 8:28; 9:11; Ephesians 1:11; 3:11; 2 Timothy 1:9). Nothing takes God by surprise. His purpose is the spiritual, eternal good of his elect and the glory of his own great name. His purpose is fixed, unalterable and immutable (Isaiah 46:9-11). It cannot be changed, thwarted, or overturned. Therefore, 'We know that all things work together for good to them that love God to them who are the called according to his purpose' (Romans 8:28). If God's eternal purpose could be altered to any degree, then no promises, prophecies, or threats recorded in the Bible could be believed. We can trust God only to the extent that we recognize his immutability. We can believe the Scriptures only to the extent that we recognize the universality and immutability of God's purpose (Romans 11:33-36).

Predestination is the purpose of God. Providence is the unfolding and accomplishment of God's purpose. Everything that God has done or has allowed to be done, is doing or allows to happen, will do or will allow to unfold is for the spiritual, eternal good of his elect, to the praise and glory of his own great name. In the end everyone will be made to see this (Revelation 4:11; 5:11-14). Beginning with Abraham, Stephen showed the unfolding of God's eternal purpose until the coming of Christ for the accomplishment of the redemption of his people. Apart from Christ and his great work of redemption, the history of the Jews and all that is recorded in the Old Testament Scriptures would be meaningless (Luke 24:27, 44-47).

3. All the events of Old Testament history pointed to the coming of Christ and redemption by him (7:1-47)

The whole purpose for which the Bible has been written is to reveal the grace and glory of God in the substitutionary, redemptive work of the Lord Jesus Christ (John 1:45). The bulk of Stephen's sermon is devoted to one theme: he shows that all the events of Old Testament history were arranged by divine providence to reveal God's eternal purpose of grace in the redemption of sinners by Christ.

God's covenant with Abraham was a partial revelation of the covenant of grace made with Christ, our surety, before the world was made (7:1-8; Hebrews 7:22; Jeremiah 31:31-34). In that covenant a seed was promised (7:5; Galatians 3:26). It was purposed that the chosen seed should fall into bondage (7:6), even as God's elect fell into the bondage of sin by Adam's transgression. Deliverance was promised (7:7) by which the glory of God would be revealed. That deliverance of Israel out of Egypt was a beautiful picture of our redemption by the blood of Christ and the power of his grace. The sign and seal of that covenant was circumcision (7:8). Circumcision was typical of the regeneration of God's elect by the Holy Spirit, by which he separates his own elect from the rest of the world and seals to their hearts all the blessings of covenant grace (Colossians 2:11; Ephesians 1:3, 13, 14).

Joseph was sent of God into Egypt to preserve his people alive (7:9-17). In all things he was a type of Christ. He was the delight of his father (Matthew 3:17; Proverbs 8:30). He was despised and rejected by his brethren (Isaiah 53:3). He was in the place of God, by God's appointment and arrangement (Genesis 50:19, 20; Acts 2:23; 4:27, 28). When his brothers bowed before Joseph they were saved alive and accepted by Pharaoh (7:13; Romans 10:9, 10).

Moses was sent to deliver God's covenant people from the bondage of Egypt (7:18-37). He too was a type of Christ (vv. 22, 35-37). He was a man approved by God (Acts 2:22). He was a prophet (John 3:2). He was a deliverer, by blood and by power. From the day that Israel came out of Egypt they wandered from God, rejected his counsel and despised his prophets. But God's purpose could not be defeated, not even by the unbelief and idolatry of the chosen nation (7:38-43; Romans 3:3, 4).

The Lord established temporary houses of worship which were to prepare the people for the coming of Christ, but they turned the ordinance of God into idolatry (7:44-47). The tabernacle, with its furnishings, first erected in the wilderness (among Gentiles), was a picture of redemption. The temple was a picture of God's church, of the glory of God dwelling in her, and of her dwelling in the glory of God for ever. These blessed objects which should have prepared the hearts of men to receive Christ, the unbelieving Jews turned into idolatrous objects of worship. They became barriers to faith!

4. Now that Christ has come and redemption has been accomplished by him, all carnal ordinances of Old Testament worship are forever abolished (7:8-50)

God has forever abolished Jewish, legal worship (Hebrews 10:1-4). Any reliance upon outward, visible symbols (statues, pictures, crosses, temples, altars, etc.) is idolatry. God cannot be worshipped by the employment of carnal rudiments of the world. All true worship is spiritual (John 4:23, 24; Philippians 3:3).

5. Continued, wilful rejection of divine truth results in eternal reprobation (7:51-53)

God will not trifle with those who trifle with him (Proverbs 1:23-33; Matthew 23:37, 38). Though the Jews, being rejected of God, rejected his Son, God's purpose was not affected (Romans 3:3, 4; 11:11, 22, 23, 26).

Our great God even overrules and uses the hands of wicked men to accomplish his purpose of grace towards his elect (7:54-60; Psalm 76:10). The stoning of Stephen was an inexcusable act of wickedness on the part of these men. Yet it was overruled by God and used by him to accomplish his great purpose of grace. It was best for Stephen. He went to glory! It was best for Saul of Tarsus. It was one of those works of prevenient grace that prepared the way for grace to come to him. It was best for God's church. Soon she would have another apostle, whose conversion, no doubt, had its roots here. It was best for the glory of God! In the light of these things we should learn to trust the wise and good providence of our God!

107

Acts 7:54 When they heard these things, they were cut to the heart, and they gnashed on him with their teeth.

Acts 7:55 But he, being full of the Holy Ghost, looked up stedfastly into heaven, and saw the glory of God, and Jesus standing on the right hand of God,

Acts 7:56 And said, Behold, I see the heavens opened, and the Son of man standing on the right hand of God.

Acts 7:57 Then they cried out with a loud voice, and stopped their ears, and ran upon him with one accord,

Acts 7:58 And cast him out of the city, and stoned him: and the witnesses laid down their clothes at a young man's feet, whose name was Saul.

Acts 7:59 And they stoned Stephen, calling upon God, and saying, Lord Jesus, receive my spirit.

Acts 7:60 And he kneeled down, and cried with a loud voice, Lord, lay not this sin to their charge. And when he had said this, he fell asleep.

Chapter 22

Stephen And Saul

Acts 7:54-60

The first martyr in the history of God's church was Stephen, a faithful deacon, a preaching deacon, but a deacon. The death of this faithful man is recorded more fully than the death of anyone else in the New Testament except that of our Lord Jesus Christ. Here is a man dying for the testimony of Christ, dying by the hands of wicked men, but dying in grace and dying graciously for the glory of God. The Spirit of God directed Luke to identify just one of Stephen's murderers. Those who stoned Stephen 'laid down their clothes at a young man's feet, whose name was Saul'. Saul was probably the man who had examined Stephen and had been baffled by his speech when he stood before the Sanhedrin (Acts 6:8-10).

Here is a striking contrast — Stephen and Saul. Both of them are in glory now. One cannot help wondering how Saul felt when Stephen's smile met him at the throne! What a joyous meeting they must have had — Stephen and Saul embracing one another! But in the text before us the two men were poles apart. They had nothing in common. Stephen was about to die. Saul was holding the clothes of those who stoned him. Saul was a proud, self-righteous Pharisee. He was proud of his pedigree, his learning, his works, his religious position and his great reputation. Stephen was a broken, humbled sinner, saved by the grace of God, whose only hope was in Christ. Saul was wrapped up in himself. Stephen was wrapped up in Christ. His heart was elated, not by looking into a mirror, but by looking to Christ, his exalted Lord. He drew his comfort, not from what he had done, but from what Christ had done for him. Saul was a religious ritualist. He placed great weight and importance on the externals of religion. To him the law, the temple, the priesthood and the ceremonies were everything. Stephen's religion was a matter of the heart, a living, spiritual union with God in Christ. He put external matters in their proper place (Philippians 3:3; Acts 7:48-50). He did not at all despise those outward forms of religion ordained of God. But he knew that religious ceremony without faith in Christ is useless (Isaiah 1:10-15). Saul thought God was impressed with rituals and ceremonies. Stephen knew what few know: 'The Lord looketh on the heart' (1 Samuel 16:7; Luke 16:15). Saul defended his religion. For the defence of his religion he was willingly cunning, cruel and callous. Stephen defended the cause of Christ, even at the cost of his own life. The cause of Christ, his church, his truth and his glory were of greater value to Stephen than life itself. Stephen was gracious to the end, ever truthful, gentle, forgiving and self-sacrificing. Here are five things to be learned from this passage of Holy Scripture and the contrast here given of Stephen and Saul.

1. A believer's life and testimony is important, influential and useful

It does matter greatly how you live in this world if you profess to be a believer, a follower of Christ. There are some people who have no knowledge of Christ and his gospel except what they hear from you and see in you. To them you represent the Son of God and the gospel of his grace. Be sure you are a good representative (Titus 2:10).

Saul's first introduction to genuine Christianity, his first experience with a true believer, was Stephen. Stephen was the first person to tell Saul about Christ and the gospel of his grace. At first he despised both the message and the messenger. But he never forgot it! In God's time it had a profound effect upon his heart. From Stephen's lips Saul heard a faithful declaration of the gospel of God's grace and glory in Christ. He saw in Stephen a believer who was thoroughly committed to Christ. He saw a believer die in faith. In God's time all these things had their impact upon him.

2. God will always preserve a witness for himself

We are always reluctant to lose any from the ranks of God's church, especially one of great service and usefulness. We appear to be fearful that the church simply cannot continue to function without certain men. But it is not so. God has always preserved sufficient witnesses for himself, and always will until Christ comes. God's cause is safe in God's hands! The church lost Stephen, a man of great usefulness. But God had his eye on Saul, a man he would make even more useful. The Lord always has a successor for any man he is pleased to use. When Elijah was taken up to heaven, Elisha was waiting to carry his mantle. God is never in short supply of men to work in his vineyard.

3. It is good for believers to remember where they were when God saved them and what they are by nature

The Holy Spirit included these words in the inspired record as a fact to be remembered: 'The witnesses laid down their clothes at a young man's feet, whose name was Saul.' They are words which were meant to keep Paul humble, and they always did. He never forgot what happened at Jerusalem that day (Acts 22:19, 20; 1 Timothy 1:12-17).

We must never forget where we were when grace found us (Isaiah 51:1). We must never forget what we were and are by nature. We must never forget what God has saved us from (Ephesians 2:1-4) and what he has done for us in Christ (1 Corinthians 6:9-11; 1 John 3:1-3). Such a memory will make us grateful. He loves much who is forgiven much (Luke 7:36-50). Such grateful remembrance will make the gospel of God's distinguishing grace precious. All who have been saved acknowledge that 'By the grace of God I am what I am' (1 Corinthians 15:10). Thank God for electing love, redeeming blood, regenerating grace and preserving power! Grace alone makes us to differ from those who are damned (1 Corinthians 4:7; Romans 9:16). This gives us hope for others too. He who saved Saul of Tarsus can save me. He who saved me can save you. He who saved us can save anyone. His blood is sufficient. His grace is sufficient. His power is sufficient. Jesus Christ is an able Saviour (Hebrews 7:25).

4. Our great God graciously overrules all things for the good of his elect and the glory of his name

As we saw in the previous chapter, the stoning of Stephen, though it was a terrible act of barbaric cruelty and sin, was best, the very best thing that could have happened, on that day. God was in total control of the situation. 'If Saul had not been there, Stephen would not have prayed for him,' said Spurgeon. 'If Stephen had not prayed, Saul would have never preached,' commented Augustine. Even the evil performed by men and devils is good for God's elect and will bring praise to his name (Psalm 76:10; Proverbs 12:21; 16:7; Romans 8:28; 1 Peter 3:12, 13).

5. When the time comes, God gives his believing people grace to die well

Those who die in the arms of Christ, who die in faith, die well. What God did for Stephen he will do essentially for all who trust Christ. Stephen died, being full of the Holy Spirit, with his heart fixed on Christ, looking up stedfastly into heaven. He died without a care in the world, trusting his sovereign substitute, calling on the name of God. He saw heaven opened. He saw the glory of God. He saw the Lord Jesus standing in the place of power to receive him. He died without any malice in his heart. He did not really die at all (John 11:25, 26). He simply dropped the body of death. He fell asleep in the arms of Christ and woke up in glory, in life!

111

Acts 8:1 And Saul was consenting unto his death. And at that time there was a great persecution against the church which was at Jerusalem; and they were all scattered abroad throughout the regions of Judaea and Samaria, except the apostles.

Acts 8:2 And devout men carried Stephen to his burial, and made great lamentation over him.

Acts 8:3 As for Saul, he made havock of the church, entering into every house, and haling men and women committed them to prison.

Acts 8:4 Therefore they that were scattered abroad went every where preaching the word.

Acts 8:5 Then Philip went down to the city of Samaria, and preached Christ unto them.

Acts 8:6 And the people with one accord gave heed unto those things which Philip spake, hearing and seeing the miracles which he did.

Acts 8:7 For unclean spirits, crying with loud voice, came out of many that were possessed with them: and many taken with palsies, and that were lame, were healed.

Acts 8:8 And there was great joy in that city.

Acts 8:9 But there was a certain man, called Simon, which beforetime in the same city used sorcery, and bewitched the people of Samaria, giving out that himself was some great one:

Acts 8:10 To whom they all gave heed, from the least to the greatest, saying, This man is the great power of God.

Acts 8:11 And to him they had regard, because that of long time he had bewitched them with sorceries.

Acts 8:12 But when they believed Philip preaching the things concerning the kingdom of God, and the name of Jesus Christ, they were baptized, both men and women.

Acts 8:13 Then Simon himself believed also: and when he was baptized, he continued with Philip, and wondered, beholding the miracles and signs which were done.

Acts 8:14 Now when the apostles which were at Jerusalem heard that Samaria had received the word of God, they sent unto them Peter and John:

Acts 8:15 Who, when they were come down, prayed for them, that they might receive the Holy Ghost:

Acts 8:16 (For as yet he was fallen upon none of them: only they were baptized in the name of the Lord Jesus.)

Acts 8:17 Then laid they their hands on them, and they received the Holy Ghost.

Acts 8:18 And when Simon saw that through laying on of the apostles' hands the Holy Ghost was given, he offered them money,

Acts 8:19 Saying, Give me also this power, that on whomsoever I lay hands, he may receive the Holy Ghost.

Acts 8:20 But Peter said unto him, Thy money perish with thee, because thou hast thought that the gift of God may be purchased with money.

Acts 8:21 Thou hast neither part nor lot in this matter: for thy heart is not right in the sight of God.

Acts 8:22 Repent therefore of this thy wickedness, and pray God, if perhaps the thought of thine heart may be forgiven thee.

Acts 8:23 For I perceive that thou art in the gall of bitterness, and in the bond of iniquity.

Acts 8:24 Then answered Simon, and said, Pray ye to the Lord for me, that none of these things which ye have spoken come upon me.

Acts 8:25 And they, when they had testified and preached the word of the Lord, returned to Jerusalem, and preached the gospel in many villages of the Samaritans.

Chapter 23

Is Your Heart Right In The Sight Of God?

Acts 8:1-25

The eighth chapter of Acts is a historic narrative. It records a brief, but very important, segment of church history, showing us how the early church endured persecution from its beginning. This chapter also records the rapid spread of the gospel of Christ from Jerusalem to Samaria and to Africa. However, this inspired, historical narrative was not designed by the Holy Spirit simply to satisfy our curiosity about the history of the early church. Like all other parts of Holy Scripture, this historical narrative was written to give us spiritual instruction in the gospel of Christ. Five lessons taught in the first twenty-five verses of this chapter demand the attention of all who are concerned for their immortal souls, the souls of perishing sinners and the glory of God.

1. The gospel of Christ is an offence to men (8:1-4)

This is a lesson often repeated in the book of Acts. We need to be reminded frequently of it. The offence of the cross has not ceased (Galatians 5:11). To those who do not believe, the cross (the doctrine of free justification through Christ, the sinner's substitute) is not only foolishness (1 Corinthians 1:21-25), it is an annoying offence that stirs up the wrath of man. Any man, any church, or any group of men that faithfully preaches ruin by the fall (the total depravity of the whole human race), redemption by the blood (the effectual atonement of Christ for the sins of his people) and regeneration by the Holy Spirit (life and faith in Christ as gifts of God's sovereign, irresistible grace) will meet with relentless opposition from lost, religious men.

2. The Lord our God has a people whom he will save (8:5-12)

The gospel of Christ has never been popularly received by men. It has always been in the minority. Human opinion and religious tradition have always been opposed to the message of God's free and sovereign grace in Christ. Most people who hear the gospel preached in the power of the Holy Spirit go on to hell as though they had never heard the message of redeeming blood

113

and saving grace. But the purpose of God is not frustrated. God has a people whom he will save (Romans 3:3, 4; Acts 18:10). His elect are scattered among all nations and generations, but they will all be saved. God will gather his own to himself (Jeremiah 32:37-40). Not one of God's elect will perish. Not one of those redeemed by Christ will be lost in the end (John 6:37-40).

3. God always causes the sinner he has purposed to save to hear the gospel of Christ (8:4)

The preaching of the gospel is, in the purpose of God, as necessary for the salvation of sinners as election, redemption and regeneration (Romans 10:13-17; James 1:18; 1 Peter 1:23-25). By the wondrous, mysterious workings of providence God always brings his elect to hear the gospel at his appointed time. He rules and overrules all things for the salvation of his chosen (John 17:2). He even allows reprobate men to persecute and scatter his church so they may be forced to carry the word of grace to chosen, redeemed sinners!

4. All supernatural, apostolic gifts ceased with the apostles (8:14-17)

Though Philip had received and exercised the miraculous gifts of the Spirit (8:6, 7), he was not able to communicate them to anyone. Only the apostles could communicate the gifts of the Spirit to others. If no one but an apostle could communicate these gifts to men (and no one else ever did!), then the gifts must have ceased once the apostles had all died. When the gifts were no longer needed they ceased to be. They were needed to prove the credibility of the apostles (Hebrews 2:3, 4). But since we now have the complete, perfect revelation of God (the Bible), there is no need for the imperfect, temporary signs the apostles possessed (1 Corinthians 13:10; 2 Peter 1:19-21).

5. Wherever the gospel is preached both true believers and those who make a false profession of faith will be found (8:12, 13, 20, 21).

Every church is a mixed multitude of true believers and those who make a false profession of faith. Wherever Christ plants wheat, Satan plants tares (Matthew 13:24-30). Wherever the Lord gathers his sheep, Satan gathers some goats. Along with those who were truly born again by the Spirit of God, Simon Magus professed to believe. But of him Peter said, 'Thou hast neither part nor lot in this matter: for thy heart is not right in the sight of God' (8:21). Simon believed the same doctrine the others believed. He was baptized like the rest. He certainly saw and recognized the power of the Holy Spirit. But Simon had one fatal deficiency: his heart was false! His heart was not right in

114

the sight of God. He was a hypocrite at heart. By profession he was a believer, but at heart he was an infidel.

Is your heart right in the sight of God? It is not enough that we believe the truth, worship God in the correct manner and obey his commands. Our faith, worship and obedience must arise from a true heart, a heart that is right in the sight of God. The Puritan Thomas Manton once said, 'Though thou pray with the Pharisee, pay thy vows with the harlot, kiss Christ with Judas, offer sacrifice with Cain, fast with Jezebel, sell thine inheritance to give to the poor with Ananias and Sapphira, all is vain without the heart, for it is the heart that enliveneth all our duties.'

First and foremost God requires our hearts (Proverbs 23:26; 4:23). Christianity is a religion of the heart. It is a heart union with the Son of God. Man by nature is content with an outward form of religion: doctrinal knowledge, a moral code, works of righteousness, ritualism, ceremonialism and emotionalism. But God requires heart worship and heart-obedience. The state of a person's soul depends upon the condition of his or her heart (Proverbs 23:7). God looks not at our religious works, but at our hearts (1 Samuel 16:7; Proverbs 21:2). He 'weigheth the spirits' (Proverbs 16:2). He says, 'I the Lord search the heart, I try the reins' (Jeremiah 17:10). We may give God a bowed head, a serious look, a strict adherence to religious duty, faithful attendance at the house of worship and a firm commitment to doctrinal truth, but until we give him our hearts our religion is an abomination to him (Isaiah 1:10-15; 66:2, 3; Luke 6:45).

Salvation is a heart work (Psalm 51:17). It is 'Christ in you, the hope of glory' (Colossians 1:27). All those things spoken of as essential to salvation are matters of the heart: conviction (Acts 2:37), repentance (Luke 13:3) and faith (Acts 8:37). But all men and women by nature have an evil heart of unbelief, departing from the living God (Ecclesiastes 9:3; Jeremiah 17:9; Genesis 6:5; Matthew 15:19). The one common way the Holy Spirit identifies the heart of men is by calling it 'a stony heart' (Ezekiel 11:19). 'A stony heart' is a hard, cold, barren, dead heart.

Only God the Holy Spirit can make a man's heart right in the sight of God. Only he can open the heart. Only he can reveal Christ in the heart. Only he can create in you a new heart. David was a man after God's own heart (Acts 13:22), because God had given him: a new heart (Ezekiel 36:26; 2 Corinthians 5:17); a broken and contrite heart (Psalm 51:17); a heart of faith in Christ (2 Samuel 23:5; Romans 10:10); a praying heart (2 Samuel 7:27); a heart of gratitude and love for Christ (Psalm 34:1-10). A heart that is right in the sight of God is a heart in which there is a constant warfare with sin (Psalm 73; Galatians 5:17; Romans 7:14-24), but it is a heart that honours God and seeks his glory above everything else (Psalm 51:1-4; 40:16).

Acts 8:26 And the angel of the Lord spake unto Philip, saying, Arise, and go toward the south unto the way that goeth down from Jerusalem unto Gaza, which is desert.

Acts 8:27 And he arose and went: and, behold, a man of Ethiopia, an eunuch of great authority under Candace queen of the Ethiopians, who had the charge of all her treasure, and had come to Jerusalem for to worship,

Acts 8:28 Was returning, and sitting in his chariot read Esaias the prophet.

Acts 8:29 Then the Spirit said unto Philip, Go near, and join thyself to this chariot.

Acts 8:30 And Philip ran thither to him, and heard him read the prophet Esaias, and said, Understandest thou what thou readest?

Acts 8:31 And he said, How can I, except some man should guide me? And he desired Philip that he would come up and sit with him.

Acts 8:32 The place of the scripture which he read was this, He was led as a sheep to the slaughter; and like a lamb dumb before his shearer, so opened he not his mouth:

Acts 8:33 In his humiliation his judgment was taken away: and who shall declare his generation? for his life is taken from the earth.

Acts 8:34 And the eunuch answered Philip, and said, I pray thee, of whom speaketh the prophet this? of himself, or of some other man?

Acts 8:35 Then Philip opened his mouth, and began at the same scripture, and preached unto him Jesus.

Acts 8:36 And as they went on their way, they came unto a certain water: and the eunuch said, See, here is water; what doth hinder me to be baptized?

Acts 8:37 And Philip said, If thou believest with all thine heart, thou mayest. And he answered and said, I believe that Jesus Christ is the Son of God.

Acts 8:38 And he commanded the chariot to stand still: and they went down both into the water, both Philip and the eunuch; and he baptized him.

Acts 8:39 And when they were come up out of the water, the Spirit of the Lord caught away Philip, that the eunuch saw him no more: and he went on his way rejoicing.

Acts 8:40 But Philip was found at Azotus: and passing through he preached in all the cities, till he came to Caesarea.

Chapter 24

Five Gospel Truths Illustrated

Acts 8:26-40

Gospel doctrine is vital. It must be preached and taught with clarity and distinctiveness. Many boast of their dislike of doctrine and appear to be utterly ignorant of it. God's people rejoice in the truth. Those who are ignorant of gospel doctrine are ignorant of Christ. They have no saving faith in him. An unknown God cannot be trusted. And the only way anyone can know and trust Christ is if he or she is taught the doctrine of Christ (Romans 10:13-17).

As gospel doctrine is essential to the saving of sinners, so too it is essential for the edification and comfort of God's saints (Ephesians 4:11-16). It is by faithful instruction in the doctrine of Christ that God's elect are built up and established in the faith.

Every true gospel preacher is a doctrinal preacher. The man who does not preach the doctrine of Christ does not preach Christ. Christ and his doctrine cannot be separated. The man who does not preach the doctrine of the gospel does not preach the gospel. Any preacher who does not expound the doctrine of Christ to his hearers is like a lamp without a light bulb — he may be pleasing to look at, but he is utterly useless!

Yet doctrine must have a personal application. Dead, dry, impersonal, unapplied doctrine is as useless as the words of those who preach nothing but the morals of vain philosophy. In the passage before us, Luke gives us five glorious gospel doctrines by illustration. After the revival at Samaria broke out, the angel of the Lord directed Philip to go 'toward the south unto the way that goeth down from Jerusalem unto Gaza'. There he met an Ethiopian eunuch returning from Jerusalem. After Philip had preached the gospel to him the eunuch declared his faith in Christ and Philip baptized him.

1. The wisdom, goodness and perfection of divine providence (8:26-28)

Providence is God's sovereign rule of the world, his gracious accomplishment of his eternal purpose of grace for the good of his elect and the glory of his name (Romans 8:28). God's providence is always mysterious, indiscernible and unexplainable by man's wisdom. But it is always wise and good. All things are perfectly arranged by God, according to his schedule. By God's arrangement, everything in the universe is connected and all the connections are on time. With God, nothing is late and nothing is early. This is beautifully illustrated here.

There were two roads going down to Gaza from Jerusalem. One was commonly travelled. The other was seldom travelled because it was a lonely, deserted road, going through the desert mountains. The angel of the Lord told Philip to take that road. 'And he arose and went: and, behold, a man of Ethiopia,' a man chosen by God came riding by! He had been in Jerusalem worshipping God. He was a Jewish proselyte, walking in the light God had given him, but spiritually lost. He came away from Jerusalem as empty as he had gone there. While at Jerusalem, no doubt he had heard much about Jesus of Nazareth and the great stir caused by his followers. He may have been warned by the Sanhedrin to stay away from the apostles. But the time of love and grace had come for him (Ezekiel 16:8). He must now be saved. So God sent Philip to meet him. At the time appointed by God, he brought Philip and the eunuch together.

2. God's eternal purpose of grace in sovereign election must be fulfilled

Before the world began God chose a people for himself, whom he determined to save. Every one of those elect sinners will, in God's time and by God's power, be brought to Christ in saving faith (Psalm 65:4; 110:3; Ephesians 1:4; 2 Thessalonians 2:13). God passed by the scribes and Pharisees, the natural descendants of Abraham, and called an African man, an Ethiopian eunuch (Psalm 68:31; Isaiah 56:4, 5). Grace always works the same way (1 Corinthians 1:26-31).

3. A picture of true evangelism in practice (8:29-35)

True evangelism arises from a firm faith in the efficacy of God's election, Christ's atonement and the Spirit's call (Acts 18:9-11). It is a work performed by the direction of God the Holy Spirit. Three things always characterize true evangelism:

First, a preacher is sent by God. Philip was the man chosen by God to be the messenger of grace to the Ethiopian eunuch. He was sent by God on an errand of mercy (Romans 10:15). The man God chose to use was a man full of the Holy Spirit, of blameless character and committed to the gospel of Christ (Acts 6:3, 5; 1 Timothy 3:1-7). He was a man willing to serve God and his church in any capacity. Philip was willing to serve as a deacon. He was willing to go to Samaria and preach there. And he was willing to walk for miles to preach the gospel to one Ethiopian. He wanted only to serve the cause of Christ. It mattered not to him where or how God used him. He just wanted to be used of God.

Secondly, the message is ordained by God. Every man sent by God to preach to anyone is sent with the message Philip carried to the eunuch. Philip preached Christ to him (8:35). God's servants have nothing else to preach (1 Corinthians 2:2). Christ crucified is 'all the counsel of God' (Acts 20:27; Luke 24:27, 44-47). If God sends a man to preach, he sends him to preach Christ in all the Scriptures.

Thirdly, the sinner is chosen by God. This Ethiopian eunuch was saved because God had chosen him (Acts 13:48; John 15:16). He is a picture of the kind of people to whom God is always gracious. He sought the Lord earnestly (Jeremiah 29:12-14). He walked in the light God gave him. He searched the Scriptures (John 5:39). And he was willing to be taught. Grace chose him. Grace prepared him for grace. And grace brought him to Christ in faith.

4. The saving faith of God's elect (8:36, 37)

True, saving faith is more than a notion received in the head. It is heart-knowledge, heart-persuasion and heart-commitment to Christ (Romans 10:9-13; 2 Timothy 1:12). This eunuch declared that he believed with all his heart 'that Jesus Christ is the Son of God'. That means that he is the one of whom the prophets speak, the Saviour typified in the law and promised by God, and that he is God in human flesh who died for sinners and rose again (1 John 5:1).

5. The significance of believer's baptism (8:36-39)

Clearly, baptism is for believers only. It is a test of submission and obedience to Christ as Lord. It is the believer's symbolic confession of faith in Christ (Romans 6:4-6). And baptism is by immersion only. Immersion is not a mode of baptism. Immersion is baptism! Commenting on this passage John Calvin wrote, 'Hence we see what was the manner of baptizing with the ancients, for they plunged the whole body into water.'

When the day was over the eunuch 'went on his way rejoicing'. He continued to follow his ordinary course of life; but now he lived by faith and lived for the glory of God. Philip went on his way too, preaching the gospel as he was led by the Spirit, until he finally settled in Caesarea (Acts 21:8).

Acts 9:1 And Saul, yet breathing out threatenings and slaughter against the disciples of the Lord, went unto the high priest,

Acts 9:2 And desired of him letters to Damascus to the synagogues, that if he found any of this way, whether they were men or women, he might bring them bound unto Jerusalem.

Acts 9:3 And as he journeyed, he came near Damascus: and suddenly there shined round about him a light from heaven:

Acts 9:4 And he fell to the earth, and heard a voice saying unto him, Saul, Saul, why persecutest thou me?

Acts 9:5 And he said, Who art thou, Lord? And the Lord said, I am Jesus whom thou persecutest: it is hard for thee to kick against the pricks.

Acts 9:6 And he trembling and astonished said, Lord, what wilt thou have me to do? And the Lord said unto him, Arise, and go into the city, and it shall be told thee what thou must do.

Acts 9:7 And the men which journeyed with him stood speechless, hearing a voice, but seeing no man.

Acts 9:8 And Saul arose from the earth; and when his eyes were opened, he saw no man: but they led him by the hand, and brought him into Damascus.

Acts 9:9 And he was three days without sight, and neither did eat nor drink.

Acts 9:10 And there was a certain disciple at Damascus, named Ananias; and to him said the Lord in a vision, Ananias. And he said, Behold, I am here, Lord.

Acts 9:11 And the Lord said unto him, Arise, and go into the street which is called Straight, and enquire in the house of Judas for one called Saul, of Tarsus: for, behold, he prayeth,

Acts 9:12 And hath seen in a vision a man named Ananias coming in, and putting his hand on him, that he might receive his sight.

Acts 9:13 Then Ananias answered, Lord, I have heard by many of this man, how much evil he hath done to thy saints at Jerusalem:

Acts 9:14 And here he hath authority from the chief priests to bind all that call on thy name.

Acts 9:15 But the Lord said unto him, Go thy way: for he is a chosen vessel unto me, to bear my name before the Gentiles, and kings, and the children of Israel:

Acts 9:16 For I will shew him how great things he must suffer for my name's sake.

Acts 9:17 And Ananias went his way, and entered into the house; and putting his hands on him said, Brother Saul, the Lord, even Jesus, that appeared unto thee in the way as thou camest, hath sent me, that thou mightest receive thy sight, and be filled with the Holy Ghost.

Acts 9:18 And immediately there fell from his eyes as it had been scales: and he received sight forthwith, and arose, and was baptized.

Acts 9:19 And when he had received meat, he was strengthened. Then was Saul certain days with the disciples which were at Damascus.

Acts 9:20 And straightway he preached Christ in the synagogues, that he is the Son of God.

Acts 9:21 But all that heard him were amazed, and said; Is not this he that destroyed them which called on this name in Jerusalem, and came hither for that intent, that he might bring them bound unto the chief priests?

Acts 9:22 But Saul increased the more in strength, and confounded the Jews which dwelt at Damascus, proving that this is very Christ.

Chapter 25

Saul's Conversion: An Example Of Grace

Acts 9:1-22

The story of Saul's conversion is recorded three times in the book of Acts, twice in his own words (22:4-16; 26:9-19) and once here in Luke's words. This man's conversion is described in great detail by the inspiration of the Holy Spirit, because the conversion of Saul of Tarsus is a pattern, an example, of all true conversions (1 Timothy 1:12-16).

People commonly talk about Saul's Damascus Road experience as though it was a rare, exceptional thing, but that is not the case at all. Without question, the physical things Saul experienced that day were exceptional. The brilliant light and audible voice from heaven have not, to my knowledge, accompanied any other person's conversion. However, Saul's spiritual experiences on the Damascus Road were not uncommon at all. In fact, all who are truly converted by the grace of God experience the very same things Saul did, essentially.

Salvation is not an experience, but a person, the Lord Jesus Christ (Luke 2:30). We must not look to our experience as the basis of faith and assurance before God. We look to Christ alone, trusting his blood, his righteousness, his intercession and the power of his grace for the salvation of our souls. Christ alone is our Saviour! Christ alone is the object of our faith! Yet salvation is something people experience. No one has the grace of God in his heart who does not experience the workings of grace in his heart. Salvation is a work of grace (Ephesians 2:8, 9). Taking Saul's conversion as our example, we see that there are five distinct acts of grace by which all who are saved have been brought to repentance and faith in Christ (Psalm 65:4).

1. A divine election (9:15)

No one has ever been saved, or ever will be, except those who are the objects of God's eternal, electing love (2 Thessalonians 2:13, 14; Acts 13:48). God's

121

operations of grace towards Saul did not begin on the Damascus Road, but long before. Saul was chosen to salvation before the world began (Ephesians 1:4-6). When God sent Ananias to preach to this newborn babe in grace, the very first thing he preached to him was election (Acts 22:13, 14). Faith in Christ is not the cause of election, but it is the fruit and the proof of election (Acts 13:48; 2 Peter 1:10). When a sinner bows to Christ, trusting him as Saviour and Lord, we say to him with confidence, 'The God of our fathers hath chosen thee' (22:14).

Election does not keep anyone from being saved, but guarantees that some people will be saved. Were there no election of grace, there would be no salvation (Romans 9:27-29). We would not and could not choose the Lord, but he chose us, and his choice of us made our choice of him certain (John 15:16). Election said, 'Saul of Tarsus will be saved.' God's merciful decree said, 'Saul will be saved at noon on the Damascus Road at the day appointed.' Predestination drew the map by which Saul must travel to the appointed place of mercy. Providence led him along the predestined path to the place and hour when Christ must be revealed to him. 'And it came to pass!'

2. A divine revelation (9:3; Galatians 1:15, 16)

Though he was chosen by God, Saul could never be saved until he was made to 'see that Just One' (22:14). So when it pleased God to reveal his Son in him, 'Suddenly there shined round about him a light from heaven.' He saw Christ and the glory of God in Christ (2 Corinthians 4:6). He saw the same thing that Moses saw (Exodus 33:18-34:7). He saw that Just One of whom he had heard Stephen speak (Acts 7:52). He was made to see, by divine revelation, the glory of God in his absolute sovereignty, infinite grace and mercy and inflexible justice, and he saw how God can be both gracious and just in saving sinners by the substitutionary blood atonement of that Just One, the Lord Jesus Christ (Psalm 85:9-11; Romans 3:24-26).

Salvation comes to sinners when they are given a revelation of Christ and the glory of God in him by the Spirit's effectual application of the gospel to their hearts. When a person sees Christ as he is and is reconciled to him in his true character he or she is saved.

3. A divine call (9:4-9)

There is a general call which men and women can and do resist (Matthew 20:16; 22:14). It goes forth indiscriminately to all who hear every time the gospel is preached. But there is an effectual call, too. No one will ever be saved until he receives this effectual, irresistible call of the Holy Spirit by which helpless, totally depraved, spiritually dead sinners are brought to life and faith in Christ by the power of God (John 5:25; Ephesians 2:1-4). Holy Scripture gives us numerous illustrations of this effectual call (Ezekiel 16:6-8; 37:1-14; John 11:43, 44; 1 Corinthians 1:26-31). Saul was one of Christ's sheep. The time had come for the Good Shepherd to call his wandering sheep. When he calls, his sheep hear his voice and follow him (John 10:1-5, 27-29).

This call of the Spirit is called 'the effectual call' because it gets the job done (Psalm 65:4; 110:3). It is a personal call (9:4, 5). Many were present, but only Saul was called. It is a convicting call (9:4, 5). The Lord convicted Saul of his sin with the words, 'Why persecutest thou me?' It is a humbling call (9:4, 6). Saul 'fell to the earth', submitting to the claims of Christ, his sovereign Lord. This call of the Spirit is also a distinguishing call (9:7). The men who were with Saul saw a light, heard a voice and were afraid. They knew something was going on, but not what. This call of grace separated and distinguished Saul from his companions (1 Corinthians 4:7). Again, the call of God is an awakening call (9:6). Once he was called of God, Saul began to call upon God. Blinded now to all earthly concerns, he began to seek the Lord with an earnest heart.

For three days he was in suspense and darkness (9:8, 9). Matthew Henry comments: 'He was all this time in the belly of hell, suffering God's terrors for his sins, which were now set in order before him. He was in the dark concerning his own spiritual state, and was so wounded in spirit for sin that he could relish neither meat nor drink.'

4. A divine illumination (9:17, 18)

God sent a preacher to Saul who told him all the truth. Then the scales of darkness and ignorance, superstition and tradition fell off his eyes, and he received his sight. When Ananias instructed him in the way of faith (Isaiah 40:1, 2) and he received his sight, what did he see? He saw Christ as his substitute, God as his Father and the Holy Spirit as his Comforter. He saw it to be his duty and his privilege to follow Christ in all things, beginning with believer's baptism, and he did it. The will of God became the rule of his life.

5. A divine conversion (9:18-22)

Saul was not disobedient to the heavenly vision. Grace converted him (Philippians 3:4-14). All that he once cherished he now renounced. His righteous deeds, his religious works and his reputation as a Pharisee, he now counted to be but manure. He turned from religion to Christ. Grace turned him from a mere form of godliness to worship and serve the living God, and he was turned for ever (Ecclesiastes 3:14). Immediately, he confessed Christ in believer's baptism (Romans 6:4-6), identified himself with the despised people of God and the gospel of his grace and became a faithful witness of Christ. He laid down his life in the cause of Christ. Grace had made him a new man (2 Corinthians 5:17). This is the way of God with men. This is the way God saves sinners: by election, revelation, calling, illumination and conversion. He saves in this way so that man's salvation will be to the praise of the glory of his grace. It is this experience of grace that identifies who God's elect are (1 Thessalonians 1:4-10).

Acts 9:23 And after that many days were fulfilled, the Jews took counsel to kill him:

Acts 9:24 But their laying await was known of Saul. And they watched the gates day and night to kill him.

Acts 9:25 Then the disciples took him by night, and let him down by the wall in a basket.

Acts 9:26 And when Saul was come to Jerusalem, he assayed to join himself to the disciples: but they were all afraid of him, and believed not that he was a disciple.

Acts 9:27 But Barnabas took him, and brought him to the apostles, and declared unto them how he had seen the Lord in the way, and that he had spoken to him, and how he had preached boldly at Damascus in the name of Jesus.

Acts 9:28 And he was with them coming in and going out at Jerusalem.

Acts 9:29 And he spake boldly in the name of the Lord Jesus, and disputed against the Grecians: but they went about to slay him.

Acts 9:30 Which when the brethren knew, they brought him down to Caesarea, and sent him forth to Tarsus.

Acts 9:31 Then had the churches rest throughout all Judaea and Galilee and Samaria, and were edified; and walking in the fear of the Lord, and in the comfort of the Holy Ghost, were multiplied.

Chapter 26

Saul Joins The Church

Acts 9:23-31

After his conversion Saul took a journey into Arabia (Galatians 1:16-18), which Luke does not mention. He did not go up to Jerusalem to receive instruction from the apostles there. Being chosen as an apostle, he had to be taught the gospel by direct revelation by Christ himself. Therefore the Lord sent Saul into Arabia where he went to school with Christ himself as his Teacher! While in Arabia he preached the gospel among the heathen. 'And after that many days were fulfilled,' Saul returned to Damascus where 'The Jews took counsel to kill him.' This is where Luke was directed by the Holy Spirit to take up his narrative. In verse 23 Saul is back in Damascus three years after his conversion on the Damascus Road.

1. Danger at Damascus (9:23-25)

As soon as Paul returned to Damascus preaching the gospel, he was in grave danger. 'The Jews took counsel to kill him' (9:23, 24). Enraged by the gospel Saul preached, they persuaded the governor in Damascus that he was a dangerous man, one that should be arrested and put to death (2 Corinthians 11:32). Thus the word of God by Ananias three years earlier began to be fulfilled, regarding the great things Saul would be required to suffer for Christ (9:16). As Matthew Henry says, 'Where God gives great grace, he commonly exercises it with great trials.' This persecution of God's servant at Damascus is instructive.

All who follow Christ walk in a path of certain trouble, affliction and sorrow. 'In the world, ye shall have tribulation (John 16:33). 'Yea, and all that will live godly in Christ Jesus shall suffer persecution' (2 Timothy 3:12). 'We must through much tribulation enter into the kingdom of God' (Acts 14:22). There are none who are honoured by God who are not reviled by the world. Reproach, slander, abuse and scorn from men are the common lot of

God's saints in this world (Matthew 5:10-12). Saul had done nothing to arouse their malice, except trust Christ, follow Christ and preach Christ. For that they tried to kill him!

The gospel of Christ, the message of salvation by grace alone, through faith alone, in Christ alone, is offensive to lost, self-righteous men and women (1 Corinthians 1:23, 24; Galatians 5:11). It offends man's pride, because it declares the total depravity and utter inability of Adam's fallen race regarding all things spiritual (Ephesians 2:1-3; Romans 5:12). The gospel of Christ offends man's sense of supremacy and self-determination, because it declares the absolute, universal sovereignty of God (Romans 9:15-18). It offends man's wisdom, because it declares salvation to be through the substitutionary sacrifice of Christ alone (Romans 3:24-26; 1 Corinthians 1:21-31). And it offends man's self-righteousness, because it declares his works of righteousness to be nothing but dung and filthy rags (Philippians 3:8; Isaiah 64:6) and makes salvation to be entirely the work of God's sovereign grace (Ephesians 2:8, 9; 2 Timothy 1:9; Titus 3:5, 6).

But God is faithful! He graciously delivered Saul from his persecutors (9:24, 25). Saul escaped out of their hands by the good providence of God (2 Corinthians 11:33). The Lord knows how to deliver the godly out of temptation. With every trial, he makes a way to escape, that we may be able to bear it (1 Corinthians 10:13).

2. Difficulty at Jerusalem (9:26-30)

When he fled from Damascus, Saul went to Jerusalem. He had escaped his persecutors only to find difficulty among God's saints! They did not persecute him, but neither did they trust him. God's people are not without their faults. Sometimes true believers say and do things that hurt and hinder one another. They have no malicious designs against one another, but they are still in this body of flesh and sometimes their fleshly nature is sadly evident.

When he arrived at Jerusalem Saul sought a place among the Lord's people (9:26). His first concern was to find the congregation of God's saints. Where they were, he would be found. 'He assayed to join himself to the disciples.' That means, Paul applied for membership in the local church at Jerusalem. He was not recruited by the church in a 'membership drive'. He asked for membership voluntarily. He loved Christ and his people and wanted to be identified with them.

John Gill wrote, 'It is the duty and interest of every gracious soul to join himself to a church of Christ, which consists of the disciples of Christ, who have learned Christ and the way of life and salvation by him ... To be joined to a church is to become an open subject of Christ's kingdom, a citizen of the heavenly Jerusalem, one of the family of God, and a member of the body of Christ visibly.'

At first the disciples were suspicious of Saul (9:26). He was not offended by their error. He understood it and forgave it. He was a gracious man. Later, he gave us instruction about receiving brethren with baseless suspicions (Romans 14:1). Believers are to receive one another upon the basis of their profession of faith in Christ, as we would receive Christ himself. We are to treat one another as we would treat Christ, because every believer is truly one with Christ. After Barnabas recommended him, Saul was received into the church (9:27). It is evident from this passage that only two things are to be regarded as qualifications for church membership: faith in Christ and believer's baptism. Nowhere in the New Testament is anything more required or anything less accepted.

While at Jerusalem Saul gained a reputation as a faithful servant of Christ (9:28-30). He spent his time in the company of God's saints and faithfully bore witness to the person and work of Christ. Yet his bold confession of Christ stirred up the wrath of the Grecians. When they tried to kill him, Saul escaped out of Jerusalem and fled to Tarsus. We learn two things from this.

First, God's sovereign providence overrules even the wicked deeds of men in the accomplishment of his purpose (Psalm 76:10). By the wrath of these men God sent Saul to preach among the Gentiles (Acts 22:17-21).

Secondly, God's servants are safe until their work is done. 'Mortals are immortal here until their work is done!'

3. Delight in the churches (9:31)

The churches of Christ had endured a long season of persecution. Then God saved the persecutor! The lion who once roared against God's little flock was made to lie down with the lambs. 'Then had the churches rest ... and walking in the fear of the Lord, and in the comfort of the Holy Ghost, were multiplied.' The churches of Christ will have times of trouble in this world; but our troubles will not last forever. Our God will make us triumphant in his time (Matthew 16:18). During these days of relative rest the people of God should be more fully employed than ever in the furtherance of the gospel, as we walk in the fear of the Lord, enjoying the comfort of the Holy Spirit.

Acts 9:32 And it came to pass, as Peter passed throughout all quarters, he came down also to the saints which dwelt at Lydda.

Acts 9:33 And there he found a certain man named Aeneas, which had kept his bed eight years, and was sick of the palsy.

Acts 9:34 And Peter said unto him, Aeneas, Jesus Christ maketh thee whole: arise, and make thy bed. And he arose immediately.

Acts 9:35 And all that dwelt at Lydda and Saron saw him, and turned to the Lord.

Acts 9:36 Now there was at Joppa a certain disciple named Tabitha, which by interpretation is called Dorcas: this woman was full of good works and almsdeeds which she did.

Acts 9:37 And it came to pass in those days, that she was sick, and died: whom when they had washed, they laid her in an upper chamber.

Acts 9:38 And forasmuch as Lydda was nigh to Joppa, and the disciples had heard that Peter was there, they sent unto him two men, desiring him that he would not delay to come to them.

Acts 9:39 Then Peter arose and went with them. When he was come, they brought him into the upper chamber: and all the widows stood by him weeping, and shewing the coats and garments which Dorcas made, while she was with them.

Acts 9:40 But Peter put them all forth, and kneeled down, and prayed; and turning him to the body said, Tabitha, arise. And she opened her eyes: and when she saw Peter, she sat up.

Acts 9:41 And he gave her his hand, and lifted her up, and when he had called the saints and widows, presented her alive.

Acts 9:42 And it was known throughout all Joppa; and many believed in the Lord.

Acts 9:43 And it came to pass, that he tarried many days in Joppa with one Simon a tanner.

Chapter 27

Æneas And Dorcas

Acts 9:32-43

Peter was on a preaching mission visiting the churches of Judea, Galilee and Samaria which had been recently established as a result of the persecution at Jerusalem. He travelled from church to church preaching the gospel of Christ, establishing them in the faith of Christ and in the truth of God.

'The saints which dwelt at Lydda' (9:32). Lydda was a town about thirty-five miles from Jerusalem in which God had been pleased to raise up a gospel church. It should be noticed that Luke and all the writers of the New Testament referred to all believers as saints. This title, 'saints', is not a title of distinction reserved for a few very eminent believers. It is a title for all believers. Every person who is born of God is a saint. The word means 'sanctified ones'! We were sanctified by God the Father in electing grace before the world began (Jude 1). He set us apart from the rest of mankind unto himself, for his own holy purposes and uses. We were sanctified by God the Son, the Lord Jesus Christ, in redemption. By his substitutionary sacrifice at Calvary the Son of God made all of God's elect holy, and God the Father, looking on us through the blood of Christ, declared us to be holy (Hebrews 10:10-14). This is our justification. Then God the Holy Spirit sanctified us in regeneration, giving us the holy nature of Christ (2 Thessalonians 2:13; 2 Peter 1:4; 1 John 3:5-9). All believers are saints and all have been sanctified. Their sanctification is the gift and work of God's free grace in Christ.

'A certain man named Æneas' (9:33-35). Æneas' healing by Peter is given as a picture of God's saving grace in Christ. This man really was healed of his physical infirmity by the power of God, but his healing was intended by God both to confirm and to illustrate his saving grace. Everything about this man and his healing corresponds to and reflects the saving grace of God experienced by every child of God.

131

1. Æneas was a chosen object of mercy

Luke describes him as 'a certain man'. In those days it was common to find paralyzed beggars laid in conspicuous places, hoping for alms or other acts of mercy from those who passed by. Where one was found, there were likely to be others (John 5:1-9). Perhaps there were many like Æneas in Lydda, but Æneas was chosen by God. Grace always comes to certain men and women, certain individuals chosen of God unto salvation (Ephesians 1:3-6; 2 Thessalonians 2:13, 14).

2. Æneas was a helplessly sick man

His disease was real. Peter was not a fake healer, but a real apostle. He healed a man who really was in an utterly helpless condition. But Æneas had not always been in such bad shape. So it is with us. God created man upright, in his own image (Genesis 1:26-28). But when Adam sinned against God, we sinned in him and we died spiritually (Romans 5:12). All men and women since the fall of Adam are in a helpless condition of sin and death. We were all born in sin (Psalm 51:5).

3. This man knew something about the Lord Jesus Christ

By some means or other, Æneas had heard about Christ. Otherwise, when Peter said, 'Jesus Christ maketh thee whole,' he would not, and could not, have believed on him (Romans 10:13-17). It is not necessary for a sinner to become a theologian to be saved, but it is necessary for him to know who Christ is and what he has done. It is not possible to trust an unrevealed, unknown Saviour!

4. Peter's word (God's word by Peter) came to Æneas' heart with divine power and personal application

Peter's word was the very word of God. God spoke to this man personally by the voice of another man, a gospel preacher. This is the way God calls sinners to Christ (John 10:1-5): ' ... Æneas, Jesus Christ maketh thee whole!' The effectual call of the Spirit (Psalm 65:4) comes to chosen sinners through the voice of gospel preachers. Sinners are saved, born again and called by the Word of God (1 Peter 1:23-25).

5. Æneas believed on the Lord Jesus Christ

He did not believe on Peter. He did not believe in the power of his own free will. But he did believe that Jesus Christ had made him whole. He proved his faith by acting upon it. 'He arose immediately!'

6. He was made whole immediately

But suppose he had not been! Suppose he had believed and yet had not been healed! Peter would have been proved an impostor. Christ would have been shamefully dishonoured. And the gospel Peter preached would have been proved a lie. The point I am making is this: it is impossible for a sinner to believe on the Lord Jesus Christ and not be saved by him (John 6:37; Hebrews 7:25).

7. Once he was healed, Æneas acted like a man who was made whole

'He arose immediately!' He no longer lay upon his bed among his former companions. He had been made new (2 Corinthians 5:17). He went all over town telling people what Christ had done for him. It was obvious to everyone! Therefore, many 'turned to the Lord'.

'Dorcas: a woman ... full of good works' (9:36-43)

Dorcas is set before us as an example of faith and godliness. She was truly a woman who lived by faith and evidenced her faith by her works (Ephesians 2:8-10; James 2:14-26). She made it her business in life to 'adorn the doctrine of God our Saviour' (Titus 2:10). Luke tells us three things about Dorcas:

1. She exemplified the gospel by her deeds of love (9:36, 39)

Dorcas was not a preacher or a teacher. She held no public office in the church (1 Timothy 2:12). But she was gifted of God as a seamstress. And she used her gifts in Christ, like love and self-denial, to make coats for God's poor saints. If I had to choose between the two, I would much rather live like Dorcas than preach like Peter (Philippians 2:1-8; 1 Corinthians 13:1-13).

2. She died in faith (9:37)

We are not told what caused her death, or where she was when she died, only that she was sick and her sickness led to her death. But she died in faith.

133

Nothing else really matters! 'Precious in the sight of the Lord is the death of his saints' (Psalm 116:15).

3. She was raised from the dead for the glory of God (9:38-43)

Dorcas was raised from the dead to die again. We who believe on the Lord Jesus shall be raised to die no more (1 Corinthians 15:51-58). When Dorcas was raised from the dead God was glorified in Joppa. And when God's elect are raised from the dead in the last day, our God will be glorified universally, forever (Revelation 5:9-13).

Acts 10:1 There was a certain man in Caesarea called Cornelius, a centurion of the band called the Italian band,

Acts 10:2 A devout man, and one that feared God with all his house, which gave much alms to the people, and prayed to God alway.

Acts 10:3 He saw in a vision evidently about the ninth hour of the day an angel of God coming in to him, and saying unto him, Cornelius.

Acts 10:4 And when he looked on him, he was afraid, and said, What is it, Lord? And he said unto him, Thy prayers and thine alms are come up for a memorial before God.

Acts 10:5 And now send men to Joppa, and call for one Simon, whose surname is Peter:

Acts 10:6 He lodgeth with one Simon a tanner, whose house is by the sea side: he shall tell thee what thou oughtest to do.

Acts 10:7 And when the angel which spake unto Cornelius was departed, he called two of his household servants, and a devout soldier of them that waited on him continually;

Acts 10:8 And when he had declared all these things unto them, he sent them to Joppa.

Acts 10:9 On the morrow, as they went on their journey, and drew nigh unto the city, Peter went up upon the housetop to pray about the sixth hour:

Acts 10:10 And he became very hungry, and would have eaten: but while they made ready, he fell into a trance,

Acts 10:11 And saw heaven opened, and a certain vessel descending unto him, as it had been a great sheet knit at the four corners, and let down to the earth:

Acts 10:12 Wherein were all manner of fourfooted beasts of the earth, and wild beasts, and creeping things, and fowls of the air.

Acts 10:13 And there came a voice to him, Rise, Peter; kill, and eat.

Acts 10:14 But Peter said, Not so, Lord; for I have never eaten any thing that is common or unclean.

Acts 10:15 And the voice spake unto him again the second time, What God hath cleansed, that call not thou common.

Acts 10:16 This was done thrice: and the vessel was received up again into heaven.

Acts 10:17 Now while Peter doubted in himself what this vision which he had seen should mean, behold, the men which were sent from Cornelius had made enquiry for Simon's house, and stood before the gate,

Acts 10:18 And called, and asked whether Simon, which was surnamed Peter, were lodged there.

Acts 10:19 While Peter thought on the vision, the Spirit said unto him, Behold, three men seek thee.

Acts 10:20 Arise therefore, and get thee down, and go with them, doubting nothing: for I have sent them.

Acts 10:21 Then Peter went down to the men which were sent unto him from Cornelius; and said, Behold, I am he whom ye seek: what is the cause wherefore ye are come?

Acts 10:22 And they said, Cornelius the centurion, a just man, and one that feareth God, and of good report among all the nation of the Jews, was warned from God by an holy angel to send for thee into his house, and to hear words of thee.

Acts 10:23 Then called he them in, and lodged them. And on the morrow Peter went away with them, and certain brethren from Joppa accompanied him.

Acts 10:24 And the morrow after they entered into Caesarea. And Cornelius waited for them, and had called together his kinsmen and near friends.

Acts 10:25 And as Peter was coming in, Cornelius met him, and fell down at his feet, and worshipped him.

Acts 10:26 But Peter took him up, saying, Stand up; I myself also am a man.

Acts 10:27 And as he talked with him, he went in, and found many that were come together.

Acts 10:28 And he said unto them, Ye know how that it is an unlawful thing for a man that is a Jew to keep company, or come unto one of another nation; but God hath shewed me that I should not call any man common or unclean.

Acts 10:29 Therefore came I unto you without gainsaying, as soon as I was sent for: I ask therefore for what intent ye have sent for me?

Acts 10:30 And Cornelius said, Four days ago I was fasting until this hour; and at the ninth hour I prayed in my house, and, behold, a man stood before me in bright clothing,

Acts 10:31 And said, Cornelius, thy prayer is heard, and thine alms are had in remembrance in the sight of God.

Acts 10:32 Send therefore to Joppa, and call hither Simon, whose surname is Peter; he is lodged in the house of one Simon a tanner by the sea side: who, when he cometh, shall speak unto thee.

Acts 10:33 Immediately therefore I sent to thee; and thou hast well done that thou art come. Now therefore are we all here present before God, to hear all things that are commanded thee of God.

Acts 10:34 Then Peter opened his mouth, and said, Of a truth I perceive that God is no respecter of persons:

Acts 10:35 But in every nation he that feareth him, and worketh righteousness, is accepted with him.

Acts 10:36 The word which God sent unto the children of Israel, preaching peace by Jesus Christ: (he is Lord of all:)

Acts 10:37 That word, I say, ye know, which was published throughout all Judaea, and began from Galilee, after the baptism which John preached;

Acts 10:38 How God anointed Jesus of Nazareth with the Holy Ghost and with power: who went about doing good, and healing all that were oppressed of the devil; for God was with him.

Acts 10:39 And we are witnesses of all things which he did both in the land of the Jews, and in Jerusalem; whom they slew and hanged on a tree:

Acts 10:40 Him God raised up the third day, and shewed him openly;

Acts 10:41 Not to all the people, but unto witnesses chosen before of God, even to us, who did eat and drink with him after he rose from the dead.

Acts 10:42 And he commanded us to preach unto the people, and to testify that it is he which was ordained of God to be the Judge of quick and dead.

Acts 10:43 To him give all the prophets witness, that through his name whosoever believeth in him shall receive remission of sins.

Acts 10:44 While Peter yet spake these words, the Holy Ghost fell on all them which heard the word.

Acts 10:45 And they of the circumcision which believed were astonished, as many as came with Peter, because that on the Gentiles also was poured out the gift of the Holy Ghost.

Acts 10:46 For they heard them speak with tongues, and magnify God. Then answered Peter,

Acts 10:47 Can any man forbid water, that these should not be baptized, which have received the Holy Ghost as well as we?

Acts 10:48 And he commanded them to be baptized in the name of the Lord. Then prayed they him to tarry certain days.

Chapter 28

Cornelius: A Man Of Faith

Acts 10:1-48

Pride and racism are intolerable evils and must never be accepted by the church of God. All who are in Christ are one in him, be they rich or poor, black or white, male or female, learned or unlearned. All true believers are brothers and sisters in Christ (Colossians 3:11; Ephesians 2:11-18; 4:1-6). In Christ there are no distinctions of race, sex, or social class, and none should exist among us. This unity of Jew and Gentile in Christ was perhaps the most difficult obstacle for the early Jewish converts to overcome, and it remains a very difficult obstacle for many today. The Jews looked upon Gentiles as being unclean and had no dealings with them, except by necessity.

For four thousand years the revelation of God was restricted to the nation of Israel. The Jews alone, with few exceptions, had the light of divine truth. Then, because of their unbelief, after Christ came, God rejected the physical nation of Israel and sent his servants to preach the gospel in all nations that he might gather his elect from the four corners of the earth (Matthew 21:3-43; 23:37, 38; 28:19). The apostle Peter was sent to preach the gospel to Cornelius, who was a Gentile, that he might be established in the faith of Christ. The lesson Peter had to learn, the lesson we all must learn, is found in verse 34. 'Of a truth I perceive that God is no respecter of persons.' The grace of God is not dependent upon, or limited by, earthly, human distinctions (John 1:11, 12; Romans 9:15). God has no regard for those things that separate and distinguish fallen men from one another.

Cornelius was a man of faith, a Gentile in whom the grace of God was evident. He had been converted from paganism to the faith of God's elect. He worshipped God according to the law of Moses. But he was ignorant of the fact that Christ had come and fulfilled the law as the sinner's substitute. He believed God (10:1, 2). He saw Christ pictured in the types and shadows of the law. He trusted Christ as he was set forth in the prophets. But he had not yet learned that Jesus of Nazareth is the Christ of God. Therefore, God sent Peter with the good news of the gospel, telling Cornelius that the Saviour for

137

whom he was looking had come and accomplished redemption. Like Simeon and Anna, Cornelius waited for the coming of Christ in faith, not knowing that Christ had come (Luke 2:25-32). Cornelius was a man in whom all the characteristics of saving faith were evident.

1. He was a man who feared God (10:1, 2)

When the Holy Spirit tells us that Cornelius 'feared God', he is telling us that he was a saved man, a child of God, a regenerate soul. Those who have the fear of God established in their hearts are saved. The Word of God holds out a multitude of promises to those who fear him. The Lord takes pleasure in them that fear him (Psalm 147:11). Those who fear God are accepted by him (Acts 10:34, 35). 'The Lord pitieth them that fear him' (Psalm 103:13). 'The eye of the Lord is upon them that fear him' (Psalm 33:18). God's hand is open to and ready to feed them that fear him. 'The secret of the Lord is with them that fear him' (Psalm 25:14). God remembers those who fear him and comes to them (Malachi 3:16; 4:2). Salvation belongs to those who fear the Lord (Psalm 85:9). Indeed, all the goodness and blessedness God has laid up for his elect in heaven belongs to all who fear him as Cornelius did (Psalm 31:19). The fear of faith is not a slavish, legal fear, but a loving, gracious reverence for the Lord God.

2. He was a charitable and generous man (10:2)

Faith that causes a person to fear God also creates in him a loving, generous spirit towards his fellow man. Cornelius 'gave much alms to the people', because he feared God. Faith produces and works by love (Galatians 5:6), and love shows itself by acts of kindness (1 Corinthians 13:1-8).

3. He was a man of earnest prayer (10:2)

His religion was not a nominal form of worship. Cornelius was earnest. He sought the Lord with all his heart (Jeremiah 29:12-14). He did so by making diligent use of the outward means of worship. At the hour of prayer he was in prayer. At the appointed feasts he was found in the outer court of the temple. He 'prayed to God alway' (cf. 1 Thessalonians 5:17). That means he lived by faith in dependence upon the Lord God. He sought the will of God in all things. Cornelius was a child of light. He walked in the light God had given him (1 John 1:7), and God gave him more light.

4. Once the will of God was made known to him Cornelius was immediately obedient to it (10:3-23)

In Old Testament times the angel of the Lord ministered to people in much the same way as God the Holy Spirit does today. He appeared to Cornelius when he was engaged in prayer and assured him of his acceptance with God (10:3, 4). Like Enoch, Cornelius pleased God by faith in Christ (Hebrews 11:6). As John Gill said, 'The prayers which he had put up in faith, and the charitable actions he had performed from a principle of love, ascended to God with acceptance.' Then the angel showed Cornelius where he could find a messenger from God for his soul and Cornelius sought him out (10:5-8). In the meantime, God prepared Peter's heart to minister to his beloved people at Caesarea (10:9-23). Cornelius needed a word from God so he sought it by earnest prayer. Peter needed the help of God to preach the gospel, he too, sought it by earnest prayer. Both men got what they needed from the Lord.

5. Cornelius received God's messenger with reverence (10:24-33)

Cornelius was anxious to hear what God would say by the voice of his servant. Knowing that God spoke to men by Peter, he gathered his family and friends to hear the Word of God. He held God's servant in high esteem. He erred in giving too much reverence to Peter (10:25), but his attitude was right (1 Thessalonians 5:12, 13; Hebrews 13:7, 17). When reproved, Cornelius submitted (10:26). He even overlooked the sinful faults of God's messenger (10:27, 28). Nothing would keep him from hearing what God had to say! He listened to Peter's preaching expecting to hear from God (10:33), and he did!

6. He believed the Word of God (10:34-43)

He believed what God taught him by his servant Peter. First, that no man has any claim upon the grace of God (10:34, 35); second, that Jesus of Nazareth is the Christ of God (10:36-40); and, third, that the Lord Jesus Christ is the exalted sovereign of the universe (10:42, 43).

7. His faith is seen in his obedience to the ordinance of Christ (10:44-48)

The Spirit of God fell upon these Gentile believers, showing Peter and the brethren from Joppa that all believers, Jews and Gentiles, are one in Christ (10:44-47; 1 Corinthians 10:16, 17). And all who believed were baptized, symbolically confessing their death, burial and resurrection with Christ (Romans 6:4-6).

Acts 10:1 There was a certain man in Caesarea called Cornelius, a centurion of the band called the Italian band,

Acts 10:2 A devout man, and one that feared God with all his house, which gave much alms to the people, and prayed to God alway.

Acts 10:3 He saw in a vision evidently about the ninth hour of the day an angel of God coming in to him, and saying unto him, Cornelius.

Acts 10:4 And when he looked on him, he was afraid, and said, What is it, Lord? And he said unto him, Thy prayers and thine alms are come up for a memorial before God.

Acts 10:5 And now send men to Joppa, and call for one Simon, whose surname is Peter:

Acts 10:6 He lodgeth with one Simon a tanner, whose house is by the sea side: he shall tell thee what thou oughtest to do.

Acts 10:7 And when the angel which spake unto Cornelius was departed, he called two of his household servants, and a devout soldier of them that waited on him continually;

Acts 10:8 And when he had declared all these things unto them, he sent them to Joppa.

Acts 10:9 On the morrow, as they went on their journey, and drew nigh unto the city, Peter went up upon the housetop to pray about the sixth hour:

Acts 10:10 And he became very hungry, and would have eaten: but while they made ready, he fell into a trance,

Acts 10:11 And saw heaven opened, and a certain vessel descending unto him, as it had been a great sheet knit at the four corners, and let down to the earth:

Acts 10:12 Wherein were all manner of fourfooted beasts of the earth, and wild beasts, and creeping things, and fowls of the air.

Acts 10:13 And there came a voice to him, Rise, Peter; kill, and eat.

Acts 10:14 But Peter said, Not so, Lord; for I have never eaten any thing that is common or unclean.

Acts 10:15 And the voice spake unto him again the second time, What God hath cleansed, that call not thou common.

Acts 10:16 This was done thrice: and the vessel was received up again into heaven.

Acts 10:17 Now while Peter doubted in himself what this vision which he had seen should mean, behold, the men which were sent from Cornelius had made enquiry for Simon's house, and stood before the gate,

Acts 10:18 And called, and asked whether Simon, which was surnamed Peter, were lodged there.

Acts 10:19 While Peter thought on the vision, the Spirit said unto him, Behold, three men seek thee.

Acts 10:20 Arise therefore, and get thee down, and go with them, doubting nothing: for I have sent them.

Acts 10:21 Then Peter went down to the men which were sent unto him from Cornelius; and said, Behold, I am he whom ye seek: what is the cause wherefore ye are come?

Acts 10:22 And they said, Cornelius the centurion, a just man, and one that feareth God, and of good report among all the nation of the Jews, was warned from God by an holy angel to send for thee into his house, and to hear words of thee.

Acts 10:23 Then called he them in, and lodged them. And on the morrow Peter went away with them, and certain brethren from Joppa accompanied him.

Acts 10:24 And the morrow after they entered into Caesarea. And Cornelius waited for them, and had called together his kinsmen and near friends.

Acts 10:25 And as Peter was coming in, Cornelius met him, and fell down at his feet, and worshipped him.

Acts 10:26 But Peter took him up, saying, Stand up; I myself also am a man.

Acts 10:27 And as he talked with him, he went in, and found many that were come together.

Acts 10:28 And he said unto them, Ye know how that it is an unlawful thing for a man that is a Jew to keep company, or come unto one of another nation; but God hath shewed me that I should not call any man common or unclean.

Acts 10:29 Therefore came I unto you without gainsaying, as soon as I was sent for: I ask therefore for what intent ye have sent for me?

Acts 10:30 And Cornelius said, Four days ago I was fasting until this hour; and at the ninth hour I prayed in my house, and, behold, a man stood before me in bright clothing,

Acts 10:31 And said, Cornelius, thy prayer is heard, and thine alms are had in remembrance in the sight of God.

Acts 10:32 Send therefore to Joppa, and call hither Simon, whose surname is Peter; he is lodged in the house of one Simon a tanner by the sea side: who, when he cometh, shall speak unto thee.

Acts 10:33 Immediately therefore I sent to thee; and thou hast well done that thou art come. Now therefore are we all here present before God, to hear all things that are commanded thee of God.

Acts 10:34 Then Peter opened his mouth, and said, Of a truth I perceive that God is no respecter of persons:

Acts 10:35 But in every nation he that feareth him, and worketh righteousness, is accepted with him.

Acts 10:36 The word which God sent unto the children of Israel, preaching peace by Jesus Christ: (he is Lord of all:)

Acts 10:37 That word, I say, ye know, which was published throughout all Judaea, and began from Galilee, after the baptism which John preached;

Acts 10:38 How God anointed Jesus of Nazareth with the Holy Ghost and with power: who went about doing good, and healing all that were oppressed of the devil; for God was with him.

Acts 10:39 And we are witnesses of all things which he did both in the land of the Jews, and in Jerusalem; whom they slew and hanged on a tree:

Acts 10:40 Him God raised up the third day, and shewed him openly;

Acts 10:41 Not to all the people, but unto witnesses chosen before of God, even to us, who did eat and drink with him after he rose from the dead.

Acts 10:42 And he commanded us to preach unto the people, and to testify that it is he which was ordained of God to be the Judge of quick and dead.

Acts 10:43 To him give all the prophets witness, that through his name whosoever believeth in him shall receive remission of sins.

Acts 10:44 While Peter yet spake these words, the Holy Ghost fell on all them which heard the word.

Acts 10:45 And they of the circumcision which believed were astonished, as many as came with Peter, because that on the Gentiles also was poured out the gift of the Holy Ghost.

Acts 10:46 For they heard them speak with tongues, and magnify God. Then answered Peter,

Acts 10:47 Can any man forbid water, that these should not be baptized, which have received the Holy Ghost as well as we?

Acts 10:48 And he commanded them to be baptized in the name of the Lord. Then prayed they him to tarry certain days.

Chapter 29

Preachers And Their Hearers

Acts 10:1-48

It is not surprising to read that while Peter preached the gospel to Cornelius and his friends, 'The Holy Ghost fell on all them which heard the word' (10:44). Such a marvellous manifestation of God's grace may be reasonably expected when men and women come to hear the Word of God with the attitude Cornelius and his friends had when they assembled to hear Peter (see 10:30-33). When preachers faithfully proclaim the gospel of the grace of God and those who hear them receive the Word of God with reverent, submissive, obedient faith, the blessings of God's grace are very likely to accompany the ministry of the Word. In this chapter, I shall use both Peter and Cornelius as examples, showing us what should reasonably be expected both from preachers and their hearers.

1. What should a person's attitude be towards those who faithfully preach the gospel?

Generally, people run to one of two extremes in their attitudes towards gospel preachers. Some hold them in contempt, despising them, ignoring them, or even opposing them, as the Judaizers in Galatia did Paul (Galatians 4:16). Others put preachers on a pedestal, as though they are to be adored and blindly followed, as Cornelius was ready to do with Peter (10:25, 26). Both these extremes are evil. Those who faithfully preach the gospel of Christ are only men. Therefore, they must not be adored and followed blindly. But every faithful gospel preacher is God's man. Therefore, he is not to be despised, ignored, or treated with contempt. The servant of God is to be known, loved and highly esteemed by those to whom he ministers (1 Thessalonians 5:12, 13). He is to be generously provided for by those who receive the benefit of his instruction (Galatians 6:6; 1 Corinthians 9:7-14; 1 Timothy 5:17, 18). And believers ought to remember their pastors in prayer, follow both their doctrine and their example and obey the messages they deliver as God's servants (Hebrews 13:7, 17, 18).

2. What did Cornelius and his friends expect from Peter?

Cornelius had received a special revelation from God, showing him that Peter was ordained by God to be his instructor in the way of life and faith in Christ (10:5, 6, 32). Therefore he regarded Peter as God's ambassador. He expected to hear from Peter all that God had commanded him to declare (2 Corinthians 5:18-21).

Every faithful servant of God should be held in this high esteem by God's saints (1 Corinthians 4:1, 2). God's preachers in our own day (pastors, elders, evangelists and missionaries) are not prophets or apostles. They do not possess prophetic or apostolic gifts, but they are God's ambassadors to sinners bound for eternity. They are sent to proclaim the same message to all men that Peter was sent to proclaim to Cornelius — justification and peace, remission and forgiveness of sins through Christ, who is Lord of all (10:36, 43; Hebrews 7:25). They are sent to preach Jesus Christ in his substitutionary redemption, sovereign reign and saving power.

You have a right to expect from every man who claims to be a gospel preacher the same thing Cornelius expected from Peter (10:33). Those who preach the gospel must be men of utmost fidelity to the Word of God and to the souls of men. They must keep back nothing that is profitable, but faithfully declare all the counsel of God (Acts 20:27). God's express command is, 'He that hath my word, let him speak my word faithfully' (Jeremiah 23:28). Three things must characterize every gospel preacher. You should expect and require these three things of any man who ministers to your soul. The preacher must be a man who knows the gospel (1 John 1:1-3); a man who preaches the gospel faithfully, regardless of cost or consequence (1 Corinthians 9:16; Ezekiel 33:7, 8); a man whose conduct is consistent with the gospel (1 Timothy 3:1-7; 4:12-16; 2 Timothy 4:1-5).

3. What did Peter find in the assembly at Caesarea?

Here are four things Peter found among Cornelius and his friends which every gospel preacher might reasonably expect to find among God's saints, when he comes before them to expound the Holy Scriptures.

First, Peter found in Cornelius a man who was truly concerned for the souls of men (10:24). Cornelius knew some people who were perishing. He knew where they could hear the gospel. And he put forth considerable effort, time and expense to get those people under the sound of the gospel. Surely, it is reasonable to expect all who fear God to behave in the same way.

Secondly, those men and women were gathered in the appointed place of worship, at the appointed hour with reverence, as in the presence of God to hear the Word of God, expecting to hear God speak to them by his servant (10:33). Like the young child Samuel in the temple, they came to the house of God saying, 'Speak, Lord, for thy servant heareth' (1 Samuel 3:9). Many do not hear from God when his servant preaches simply because they do not come to the house of God seeking a message from the Lord.

Thirdly, Peter found in this band of people a readiness to receive the Word of God with meekness. Not one of them arrived late (10:33). As far as they were concerned nothing was so important as the hearing of the gospel. They readily received God's message (Isaiah 66:1, 2). They did not try to mould God's message to their way of thinking. They moulded their thoughts to the Word of God.

The congregation at Caesarea was willingly determined to obey God. What God said, they immediately believed. What God required, they immediately gave. What God commanded, they immediately did. They submitted to Christ as Lord of all, trusted Christ for the remission of sins and confessed Christ in believer's baptism. These men and women did not merely acknowledge the truth of the Word of God. They took it as their only rule of faith and practice. They addicted themselves to it. We must do the same! Hold fast the truth of God (2 Timothy 1:8-13) and proclaim it everywhere (Matthew 28:18-20).

4. What was the result of this meeting?

Peter was faithful to God, his Word and the souls of men. Cornelius and his friends received the Word gladly. The result was glorious! The Lord God graciously visited and poured out his Spirit upon the band of chosen sinners (vv. 44, 45).

Blessed is the man who has the privilege of hearing a man like Peter faithfully preach the gospel. And blessed is the preacher who ministers to such a congregation as Peter found in Cornelius' house. Wherever such preachers and such hearers are found, God the Holy Spirit is present and will be manifest!

Acts 10:9 On the morrow, as they went on their journey, and drew nigh unto the city, Peter went up upon the housetop to pray about the sixth hour:

Acts 10:10 And he became very hungry, and would have eaten: but while they made ready, he fell into a trance,

Acts 10:11 And saw heaven opened, and a certain vessel descending unto him, as it had been a great sheet knit at the four corners, and let down to the earth:

Acts 10:12 Wherein were all manner of fourfooted beasts of the earth, and wild beasts, and creeping things, and fowls of the air.

Acts 10:13 And there came a voice to him, Rise, Peter; kill, and eat.

Acts 10:14 But Peter said, Not so, Lord; for I have never eaten any thing that is common or unclean.

Acts 10:15 And the voice spake unto him again the second time, What God hath cleansed, that call not thou common.

Acts 10:16 This was done thrice: and the vessel was received up again into heaven.

Chapter 30

'Not so, Lord'

Acts 10:9-16

The Lord God let down a sheet from heaven 'wherein were all manner of four-footed beasts of the earth, and wild beasts, and creeping things, and fowls of the air. And there came a voice to Peter, Rise, Peter; kill, and eat. But Peter said, Not so, Lord.' Once more impetuous Peter made a terrible blunder. We must not be judgmental or censorious of him in his error. Who are we to put ourselves in the place of judgment over God's saints? (See Romans 14:4). Few men are half the man Peter was. But he was a man, and his errors as a man are written in the Scriptures for our learning and admonition (Romans 15:4). I do not doubt that Peter meant well, though he did wrong. His words were not intended by him to suggest all the evil that others have seen in them. Still, his error was significant enough for the Lord God to rebuke him sharply (10:15, 16). The Lord God told Peter to do something and Peter said, 'Not so, Lord!' The simple fact is that all God's people in this world have a constant struggle with sin, rebellion and unbelief, because we all still live in the body of flesh. No believer is the servant of sin (Romans 6:17, 18), but no believer lives without sin (1 John 1:8-10). Though redeemed by the blood of Christ, called by grace and robed in righteousness, God's saints in this world are sinners still. Sin is mixed with and mars all we do. David was a man after God's own heart, but he still had a great struggle with personal sin (Psalm 32:1-5; 51:1-17; 73:1-26). Paul was perhaps the greatest of all the apostles, but his warfare with sin was real (Romans 7:14-24). Peter was a man who died for Christ, but he also was a sinner until he drew his last breath in this world. We would be wise to learn from his mistake.

1. Though he is in Christ, the believer still bears the image of Adam

Though we have a new nature created in us by the work of God the Holy Spirit in regeneration, the old nature has not been eradicated. Though Christ lives in us and reigns in our hearts as King, old man Adam still lives in us.

147

He has been nailed to the tree and crucified, but he is a long time dying and struggles hard to gain supremacy. Believers are new men in Christ, but we are still men and sin dwells in us. We are saved sinners, redeemed sinners, sanctified sinners, forgiven sinners, but we are all sinners still! As it was with Peter, so it is with every believer — our struggle with sin is both real and constant (Galatians 5:17).

Peter was saved by the grace of God, but he was still Peter. If I had never read this passage of Scripture and someone related the story to me, without telling me who had spoken so rashly to the Lord, I think I would have recognized that it was Peter. Who else would have openly said, 'Not so, Lord'? Yet, we are all very much like him. Though grace reigns in us, the beast of sin still rages in us. There is a new man created in us, but the old man is still there. The inclinations to evil are not dead. We shall, each of us, have to struggle with the peculiar weakness of our old nature for as long as we live in this world. It is true, even among God's saints in this world, 'The very best of men are only men at best.'

This was not the first time Peter rebuked his Lord in ignorance (Mark 8:31-33). This was not the first time he impulsively refused his Master's command (John 13:8). We are all too much like Peter in this regard, saying, 'Not so, Lord,' foolishly imagining that we know better than God what ought to be! When we argue with God's providence, question his Word, or do not obey his will, we are saying, 'Not so, Lord!' In our hearts we know that the Lord knows best. Yet we often speak and act as if we knew best! Neither was this the first time Peter flatly, almost arrogantly, contradicted his Lord (Matthew 26:31-35). Like other believers, Peter was redeemed, regenerated and filled with the Spirit and, at the same time, he was rash, impudent, impulsive and sinful.

Yet Peter did have his good points. Grace was evident in this feeble man's heart. Grace was the ruling principle in him. This is evident in the fact that Peter acknowledged his fault. Luke would not have known what happened in Joppa if Peter had not told him (Acts 11:4-9). Peter was rash, but he was real, too. He was blunt, but he was bold. He was hasty, but he was honest. There was no cunning or craftiness about him.

What should we learn from these things?

1. A person may have many faults and yet be a true believer.

2. As our Lord was patient and longsuffering with Peter, and as he is with us, so we ought to be patient and longsuffering with one another (Ephesians 4:32-5:1).

3. Though we are in Christ, we must guard against the evil tendencies of our old nature (Colossians 3:12-17; Romans 6:11-14). The flesh is never dormant!

2. Though we are saved by the grace of God, our flesh still rebels against grace

Peter's 'Not so, Lord,' was the response of his flesh to the great principle of the gospel that God had just set before him — the total abolition of law worship. Peter had to learn that we are not under law but under grace (Romans 6:14, 15), and it took him a while to learn it (Galatians 2:11-16).

Legalism is natural to man. Our flesh kicks against the glorious free grace of God in Christ. It is the spirit of legalism remaining in us that causes us to lose our assurance or gain it by the evil or good we do. It is the spirit of legalism that causes us to neglect our duties and responsibilities (prayer, the Lord's Table, etc.) because of personal inadequacy . It is the spirit of legalism that sets up rules of life for others to live by, which God has not given in his Word. It is the spirit of legalism that tries to motivate believers with threats of punishment and promises of reward. It is the spirit of legalism that causes men to set themselves up as the judges of God's saints. When will men learn that Christ is the end of the law? (Romans 10:4). We are not under the law, but under grace! We are not slaves, but children in the house of God. God's elect are not lawless antinomians, but we are no longer debtors to the law to live after the law. Christ fulfilled the law for us, and we are free from the law!

Peter also had to learn that all men and women are equal before God (10:34). God has no regard for those things that separate men and women from one another, and neither should we have (James 2:1-9; Acts 17:26).

3. Though we are new creatures in Christ, the believer's old nature shows itself in many ways

It does so by rebellion against gospel doctrine; by rebellion against revealed duty; by murmuring against God's providence; by proudly despising our place of service! Let us ever put off these things of the flesh and put on Christ!

So long as we are in this body of flesh we shall have to struggle with sin. God will not eradicate, or even alter, the evil tendencies of our flesh. Yet, though we are weak, fleshly and sinful, God's grace is sufficient (2 Corinthians 12:3-9).

Acts 10:34 Then Peter opened his mouth, and said, Of a truth I perceive that God is no respecter of persons:

Acts 10:35 But in every nation he that feareth him, and worketh righteousness, is accepted with him.

Chapter 31

'God is no respecter of persons'

Acts 10:34, 35

'God is no respecter of persons.' That means that in the disposition of his saving grace, God is totally sovereign, giving it freely to whom he will (Romans 9:15, 16). Neither earthly condition, hereditary descent, nor outward circumstances secure God's grace, nor even make one person more likely to be saved than another (John 1:11-13). Neither will those earthly considerations prohibit God's saving grace, nor make a person less likely to be saved (1 Corinthians 1:26-29). God has no regard for those things that distinguish one man from another. His grace is not attracted by anything good in man. Neither is his grace repelled by anything evil in man.

1. As God is no respecter of persons, there is no place in the church of God for respect to men's persons

Our love, generosity, care and fellowship must not be determined by a person's position, wealth, race, or social standing. We are not to court the rich or the poor. We must learn to treat all men alike. We all sprang from one common father, Adam (Acts 17:26). Had it not been for the sin and fall of our father Adam, all mankind would be one happy, loving family. Were it not for sin, we would have no divisions among us. It is sin that has produced pride, racism and social snobbery. Because of the sin of one of Noah's sons, God divided all mankind into three races and divided to each race its providential estate in this world (Genesis 9:18-27). But in Christ, and in the church of Christ, these distinctions of providence have no significance (Colossians 3:11; Ephesians 2:14-22). The sons and daughters of Shem, Ham and Japheth are one in Christ. In Christ there is no such thing as Jew or Gentile, black or white, African, Asian or European, male or female, bond or free, rich or poor, learned or unlearned. God gathers his elect from all races, all classes, all social orders and all ages, and bestows his grace upon people

151

from all walks of life as it pleases him (Revelation 5:9). This is the thing that Peter had to learn and that we all must learn. 'God is no respecter of persons: but in every nation he that feareth him and worketh righteousness, is accepted with him.'

2. What does the Holy Spirit mean when he says by Peter that 'God is no respecter of persons'?

If interpreted in its context, like all other parts of Holy Scripture, this passage plainly asserts the freeness and sovereignty of God in the exercise of his grace. These words do not mean that God treats all men alike in providence and grace. 'God's grace is his own, and he dispenses it according to his own sovereign will and pleasure,' wrote Charles Simeon. God does distinguish between men (1 Corinthians 4:7) in election (2 Thessalonians 2:13), in redemption (John 10:11, 26), in providence (Romans 8:28) and in effectual calling (Matthew 22:14). God chose Isaac and rejected Ishmael. He loved Jacob and hated Esau. The fact is, God gives light and withholds light, gives grace and withholds grace, entirely according to his sovereign will, without regard to man's person (Matthew 11:20-26; Hebrews 2:16).

These words do not teach that salvation is by works. When Peter speaks of fearing God and working righteousness for acceptance with God, he is not teaching that men may gain divine favour by works of moral goodness. If salvation could be accomplished by human works of righteousness, then Christ died in vain (Galatians 2:21). If works contribute anything to salvation, then grace is altogether eliminated (Romans 11:6). Grace and works cannot exist together. They are opposed to one another. The one implies that salvation is paid to us as a debt. The other asserts that salvation is freely, gratuitously bestowed upon us as a gift. The Word of God plainly asserts that man's works have nothing to do with God's saving grace (Romans 3:20; Galatians 2:16; 2 Timothy 1:9; Titus 3:5).

This text does not teach that as long as a person is sincere he will be saved, no matter what his religion is. All who are ignorant of Christ and the gospel of his grace are lost, perishing in their ignorance, without excuse (Romans 1:18-20). Cornelius was saved, accepted by God in Christ because he worshipped as he was supposed to do at the time. Believing the revelation God had given, he trusted Christ, of whom the law and the prophets spoke. There are none today in his peculiar circumstances. This man's character is not to be applied to religious men and women who deny the revelation of God in Holy Scripture.

The words of our text mean that God does not prefer or despise anyone because of his or her earthly conditions. The Jews thought they were the only people to whom God would ever be gracious. They regarded all Gentiles as dogs; cursed and rejected by God. But Peter assures us here that all are alike before God. All people need God's saving grace (Romans 3:23). The grace of God comes to all the same way, through Christ, the sinner's substitute (Ephesians 1:3-6). All who are saved must come to God the same way, by faith in Christ (Acts 4:12). And all who come to God by faith in Christ are equally accepted in him. All are one with Christ. And all are one in Christ (Galatians 3:28). As Thomas Manton said, 'Some lie nearer, others more remote from the sun, but they are all alike near to the Sun of Righteousness.'

3. Who are those that fear God and work righteousness?

Cornelius is described as a devout man who feared God and worked righteousness. But it is contrary to everything revealed in the Bible to imagine that his fear of God and works of righteousness were the foundation of his acceptance with God (Titus 3:4, 5). The only people in the world who fear God and do works of righteousness are those who have been saved by the grace of God, accepted in Christ, washed in his blood and robed in his righteousness. These are the fruits of grace, not the causes of grace. The grace of God that brings salvation causes saved sinners to do works of righteousness (Ephesians 2:8-10; Titus 2:11-14). But grace does not come as the result of works!

4. What does it mean to be accepted by God?

Peter speaks in our text of sinners being 'accepted with' God. The only way sinners can ever be accepted by God is in Christ (Ephesians 1:6). God accepts every gift given and every act performed for him by every believer through the merits of Christ (1 Peter 2:5). As he is pleased with Christ, so he is pleased with all who are in Christ by his grace (Matthew 17:5), because all that Christ has is ours in him by divine imputation. Hence, to be 'accepted with God' means that it will be a righteous thing for God to reward every believer with all the blessedness of eternal glory in the Day of Judgment (Romans 8:17).

5. What lessons are to be learned from this text and from God's dealings with Cornelius?

Without question, the Holy Spirit has recorded these things to teach us three very important lessons.

First, God's saving grace is absolutely free and sovereign. No earthly distinctions will secure God's favour, and no earthly woes will prevent it.

Secondly, no one will ever seek the Lord in vain (Isaiah 45:19). Any who walk in the light God gives them will get more light. No one can put God under obligation. We can never merit anything from him but wrath. Yet this is certain — all who truly seek the Lord will find him (Jeremiah 29:13).

Thirdly, if God has no regard for anyone's person, neither should we have. We must neither court the rich nor despise the poor, or vice versa. We are to receive all as brothers and sisters in Christ who worship the Lord our God, and treat them as the children of God.

'God is no respecter of persons'

Acts 10:34 Then Peter opened his mouth, and said, Of a truth I perceive that God is no respecter of persons:

Acts 10:35 But in every nation he that feareth him, and worketh righteousness, is accepted with him.

Acts 10:36 The word which God sent unto the children of Israel, preaching peace by Jesus Christ: (he is Lord of all:)

Acts 10:37 That word, I say, ye know, which was published throughout all Judaea, and began from Galilee, after the baptism which John preached;

Acts 10:38 How God anointed Jesus of Nazareth with the Holy Ghost and with power: who went about doing good, and healing all that were oppressed of the devil; for God was with him.

Acts 10:39 And we are witnesses of all things which he did both in the land of the Jews, and in Jerusalem; whom they slew and hanged on a tree:

Acts 10:40 Him God raised up the third day, and shewed him openly;

Acts 10:41 Not to all the people, but unto witnesses chosen before of God, even to us, who did eat and drink with him after he rose from the dead.

Acts 10:42 And he commanded us to preach unto the people, and to testify that it is he which was ordained of God to be the Judge of quick and dead.

Acts 10:43 To him give all the prophets witness, that through his name whosoever believeth in him shall receive remission of sins.

Acts 10:44 While Peter yet spake these words, the Holy Ghost fell on all them which heard the word.

Chapter 32

'He commanded us to preach'

Acts 10:34-44

Peter was in Caesarea preaching the gospel to Cornelius and his friends. In verse 42 he declares why he was there. 'He commanded us to preach unto the people.' Before the Lord Jesus ascended back into heaven he left his church, his apostles and all after them who would serve him with a specific responsibility, 'He commanded us to preach unto the people.' That is the singular responsibility of every local church and of every servant of God (Matthew 28:18-20; Mark 16:15, 16; Luke 24:46-48; John 20:21-23; Acts 1:8).

As we have already seen, the apostle Peter had many faults and failures. He was, like all other gospel preachers, only a man. Yet he was faithful to the charge and responsibility God gave him. It mattered not where the Lord sent him, he went forth preaching the gospel. It mattered not who his hearers were, he preached the gospel to them. It mattered not what the results might be, Peter was a preacher, so he preached the gospel wherever God's providence opened the door. He was happy to preach to thousands in the temple, to the powerful Sanhedrin, or in the home of a Roman soldier who had gathered a few friends to hear the good news. What an example he sets before us!

The church of God must never lose sight of the purpose for her existence in this world (1 Timothy 3:15). The church is to be a sounding board for the gospel (1 Thessalonians 1:8), no more and no less. The church of this age has lost sight of her mission. That is why she is so weak and pathetic. The church of the living God is not a social club, an entertainment centre, or a political force. The church of God is, by divine commission, a preaching centre! The ministry of the church is preaching!

As preaching is the business of the church collectively, so preaching is the business of God's preachers specifically (2 Timothy 4:1-5). God's servants are not called to be counsellors, psychologists, social workers, or promoters of religion. God's servants are watchmen to warn of impending danger. They are preachers, men with a message from God for his people. It is the responsibility of every man who is called by God to preach the gospel to disentangle himself from the affairs of this world, and to give himself relentlessly to the business of preaching the gospel (1 Timothy 4:12-16; 2 Timothy 2:4).

All who are sent by God to preach the gospel preach the same thing. In the sermon described in our text Peter declared that he was preaching by divine commission, and God the Holy Spirit shows us what every God-sent preacher preaches. Peter is here set before us as an example, or pattern, of all true gospel preachers in three things.

1. He was sent by God. God himself put Peter into the ministry. God alone determined what he preached, where he preached and when he preached.

2. He preached with divine authority. 'Every true minister must speak because he is commanded to speak; he must speak what he is commanded to speak; and he must be prepared to fall back upon the authority of the Word of God continually,' said C.H. Spurgeon. The preacher's doctrine must be the doctrine of God, plainly revealed in Holy Scripture (Isaiah 8:20).

3. His message was always the same in its essence. Peter preached the person and work of the Lord Jesus Christ (cf. 2:14-40; 3:12-26; 4:8-12). Jesus Christ himself is the theme of Holy Scripture and the theme of every sermon that is of God (Luke 24:44-47; John 1:45).

The mission of the church is preaching. The work of the preacher is preaching. But what is to be preached? What kind of preaching is both honouring to God and useful to the souls of men and women facing the prospect of eternity? For the answer to those questions we need only to look into the Word of God and read the sermons of those apostles who preached with the inspiration and power of God the Holy Spirit. Acts 10:34-44 sets before us an example of apostolic preaching. By this standard all preaching, all preachers and all churches must be judged to determine whether they follow the pattern of the New Testament.

1. Apostolic preaching is the declaration of the sovereignty and the freeness of divine grace (10:34, 35)

The grace of God is both sovereign and free. God is not gracious to sinners because of who they are, what they do, or what they have. God does not accept or reject any because of anything in them (John 1:11-13). He alone has determined to whom he will be gracious (Romans 9:15-18). Verse 35 describes the character of God's elect, not the cause of his saving grace. All who are born of God fear him, work righteousness and are accepted by him through the merits of Christ, the sinner's substitute.

2. New Testament preaching is the proclamation of peace and reconciliation to God through Jesus Christ (10:36)

The gospel is 'the word of reconciliation' (2 Corinthians 5:16-21). All people are by nature God's enemies. We must be reconciled to God and brought to terms of peace with him, or perish under his wrath. The only way peace can be obtained is by Jesus Christ. He obtained peace by his blood for all God's elect (Ephesians 2:14, 15; Colossians 2:14, 15). He offers peace to sinners in the gospel (Matthew 11:28-30). When he comes to sinners in saving power, the Prince of peace brings peace (Romans 5:1; Colossians 1:20, 21).

3. All who preach the gospel declare the absolute lordship and universal reign of Christ

'He is Lord of all' (10:36). God the Father has turned the universe over to the rule of his Son, the Lord Jesus Christ, as the God-man mediator (John 17:2; Romans 14:9). As the reward of his finished work of redemption, the Lord Jesus Christ, as a man, possesses universal dominion (Isaiah 53:10-12) and exercises that dominion for the saving of his people. He is Lord of all men, all providence, all creation and all events. The only way sinners can be saved is by bowing to his dominion as Lord (Luke 14:25-33). That is what faith is.

4. To preach the gospel is to expound to sinners the meaning and significance of our Saviour's death (10:37-41)

W.A. Criswell wrote, 'When a man preaches the historical facts of Jesus, he is preaching Jesus. When he affirms the historical facts of the Christian faith, he is preaching the Christian faith. When he believes the historical facts of the Christian faith, he is believing the faith itself.' That is the deadly error of this age! Preaching is not the declaration of facts, but of a person. We exercise faith in a person, not in facts. To preach the gospel is to declare the meaning of Christ's work. Peter explained to Cornelius the meaning of all the facts he had heard about Jesus of Nazareth, and affirmed his personal knowledge of the risen Christ (1 John 1:1-3).

5. Gospel preaching involves the declaration of impending judgment (10:42)

'Hear the Word of God,' wrote Matthew Poole, 'and be persuaded of this, that Christ, whose gospel and word you hear, will judge you according unto it' (See John 5:26, 27; Acts 17:31; 2 Corinthians 5:10, 11; 2 Timothy 4:1). In that great day, all who are saved will be justly saved through the merits of Christ, and all who are damned will be justly damned because of their own sin (Revelation 22:11).

6. To preach the gospel is to declare the complete remission of sins through Jesus Christ for all who believe (10:43)

God delights in mercy. Therefore he pardons iniquity (Micah 7:18). And he does so justly through the blood of the Lord Jesus Christ (1 John 1:9).

These six things characterize the message of all true churches and preachers, and form the essence of every believer's testimony to men. But all our preaching and witnessing is vain unless God the Holy Spirit makes the word of grace effectual (10:44).

'He commanded us to preach'

Acts 11:1 And the apostles and brethren that were in Judaea heard that the Gentiles had also received the word of God.

Acts 11:2 And when Peter was come up to Jerusalem, they that were of the circumcision contended with him,

Acts 11:3 Saying, Thou wentest in to men uncircumcised, and didst eat with them.

Acts 11:4 But Peter rehearsed the matter from the beginning, and expounded it by order unto them, saying,

Acts 11:5 I was in the city of Joppa praying: and in a trance I saw a vision, A certain vessel descend, as it had been a great sheet, let down from heaven by four corners; and it came even to me:

Acts 11:6 Upon the which when I had fastened mine eyes, I considered, and saw fourfooted beasts of the earth, and wild beasts, and creeping things, and fowls of the air.

Acts 11:7 And I heard a voice saying unto me, Arise, Peter; slay and eat.

Acts 11:8 But I said, Not so, Lord: for nothing common or unclean hath at any time entered into my mouth.

Acts 11:9 But the voice answered me again from heaven, What God hath cleansed, that call not thou common.

Acts 11:10 And this was done three times: and all were drawn up again into heaven.

Acts 11:11 And, behold, immediately there were three men already come unto the house where I was, sent from Caesarea unto me.

Acts 11:12 And the Spirit bade me go with them, nothing doubting. Moreover these six brethren accompanied me, and we entered into the man's house:

Acts 11:13 And he shewed us how he had seen an angel in his house, which stood and said unto him, Send men to Joppa, and call for Simon, whose surname is Peter;

Acts 11:14 Who shall tell thee words, whereby thou and all thy house shall be saved.

Acts 11:15 And as I began to speak, the Holy Ghost fell on them, as on us at the beginning.

Acts 11:16 Then remembered I the word of the Lord, how that he said, John indeed baptized with water; but ye shall be baptized with the Holy Ghost.

Acts 11:17 Forasmuch then as God gave them the like gift as he did unto us, who believed on the Lord Jesus Christ; what was I, that I could withstand God?

Acts 11:18 When they heard these things, they held their peace, and glorified God, saying, Then hath God also to the Gentiles granted repentance unto life.

Chapter 33

Peter's Defence Before His Brethren

Acts 11:1-18

God's servants always meet with opposition in the world. They expect it (John 15:20, 21). The prophets of the Old Testament, the apostles of the New and faithful gospel preachers throughout the ages have constantly been the objects of mockery, derision, slander and persecution. The message of the cross has always been offensive to men, and still is. The doctrine of God's free and sovereign grace in Christ has never been approved of by the masses. The church of God has a message from God to deliver to men and women who are his enemies. We expect opposition from God's enemies. But in Acts 11:1-18 Peter is standing in the midst of his brethren at a church meeting, defending his ministry before people who should have rejoiced in it! He could handle opposition from the Pharisees, the Sadducees and the Libertines easily enough. He expected it. But it must have been an astonishing, painful thing for him to meet with opposition in the church of Christ and to have to defend himself before his own brethren.

Being led by God to do so, Peter went to Caesarea and preached the gospel to a congregation of uncircumcised Gentiles. Because they believed the message of grace and redemption through Christ, the sinner's substitute, these Gentiles were baptized by Peter in the name of the Lord. When the Jewish believers heard about what Peter had done, instead of rejoicing in God's grace, they were very angry! In this passage Peter explains what God had done. The Holy Spirit has recorded this sad incident in the history of God's church to teach us several important lessons.

1. God's people in this world have many faults (11:1-3)

Here is a marvellous revelation of human nature. The church at Jerusalem was in an uproar, not because of some grave doctrinal error or sinful deed, but because Peter had eaten with Gentiles! The uproar was so great that later it caused Peter himself to err (Galatians 2:11-16). They ignored the facts that

163

God's name was worshipped and honoured at Caesarea, that this thing was done by God's direction, that the saving grace of God had reached many and that God's mercy was going out to the whole world. Nothing was said about any of these things! They were ready to condemn Peter because he had been in the home of an uncircumcised Gentile and had eaten with him.

This church that had once been 'with one accord' and filled with the power of the Holy Spirit, once so mightily used of God, was now ready to sit in judgment over God, his servant and his work! It was filled with strife over nothing! By the time we get to the end of the chapter, God had reduced them to utter poverty, living on the charity of the Gentile believers they here derided (11:27-30). This incident in the church at Jerusalem is recorded to warn us. We must carefully and constantly guard against the evil tendencies of our proud flesh towards harshness, slander and division (Ephesians 4:1-7, 30-32; 5:1, 2). Be very careful in your assessment of your brother's actions (Matthew 7:1-5). Make allowances for, and be lenient with, one another. Grace teaches people to be gracious!

2. Human nature will always try to mix works and grace (11:4-17)

This was the real problem. These Jewish believers thought uncircumcised Gentiles could not be accepted by God. The only way Peter could exonerate himself was to tell them exactly what had happened, exactly what God had taught him in his vision at Joppa and exactly how Cornelius and his band had responded to the gospel, and to say, 'Brethren, God did this!'

The sad fact is that Judaizers, legalists, have always plagued the church of God in this world. It is the natural tendency of proud human flesh to say, 'Grace is not enough. God requires something from man.' While declaring that salvation is by grace, they add law-keeping, sabbath-observance, and adherence to religious traditions and customs to the grace of God. In doing so, they destroy the doctrine of grace. Anything done by man, when added to Christ, or added to the grace of God for justification, sanctification, or any other aspect of salvation, makes the blood of Christ and the grace of God to be of no effect (Galatians 5:1-4).

Grace and works will not mix (Romans 11:6: Ephesians 2:8-10). Grace produces good works. But grace is not caused by, dependent upon, or even influenced by our works! All preachers of works-salvation are enemies of God, of Christ, of the gospel and of men's souls. They are to be held in utter contempt by the church of God (Galatians 1:6-8; 5:12; Philippians 3:2). God's gospel simply declares with regard to the whole work of salvation, 'God did it!' God thought it; God bought it; God wrought it!

3. God's people, though they have many faults, submit to and receive spiritual instruction

'When they heard these things, they held their peace and glorified God' (11:18). Having been corrected, these brethren acknowledged their error and turned from it. True believers do err in many ways (1 John 1:8, 10). But believers do not hold the Word of God in contempt. Like David, when God confronts them with their sin, they bow to the Word of God (2 Samuel 11:26-12:24).

4. God's saving grace always produces genuine repentance (11:18)

Repentance, like faith, is a gift of God. It is not something men work up. It is not something that can be produced by human power and reason. Repentance is something God grants to sinners through Jesus Christ by the preaching of the gospel (Acts 5:31). Legal fear is not repentance; both Cain and Simon Magus had that. Moral reformation is not repentance; the Pharisees had that. Trembling at the Word of God is not repentance; Felix had that. Remorse for sin is not repentance; Judas had that. A desire for heaven is not repentance; Esau had that. What is repentance? It involves at least these four things:

1. Conviction (John 16:8-14). No one will ever repent until he is convinced by the Spirit of God of his sin, Christ's righteousness and God's judgment of sin by Christ's accomplished redemption.
2. Conversion (1 Thessalonians 1:9). Repentance is a turning of the heart to God, as he is revealed in Christ, in reconciliation and love.
3. Commitment (Mark 8:34-38). There is no repentance towards God where there is no commitment to Christ as Lord.
4. Continuation (Matthew 5:22). Every true penitent keeps on repenting, coming to Christ, following Christ and consecrating himself to Christ. Like faith, true repentance never ceases. It seeks Christ until it has Christ in the fulness, perfection and joy of heavenly glory.

Acts 11:19 Now they which were scattered abroad upon the persecution that arose about Stephen travelled as far as Phenice, and Cyprus, and Antioch, preaching the word to none but unto the Jews only.

Acts 11:20 And some of them were men of Cyprus and Cyrene, which, when they were come to Antioch, spake unto the Grecians, preaching the Lord Jesus.

Acts 11:21 And the hand of the Lord was with them: and a great number believed, and turned unto the Lord.

Acts 11:22 Then tidings of these things came unto the ears of the church which was in Jerusalem: and they sent forth Barnabas, that he should go as far as Antioch.

Acts 11:23 Who, when he came, and had seen the grace of God, was glad, and exhorted them all, that with purpose of heart they would cleave unto the Lord.

Acts 11:24 For he was a good man, and full of the Holy Ghost and of faith: and much people was added unto the Lord.

Acts 11:25 Then departed Barnabas to Tarsus, for to seek Saul:

Acts 11:26 And when he had found him, he brought him unto Antioch. And it came to pass, that a whole year they assembled themselves with the church, and taught much people. And the disciples were called Christians first in Antioch.

Acts 11:27 And in these days came prophets from Jerusalem unto Antioch.

Acts 11:28 And there stood up one of them named Agabus, and signified by the Spirit that there should be great dearth throughout all the world: which came to pass in the days of Claudius Caesar.

Acts 11:29 Then the disciples, every man according to his ability, determined to send relief unto the brethren which dwelt in Judaea:

Acts 11:30 Which also they did, and sent it to the elders by the hands of Barnabas and Saul.

Chapter 34

'The disciples were called Christians'

Acts 11:19-30

Acts 11 is a turning-point in the history of the early church. The church at Antioch, established under the ministry of Barnabas (11:22-24), was the first gospel church to be established among the Gentiles. Paul and Barnabas worked together in Antioch for about a year. During that time the church grew enormously. The church at Jerusalem was no longer the centre of evangelism. When that church was on the decline, when the time had come for the gospel to be carried to the Gentile world, God raised up this church at Antioch. It took up the banner of gospel truth and held it high for five hundred years until the entire city was destroyed by an earthquake in 526. It was this church which sent out Paul and Barnabas, the first missionaries, to proclaim the gospel to the world (Acts 13). Before they were done, these men carried the gospel to the entire civilized world. The events at Antioch recorded in these verses and the lessons here taught and illustrated by the Spirit of God may be summarized by four statements.

1. By the arrangement of his wise and good providence God graciously caused his elect to hear the gospel at the time he had appointed when he would save them

God has a purpose in everything he does, and his purpose is always good. The Lord God sent persecution to his church at Jerusalem so that he might be gracious to his chosen among the Gentiles (cf. Acts 8:1-4; 11:19; Romans 8:28). At the time of love God will cause his chosen ones to hear the gospel and believe (Ezekiel 16:8; Psalm 65:4). These believers who were greatly afflicted by God's hand of providence were yet obedient to him. Though they were persecuted, they went everywhere 'preaching the Lord Jesus' (11:20). In the midst of trouble and sorrow they were faithful witnesses. Though they could not have understood the purpose of God in their trials, they did understand their responsibility and faithfully performed it. 'And the hand of the Lord was with them' (11:21). God never forsakes his own (Isaiah 41:10-

14). Our heavenly Father does not always tell us what he is doing, but he assures us that all he is doing is for our good, the good of his elect in general and his own glory. As the result of the persecution at Jerusalem the gospel was preached at Antioch, 'And a great number believed and turned unto the Lord.'

2. The Lord gave his church at Antioch pastors according to his heart, who fed the saints with knowledge and understanding (11:22-26; Jeremiah 3:15)

First, he sent Barnabas to them, 'a good man', generous, charitable and kind, 'full of the Holy Ghost' (Ephesians 4:18-21) and 'full ... of faith'. He believed God and had proved himself faithful to God. Barnabas served the church of God wherever he was needed, with everything he had, long before he was sent out to preach the gospel. He was not a novice, but a man of proven faithfulness. Let no man be sent into the work of the gospel ministry who has not been proved to be a faithful man (1 Timothy 3:1-6; Titus 1:6-9). This faithful pastor rejoiced in the grace of God upon his people and 'exhorted them all, that with purpose of heart they would cleave unto the Lord' (11:23). Then Barnabas went to Tarsus and persuaded Paul to come to Antioch to help him in the work. As stated before, they worked together as a pastoral team at Antioch for a full year (11:25, 26).

3. Through the faithful ministry of these two gospel preachers God saved many, as it pleased him (11:21, 24, 26)

This is God's method of grace (Romans 10:17; 1 Corinthians 1:21; James 1:18; 1 Peter 1:23-25). God has a people in this world whom he will save: his elect, his redeemed! At the time appointed, God will cause his chosen ones to hear the gospel. And he will give them life, faith and repentance through the preaching of the gospel, by the power of his Holy Spirit.

4. The disciples were called Christians first at Antioch (11:26-30)

Until this time the Christian religion had been looked upon as a sect of Judaism, like the Pharisees and Sadducees. The early believers were Jews. They were circumcised. They lived among the Jews. They kept the Mosaic feasts, holy days, rituals and ceremonies and worshipped in the temple and in synagogues. The trappings of legal worship were not dropped, or destroyed all at once (Hebrews 8:13). But something new, something totally different happened at Antioch. These converts were not Jews, but Gentiles. They had no background in Judaism and no relationship to the Mosaic law. They had lived as pagans and idolaters, who engaged in the most godless, depraved lifestyles imaginable. Among these people God was pleased to raise up a church. Vile Gentiles had been given repentance and faith in Christ. They became followers of Christ. And their pagan neighbours invented a new name to describe this strange group of people. They called them 'Christians'.

What does that name mean? A Christian is a person, like Christ, anointed by God (1 John 2:27). As an Augustinian is one who follows Augustine, so a Christian is one who follows Christ. As a baker is one whose business is baking, so a Christian is one whose business is Christ. A Christian is a voluntary slave to Christ in his household.

There was something about the believers at Antioch which caused their neighbours and relatives to look upon them with scorn, and say with contempt and derision, 'They are Christians!' What was it? What made these people so unique, so different? It was not their dress, their speech, their diet, or even their social life that made them peculiar. If we carefully study the usage of this word 'Christian' here and the other two places where it is found in the Bible (Acts 26:28; 1 Peter 4:16), six things will become obvious:

1. A Christian is a person who believes on the Lord Jesus Christ as he is revealed in the gospel (11:20, 21; Acts 26:28). Believing the gospel message, we trust ourselves to the hands of Christ. We believe the gospel; but we trust Christ alone for salvation, eternal life and everlasting acceptance with God.

2. A Christian bows to Christ as his Lord and King (11:21). Faith surrenders to the claims of Christ as Lord and willingly resigns to his rule (Luke 14:25-33).

3. A Christian is one who with purpose of heart cleaves unto the Lord (11:23). Believers persevere in faith. They cling to Christ, saying, 'Lord, to whom shall we go' (John 6:68). We have no other hope.

4. A Christian is one who assembles with God's people in the name of Christ (11:26). Sheep are social creatures. Goats roam alone! Believers identify themselves with Christ and one another in baptism (Romans 6:4-6), gather together in worship (Hebrews 10:25), break bread in communion (1 Corinthians 11:24-28) and are united in the cause of Christ.

5. A Christian is one who walks in love with his brethren (11:27-30). God's people love each other. 'He that loveth not knoweth not God' (1 John 4:8; 5:1).

6. A Christian is one who patiently bears suffering and reproach for the glory of God (1 Peter 4:16). They follow the example of Christ even in the things they suffer (1 Peter 2:21).

Acts 11:28 And there stood up one of them named Agabus, and signified by the Spirit that there should be great dearth throughout all the world: which came to pass in the days of Claudius Caesar.

Acts 11:29 Then the disciples, every man according to his ability, determined to send relief unto the brethren which dwelt in Judaea:

Acts 11:30 Which also they did, and sent it to the elders by the hands of Barnabas and Saul.

Chapter 35

A Lesson In Giving

Acts 11:28-30

Agabus the prophet informed the saints at Antioch that there was going to be a great famine in the world, 'which came to pass in the days of Claudius Caesar. Then the disciples, every man according to his ability, determined to send relief unto the brethren which dwelt in Judea: which also they did, and sent it to the elders by the hands of Barnabas and Saul.' These children of God are held up by the Holy Spirit as examples to us. They exemplify the grace of giving.

They were informed by Agabus of a need and were moved by the Holy Spirit, speaking through Agabus, to do what they could to help their brethren in Judea (11:28). Then they spontaneously determined, without any pressure but the pressure of love and grace in their hearts, to give for the relief of their Jewish brethren, people they had never met (11:29).

The believers at Jerusalem had already sold their possessions and given everything they had to support their brethren and to see that the gospel was preached throughout the world (Acts 4:34-37). Had it not been for the generosity of the believers at Jerusalem there would have been no believers at Antioch! Now the saints at Antioch, in gratitude to God and their brethren from whom they had received the gospel, determined in their hearts to help their brethren in Judea when the need arose. Every man resolved to give according to his own ability. Each person's giving was spontaneous, free and unconstrained. Spontaneous giving is not careless giving. It is giving that is prompted by the Spirit of God, guided by the Word of God and carried out with thoughtful determination and purpose of heart (2 Corinthians 9:7). By giving to meet the needs of their brethren, these saints at Antioch were following the example of Christ himself (Philippians 1:1-8; 2 Corinthians 8:7-9). Taking the believers at Antioch as an example, I want to draw your attention to eight things plainly revealed in the Word of God about giving.

171

1. If we would give anything for the glory of God and the honour of Christ, our gifts must be motivated by love and gratitude towards the Lord Jesus Christ (2 Corinthians 8:7-9)

The apostle Paul refused to give any commandment about giving. He simply says that our giving is to be a proof, or demonstration, of our love for Christ. We prove the sincerity of our professed love to Christ by what we give and why we give it. In this dispensation of grace, God has given us no laws telling us how much we are to give. Like all other acts of worship, our gifts must be motivated by love. 'The love of Christ constraineth us' (2 Corinthians 5:14). Love for Christ is the key. Love is generous, overflowing and sacrificial. Love sets its own guidelines. Love is a law unto itself. Love determines what the believer gives, how much he gives and how often he gives.

2. If we would give as unto the Lord, our gifts must arise from a willing heart (2 Corinthians 8:12)

That which is given out of a sense of duty, responsibility, debt, or legal constraint is not free. Only when our gifts come from willing hearts, only when they are given freely and cheerfully, are they accepted by God. The quantity given is totally insignificant to the Lord. It is not the amount given, but the motive of the gift that matters (Exodus 35:4, 5, 29).

3. We should all give according to our ability, in proportion to our blessings (1 Corinthians 16:2)

Carnal men and religious legalists talk about percentages and specific amounts. But the New Testament never speaks of such things. Our gifts to the cause of Christ, the preaching of the gospel and the poor among us are to be based upon our ability. God's people are not tax-payers or tithers, but sons! We do not owe ten per cent of our income to the government of God's kingdom. God's kingdom, his church, is our family. When we give, we are giving to meet the needs of our family. What miser will be stingy with his own family?

There should be an equality in giving too (2 Corinthians 8:13, 14). A few people should not be expected to carry the load for all. Each should do what he or she has the ability to do in the support of Christ's kingdom. Yet the poor should not be expected to carry the same load as the wealthy.

4. All God's people should give for the support of the gospel (1 Corinthians 16:2; 2 Corinthians 9:7)

Men and women, rich and poor, old and young, all who believe the gospel should give a portion of their earthly goods for the support of the gospel. We should all be willing to share what we have for the common good of God's church.

5. If we would honour Christ in our giving, we must be both liberal and sacrificial in giving (2 Corinthians 9:5, 6)

Believers are liberal and generous because they have been treated liberally and generously by God (Romans 5:21; 1 Corinthians 6:9-11). Giving is like sowing seed in the earth. A wise farmer sows his best seed and scatters it generously. That is the way we are to give (Galatians 6:6-10). We have given nothing until we have taken what we want, what we need, what we can use for ourselves, and have given it to our Lord (Mark 12:41-44).

6. Any gift that is accepted by Christ as an act of worship, faith and commitment to him must be voluntary (2 Corinthians 9:7)

The Word of God leaves it entirely up to you what you give, to whom you give it, where you give, the way you give and when you give. There is nothing legal about it. God's people are not in bondage. 'God loveth a cheerful giver!' He will not have legal gifts of a grudging spirit.

7. Whether our gifts are made in public offerings of worship, to private individuals, or to specific causes, we are to give as unto the Lord (Matthew 6:1-5)

Do nothing to be seen by men or honoured by men. That which is done unto the Lord, for the honour of God, will be seen and honoured by him (Mark 14:3-9). In all acts of worship (prayer, giving, fasting, Bible reading, etc.) strive to maintain privacy. The minute you advertise what you do for Christ you expose a hypocrite's motive!

8. This kind of giving is well-pleasing to God (Philippians 4:18; Hebrews 13:16)

Give out of a loving and grateful heart, hoping for nothing in return. Of these two things you may be assured:

173

1. You will never suffer loss by generosity (Luke 6:38). 'The only way to have more than enough to spare is to give more than you can spare,' said Oswald Smith. And C.H. Spurgeon said, 'Many a man becomes empty-handed because he does not know the art of distribution' (cf. Psalm 37:16-26).

2. The more you can be trusted with to use for the kingdom of God, the glory of Christ, and the furtherance of the gospel, the more you will have to use. If you are willing to give, God will supply you with the ability to give (2 Corinthians 9:10; Philippians 4:19).

A Lesson In Giving

Acts 12:1 Now about that time Herod the king stretched forth his hands to vex certain of the church.

Acts 12:2 And he killed James the brother of John with the sword.

Acts 12:3 And because he saw it pleased the Jews, he proceeded further to take Peter also. (Then were the days of unleavened bread.)

Acts 12:4 And when he had apprehended him, he put him in prison, and delivered him to four quaternions of soldiers to keep him; intending after Easter to bring him forth to the people.

Acts 12:5 Peter therefore was kept in prison: but prayer was made without ceasing of the church unto God for him.

Acts 12:6 And when Herod would have brought him forth, the same night Peter was sleeping between two soldiers, bound with two chains: and the keepers before the door kept the prison.

Acts 12:7 And, behold, the angel of the Lord came upon him, and a light shined in the prison: and he smote Peter on the side, and raised him up, saying, Arise up quickly. And his chains fell off from his hands.

Acts 12:8 And the angel said unto him, Gird thyself, and bind on thy sandals. And so he did. And he saith unto him, Cast thy garment about thee, and follow me.

Acts 12:9 And he went out, and followed him; and wist not that it was true which was done by the angel; but thought he saw a vision.

Acts 12:10 When they were past the first and the second ward, they came unto the iron gate that leadeth unto the city; which opened to them of his own accord: and they went out, and passed on through one street; and forthwith the angel departed from him.

Acts 12:11 And when Peter was come to himself, he said, Now I know of a surety, that the Lord hath sent his angel, and hath delivered me out of the hand of Herod, and from all the expectation of the people of the Jews.

Acts 12:12 And when he had considered the thing, he came to the house of Mary the mother of John, whose surname was Mark; where many were gathered together praying.

Acts 12:13 And as Peter knocked at the door of the gate, a damsel came to hearken, named Rhoda.

Acts 12:14 And when she knew Peter's voice, she opened not the gate for gladness, but ran in, and told how Peter stood before the gate.

Acts 12:15 And they said unto her, Thou art mad. But she constantly affirmed that it was even so. Then said they, It is his angel.

Acts 12:16 But Peter continued knocking: and when they had opened the door, and saw him, they were astonished.

Acts 12:17 But he, beckoning unto them with the hand to hold their peace, declared unto them how the Lord had brought him out of the prison. And he said, Go shew these things unto James, and to the brethren. And he departed, and went into another place.

Acts 12:18 Now as soon as it was day, there was no small stir among the soldiers, what was become of Peter.

Acts 12:19 And when Herod had sought for him, and found him not, he examined the keepers, and commanded that they should be put to death. And he went down from Judaea to Caesarea, and there abode.

Acts 12:20 And Herod was highly displeased with them of Tyre and Sidon: but they came with one accord to him, and, having made Blastus the king's chamberlain their friend, desired peace; because their country was nourished by the king's country.

Acts 12:21 And upon a set day Herod, arrayed in royal apparel, sat upon his throne, and made an oration unto them.

Acts 12:22 And the people gave a shout, saying, It is the voice of a god, and not of a man.

Acts 12:23 And immediately the angel of the Lord smote him, because he gave not God the glory: and he was eaten of worms, and gave up the ghost.

Acts 12:24 But the word of God grew and multiplied.

Acts 12:25 And Barnabas and Saul returned from Jerusalem, when they had fulfilled their ministry, and took with them John, whose surname was Mark.

Chapter 36

The Good Providence Of Our God

Acts 12:1-25

Nothing is more comforting and beneficial to believers than a clear understanding of, and confidence in, God's providence. B.B. Warfield expressed it like this: 'A firm faith in the universal providence of God is the solution of all earthly problems. It is almost equally true that a clear and full apprehension of the universal providence of God is the solution of most theological problems.'

1. Divine providence is God's sovereign rule over all things

Providence is God's government of his creation. In providence God graciously and wisely brings to pass all that he purposed in eternity and all that he has promised in the Scriptures. Predestination (Romans 8:29, 30; Ephesians 1:5, 11) is the sovereign, eternal purpose of God. Providence is the unfolding of that purpose in time. It is God's sovereign, absolute arrangement and disposal of all things for the eternal, spiritual good of his elect and the glory of his own great name (Romans 8:28; 11:36). 'All things are of God' (2 Corinthians 5:18). Learn that and you have learned the only thing that can sustain your heart in peace when your life is full of trouble. Faith in God's sovereign providence is the only antidote there is to anxiety and fear. 'Happy is the man,' wrote William Cowper, 'who sees God employed in all the good and ill that chequers life.'

Acts 12 exemplifies and illustrates God's wise, adorable and good providence in a very instructive manner. Herod the king had killed James, the brother of John, and was about to kill Peter. But the angel of the Lord delivered Peter from Herod's sword. Our purpose in studying this chapter is to demonstrate clearly the fact that God's providence wisely and graciously ruled in all the events recorded in these twenty-five verses. The death of James, the arrest of Peter, the prayers of the church, the deliverance of Peter

177

by the angel and the death of Herod were all the works of God's good providence. The events of this chapter demonstrate the glorious sovereignty of our God in all things (Psalm 115:3; 135:6; Isaiah 14:24; 45:7; 46:9, 10; Daniel 4:34-37). This passage of Holy Scripture is an illustration of Psalm 76:10, where it is written, 'Surely the wrath of man shall praise thee: the remainder of wrath shalt thou restrain.'

2. Divine providence brought a terribly painful trial upon the very people who were the objects of God's eternal love (12:1-4)

God sent famine throughout the world in the days of Claudius Caesar, and Herod Agrippa began to persecute the church. It was his intention to destroy the body of Christ, just as his predecessor had tried to destroy Christ himself by murdering all the male babies in the land of Judea (Matthew 2:16). He had already killed James, the brother of John. That pleased the Jews so much that he had Peter arrested, planning to kill him after Easter, the Passover.

God's saints are not sheltered from trials and heartaches in this world. They suffer all the common trials of men. When the drought and famine came, it came upon both the righteous and the wicked. The fact is, as long as we live in this sin-cursed world we shall suffer the consequences of sin, just like all other people. Believers as well as unbelievers fall sick, endure sorrow and die. Faith in Christ does not eliminate pain in life! In addition to the ordinary trials of life, believers suffer the reproach of the gospel for Christ's sake (Matthew 10:22; 24:9; Mark 13:13; Luke 21:17). It is not possible to faithfully confess Christ and the gospel of God's free and sovereign grace in him without incurring the wrath of those who hate him (John 16:33). The cross of Christ is offensive to men (Galatians 5:11).

The believer knows that his trials, whatever they are, are sent by God (Job 2:10). Nothing happens in this world except that which our God has decreed for the good of his people. Our God rules all things in this world, the elements of nature, the thoughts of men and the deeds of all his creatures (Proverbs 16:1, 4, 9, 33; 21:1). Let every tried believer be assured of these five things:

1. God sent your trial (Romans 8:28).
2. God will sustain you through your trial (1 Corinthians 10:13).
3. God will be with you in your trial (Isaiah 41:10).
4. God will bring your trial to a good end (1 Peter 1:7).
5. God will get glory to himself through your trial (Romans 11:36).

3. The trial of providence caused God's saints to seek him in prayer (12:5, 12)

Our trials are ordained by God for many reasons. Just as fire purifies gold, the believer's trials have a sanctifying effect upon him. One blessed result of earthly woes is this: they cause believers to pour out their hearts to God in prayer (Psalm 107). When Peter was cast into prison, 'Prayer was made without ceasing of the church unto God for him.' William Cowper wrote:

> God in Israel sows the seeds
> Of affliction, pain and toil;
> These spring up and choke the weeds
> That would else o'erspread the soil.
>
> Trials make the promise sweet;
> Trials give new life to prayer;
> Trials bring me to his feet,
> Lay me low, and keep me there.

4. Faith in God's good providence gave Peter confidence, assurance, contentment and peace in the midst of great adversity (12:6)

Peter was scheduled to be executed by a cruel tyrant, but he was peaceful, so peaceful that he slept soundly on the eve of his scheduled execution. He slept so soundly that the angel had to hit him on the side to wake him up. How could he have been so tranquil, so peaceful, so free of care? He believed God! Peter lived by faith. He knew three things which enabled him to sleep peacefully in the midst of great adversity:

1. He belonged to God. By election, redemption and regeneration God had made Peter his.
2. He was in the hands of God. Peter was in the hands of God's care and his persecutors were in the hands of God's control.
3. God had promised to do him good. If the Lord delivered him, that would be good. He would go on serving his Master. If Herod killed him, that would be better. He would go to be with his Master (Romans 8:31; Psalm 56:3).

179

5. The same hand that delivers God's elect destroys God's enemies (12:7, 23)

The angel of the Lord was sent to deliver Peter and to destroy Herod. Both men were smitten by the same angel, but one was saved by him and the other slain. So it is with God's providence. God's providence towards his elect is all mercy. Towards those who believe not, it is all wrath (Psalm 92). The angels of God are messengers of mercy to serve and protect God's chosen sons and daughters (Hebrews 1:14). But to the reprobate they are messengers of wrath and executioners of justice (Matthew 13:41, 42).

6. Because our God sovereignly rules all things in providence, we are assured that his purpose of grace will be accomplished (12:24, 25)

Acts 12 begins with Herod fighting against God, trying to stop the spread of the gospel. It ends with Herod being slain by God and the gospel spreading triumphantly. This is how it will be until the end! The church of God is safe, the gospel of God is safe, the glory of God is safe, because God is on his throne! John Newton once wrote, 'If you think you see the ark of God falling, you can be sure it is due to a swimming in your head.'

The Good Providence Of Our God

Acts 13:1 Now there were in the church that was at Antioch certain prophets and teachers; as Barnabas, and Simeon that was called Niger, and Lucius of Cyrene, and Manaen, which had been brought up with Herod the tetrarch, and Saul.

Acts 13:2 As they ministered to the Lord, and fasted, the Holy Ghost said, Separate me Barnabas and Saul for the work whereunto I have called them.

Acts 13:3 And when they had fasted and prayed, and laid their hands on them, they sent them away.

Acts 13:4 So they, being sent forth by the Holy Ghost, departed unto Seleucia; and from thence they sailed to Cyprus.

Acts 13:5 And when they were at Salamis, they preached the word of God in the synagogues of the Jews: and they had also John to their minister.

Acts 13:6 And when they had gone through the isle unto Paphos, they found a certain sorcerer, a false prophet, a Jew, whose name was Barjesus:

Acts 13:7 Which was with the deputy of the country, Sergius Paulus, a prudent man; who called for Barnabas and Saul, and desired to hear the word of God.

Acts 13:8 But Elymas the sorcerer (for so is his name by interpretation) withstood them, seeking to turn away the deputy from the faith.

Acts 13:9 Then Saul, (who also is called Paul,) filled with the Holy Ghost, set his eyes on him,

Acts 13:10 And said, O full of all subtilty and all mischief, thou child of the devil, thou enemy of all righteousness, wilt thou not cease to pervert the right ways of the Lord?

Acts 13:11 And now, behold, the hand of the Lord is upon thee, and thou shalt be blind, not seeing the sun for a season. And immediately there fell on him a mist and a darkness; and he went about seeking some to lead him by the hand.

Acts 13:12 Then the deputy, when he saw what was done, believed, being astonished at the doctrine of the Lord.

Acts 13:13 Now when Paul and his company loosed from Paphos, they came to Perga in Pamphylia: and John departing from them returned to Jerusalem.

Chapter 37

The Work To Which God Has Called Us

Acts 13:1-13

The revealed purpose of God for his church is that it should be the means by which the gospel of his free and sovereign grace in Christ is preached throughout the world (Matthew 28:18-20; Mark 16:15, 16; Luke 24:45-48; Acts 1:8). Every local church has, by divine mandate, a singular purpose for existence, and that purpose is that it be a lighthouse, a sounding-board for the gospel. The church of Christ is to be a preaching centre, in which the gospel of Christ is preserved from generation to generation and from which it is preached unto all men (1 Timothy 3:15). Every believer is called by God to be a witness for him (John 20:21; Isaiah 44:8). Our business, goal and occupation in life, is to seek the Lord's sheep, the salvation of God's elect.

I can think of no reason for God leaving his people in this world except to use them for the saving of chosen, redeemed sinners. Every believer is completely fit for heaven (Colossians 1:12). We are completely forgiven of all sin, perfectly righteous and approved of by God through the sin-atoning blood and imputed righteousness of the Lord Jesus Christ. And we have been given a righteous nature in regeneration. Righteousness has been imparted to us by the Spirit of God. Why then has God left us in this world to live in this body of flesh? It is because he has chosen to use saved sinners to carry the gospel to other sinners for the saving of his elect!

In Acts 13 the Holy Spirit records for our learning the beginning of world evangelism. In this chapter God's eternal purpose that the gospel be preached in all the world began to be fulfilled. Prior to this the centre of the church was Jerusalem. From this point forward (in the book of Acts) it is the Gentile city of Antioch. Prior to this the primary spokesman was Peter, the apostle of the circumcision. From this point on it is Paul, the apostle of the uncircumcision. Prior to this the gospel had been preached basically to the Jews only. From this point on it is preached to the Gentiles. Prior to this the church was still bound with many of the fetters of Jewish legal worship. From this point forward the chains of bondage are completely broken.

Acts 13 marks the point in history when the Lord God began gathering his elect from the four comers of the earth by the preaching of the gospel of his dear Son. In our study of this chapter we shall consider seven things about the work to which God has called us.

1. God has an elect people whom he has determined to save in every part of the world

It never was God's intention, desire, will, or purpose that the gospel of his grace be preached only among the Jews. God's church and kingdom are made up of men and women of every nation, kindred, tribe and language upon the earth (Revelation 5:9). There are some among all people to whom God will be gracious, some who must be saved, because God purposed to save them. It has always been the purpose of God to gather his elect from the four corners of the earth. The Israel of God, his church, is made up of those who are 'Elect from every nation, yet one o'er all the earth!' The Word of God plainly asserts that God's elective purpose has never been limited to a singular race, or class of men. His purpose of grace includes people from every race, from all parts of the world, Jews and Gentiles, blacks and whites, rich and poor, male and female, learned and unlearned (Genesis 22:17, 18; Exodus 19:46; Isaiah 11:10; 49:6; Hosea 1:10; John 3:16; Acts 9:15; Galatians 1:15, 16). God will fulfil his covenant. He will accomplish his purpose. All his elect must be saved. Therefore he has sent his church into the world to preach the gospel. What wondrous, condescending grace! Certainly, the sovereign, almighty Lord God could have saved his elect without the use of means. But he has chosen to use saved sinners to carry the gospel to chosen, redeemed sinners who must be saved (Acts 26:16-18).

2. The instrument by which God accomplishes his purpose of grace in this world is his church (13:1-5)

God's purpose of grace is accomplished through his church. The church of Christ is separated and called by God to the work of proclaiming the gospel. Throughout history men have attempted to bypass the church and do the work of evangelism outside and apart from the church. But God's work must be done in God's prescribed way. No organization can replace the church of Christ. No one else can or should do the work God has called us to do. And the work of evangelism cannot be done by any means other than the preaching of the gospel, either publicly or privately. The church of the living God is the pillar of the truth, the preserver of the truth and the proclaimer of the truth (1 Timothy 3:15). We are the stewards of the mysteries of God (1 Corinthians 4:1, 2; 1 Peter 4:10). God has entrusted his church with the gospel. It is our responsibility to proclaim it faithfully.

3. The Lord God always raises up preachers within his church sufficient to accomplish his purpose of grace (13:1-5)

We sometimes think there is a deficiency of preachers, but there is not. When God has a work to do, he always raises up the men needed to do it, and gifts them with whatever is needed to do the work. These verses show us five things that are true of all true gospel preachers.

First, they are called by God. Second, they are recognized by the church of God as men gifted and called to the work of the ministry. Third, they are separated unto the work of the gospel. Fourth, they are filled with and led by the Spirit of God. Finally, they preach the Word of God faithfully.

4. Gospel preaching by the power of the Holy Spirit is effectual (13:6-12)

None of God's servants labours in vain (Isaiah 55:11). Some believe and some do not believe (Acts 28:24). Either way, when the gospel is preached God is honoured and his purpose is accomplished (2 Corinthians 2:14-17).

5. God's ordained means for saving his elect is preaching of the gospel

This is God's method of grace. He has chosen to save those who believe by the foolishness of preaching (Romans 1:16; 10:14-17; 1 Corinthians 1:21-23; Hebrews 4:12; James 1:18; 1 Peter 1:23-25). The faithful proclamation of God's holy, sovereign character, man's lost and ruined condition and Christ's effectual, substitutionary atonement is the message by which the Word of God is preached unto men.

6. Faithful witnesses will meet with much opposition and suffer painful disappointments in this world (13:6-8, 13)

Like Paul and Barnabas, we shall be opposed by false prophets and false religion. And we shall sometimes be disappointed by our brethren. Men of sinful flesh will disappoint one another, even believers, like John Mark (13:13; 15:36-39; 2 Timothy 4:11). But we must not be discouraged. We must persevere in the work to which God has called us.

7. The purpose of God and the cause of Christ will be triumphant at last

God will have his elect (John 6:37-40). Christ will have his ransomed people (Isaiah 53:10, 11). The Spirit will have those whom he has called (Ephesians 1:13, 14). Our labour is not in vain in the Lord!

Acts 13:14 But when they departed from Perga, they came to Antioch in Pisidia, and went into the synagogue on the sabbath day, and sat down.

Acts 13:15 And after the reading of the law and the prophets the rulers of the synagogue sent unto them, saying, Ye men and brethren, if ye have any word of exhortation for the people, say on.

Acts 13:16 Then Paul stood up, and beckoning with his hand said, Men of Israel, and ye that fear God, give audience.

Acts 13:17 The God of this people of Israel chose our fathers, and exalted the people when they dwelt as strangers in the land of Egypt, and with an high arm brought he them out of it.

Acts 13:18 And about the time of forty years suffered he their manners in the wilderness.

Acts 13:19 And when he had destroyed seven nations in the land of Chanaan, he divided their land to them by lot.

Acts 13:20 And after that he gave unto them judges about the space of four hundred and fifty years, until Samuel the prophet.

Acts 13:21 And afterward they desired a king: and God gave unto them Saul the son of Cis, a man of the tribe of Benjamin, by the space of forty years.

Acts 13:22 And when he had removed him, he raised up unto them David to be their king; to whom also he gave testimony, and said, I have found David the son of Jesse, a man after mine own heart, which shall fulfil all my will.

Acts 13:23 Of this man's seed hath God according to his promise raised unto Israel a Saviour, Jesus:

Acts 13:24 When John had first preached before his coming the baptism of repentance to all the people of Israel.

Acts 13:25 And as John fulfilled his course, he said, Whom think ye that I am? I am not he. But, behold, there cometh one after me, whose shoes of his feet I am not worthy to loose.

Acts 13:26 Men and brethren, children of the stock of Abraham, and whosoever among you feareth God, to you is the word of this salvation sent.

Acts 13:27 For they that dwell at Jerusalem, and their rulers, because they knew him not, nor yet the voices of the prophets which are read every sabbath day, they have fulfilled them in condemning him.

Acts 13:28 And though they found no cause of death in him, yet desired they Pilate that he should be slain.

Acts 13:29 And when they had fulfilled all that was written of him, they took him down from the tree, and laid him in a sepulchre.

Acts 13:30 But God raised him from the dead:

Acts 13:31 And he was seen many days of them which came up with him from Galilee to Jerusalem, who are his witnesses unto the people.

Acts 13:32 And we declare unto you glad tidings, how that the promise which was made unto the fathers,

Acts 13:33 God hath fulfilled the same unto us their children, in that he hath raised up Jesus again; as it is also written in the second psalm, Thou art my Son, this day have I begotten thee.

Acts 13:34 And as concerning that he raised him up from the dead, now no more to return to corruption, he said on this wise, I will give you the sure mercies of David.

Acts 13:35 Wherefore he saith also in another psalm, Thou shalt not suffer thine Holy One to see corruption.

Acts 13:36 For David, after he had served his own generation by the will of God, fell on sleep, and was laid unto his fathers, and saw corruption:

Acts 13:37 But he, whom God raised again, saw no corruption.

Acts 13:38 Be it known unto you therefore, men and brethren, that through this man is preached unto you the forgiveness of sins:

Acts 13:39 And by him all that believe are justified from all things, from which ye could not be justified by the law of Moses.

Acts 13:40 Beware therefore, lest that come upon you, which is spoken of in the prophets;

Acts 13:41 Behold, ye despisers, and wonder, and perish: for I work a work in your days, a work which ye shall in no wise believe, though a man declare it unto you.

Chapter 38

The Message Of The Gospel

Acts 13:14-41

When the rulers of the synagogue at Antioch in Pisidia asked Paul and Barnabas if they had 'any word of exhortation for the people', Paul seized the opportunity (13:14-16). His sermon is recorded for us in verses 17-41. It is essentially the same message he had heard Stephen preach in chapter 7.

The Jews were very interested in two things: the Old Testament Scriptures and the promise of the Messiah. Paul met them at the place of their interest and preached Christ to them. He did not debate with them. He simply preached Christ to them. He did so boldly in simple, unmistakable, irrefutable terms. He spoke with such clarity that when he came to the end of his sermon everyone in the synagogue understood exactly what he had said. Thus, by example as well as by precept, Paul shows us what preaching is. It is the bold and clear declaration of the free grace of God towards sinners through the person and work of the Lord Jesus Christ (1 Corinthians 2:1-8). In this passage the apostle Paul declared the message of the gospel in five points.

1. The glorious sovereignty of God (13:17-19)

When Paul stood to preach the gospel the first words that fell from his lips declared the sovereignty of God.

First, he spoke of God's sovereignty in election. 'The God of this people of Israel chose our fathers' (13:17). In the Old Testament God chose to make himself known only to the children of Israel, passing by all other nations. His choice of Israel was a matter of unconditional grace and absolute sovereignty (Deuteronomy 7:7-9). So also, in his sovereign, electing love, God chose to save a great multitude from Adam's fallen race through the Lord Jesus Christ (Ephesians 1:3-6; 2 Thessalonians 2:13, 14).

Secondly, Paul spoke of God's sovereignty in redemption. 'With an high arm he brought them out of [Egypt]' (13:17). God's deliverance, or redemption, of Israel out of Egypt was typical of the redemption and salvation of his elect by Christ. As such, it was an act of particular, distinguishing, irresistible and effectual grace. No sacrifice was provided for,

187

no mercy was offered to, no grace was exercised towards the Egyptians. Everything that God did in the affair was for an elect, chosen people. So too, in the redemptive work of Christ and in the saving operations of his Spirit, everything is for God's elect. Christ died for and redeemed God's elect (Isaiah 53:8; John 10:11, 15). The Holy Spirit regenerates and calls God's elect, those redeemed by Christ (Psalm 65:4). Even the intercessory prayers of Christ are made only for God's elect (John 17:9, 20). Those whom God purposed to bring out of Egypt, he brought out. Not even a hoof of the herds of Israel was left behind (Exodus 10:26). And all whom God purposed to redeem by Christ were redeemed by him (Galatians 3:13) and will be saved by him (John 6:37-40). Not one will be lost (Romans 8:28-30).

Thirdly, the apostle declared God's sovereignty in the operations of his grace and the works of providence. The inheritance of Israel in the land of Canaan was entirely the gift of God's sovereign grace. 'He divided their land to them by lot' (13:19). That means he did it without man's choice or will (Proverbs 16:33). Israel did not conquer the land of Canaan. God conquered their enemies before them. Israel simply took possession of the land at God's command and received their inheritance by his decree. So too, God's elect do not conquer their enemies; the world, the flesh and the devil. Christ did that for us. We do not win eternal salvation. Christ won it for us! The believer simply takes possession of these things by faith at God's command.

2. The total depravity and sinfulness of man (13:18-21)

The history of Israel is a history of human sin and divine mercy (Psalm 78; 105). The people whom God chose and redeemed as types of his elect were a sinful, undeserving, rebellious people. Paul here declares that God's elect, like all other men, are fallen, depraved, justly condemned children of Adam (Romans 5:12; Ephesians 2:1-4).

3. The sure accomplishment of God's eternal purpose (13:22, 23)

Throughout this brief survey of Old Testament history Paul was driving one point home to his hearers: God's purpose of grace is sure. God promised a Redeemer, a King and a Saviour, and he must come! Our great God so wisely and sovereignly rules this world that even the depraved hearts and sinful acts of men cannot thwart his purpose. In fact, they are instruments by which God fulfils his eternal purpose of grace (Psalm 76:10). This is Paul's doctrine: in spite of our sin, rebellion and unbelief, God is faithful! 'God according to his promise raised unto Israel a Saviour, Jesus.'

188

4. The person and work of the Lord Jesus Christ (13:24-39)

Paul's message was 'Jesus Christ, and him crucified' (1 Corinthians 2:2). Everything he had said in the preceding verses was leading up to this point. In this part of his message the apostle tells us five things about the person and work of the Lord Jesus Christ.

First, Christ came (13:24-27). John the Baptist had just one mission. He was sent to prepare the way for and identify the Lord Jesus Christ. When he saw the Lord, John pointed to him and said, 'Behold the Lamb of God which taketh away the sin of the world ... This is the Son of God!' (John 1:29, 34). God himself assumed human flesh! 'The Word was made flesh, and dwelt among us' (John 1:14). The Son of God came into this world to save sinners by the sacrifice of himself.

Secondly, Christ died (13:27-29). Though he was clearly an innocent, righteous man, one who 'knew no sin' (2 Corinthians 5:21), he was despised and rejected by men and put to death under the penalty of the law, according to the Scriptures. The Son of God died by the hands of wicked men, but he died according to the purpose of God (Acts 2:23). As the sinner's substitute he died as a common criminal under the wrath of God, to satisfy the justice of God for his people. Christ died to save guilty sinners from the wrath of God (Isaiah 53:4-11; Romans 5:6-8; Galatians 3:13; 1 Peter 1:18-20; 3:18).

Thirdly, Christ arose (13:30-37). The resurrection of Christ is God's public declaration that he is the Son of God, the Messiah, the Son of David, that he has put away the sins of his people which were imputed to him by the satisfaction of divine justice, and that the 'sure mercies of David' (the sure mercies of God in Christ), will be bestowed upon all his people.

Fourthly, Christ reigns (13:33, 34). Jesus Christ is King! He reigns as the Son of David, the Son of Man upon the throne of God to give eternal life, to dispense 'the sure mercies of David' to chosen sinners (John 17:2).

Fifthly, Christ saves (13:38, 39). The gospel of the free grace of God in Christ is the message of redemption accomplished by the substitutionary sacrifice of the Son of God. It is the proclamation of the free forgiveness of sins and complete justification for all who believe upon the grounds of justice satisfied and righteousness imputed (1 John 1:9; Romans 3:24-26).

5. The responsibility of man (13:26, 40, 41).

'To you is the word of this salvation sent.' It is the responsibility of all to believe it. If you do, if you trust the Lord Jesus Christ, you will live forever. If you refuse to believe, if you reject the gospel and despise the Son of God, unutterable woe will be your eternal portion (Mark 16:16).

Acts 13:42 And when the Jews were gone out of the synagogue, the Gentiles besought that these words might be preached to them the next sabbath.

Acts 13:43 Now when the congregation was broken up, many of the Jews and religious proselytes followed Paul and Barnabas: who, speaking to them, persuaded them to continue in the grace of God.

Acts 13:44 And the next sabbath day came almost the whole city together to hear the word of God.

Acts 13:45 But when the Jews saw the multitudes, they were filled with envy, and spake against those things which were spoken by Paul, contradicting and blaspheming.

Acts 13:46 Then Paul and Barnabas waxed bold, and said, It was necessary that the word of God should first have been spoken to you: but seeing ye put it from you, and judge yourselves unworthy of everlasting life, lo, we turn to the Gentiles.

Acts 13:47 For so hath the Lord commanded us, saying, I have set thee to be a light of the Gentiles, that thou shouldest be for salvation unto the ends of the earth.

Acts 13:48 And when the Gentiles heard this, they were glad, and glorified the word of the Lord: and as many as were ordained to eternal life believed.

Acts 13:49 And the word of the Lord was published throughout all the region.

Acts 13:50 But the Jews stirred up the devout and honourable women, and the chief men of the city, and raised persecution against Paul and Barnabas, and expelled them out of their coasts.

Acts 13:51 But they shook off the dust of their feet against them, and came unto Iconium.

Acts 13:52 And the disciples were filled with joy, and with the Holy Ghost.

Chapter 39

Our Labour Is Not In Vain

Acts 13:42-52

When Paul and Barnabas preached the gospel at Antioch in Pisidia, the Jews 'were filled with envy' and spoke against the gospel, contradicting it and blaspheming God. They wilfully and deliberately refused to believe the revelation of God concerning his Son. Despising Christ, despising the gospel of the grace of God and despising the messengers of grace, they brought destruction upon themselves. But Paul and Barnabas were not turned away from their noble work. Neither the instability of their brother and friend, John Mark, nor the unbelief and opposition of the Jews could deter them from their work. The Jews would not hear them, so they turned to the Gentiles and preached the gospel to them. Thus they were instruments in God's hand by which he accomplished his eternal purpose of grace in the saving of his elect among the Gentiles (Isaiah 55:11). There are five lessons clearly taught in this passage of Holy Scripture.

1. All who believe the gospel should seize every opportunity to preach the gospel (13:42-44)

After Paul had finished preaching, the Jews walked out in angry protest. But there were some Gentiles present whose hearts were affected by the message. They asked Paul and Barnabas to preach to them through the week and on the next sabbath, which they gladly did. While at Antioch they preached in the Jewish synagogue and on the streets to the great multitudes who gathered to hear them and to individuals as God gave them opportunity. They looked for opportunities to speak to sinners heading for eternity about their souls and to preach Christ to them. And they seized every opportunity God gave them. In that regard they are examples to all believers in this world. Every pastor, every gospel preacher, must relentlessly give himself to the work of the ministry, to the business of faithfully preaching the gospel (1 Timothy 4:12-16; 2 Timothy 4:1-5). And every believer should look for and seize every opportunity to bear faithful witness to perishing sinners concerning the things of Christ (John 20:21; Acts 1:8). We all make excuses for not witnessing to the people around us, but we are without excuse. If we refuse to honestly and openly confess Christ to others, it is either because we do not care that people are perishing without him, or because we fear their reaction to us, or because we do not really believe in the power of the gospel. Many who would gladly preach to thousands where they might be applauded often refuse to preach to one for fear of scorn!

2. All who faithfully preach the gospel will meet with opposition in this world (13:45, 46)

It is not possible to preach the gospel of Christ faithfully without offending the enemies of Christ. People who are opposed to Christ will be opposed to anyone who faithfully represents Christ to them (1 Corinthians 1:22-24). When men and women oppose God's preachers, those who faithfully preach the gospel of Christ, they are fighting against God (1 Samuel 8:7). The Jews at Antioch did not merely reject Paul and Barnabas. They did not merely reject a sermon they did not like. They rejected the Lord Jesus Christ and the message of God's free grace in him. In doing so they judged themselves unworthy of everlasting life. John Gill commented: 'The Jews, by this act of theirs in rejecting the Gospel, did as it were pass sentence upon themselves that they ought not to be saved, since they despised the means of salvation.'

This is a very solemn matter! These men and women, by their rejection of the gospel, became reprobate. God left them to their just condemnation and hardened their hearts in unbelief (Hosea 4:17; John 12:39, 40; Romans 11:8-11). The judgment of God that fell upon them should be alarming to any who hear but refuse to believe the gospel of God's free grace in Christ. To reject the gospel of Christ is to court reprobation. It is to court the judgment of God. Wilful unbelief, the wilful rejection of the gospel, involves four things:

1. It calls God a liar (1 John 5:10).
2. It despises the precious blood of Christ (Hebrews 10:29).
3. It fights against God (Isaiah 63:10).
4. It is the judgment of self as one worthy of eternal damnation.

A person's rejection of the gospel, the rejection of Christ, is a decided, deliberate act of his own will. The unbelieving heart is so obstinately proud that it chooses destruction before it will bow to the rule of Christ. God declares that in hell the damned who suffer his wrath eat the fruit of their own free will (Proverbs 1:31).

3. A man's faithfulness in preaching the gospel is not to be determined by his success, but by his obedience to the commandment of God (13:47)

When Paul and Barnabas found that their message had been rejected, they did not turn away from their work. It never entered their minds to do so. They did not compromise their message. It never occurred to them that they might be more successful if they were a bit less dogmatic in their doctrine. They simply did what they had always done — they went on preaching the gospel. They changed nothing, not their message, their method, or their manners.

The prophecy referred to in verse 47 (Isaiah 49:6) refers to Christ himself, but Paul applies it to all who preach the gospel because all true gospel preachers are labourers together with Christ (1 Corinthians 3:9). In the Word of God those who preach the gospel are so closely connected to Christ in their work that they are called both lights and saviours (Matthew 5:14; Obadiah 21; 1 Timothy 4:16).

God requires only one thing of his servants — faithfulness. He does not require success. But he does require faithfulness. It is the responsibility of every child of God and every servant of God to serve faithfully the honour of God, the will of God and the people of God, as providence directs and the Holy Spirit leads (1 Corinthians 4:1, 2; 2 Corinthians 4:1-7). Let us ever be found faithful to the glory of God, the gospel of Christ and the souls of men with the talents we have, in the place where God puts us.

4. As God's servants faithfully preach the gospel of Christ he sovereignly accomplishes his purpose of grace (13:48, 49)

Some believe and some do not believe, but God's purpose is always accomplished. Though the Jews did exactly what they wanted to do, yet by their unbelief the gospel has been sent to chosen sinners throughout the world (Romans 11:22, 23, 32-36).

Verses 48 and 49 demonstrate four gospel truths with striking clarity:

1. Unbelief is the cause of eternal damnation (13:46; John 3:36).
2. Election is the cause of saving faith (2 Thessalonians 2:13, 14).
3. All who obey the gospel in time were ordained to eternal life in eternity (1 Thessalonians 1:4, 5).
4. The preaching of the gospel always accomplishes God's purpose and glorifies him (1 Corinthians 2:14-16).

God will save his elect. He will glorify himself. He will honour his word (1 Corinthians 15:58).

193

5. By the faithful discharge of their responsibilities God gives his servants confidence and joy before him (13:50-52)

When they were thrown out of Antioch for preaching the gospel Paul and Barnabas 'shook off the dust of their feet' against their persecutors, being free from their blood (Luke 9:5; Ezekiel 33:8, 9), and went on to proclaim God's saving grace in another place. And they were 'filled with joy and with the Holy Ghost'. They had faithfully discharged their responsibilities as God's servants. Therefore they rejoiced before him (2 Timothy 4:6-8).

Acts 14:1 And it came to pass in Iconium, that they went both together into the synagogue of the Jews, and so spake, that a great multitude both of the Jews and also of the Greeks believed.

Acts 14:2 But the unbelieving Jews stirred up the Gentiles, and made their minds evil affected against the brethren.

Acts 14:3 Long time therefore abode they speaking boldly in the Lord, which gave testimony unto the word of his grace, and granted signs and wonders to be done by their hands.

Acts 14:4 But the multitude of the city was divided: and part held with the Jews, and part with the apostles.

Acts 14:5 And when there was an assault made both of the Gentiles, and also of the Jews with their rulers, to use them despitefully, and to stone them,

Acts 14:6 They were ware of it, and fled unto Lystra and Derbe, cities of Lycaonia, and unto the region that lieth round about:

Acts 14:7 And there they preached the gospel.

Acts 14:8 And there sat a certain man at Lystra, impotent in his feet, being a cripple from his mother's womb, who never had walked:

Acts 14:9 The same heard Paul speak: who stedfastly beholding him, and perceiving that he had faith to be healed,

Acts 14:10 Said with a loud voice, Stand upright on thy feet. And he leaped and walked.

Acts 14:11 And when the people saw what Paul had done, they lifted up their voices, saying in the speech of Lycaonia, The gods are come down to us in the likeness of men.

Acts 14:12 And they called Barnabas, Jupiter; and Paul, Mercurius, because he was the chief speaker.

Acts 14:13 Then the priest of Jupiter, which was before their city, brought oxen and garlands unto the gates, and would have done sacrifice with the people.

Acts 14:14 Which when the apostles, Barnabas and Paul, heard of, they rent their clothes, and ran in among the people, crying out,

Acts 14:15 And saying, Sirs, why do ye these things? We also are men of like passions with you, and preach unto you that ye should turn from these vanities unto the living God, which made heaven, and earth, and the sea, and all things that are therein:

Acts 14:16 Who in times past suffered all nations to walk in their own ways.

Acts 14:17 Nevertheless he left not himself without witness, in that he did good, and gave us rain from heaven, and fruitful seasons, filling our hearts with food and gladness.

Acts 14:18 And with these sayings scarce restrained they the people, that they had not done sacrifice unto them.

Acts 14:19 And there came thither certain Jews from Antioch and Iconium, who persuaded the people, and, having stoned Paul, drew him out of the city, supposing he had been dead.

Acts 14:20 Howbeit, as the disciples stood round about him, he rose up, and came into the city: and the next day he departed with Barnabas to Derbe.

Acts 14:21 And when they had preached the gospel to that city, and had taught many, they returned again to Lystra, and to Iconium, and Antioch,

Acts 14:22 Confirming the souls of the disciples, and exhorting them to continue in the faith, and that we must through much tribulation enter into the kingdom of God.

Acts 14:23 And when they had ordained them elders in every church, and had prayed with fasting, they commended them to the Lord, on whom they believed.

Acts 14:24 And after they had passed throughout Pisidia, they came to Pamphylia.

Acts 14:25 And when they had preached the word in Perga, they went down into Attalia:

Acts 14:26 And thence sailed to Antioch, from whence they had been recommended to the grace of God for the work which they fulfilled.

Acts 14:27 And when they were come, and had gathered the church together, they rehearsed all that God had done with them, and how he had opened the door of faith unto the Gentiles.

Acts 14:28 And there they abode long time with the disciples.

Chapter 40

Two Faithful Gospel Preachers

Acts 14:1-28

After preaching the gospel at Antioch in Pisidia, Paul and Barnabas came to Iconium and preached Christ there. There was a great division among the people at Iconium over the message of God's saving grace in Christ. God's servants were assaulted and abused and would have been stoned had they not fled to Lycaonia. 'And there they preached the gospel.'

At Lystra Paul healed a lame man by the power of God and all the people came to worship him and Barnabas as gods. 'They called Barnabas, Jupiter, and Paul, Mercurius, because he was the chief speaker. 'Had Paul and Barnabas not prevented it, the people of Lystra would have sacrificed animals to them! Yet when Paul denounced their idolatry and preached the living God to them, they stoned him, dragged him out of the city and left him for dead. But he arose and came back into the city.

The next day he and Barnabas left on another preaching mission. They went to Derbe, back to Lystra, to Iconium and to Antioch in Pisidia again, preaching the gospel of Christ, confirming the brethren and ordaining elders in every church. After that they passed through Pisidia and preached the Word in Pamphylia, Perga and Attalia. Then they returned to Antioch in Syria to give a report of all that had taken place on their first missionary journey (14:27, 28; cf. 13:1-3).

This brief summary of Acts 14 clearly demonstrates the fact that Paul and Barnabas were faithful gospel preachers of the apostolic age. They are held up by the Holy Spirit as examples to all who preach the gospel. The entire book of Acts is a history of preaching in the early church. It is evident that the Spirit of God intends churches and individual believers to be well informed about the work and responsibilities of faithful gospel preachers.

If God speaks to men it will be through the lips of a man preaching the gospel. Therefore there are certain questions which should be of great interest to all people, all believers and all local churches. What preachers should we hear? What kind of man is a preacher to be? What is involved in the work of the ministry? How can believers best pray for, support and assist those men who preach the gospel? These questions are clearly answered in the Word of God (1 Timothy 3:1-7; 4:12-16; 2 Timothy 4:1-4; Titus 1:5-9). They are also answered by example. In Acts 14 the Holy Spirit holds Paul and Barnabas up as examples of true and faithful preachers of the gospel.

1. What did these two men preach?

Paul and Barnabas preached to a great number of people in many different places. They preached to Jews and Gentiles, rich and poor, learned and unlearned, men and women, young and old, religious people and profane people, influential people and despised people, believers and unbelievers. Yet their message was always the same. Wherever they were, 'There they preached the gospel' (14:7; 1 Corinthians 1:17-24). All true gospel preachers have just one message: 'Christ crucified' (1 Corinthians 2:1-5). Regarding that message they all see eye to eye and speak with one voice (Isaiah 52:7, 8). Christ crucified is the theme of Holy Scripture and the theme of every gospel preacher (Luke 24:27, 44-47). Richard Sibbes once said, 'Preaching is the chariot that carries Christ up and down the world.' Writing to preachers, Richard Baxter was exactly right when he said, 'If we can but teach Christ to our people, we teach them all.' The preaching of Christ crucified involves, at the very least, the clear declaration of these three things:

1. The glory of his person as the God-man mediator (John 1:1-3, 14, 18; 2 Corinthians 8:9; Philippians 2:5-8; 1 Timothy 6:14-16; Hebrews 1:1-3; 1 John 5:7).
2. The efficacy of his work as the sinner's substitute (Isaiah 53:10, 11; Romans 5:19; 8:34; Galatians 3:13; Hebrews 9:12; 10:10-14).
3. The universal sovereignty of his dominion (John 17:2; Romans 14:9; 1 Corinthians 15:25; Philippians 2:9-11; Hebrews 10:12, 13).

Every preacher must be judged, or examined, first and foremost, by the theme of his ministry. If the theme of his ministry is not distinctively and pre-eminently the person and work of the Lord Jesus Christ, he is not the servant of God!

2. What happened when Paul and Barnabas preached Christ crucified?

When men preach the gospel in the power of the Holy Spirit one of two things always happens: either the hearers bow to Christ in faith, or they rebel against Christ in obstinate unbelief. It is impossible to stand before the throne of the sovereign Christ with indifference (Acts 13:48, 50; 14:1-5, 19, 20; 2 Corinthians 2:14-16). As it has been, so it is now and always will be: to the Jews, and all who trust in their religion, Christ crucified is a stumbling-block; to the Gentiles, the intellectuals, the imaginary wise people of the world, Christ crucified is foolishness. But to those who are called by God, those who are saved by God's grace, Christ crucified is the wisdom of God revealed and the power of God experienced in their souls (1 Corinthians 1:23, 24). Everywhere they went Paul and Barnabas preached Christ and him crucified to all who would hear them. The response of the people was always the same. Some believed and some did not believe. So it is to this day — wherever Christ is preached there is 'a division among the people because of him' (John 7:43).

3. What was the attitude of God's servants towards the ministry?

Though they met with much opposition everywhere they went, Paul and Barnabas proved themselves to be men of uncompromising dedication (14:19-21). Though Paul was stoned and left for dead at Lystra, he went right back into the city, and later returned again to preach the gospel to the very people who had stoned him (14:21). They were thoroughly committed to the work God had put into their hands (20:24).

Being committed to the work of preaching the gospel, they were men of unswerving faithfulness (2 Corinthians 4:1-7). Regardless of circumstances, regardless of the consequences of their actions, Paul and Barnabas faithfully sought the will and glory of God, faithfully ministered to the souls of men and faithfully proclaimed the doctrine of the gospel.

They were men of unquestioning faith. Believing God, they went about their work trusting him to open the door before them, provide their needs and protect them. Faith makes the servants of God independent of all men (13:51; Genesis 14:21-23). Faith makes gospel preachers bold, even in the face of numerous, influential and powerful enemies (Acts 15:26). They live and preach with boldness. William Gurnall wrote, 'A preacher without boldness is like a smooth file' — utterly useless! Faith in Christ makes men bold in the cause of God, for the honour of Christ and in defence of the truth of the gospel.

4. What motivated Paul and Barnabas in their work?

Clearly, they were not motivated by money, power, or fame. They gained none of these things. What motivated them and motivates all who are truly

199

the servants of God was a desire for the glory of God in Christ to be made known unto men (2 Corinthians 4:3-6; 1 Kings 18:36, 37), an ambition for the salvation of God's elect (1 Corinthians 9:22) and a genuine concern for the spiritual and eternal welfare of God's church and kingdom (Acts 14:22-26).

5. What was the source of their strength?

It is evident that Paul and Barnabas were men of great courage and strength. They seem to have feared nothing. Nothing appears to have discouraged them. Nothing could stop them (14:27). What gave them such courage and strength? Three things. First, they rested in God's providence. When they told their brethren all that happened to them and with them, they said, 'God did it!' Secondly, they relied upon God's power. They realised that it was God alone who had opened the door before them. And, thirdly, they recognized God's purpose in all things — in their trials as well as their triumphs. What can you do with men like that? You can stand back and watch them, or you can join them in their labours, but you cannot stop them. To fight against them is to fight against God!

Acts 15:1 And certain men which came down from Judaea taught the brethren, and said, Except ye be circumcised after the manner of Moses, ye cannot be saved.

Acts 15:2 When therefore Paul and Barnabas had no small dissension and disputation with them, they determined that Paul and Barnabas, and certain other of them, should go up to Jerusalem unto the apostles and elders about this question.

Acts 15:3 And being brought on their way by the church, they passed through Phenice and Samaria, declaring the conversion of the Gentiles: and they caused great joy unto all the brethren.

Acts 15:4 And when they were come to Jerusalem, they were received of the church, and of the apostles and elders, and they declared all things that God had done with them.

Acts 15:5 But there rose up certain of the sect of the Pharisees which believed, saying, That it was needful to circumcise them, and to command them to keep the law of Moses.

Acts 15:6 And the apostles and elders came together for to consider of this matter.

Acts 15:7 And when there had been much disputing, Peter rose up, and said unto them, Men and brethren, ye know how that a good while ago God made choice among us, that the Gentiles by my mouth should hear the word of the gospel, and believe.

Acts 15:8 And God, which knoweth the hearts, bare them witness, giving them the Holy Ghost, even as he did unto us;

Acts 15:9 And put no difference between us and them, purifying their hearts by faith.

Acts 15:10 Now therefore why tempt ye God, to put a yoke upon the neck of the disciples, which neither our fathers nor we were able to bear?

Acts 15:11 But we believe that through the grace of the Lord Jesus Christ we shall be saved, even as they.

Acts 15:12 Then all the multitude kept silence, and gave audience to Barnabas and Paul, declaring what miracles and wonders God had wrought among the Gentiles by them.

Acts 15:13 And after they had held their peace, James answered, saying, Men and brethren, hearken unto me:

Acts 15:14 Simeon hath declared how God at the first did visit the Gentiles, to take out of them a people for his name.

Acts 15:15 And to this agree the words of the prophets; as it is written,

Acts 15:16 After this I will return, and will build again the tabernacle of David, which is fallen down; and I will build again the ruins thereof, and I will set it up:

Acts 15:17 That the residue of men might seek after the Lord, and all the Gentiles, upon whom my name is called, saith the Lord, who doeth all these things.

Acts 15:18 Known unto God are all his works from the beginning of the world.

Acts 15:19 Wherefore my sentence is, that we trouble not them, which from among the Gentiles are turned to God:

Acts 15:20 But that we write unto them, that they abstain from pollutions of idols, and from fornication, and from things strangled, and from blood.

Acts 15:21 For Moses of old time hath in every city them that preach

201

him, being read in the synagogues every sabbath day.

Acts 15:22 Then pleased it the apostles and elders, with the whole church, to send chosen men of their own company to Antioch with Paul and Barnabas; namely, Judas surnamed Barsabas, and Silas, chief men among the brethren:

Acts 15:23 And they wrote letters by them after this manner; The apostles and elders and brethren send greeting unto the brethren which are of the Gentiles in Antioch and Syria and Cilicia:

Acts 15:24 Forasmuch as we have heard, that certain which went out from us have troubled you with words, subverting your souls, saying, Ye must be circumcised, and keep the law: to whom we gave no such commandment:

Acts 15:25 It seemed good unto us, being assembled with one accord, to send chosen men unto you with our beloved Barnabas and Paul,

Acts 15:26 Men that have hazarded their lives for the name of our Lord Jesus Christ.

Acts 15:27 We have sent therefore Judas and Silas, who shall also tell you the same things by mouth.

Acts 15:28 For it seemed good to the Holy Ghost, and to us, to lay upon you no greater burden than these necessary things;

Acts 15:29 That ye abstain from meats offered to idols, and from blood, and from things strangled, and from fornication: from which if ye keep yourselves, ye shall do well. Fare ye well.

Acts 15:30 So when they were dismissed, they came to Antioch: and

when they had gathered the multitude together, they delivered the epistle:

Acts 15:31 Which when they had read, they rejoiced for the consolation.

Acts 15:32 And Judas and Silas, being prophets also themselves, exhorted the brethren with many words, and confirmed them.

Acts 15:33 And after they had tarried there a space, they were let go in peace from the brethren unto the apostles.

Acts 15:34 Notwithstanding it pleased Silas to abide there still.

Acts 15:35 Paul also and Barnabas continued in Antioch, teaching and preaching the word of the Lord, with many others also.

Acts 15:36 And some days after Paul said unto Barnabas, Let us go again and visit our brethren in every city where we have preached the word of the Lord, and see how they do.

Acts 15:37 And Barnabas determined to take with them John, whose surname was Mark.

Acts 15:38 But Paul thought not good to take him with them, who departed from them from Pamphylia, and went not with them to the work.

Acts 15:39 And the contention was so sharp between them, that they departed asunder one from the other: and so Barnabas took Mark, and sailed unto Cyprus;

Acts 15:40 And Paul chose Silas, and departed, being recommended by the brethren unto the grace of God.

Acts 15:41 And he went through Syria and Cilicia, confirming the churches.

202

Chapter 41

The Conference At Jerusalem

Acts 15:1-41

Throughout the history of Christianity there have been numerous church councils. Some have been of monumental significance, but most have been of very little consequence. Denominational churches have regular councils for the purpose of determining both doctrine and practices among the churches of the denomination. In those councils three things always take place: debate, negotiation and compromise. In order for opposing parties to get along and function together in a united, co-operative programme, there must be compromise on both sides. That is the way denominations survive. But with men of principle and conviction there can be no compromise. The truth of God is not debatable! It is not possible for a person or a church believing the gospel to co-operate with people in religious works and activities who do not believe the gospel.

The conference at Jerusalem was not that kind of religious council. The apostles and elders met at Jerusalem not to debate doctrine, but to declare the truth of God with a unified voice. In that day, as in ours, there were legalists in the church who tried to mix law and grace, trying to bring God's elect under the yoke of legal bondage, subverting their souls. Therefore the church at Jerusalem held a conference. Many apostles, elders and preachers attended, but there were only three principal spokesmen: Peter, Paul and James. They spoke as one and the church made a unified denunciation of legalism. In Acts 15 Luke gives us the historical narrative of the conference. Paul explains the theological issues of it in Galatians 2.

As stated above, the conference at Jerusalem was not a church council to debate doctrine. When Paul went up to Jerusalem his mind was already made up. He refused to budge an inch, or give any ground at all to the legalists (Galatians 2:5, 21). He went to Jerusalem only so that the doctrine of the believer's absolute freedom in Christ from the law of Moses might be publicly avowed, even by those whose primary sphere of ministry was among the Jews. At the Jerusalem conference the apostles and elders and the church as a whole, being led by the Holy Spirit (15:28), publicly denounced legalism and stripped all preachers of law and legality of all credibility.

1. The confrontation with the legalists (15:1-3)

There were some self-appointed, freelance preachers who came from Jerusalem to Antioch perverting the gospel, teaching salvation by the works of the law. They were Pharisees who professed faith in Christ. They claimed to believe the gospel doctrine of salvation by grace alone, through faith alone, in Christ alone. But they mixed works with grace and said, 'Unless you keep the law you cannot be saved.' Paul, Barnabas and the church at Antioch, by their example, demonstrate that the doctrine and spirit of legalism must never be tolerated (Galatians 2:1-5). Paul declares the legalists to be 'false brethren'. It matters not whether men teach obedience to the law as a basis of justification, the measure of sanctification, the believer's rule of life, the motive for Christian service, or the ground of reward in heaven — all attempts to put believers under the yoke of the law are intolerably evil. The Word of God states emphatically and plainly that in Christ we are free from, and no longer under, the law (Romans 6:14, 15; 7:4; 10:4; Galatians 3:24-26; 5:1-4; Colossians 2:8-23; 1 Timothy1:5-10).

Never, not even once, in the New Testament is a believer commanded to do anything on the basis of, or being motivated by, the law. So far is the law from being a rule of life that Paul declares it is 'the ministration of death' (2 Corinthians 3:7). Legalists say, 'The preaching of the law promotes holiness.' But Paul says the law is 'the strength of sin' (1 Corinthians 15:56). Let no one be confused. The issue is not godliness or ungodliness. The issue is not what a believer does. The issue is the motive of the heart. Legalists are motivated by fear of punishment and desire for reward. Believers are motivated by love for Christ (2 Corinthians 5:14).

2. The conference of the leaders (15:4-21)

There were many gifted men in the church in those days, but three stood out as men gifted by God and specifically chosen by him to be his messengers to that first generation of Christians. The first preacher was Peter, the apostle to the Jews (15:7-11). His message had two main points: God purifies the hearts of men by faith in Christ (15:9); and salvation is by grace alone (15:11). In verse 12 Paul rose to speak, declaring what wonders God had done through him and Barnabas among the Gentiles (cf. 15:4). Barnabas may have addressed the conference briefly, but Paul probably spoke for both Barnabas and himself. The third man to speak at the conference was James, our Lord's half-brother, pastor of the church at Jerusalem (15:13-21). It was fitting that he bring the concluding message. He gave the opinion of the apostles, the opinion of the Holy Spirit, the opinion of the New Testament regarding the issue at hand (the relation of the law to believers in the New Testament age) in four points.

1. The calling of the Gentiles in one body with the Jews was foretold by the prophets (15:13-17; Isaiah 11:10; Amos 9:11, 12).

2. The fall of Israel and the calling of the Gentiles was according to the eternal purpose of God (15:18; Romans 11:25, 26).

3. Believers in the Gentile world must never be troubled with the yoke of bondage, which no man other than Jesus Christ the God-man has ever kept (15:19; cf. 15:10).

4. In matters of indifference it was recommended that the Gentile believers should abstain from those things that might hinder the preaching of the gospel and offend weaker brethren (15:20, 21).

Certainly fornication is not a matter of indifference. It is a horribly evil thing. Yet it was treated as a matter of indifference since to the Gentiles, who were uninstructed in the law of God, it was commonly looked upon as such.

3. The circulation of the letter (15:22-34)

The church at Jerusalem drafted a letter to be sent to the churches in the Gentile world. To confirm the truthfulness of the letter they sent Judas and Silas back to Antioch with Paul and Barnabas. The letter denounced all preachers of the law as false prophets (15:24), commended Paul and Barnabas as faithful servants of God (15:25, 26) and assured God's saints that their liberty in Christ was approved of God (15:28, 29). When it was read in churches this letter was the cause of great joy among God's saints (15:31).

4. The conflict between two labourers (15:36-41)

Paul and Barnabas had worked together for a long time. They stood shoulder to shoulder in the heat of battle. They had, at least for the time being, settled the issue of legalism. But Satan is a crafty foe. He could not frighten either man by persecution. He could not divide the two doctrinally. But the old serpent found a weak point and exploited it to divide these two brethren — John Mark, Barnabas' nephew. Perhaps Barnabas was too lenient with Mark. Perhaps Paul was too severe. We are not told. But these two friends left one another in an angry dispute. What a shame! Yet God providentially overruled this evil for the good of his church and the furtherance of the gospel (Psalm 76:10). Instead of one missionary team, now there were two. God blesses in spite of our failures!

Acts 15:8 And God, which knoweth the hearts, bare them witness, giving them the Holy Ghost, even as he did unto us;

Acts 15:9 And put no difference between us and them, purifying their hearts by faith.

Chapter 42

Gospel Purification

Acts 15:8, 9

Every true believer desires to worship God with a pure heart and honour him with a life of purity. According to the apostle John, the believer's hope of eternal life in Christ inspires in him an insatiable desire for purity. 'Every man that hath this hope in him' (the hope of seeing Christ and being like Christ) 'purifieth himself, even as he is pure' (1 John 3:3). But how is this purification accomplished? That is the question I want to answer in this chapter.

In the Old Testament, under the types and shadows of the Mosaic dispensation, there were many forms of ceremonial purification which the children of Israel were required to obey meticulously. The instruments of service in the tabernacle and later in the temple were ceremonially purified by being washed with water and sprinkled with blood. The priests and their garments were purified by ceremonial washings. Women were required to purify themselves before marriage, after childbirth and following every period of menstruation. And the people were required to purify themselves before observing the appointed feasts and holy ordinances of divine worship. But the first and most important means of legal, ceremonial purification was circumcision. This seal of God's covenant with Abraham symbolically pictured the purification of God's elect by the Holy Spirit in regeneration (Philippians 3:3; Colossians 2:11).

Those Old Testament ceremonies of purification were all outward. They did nothing to purify the heart. They only pictured the purification of the heart by the grace of God. However, by the end of the legal dispensation, by the time Christ appeared, the Jews' religion had degenerated into base idolatry, self-righteousness and will-worship. They looked upon the mere observance of outward ceremonies as the actual purifying of their hearts and made their outward religious services the basis of their acceptance with God! They thought God would accept them because they were outwardly,

207

ceremonially clean, even though their hearts were vile (Matthew 23:25-28; Luke 16:15).

Though those rituals were only temporary symbols and pictures of gospel purification, there were many in the early church who were still Pharisees. They insisted that the Gentile believers be compelled to be circumcised and to keep the law of Moses (Acts 15:1, 5). It was bad enough to have Pharisees outside the church persecuting it, but when the legalists joined the church and tried to pervert the gospel, subverting men's souls, the evil was intolerable (Acts 15:24; Galatians 1:6-8; 2:4, 5; 3:1-3; 5:2, 4, 12). Those 'false brethren', as Paul calls them, are still with us today. They are still stirring up strife and endeavouring to bring all believers into legal bondage. They make holiness and purity a matter of outward, legal obedience to the law of Moses, or (even worse) to the religious laws and customs of men. It is the spirit and doctrine of legalism that the early church confronted and denounced at the Jerusalem conference. It is an evil that must not be tolerated. Peter plainly declares that those who preach and teach legalistic doctrine are guilty of tempting God, walking directly contrary to his revealed will (Acts 15:10; Colossians 2:16-23; 1 Timothy 4:1-5).

In Acts 15:8, 9 the apostle reproves the Judaizers and denounces their doctrine by reminding those present at the conference of God's work of grace upon Cornelius and his household, all of whom were uncircumcised Gentiles (Acts 10:43, 44). Speaking by the Spirit of God, Peter plainly declared two facts that many today are either ignorant of or fail to appreciate.

1. In Christ all God's elect are one, and being one in Christ, all believers are equal before the Lord

'God ... put no difference between us and them.' There are no second-class citizens in the kingdom of heaven (Ephesians 2:11-19; 4:1-7; Colossians 3:11). Our standing and acceptance with God are determined entirely by our relationship to the Lord Jesus Christ, our substitute, not by something we do. We are complete in him (Colossians 2:10). Our experiences may vary and our understanding of spiritual things on this earth may differ, but there is 'no difference between us' in the sight of God. In Christ all true believers are loved with the same love (1 John 3:1), chosen by the same grace (Ephesians 1:4-6), blessed with the same privileges (Ephesians 1:3), redeemed by the same blood (1 Peter 1:18-20), quickened by the same Spirit (Ephesians 2:1-5), robed in the same righteousness (Jeremiah 23:6), partakers of the same divine nature (2 Peter 1:4), adopted into the same family (Galatians 4:4-6), built upon the same foundation (Ephesians 2:20-22), children of the same Father (Matthew 6:9), servants of the same Master (1 Corinthians 7:20-23), possessors of the same hope (Romans 8:24, 25), partakers of the same promises (2 Corinthians 1:20), heirs of the same inheritance (Romans 8:17) and beneficiaries of the same intercessor (John 17:20-26).

2. God purifies the hearts of his people by faith in the Lord Jesus Christ

'God put no difference between us and them, purifying their hearts by faith.' By nature our hearts are defiled and filthy (Matthew 15:17-19; Romans 8:7). As John Gill says, 'This defilement of the heart reaches to all the members of the body, and the faculties of the soul' (cf. Romans 3:9-19). The total depravity of the human heart is an inescapable fact.

The work of purifying the heart can be performed by God alone. Peter did not say, 'Cornelius purified his heart,' but 'God purified his heart'! Ceremonial cleansing, moral reformation, sorrowful repentance, baptism and religious services can never purify the heart of man. Only the application of Christ's blood to the heart by God's almighty grace can purify it (Hebrews 9:12-14; Titus 3:4-7).

The means of purification is God-given faith in Christ. 'Faith changes the current of our love, and alters the motive which sways us: this is what is meant by purifying the heart. It makes us love that which is good and right, and moves us with motives free from self and sin. This is a great work indeed!' said C.H. Spurgeon. Faith in Christ purifies the heart by:

1. Freeing us from the guilt of sin and terror of the law (Hebrews 9:14; 1 John 3:21);

2. Providing an overwhelming realisation of the love of Christ for us (2 Corinthians 5:14);

3. Bringing us into intimate communion with Christ (Song of Solomon 1:2; 2:4, 6);

4. Enabling us to realise, in some measure, the manifold blessings and privileges we enjoy in Christ by the grace of God (Ephesians 1:3-14);

5. Fixing our hearts upon Christ and the heavenly, eternal things promised to us in him (2 Corinthians 4:17-5:1; Colossians 3:1-3; 1 John 3:1-3).

This purification of the believer's heart is a continual, daily exercise of divine grace (John 13:6-10). As we make our pilgrimage through this world, we are continually gathering the dirt of sin upon us. Therefore we must continually go to the precious fountain and be washed in the blood of Christ (1 John 1:9).

Acts 15:11 But we believe that through the grace of the Lord Jesus Christ we shall be saved, even as they.

Chapter 43

'We believe ... '

Acts 15:11

Peter was an apostle of Christ. The words he spoke at the Jerusalem conference, like those which he wrote in his epistles, were inspired by God the Holy Spirit (15:28). The words of Acts 15:11, being inspired of God, are recorded for our learning and admonition. The apostle stood and said, 'We believe ... '. He spoke with bold, unbending, unyielding, uncompromising dogmatism. Speaking as an apostle of Christ, Peter was not speaking for himself alone, but for all the apostles, all the church of God, all true gospel preachers and all true Christians. When he said, 'We believe,' he was saying, 'This is the truth of God. It must be believed by all. Anything contrary to this is heresy, damnable and destructive to men's souls. This is what all true Christians believe. Those who do not believe and teach this are not Christians.' This then is the doctrine of God: 'We believe that through the grace of the Lord Jesus Christ we shall be saved, even as they.' With regard to this gospel doctrine of salvation by grace alone we must be perfectly clear in our understanding, unhesitating in our witness and intolerant of any deviation from the message of God's pure, free, sovereign, effectual grace in Christ. This is an apostolic confession of faith. Concerning less important issues God's saints may and do differ and yet remain in essential harmony and fellowship. No one has a perfect knowledge of divine truth. But the gospel doctrine of salvation by grace alone is vital. With regard to this vital issue the doctrine of the church is stated plainly. 'We believe that we shall be saved by the grace of the Lord Jesus Christ, even as they.' All who deviate from this deviate from the doctrine of the apostles and from Christ himself!

The apostles of Christ obviously did not believe much of what is taught today about the way of salvation. Peter's statement is complete. It includes all that is vital to the souls of men. But some things are obviously and deliberately omitted.

There is no mention of any religious ritual or ceremony. The two ordinances which Christ left us, baptism and the Lord's Supper, are important aspects of worship and obedience. Believer's baptism is the believer's public confession of faith in, and allegiance to, Christ (Romans 6:4-6). The Lord's Supper is the church's celebration of redemption by Christ, a symbolic picture of the gospel and a visible reminder of our Saviour's glorious person and work (1 Corinthians 11:24-26). No mention is made of personal obedience to the law of God. That was the issue at the Jerusalem conference. Surely, if obedience to the law had any bearing upon salvation, sanctification, or our relationship to God, Peter would have mentioned it here. But we are not under the law and must never attempt to put any believer under the yoke of bondage (15:10). There is no mention of personal righteousness. The creed of the world is: 'Do the best you can and God will accept you.' To deny that creed is treason against human pride. Every child of Adam is born a Pharisee. Self-righteousness is bred in us. It will manifest itself in time. But those who promote self-righteousness are guilty of treason towards God.

And no mention is made of man's free will. It is true that all believers choose Christ, trust Christ and come to Christ. But it is heretical to assert that man's free will is the cause of God's saving grace (John 1:11-13; Romans 9:15-18; 2 Timothy 1:9).

Peter's doctrine is the doctrine of grace. He tells us that salvation is, from beginning to end, all of grace. This is the doctrine of Christ and his apostles. This is the doctrine of the Bible. Any denial of the doctrine of salvation by grace alone is a denial of the gospel of Christ. All attempts to mix grace and works is antichrist. Seven things are implied and taught in Peter's words.

1. The sovereignty of God's grace

He tells us that saving grace belongs to the Lord Jesus Christ. He gives it to whomsoever he will (John 5:21; 17:2).

2. The total depravity of man

When Peter speaks of people being 'saved', the implication is that they do not have the ability to save themselves (Romans 5:12; Ephesians 2:1-3).

3. God's unconditional election

Though Peter does not mention the word 'election' in this passage it must be remembered that his mind had not been corrupted by free-will, works religion. To Peter and the rest of the apostles the word 'grace' always included election. They understood that the grace of God is eternal, unmerited and immutable (1 Peter 1:2-5).

4. Christ's limited atonement

When Peter speaks of 'grace', it is that grace which comes flowing to sinners from the wounds of the crucified Christ, that grace which was effectually obtained for God's elect when Christ died as their substitute and obtained eternal salvation for them (Hebrews 9:12; 1 Peter 1:18-21; 2:24). There are two points about the redemptive work of Christ upon which we must be clear. First, redemption was obtained for a particular people (Isaiah 53:8; John 10:11, 15, 26). Second, it was effectually accomplished when Christ died (Hebrews 9:10; Isaiah 53:10-12). Any who fail to see the fulness and efficacy of Christ's redemptive work cannot see any other gospel truth clearly.

5. God's irresistible grace

Peter said, 'We shall be saved.' He does not speak of God's saving grace as a possibility, but as a matter of certainty. Salvation is not something God hopes to do. It is something God does (Psalm 65:4; 110:3).

6. The final perseverance of the saints

Peter was not in any doubt about what he believed. He knew that salvation is God's work. He knew it was forever (Ecclesiastes 3:14). He knew God's promise (John 10:27-29), power (1 Peter 1:5) and immutability (Malachi 3:6) demand the absolute, infallible, eternal security of his elect.

7. The equality of all believers

When Peter said, 'We shall be saved by the grace of the Lord Jesus Christ, even as they,' he seems to imply that the Jewish believers have no preference over the Gentile believers. In Christ all are one! All are saved by grace alone (Colossians 3:11). This is the confession of every true believer. All who are saved are saved by grace alone and gladly acknowledge it (1 Corinthians 15:10). Self-righteous moralists, religious ritualists and profligate sinners must all be saved the same way. Grace is unconditional! It is not attracted by good works and it is not repelled by the lack of good works. Grace washes all believers in the blood of Christ, robes all in the righteousness of Christ and makes all accepted in Christ. Some are more gifted than others, but none is more accepted. Some are more faithful than others, but none is more favoured. Some are more confident than others, but none is more beloved and none is more secure. This is our doctrine: 'We believe that through the grace of the Lord Jesus Christ we shall be saved, even as they.'

Acts 16:1 Then came he to Derbe and Lystra: and, behold, a certain disciple was there, named Timotheus, the son of a certain woman, which was a Jewess, and believed; but his father was a Greek:

Acts 16:2 Which was well reported of by the brethren that were at Lystra and Iconium.

Acts 16:3 Him would Paul have to go forth with him; and took and circumcised him because of the Jews which were in those quarters: for they knew all that his father was a Greek.

Acts 16:4 And as they went through the cities, they delivered them the decrees for to keep, that were ordained of the apostles and elders which were at Jerusalem.

Acts 16:5 And so were the churches established in the faith, and increased in number daily.

Acts 16:6 Now when they had gone throughout Phrygia and the region of Galatia, and were forbidden of the Holy Ghost to preach the word in Asia,

Acts 16:7 After they were come to Mysia, they assayed to go into Bithynia: but the Spirit suffered them not.

Acts 16:8 And they passing by Mysia came down to Troas.

Chapter 44

A Spirit-Filled Ministry

Acts 16:1-8

The supernatural gifts of the Holy Spirit by which the apostles were confirmed as the messengers of Christ (Hebrews 2:4) ceased when the canon of Holy Scripture was complete and the apostles had all died (1 Corinthians 13:10). The Bible is the perfect, complete revelation of God. Nothing can be added to it or taken from it (Revelation 22:19). Since there are no inspired apostles today writing out a new word of revelation from God, there is no need for those gifts of a supernatural, miraculous nature by which the apostles were identified as apostles. However, the ministries of God's servants today are just as truly Spirit-filled ministries as were those of his servants in the apostolic era. Every true gospel preacher, being called and directed in his labours by God the Holy Spirit, exercises a Spirit-filled ministry as he preaches the gospel of Christ in the power of the Holy Spirit. Acts 16:1-8 gives us an example of such a ministry. This chapter begins with Paul and Silas coming to Derbe and Lystra. It is the beginning of Paul's second missionary journey. We are told nothing more about Barnabas, but Paul and Silas continued faithfully to preach the gospel of Christ, being led by God the Holy Spirit in all things. That is what a Spirit-filled ministry is. It is a ministry dictated by the Holy Spirit, a ministry controlled by, and in submission to, the Spirit of God (Ephesians 5:18). In these eight verses Luke shows us four things that characterize a Spirit-filled ministry.

1. A man prepared by God (16:1-3)

Wherever you find a Spirit-filled ministry you will find a man prepared by God for the work of the ministry. No man is called by God to preach the gospel who has not been prepared and qualified by God for the work (1 Timothy 3:1-7). When Paul came to Derbe and Lystra, he found a young man named Timothy, whom he ordained to the work of the gospel ministry (1 Timothy 4:14; 2 Timothy 1:6). Neither Paul nor Timothy knew how the Lord might be pleased to use him, but Timothy was a young man whom God had called and gifted for the work of preaching the gospel.

The Lord began preparation of Timothy in his earliest years by special providence. Timothy's mother Eunice was a Jewish woman who was a believer. His grandmother Lois had also been converted by the grace of God. From his earliest days of childhood Timothy had been taught the Holy Scriptures, which are able to make sinners wise unto salvation through faith in the Lord Jesus Christ (2 Timothy 1:5; 3:15). Eunice gave her son the name 'Timothy', which means 'honoured of God'. Like Hannah of old, Eunice got her son from the Lord and gave him to the Lord. From his boyhood he was taught the Word of God.

It should be the greatest concern of parents to instruct their children in the gospel of Christ and train them up in the nurture and admonition of the Lord (Ephesians 6:4). If parents would train their children as they ought, they must: Train them in the way they should go — not the way they want to go (Proverbs 22:6). Discipline them firmly and consistently, insisting that they behave in the way they should (Proverbs 22:15; 23:12-14; 29:15). Walk before them in the way of faith and obedience, showing them the way by example (Genesis 18:19). Pray for God's wisdom, direction and grace in training their children, and for his merciful blessings upon the training they give (Genesis 17:18). Commit them to the hands of God (1 Samuel 1:24-28).

We see in Timothy's parents a display of God's marvellous providence and grace. Though his mother and grandmother were both believers, his father was an unbelieving Gentile. Eunice's marriage to him was an act of disobedience to God (Deuteronomy 7:3; 2 Corinthians 6:14). But providence took the sinful union of an unbelieving man and a believing woman and prepared a messenger of sovereign grace! As God overruled David's adultery with Bathsheba and gave them Solomon, so he overruled Eunice's disobedience and gave her Timothy. Thank God, he does not remember the sins of his people against them! Indeed, as John Trapp put it, 'God can (and often does) turn our sins to our good and comfort.' Like a wise physician, our Lord takes the most deadly poison and makes it a medicine for our health.

In the fulness of time Timothy was also prepared by grace for the work to which God had ordained him. He who preaches grace to others must first experience grace in his heart, and Timothy did. He was a devoted disciple of Christ, a man of blameless reputation in the community where he lived and 'well reported of by the brethren' (cf. 1 Timothy 3:7). Timothy was willing to serve God's cause in any capacity. That service which Mark despised as shameful, Timothy counted an honour (13:5; 15:38). God uses men like that!

Timothy was further prepared for the work of the gospel ministry by his willing submission to a man of proven faithfulness (16:3). Before a man can lead men, he must learn to follow. Before Elisha could be a prophet he had to sit at the feet of, and serve, the prophet Elijah. And before Timothy could be entrusted with the care of the churches he had to prove his care for the churches by serving Paul. He even submitted to the painful ordeal of circumcision, because Paul, God's faithful servant, said it would be best for the gospel's sake (1 Corinthians 9:19-23). Timothy was a man prepared by providence, grace and obedience for the work of preaching the gospel.

2. A message proclaimed from God (16:4)

That man who preaches by the Spirit of God is God's messenger, God's ambassador to men. He has a message from God and faithfully delivers it (2 Corinthians 5:18-21). Spirit-filled preachers all have the same message — the gospel of Christ. They are to be heard, received and treated as ambassadors of God. They declare 'the decrees' ordained of the apostles by inspiration of the Holy Spirit (15:11, 28): the Scriptures alone; Christ alone; grace alone! All God's servants preach God's gospel: ruin by the Fall, redemption by the blood of Christ and regeneration by the Holy Spirit. A Spirit-filled ministry is characterized by the message of God's free and sovereign grace in Christ.

3. A ministry performed by God (16:5)

Paul and Silas went about preaching the gospel. They did not employ entertainers to make the gospel more appealing, have puppet shows to reach the children, host ball teams for the men, or organize bowling leagues for the women. They simply preached the gospel and waited for God to work, and he did (2 Corinthians 10:4, 5). John Trapp said, 'Some were converted by their ministry, others confirmed. This is still the fruit of faithful preaching.' This much is certain: whenever a man preaches the gospel in the power of the Holy Spirit something happens for the glory of God (2 Corinthians 2:14-17).

4. A messenger propelled by God (16:6-8)

Faithful gospel preachers are led by the Holy Spirit. God's servants will not allow their own desires or the influences of men to determine the course, place, or message of their ministry. Paul wanted to go to Asia, but the Holy Spirit would not allow it. He tried to go to Bithynia, but was providentially hindered. It was the purpose of God that the gospel be carried to Troas and then to Macedonia. There are places in this world where God's servants are 'forbidden of the Holy Ghost to preach the word'. 'This was a heavier judgment upon those coasts,' wrote Trapp, 'than to be denied a harvest, or the light of the sun. Prize the preaching of the gospel as a singular privilege. They that are without a teaching priest are without God (2 Chronicles 15:3).' Blessed beyond measure are those people to whom God sends his servants to preach his Word faithfully (Amos 8:11, 12; Isaiah 52:7).

Acts 16:6 Now when they had gone throughout Phrygia and the region of Galatia, and were forbidden of the Holy Ghost to preach the word in Asia,

Acts 16:7 After they were come to Mysia, they assayed to go into Bithynia: but the Spirit suffered them not.

Acts 16:8 And they passing by Mysia came down to Troas.

Acts 16:9 And a vision appeared to Paul in the night; There stood a man of Macedonia, and prayed him, saying, Come over into Macedonia, and help us.

Acts 16:10 And after he had seen the vision, immediately we endeavoured to go into Macedonia, assuredly gathering that the Lord had called us for to preach the gospel unto them.

Acts 16:11 Therefore loosing from Troas, we came with a straight course to Samothracia, and the next day to Neapolis;

Acts 16:12 And from thence to Philippi, which is the chief city of that part of Macedonia, and a colony: and we were in that city abiding certain days.

Acts 16:13 And on the sabbath we went out of the city by a river side, where prayer was wont to be made; and we sat down, and spake unto the women which resorted thither.

Chapter 45

The Macedonian Call

Acts 16:6-13

After establishing the churches in Lystra and Derbe in the faith of the gospel, Paul and Silas went throughout Phrygia and the region of Galatia preaching the grace of God in Christ. Paul wanted to carry the good news of redeeming, saving grace into Asia, but the Holy Spirit gave him no liberty to do so (16:6). So he travelled on to Mysia and tried to go into Bithynia, but again the Spirit of God closed the door (16:7). Following the direction of God's providence and the leadership of the Holy Spirit, Paul and his companions 'came down to Troas' (16:8).

In the evening, as Paul was seeking God's direction for his ministry, a vision was given to him. By the special, supernatural revelation of God the Holy Spirit, he saw a man from Macedonia standing before him who said, 'Come over into Macedonia, and help us' (16:9).

Paul took this to be a call from God (16:10). He had earnestly sought the will of God, and now he knew it. God had called him to preach the gospel to the perishing men and women of Macedonia. Immediately he went to Philippi, the first city he could get to in Macedonia (16:11, 12). There he went to the place in that city where he was most likely to get a hearing and preached the gospel to a gathering of a few women (16:13). Paul did not stop to do deputation work to raise money. He did not seek the approval or permission of a mission board. He knew that God had called him and he trusted God both to provide for him and to make his labour effectual. It was his responsibility to preach the gospel to the perishing sinners of Macedonia. That was the one thing he knew he must do. He had to be obedient to the call of God (1 Corinthians 9:16).

Here is the Macedonian call; 'Come over and help us.' It is a call that has application to the church of God today. There is much for us to learn from this call and Paul's response to it about the evangelistic, missionary responsibilities of the church.

219

1. Men and women who do not know the gospel of Christ are lost, perishing in ignorance, under the wrath of God

The lost condition of perishing sinners is, to the people of God, a cry for help. This man of Macedonia represented a people who had everything imaginable in a natural sense. He represented a country and empire of incomparable greatness. Macedonia was the land of Philip, King of Macedonia and his son, Alexander the Great. This man represented the Greek world, the world of refinement, learning, wealth and culture. The Greeks were also a very religious people. No one could question their devotion, fervency and sincerity as religious people. They gave a great portion of their time, work and money to religious work and worship. They built the famous Parthenon in Athens and the great temple at Ephesus. In Athens alone the Greeks had 30,000 gods! When Paul saw their worship and devotion, he said, 'I perceive that in all things ye are too superstitious [religious]' (17:22). The Greeks had every advantage socially and economically. Yet, like the rich young ruler, they lacked one thing. They had no knowledge of the Lord Jesus Christ. They were ignorant of soul-saving gospel truth. The lost condition of the refined Greeks demonstrates one fact with clarity: all who are ignorant of the gospel of Christ are lost, perishing in their sins and under the wrath of God! The ignorant barbarian is lost (Romans 1:18-21). Our religious and irreligious relatives, neighbours and friends who do not know the Lord Jesus Christ are lost (Romans 10:1-17). Their lost condition is a cry for help. It is our responsibility to preach the gospel to them.

2. The greatest blessing God can ever bestow upon any people is to send them a faithful gospel preacher (Isaiah 52:7)

The Holy Spirit would not let Paul go to Asia or Bithynia. But he sent him to Macedonia. What a blessing! There were some chosen sinners in Macedonia whom Christ had redeemed. The time had come when they must be called to life and faith in Christ by the power of the Holy Spirit through the preaching of the gospel. 'Ministers,' wrote John Trapp, 'are those by whom God helpeth his perishing people, and putteth them out of the devil's danger. Hence they are called saviours (Obadiah 21; 1 Timothy 4:16), redeemers (Job 33:24, 28), co-workers with Christ (2 Corinthians 6:1).'

God saves his elect through the instrumentality of gospel preaching. He who ordained the salvation of chosen sinners also ordained the means whereby it must be accomplished (Romans 10:17; 1 Corinthians 1:21; 2 Thessalonians 2:13, 14; James 1:18; 1 Peter 1:23-25). Wherever an elect sinner is found, at the time appointed, a gospel preacher will be sent. One sign of God's anger, wrath and displeasure upon reprobate men is that he sends them no gospel preachers, or that he withdraws from them the ministry of a faithful man (Hosea 4:17).

3. It is the responsibility of believers to preach the gospel of Christ to sinners bound for eternity (Mark 16:15, 16)

Every gospel preacher is responsible to keep the charge of God upon him (1 Timothy 4:12-16; 2 Timothy 4:1-5). Every local church must devote itself to the furtherance of the gospel (Matthew 28:18-20). And every believer must assume his responsibility to make the gospel of Christ known in his own generation. God has given you the light that you may show others the way. He has given you the message of his free and sovereign grace in Christ. It is your responsibility to make it known in the generation in which you live. You cannot make anyone believe the gospel. That is not your responsibility. But you can see that they hear it. And that is your responsibility (Acts 1:8).

4. As you endeavour to make the gospel known, seek and submit to the direction of God the Holy Spirit (16:6-10)

If you seek the will of God and wait upon the Lord that you may know how to serve him, he will show you his will (Proverbs 3:5, 6). By the direction of his Word, the impulses of his Spirit, and the indications of his providence, God will make his will known to all who seek it. When God reveals his will to you, you will know it. And when you know you are doing the will of God you can do it with boldness, without fear of failure. If God is in the initiation of a thing, he will be in its execution. He will see it through to its appointed end. If God shuts a door or opens one, we must readily follow his direction.

5. God will both direct and honour the efforts of his people for the furtherance of the gospel

God always honours those who honour him (1 Samuel 2:30). You do not labour in vain, if you seek to serve Christ (1 Corinthians 15:58). When Paul went to Macedonia he was thrown in jail, but God honoured his faithful service in the saving of two precious souls, Lydia and the Philippian jailor. His ministry there was a great success! He did exactly what God sent him there to do.

Be faithful to the work God has entrusted to your hands, whatever it is. You will not fail. God is with you. His Word, which he sends out through you, will not return unto him void (Isaiah 55:11).

Acts 16:13 And on the sabbath we went out of the city by a river side, where prayer was wont to be made; and we sat down, and spake unto the women which resorted thither.

Acts 16:14 And a certain woman named Lydia, a seller of purple, of the city of Thyatira, which worshipped God, heard us: whose heart the Lord opened, that she attended unto the things which were spoken of Paul.

Acts 16:15 And when she was baptized, and her household, she besought us, saying, If ye have judged me to be faithful to the Lord, come into my house, and abide there. And she constrained us.

Chapter 46

'A certain woman named Lydia'

Acts 16:13-15

There were many women at Philippi, and several who gathered every sabbath day for prayer by the riverside, but among the many there was 'a certain woman named Lydia', who had been separated and distinguished from the rest by the grace of God. This 'certain woman', chosen by God and redeemed by Christ, must be regenerated by the Spirit and called to Christ. Before the world began the Lord God had appointed a time and a place for this woman's salvation. Now the time of mercy had come. The place grace had chosen was a riverside just outside the city of Philippi. Exactly at the time appointed, 'the time of love' (Ezekiel 16:8), God brought Paul, his messenger of grace, to that little clearing by the riverside to preach the gospel to Lydia, 'whose heart the Lord opened'. This brief narrative of Lydia's conversion is here recorded by divine inspiration to teach us at least five things.

1. Grace always has its way

Salvation is by grace alone. That is stated so plainly and emphatically in the Scriptures that very few people openly deny it (Ephesians 2:8, 9; 2 Timothy 1:9; Titus 3:3-5). However, there are few people in this world who understand the meaning of the word 'grace' as it is used in the Bible. Grace is more than a divine attribute. It is a divine determination, a divine work and a divine gift. It is not merely a desire in God's heart to save. It is the operation of God's arm, accomplishing salvation.

The grace of God is sovereign (Romans 9:16). God alone determined whom he would save. His choice and election of some to eternal life was an act of his free, unconditional love (Jeremiah 31:3; Ephesians 1:3, 4). Grace is never caused by, dependent upon, or determined by man.

The grace of God is eternal (2 Timothy 1:9). The people to whom grace would come, the blessings grace would bring and the works grace would accomplish were all determined by God before the worlds were made (Ephesians 1:11).

223

The grace of God is irresistible and effectual (Psalm 65:4; 110:3; Isaiah 46:9-13). 'The marvel of God's grace is that it will not take "No" for an answer from some men,' said Walter Chantry. Grace is more than divine goodness. It is the omnipotent power of divine goodness. Grace is not something God offers to sinners. It is something God performs in them!

The grace of God gives God alone all praise, honour and glory for his saving operations (1 Corinthians 1:30, 31). Grace attributes nothing to man but sin. Grace honours the triune God for salvation: the glorious Father, as the covenant-keeping God of heaven and earth; the gracious Son, as the Redeemer of his people; and the Holy Spirit, as the Author of regeneration.

Grace is always on time (Ezekiel 16:6-8). At the time appointed when the chosen sinner must be saved, grace comes calling, creating life and faith, causing the dead sinner to come to Christ. No wonder the psalmist sang, 'Blessed is the man whom thou choosest, and causest to approach unto thee' (Psalm 65:4). Every saved sinner is a trophy of grace for the praise of God (Ephesians 2:7).

2. Divine providence sovereignly rules all for the salvation of God's elect

This lesson is demonstrated repeatedly, throughout the book of Acts. In the passage we are studying we see grace making its way to 'a certain woman named Lydia'. Grace marked out its object Lydia! Grace set the time — a certain sabbath day. Grace determined the place — a riverside at Philippi. But how would Paul, the messenger of grace, and Lydia, the object of grace, be brought together at Philippi?

Paul was brought to Philippi by a very remarkable work of divine providence. His intentions were in another direction altogether, but God's intention was to bring him to Philippi. The strife with Barnabas caused him to go in one direction and Barnabas in another (15:36-41). Paul wanted to go to Asia. Lydia lived there, in Thyatira, but she was not at home at the time. So the Holy Spirit forbade Paul to go there. Then Paul tried to go to Bithynia but, again, the Spirit of God would not allow it (16:6, 7). At last, he was called over into Macedonia, and the first city in his path was Philippi (16:9, 10). He must needs go through Philippi, because there were chosen sinners there for whom the time of grace had come. At exactly the same time, divine providence brought Lydia to Philippi. She had come on business, because God almighty was doing business for her! Ever trust and admire God's wise, adorable providence! Often we murmur because we look at our circumstances. May God teach us to look instead to his purpose and to trust it (John 17:2; Romans 8:28).

3. Those who walk in the light God gives them will be given more light

Salvation is by grace alone. Yet every person is responsible to obey the gospel. Here are three inescapable facts revealed in Holy Scripture: first, all are responsible to trust Christ (Acts 17:30); second, no one will ever trust Christ unless God gives them faith (John 5:40; 6:44); and, third, any sinner in all the world who will come to Christ may come to Christ and, coming to Christ, will be saved by Christ (John 6:37; Romans 10:13).

Lydia did not open her own heart. That was the work of God. But she was not indifferent to her soul's welfare. She did what she knew she should do. When she came to Philippi she sought out people who sought to worship God They were only a band of women with no house of worship (16:13). When Paul spoke the Word of God, she listened (16:14). Lydia was earnest about her soul. She sought the Lord, and seeking him she found him (Jeremiah 29:12, 13). You would be wise to follow her example (Proverbs 1:23-33).

4. God uses faithful men for the salvation of his elect

As we have seen many times in the study of Acts, God's ordained means of grace to sinners is preaching of the gospel (Romans 10:13-17; 1 Corinthians 1:21; 1 Timothy 4:16). Paul faithfully performed the work God had committed to him (1 Corinthians 4:1-7; 2 Corinthians 4:1-7). In all things he sought the will of God and laboured for the glory of God. He did not seek anything for himself, but faithfully served Christ in the place where God put him, ministering to the people God entrusted to his care, and counted it his great privilege to do so (Ephesians 3:8).

5. The Lord God alone can open the hearts of sinners

Providence brought Paul and Lydia together. Lydia came to the place of prayer, because she sought to worship God. But their meeting on the sabbath day would have been a meaningless, insignificant exercise of religion except for one thing: the Lord was there! He was there working by his almighty, effectual, irresistible grace. Lydia was a woman 'whose heart the Lord opened'. He alone could do it. He who is the heart's Maker is the heart's Master. Christ alone holds the key to a person's heart, knows how to put the key in and opens the heart's door to let himself in! The Lord opened Lydia's heart to hear, understand and believe the message of grace in the gospel. Her faith in Christ was manifest by two things (16:15). First, she obeyed Christ, confessing him in believer's baptism, then she loved those who served her soul (Isaiah 52:7). Grace made her generous and hospitable.

Acts 16:16 And it came to pass, as we went to prayer, a certain damsel possessed with a spirit of divination met us, which brought her masters much gain by soothsaying:

Acts 16:17 The same followed Paul and us, and cried, saying, These men are the servants of the most high God, which shew unto us the way of salvation.

Acts 16:18 And this did she many days. But Paul, being grieved, turned and said to the spirit, I command thee in the name of Jesus Christ to come out of her. And he came out the same hour.

Acts 16:19 And when her masters saw that the hope of their gains was gone, they caught Paul and Silas, and drew them into the marketplace unto the rulers,

Acts 16:20 And brought them to the magistrates, saying, These men, being Jews, do exceedingly trouble our city,

Acts 16:21 And teach customs, which are not lawful for us to receive, neither to observe, being Romans.

Acts 16:22 And the multitude rose up together against them: and the magistrates rent off their clothes, and commanded to beat them.

Acts 16:23 And when they had laid many stripes upon them, they cast them into prison, charging the jailor to keep them safely:

Acts 16:24 Who, having received such a charge, thrust them into the inner prison, and made their feet fast in the stocks.

Acts 16:25 And at midnight Paul and Silas prayed, and sang praises unto God: and the prisoners heard them.

Acts 16:26 And suddenly there was a great earthquake, so that the foundations of the prison were shaken: and immediately all the doors were opened, and every one's bands were loosed.

Acts 16:27 And the keeper of the prison awaking out of his sleep, and seeing the prison doors open, he drew out his sword, and would have killed himself, supposing that the prisoners had been fled.

Acts 16:28 But Paul cried with a loud voice, saying, Do thyself no harm: for we are all here.

Acts 16:29 Then he called for a light, and sprang in, and came trembling, and fell down before Paul and Silas,

Acts 16:30 And brought them out, and said, Sirs, what must I do to be saved?

Acts 16:31 And they said, Believe on the Lord Jesus Christ, and thou shalt be saved, and thy house.

Acts 16:32 And they spake unto him the word of the Lord, and to all that were in his house.

Acts 16:33 And he took them the same hour of the night, and washed their stripes; and was baptized, he and all his, straightway.

Acts 16:34 And when he had brought them into his house, he set meat before them, and rejoiced, believing in God with all his house.

Acts 16:35 And when it was day, the magistrates sent the serjeants, saying, Let those men go.

Acts 16:36 And the keeper of the prison told this saying to Paul, The magistrates have sent to let you go: now therefore depart, and go in peace.

Acts 16:37 But Paul said unto them, They have beaten us openly uncondemned, being Romans, and have cast us into prison; and now do they thrust us out privily? nay verily; but let them come themselves and fetch us out.

Acts 16:38 And the serjeants told these words unto the magistrates: and they feared, when they heard that they were Romans.

Acts 16:39 And they came and besought them, and brought them out, and desired them to depart out of the city.

Acts 16:40 And they went out of the prison, and entered into the house of Lydia: and when they had seen the brethren, they comforted them, and departed.

Chapter 47

Why Were Paul And Silas Imprisoned?

Acts 16:16-40

Though they had done nothing at Philippi except preach the gospel of Christ and cast an unclean spirit out of a young woman, Paul and Silas were arrested, unjustly beaten and publicly humiliated as common criminals. Why? Were they out of God's will? Had the Lord forsaken them? Was the angry mob out of God's control? Had Satan managed to thwart God's purpose? Nonsense! 'Our God is in the heavens: he hath done whatsoever he hath pleased' (Psalm 115:3). Paul and Silas were arrested and thrown into prison at Philippi in violation of Roman law (16:35-39), because the jailer in that prison was one of God's elect and the appointed time of mercy and love had come when he must be converted by the grace of God.

1. God sovereignly rules all things for the good of his elect (16:16-24)

The first lesson taught and illustrated in this passage is one that is frequently set before us throughout the book of Acts. There was an elect soul at the Philippi prison to whom Paul must preach the gospel. But their paths would never have crossed had God not sovereignly intervened to bring it about. In order to accomplish his purpose of grace, God overruled the ranting of a demon-possessed woman and the malice of an angry mob (Psalm 76:10; Romans 8:28).

God's servants refused the praise of a fortune-teller (16:16-18). Refusing to be associated with this satanic woman and her satanic religion, Paul turned and cast the demon out of her by the power of Christ. Three things need to be understood. First, all forms of sorcery, witchcraft and fortune-telling are forbidden in the Scriptures as satanic devices (Leviticus 19:26, 31; 20:6; Deuteronomy 18:9-14; Isaiah 8:19; Malachi 3:5). Second, God's servants will not receive the praise and commendation of those who do not worship the Lord God. And, third, exorcism, like healing and the gift of tongues, was

227

an apostolic gift, confirming the apostles as God's messengers in the apostolic age (Hebrews 2:3, 4). Those gifts are not active in the church today because they are no longer needed (1 Corinthians 13:10).

Even the wrath and wicked deeds of reprobate men accomplish the purpose of God (16:19-24). The girl spoke what Satan inspired her to speak and the men of the city did exactly what their anger and greed led them to do, but God wisely and sovereignly used them to bring Paul to preach the gospel to a chosen sinner so he might be saved (Psalm 76:10). Election determined who would be saved (Ephesians 1:3-6). Predestination determined all things for the accomplishment of God's gracious purpose (Ephesians 1:11). Providence is God's wise and orderly disposition of all things in the sovereign accomplishment of his purpose (Romans 8:28-30). As it is written, 'All things are of God' (2 Corinthians 5:18).

2. Faith in Christ causes believers to submit joyfully to the will of God (16:25-28)

Paul and Silas recognized that their imprisonment was as much the work of God as the daily provision for their needs. Therefore they were both confident and joyful. In their time of trouble they did not seek a Christian counsellor, psychiatrist, or therapist. They did not become emotional wrecks. They believed God. Therefore they prayed. Happy are those souls who learn thus to deal with their troubles (Hebrews 4:15, 16; 1 Peter 5:6, 7).

Moreover, these men offered to God the sacrifices of praise and thanksgiving in the midst of great trouble. They 'sang praises unto God: and the prisoners heard them'. Why should they not? Believing God, they were full of joy. They knew their imprisonment was the will of God and that God's will is always good. Therefore they gave thanks (1 Thessalonians 5:16-18). The believer's joy is the joy of faith (Philippians 1:25). It is not circumstantial, but spiritual. It is a joy that glows in the dark.

The Lord has a way of assuring his tried and afflicted people that all is well, that he is upon his throne and that he is with them. He graciously demonstrated his presence with, and approval of, Paul and Silas by a remarkable, providential intervention. He sent an earthquake that did no harm, but only good (16:26). Immediately, Paul thought of his captor, whom he knew was likely to kill himself if his prisoners escaped (16:26, 27). What an example he was, even in great trial! In the midst of his trouble, Paul carefully sought the comfort and welfare of a man who was his enemy.

3. God promises eternal salvation to all who believe on the Lord Jesus Christ (16:29-34)

The jailer cried, 'Sirs, what must I do to be saved?' Like all natural men, when seized with the fear of death and the wrath of God, this man thought he could and should do something to obtain God's salvation. Paul did not rebuke him for his error, but rather said simply, 'Believe on the Lord Jesus Christ, and thou shalt be saved, and thy house.' Essentially, his words mean: 'You cannot do anything to be saved. You must trust Christ alone as your Lord and Saviour. Believe on him and you will be saved. And if the members of your family trust him, they too will be saved!' Having made that declaration, Paul proceeded to instruct the chosen sinner and his household in the gospel of Christ (16:32). Once they heard the message of grace and redemption in Christ, both the jailer and all his household were converted by the grace of God (16:33, 34). They all believed on Christ. They all confessed him in believer's baptism. They all rejoiced in God their Saviour. And they all did what they could to comfort and assist the men who brought the message of grace to them.

4. The only difference between those who believe and those who do not believe is the distinguishing grace of God (16:35-39)

The magistrates had seen the same things the jailer did. They felt the earthquake. They were filled with fear. But their hearts were unbroken. What made the difference between them and the jailer? Why did he believe God while they refused to believe? The answer is grace! (1 Corinthians 4:7; 15:10). He was one of the Lord's sheep. They were not (John 10:25-27). Grace sought him out. Grace gave him life. Grace gave him faith. Grace made him a new creature (2 Corinthians 5:17).

5. The believer's trials equip him to comfort others in their time of trial (16:40)

Paul and Silas gathered their brothers and sisters together to comfort them and strengthen their hearts in the faith. I am sure Paul told them what God had done, how that the Lord was with them in their trouble and how grace had come to the jailer's house. Just before leaving them, the apostle must have urged them ever to cling to Christ and trust him, assuring them that no matter what their outward circumstances might be, all is well, eternally well, because God is accomplishing his purpose of grace (Romans 8:28-39).

Acts 16:30 And brought them out, and said, Sirs, what must I do to be saved?

Acts 16:31 And they said, Believe on the Lord Jesus Christ, and thou shalt be saved, and thy house.

Acts 16:32 And they spake unto him the word of the Lord, and to all that were in his house.

Acts 16:33 And he took them the same hour of the night, and washed their stripes; and was baptized, he and all his, straightway.

Acts 16:34 And when he had brought them into his house, he set meat before them, and rejoiced, believing in God with all his house.

Chapter 48

'Believing in God with all his house'

Acts 16:30-34

The Philippian jailer said to Paul and Silas, 'Sirs, what must I do to be saved?' His concern was not how he could be saved from temporal death, but from spiritual and eternal death. He was moved, not by the fear of Caesar, but by the fear of God. Fearing God and eternal death, he may have phrased his question as he did because he thought (as all men do by nature) that he must do something to obtain God's salvation. But Paul and Silas answered with emphatic clarity and simplicity, 'Believe on the Lord Jesus Christ, and thou shalt be saved, and thy house,' teaching him and us that salvation is not by works, but by faith (Romans 3:20, 28; Ephesians 2:8, 9; 2 Timothy 1:9).

1. What must we believe?

Really the question is not 'what', but 'Whom must we believe?' Salvation does not come as the result of believing certain doctrines, no matter how true and necessary they are. Neither does salvation come by believing certain historical facts, no matter how vital those facts may be. Salvation comes to those who believe, who trust a person, the Lord Jesus Christ (2 Timothy 1:12; 1 John 5:1). In order to believe on Christ a person must know the truth about Christ, as it is revealed in the gospel. But saving faith is more than mere agreement with, or acceptance of, revealed truth. It is believing a person. It is trusting Christ himself (Isaiah 45:22). This is the way faith is represented to us throughout the Scriptures (Matthew 16:16, 18; John 20:21; Acts 8:37; 1 John 5:10-13). 'True faith is not barely a believing that Christ is the Son of God, but a believing in him as such,' is how John Gill put it. Saving faith is believing in Christ, the incarnate Son of God, as your all-sufficient, effectual, sin-atoning substitute (2 Corinthians 5:21; Galatians 3:13; 1 Peter 2:24).

2. What is it to believe on the Lord Jesus Christ?

Men often make simple things difficult by trying to explain them. Certainly there is a danger of that when discussing faith. Yet the word 'believe', as it is

231

used in the Bible, is not the same thing as men imagine it to be today. So some explanation is needed. For example, Webster's Dictionary defines 'believe' like this: 'To place credence, apart from personal knowledge; to expect or hope; to be more or less firmly persuaded of the truth of anything; to think or suppose.' In that sense most people believe in Christ. Most believe that he lived in righteousness as a perfect man, that he died on the cross to save sinners, that he rose from the dead the third day and that he ascended into heaven. But that is not the meaning of the word 'believe' as it is used in the Word of God. Actually, there is no single English word that can accurately translate the Greek word used in Acts 16:31 for 'believe'. That word means 'adhere to, cleave to, trust, have faith in and rely upon'. The apostle's words to the jailer might be more accurately translated: 'Have an absolute, personal reliance upon the Lord Jesus Christ, and you will be saved.' The Amplified Version gives the sense of Paul's words most clearly: 'Believe in and on the Lord Jesus Christ — that is, give yourself up to him, take yourself out of your own keeping and entrust yourself to his keeping, and you will be saved.'

Believing on Christ, faith in him, involves four things: knowledge, assent, trust and perseverance.

1. Knowledge: no one can trust an unknown, unrevealed Saviour. Before anyone can, or will, trust Christ, Christ must be made known to him or her by the preaching of the gospel (Romans 10:14-17). It is not possible for a person to believe on Christ until he has been informed about Christ, until he knows who Christ is, what he did and why he did it. Faith is not a leap in the dark. Faith is based upon divine revelation. But there must be more.

2. Assent: our hearts must give assent to God's revelation. There is no faith until the heart is reconciled to, and in agreement with, the truth of God revealed in Holy Scripture. We must be reconciled to God and his revelation concerning the vital issues of salvation; sin, righteousness and judgment (2 Corinthians 5:20; John 16:8-11).

3. Trust: saving faith is believing in, relying upon, trusting Christ. It is a heart-confidence in the Son of God. This trust, this confidence, is what Paul expressed in his last epistle (2 Timothy 1:12; 4:6-8). To trust Christ is to confidently rest your soul upon his righteousness, his atonement, his intercession, his grace and his dominion as your Lord and Saviour.

4. Perseverance: faith is not an event in life. It is the character of the believer's life. The just live by faith. The believer never stops trusting Christ. Every child of God, like the saints of old, will 'die in faith' (Hebrews 11:13). Faith that does not persevere to the end is a false faith.

It is the very simplicity and easiness of faith that makes it so difficult for proud sinners to be saved. God says, 'Believe and live.' But proud man says, 'No, I must do something. I will not be saved entirely by the grace of God. I will not entirely trust my soul upon the merits of Christ.' Yet there is no other way to be saved! Sinners are saved by trusting Christ, the Son of God, by committing themselves to the merit and power of the substitute who lived, died and lives again for sinners. Salvation by grace alone, through faith alone, in Christ alone is so humbling to proud, self-righteous men and women that no one can or will trust Christ unless and until God the Holy Spirit gives them life and creates faith in them. Yes, faith in Christ is the gift of God (Ephesians 1:19; 2:8, 9; Philippians 1:29; Colossians 2:12).

3. What is that salvation which comes to sinners by faith in Christ?

It is complete deliverance from all sin and all the consequences of sin by the grace of God through the merits of Christ's righteousness and shed blood as our substitute (John 3:18, 36; Romans 8:1; 1 John 5:10-13). To be saved is to be delivered from death to life, from the bondage of sin to the liberty of righteousness, from the tyranny of the law to the blessedness of grace and at last into 'the glorious liberty of the sons of God' (Romans 8:21).

One more question arises as we read Acts 16 and needs to be answered.

4. Does this passage teach household salvation? (16:31-34)

The grace of God does not run in blood lines, and it is not possible for parents to secure faith for their sons and daughters. Many truly godly men, like David, have gone to their graves knowing their sons and daughters lived and died as rebels against God (2 Samuel 23:5). Salvation is by the will and purpose of God (John 1:12, 13; Romans 9:16). Faith is the gift of his grace. The Philippian Jailer was saved because he believed God. All who were in his house were saved because they too believed God. As soon as the jailer heard and believed the gospel of Christ, he brought Paul and Silas upstairs to his house. He gathered his wife, children and servants around his table in the middle of the night, and arranged for them to hear the message of grace too. When they heard, they believed and confessed Christ in believer's baptism.

Every believing parent is responsible to do for his household what the jailer did for his. If we would see our families saved by the grace of God, we must see that they hear the gospel preached. That much we are responsible to do. That much we can do. That much we must do! But the salvation of our households is entirely dependent upon, and determined by, the will and grace of our God.

Acts 17:1 Now when they had passed through Amphipolis and Apollonia, they came to Thessalonica, where was a synagogue of the Jews:

Acts 17:2 And Paul, as his manner was, went in unto them, and three sabbath days reasoned with them out of the scriptures,

Acts 17:3 Opening and alleging, that Christ must needs have suffered, and risen again from the dead; and that this Jesus, whom I preach unto you, is Christ.

Acts 17:4 And some of them believed, and consorted with Paul and Silas; and of the devout Greeks a great multitude, and of the chief women not a few.

Acts 17:5 But the Jews which believed not, moved with envy, took unto them certain lewd fellows of the baser sort, and gathered a company, and set all the city on an uproar, and assaulted the house of Jason, and sought to bring them out to the people.

Acts 17:6 And when they found them not, they drew Jason and certain brethren unto the rulers of the city, crying, These that have turned the world upside down are come hither also;

Acts 17:7 Whom Jason hath received: and these all do contrary to the decrees of Caesar, saying that there is another king, one Jesus.

Acts 17:8 And they troubled the people and the rulers of the city, when they heard these things.

Acts 17:9 And when they had taken security of Jason, and of the other, they let them go.

Acts 17:10 And the brethren immediately sent away Paul and Silas by night unto Berea: who coming thither went into the synagogue of the Jews.

Chapter 49

Three Weeks In Thessalonica

Acts 17:1-10

Acts 16 closes with Paul and Silas quietly departing from Philippi. The magistrates there were politically embarrassed when they found out that Paul and Silas, whom they had beaten and imprisoned, were Roman citizens. Had they chosen to do so, Paul and Silas could have caused them much trouble legally and politically. But after receiving a public apology they left the town quietly, once they had visited and comforted Lydia, the first European convert, and the brethren (16:39, 40). Philippi would never be the same again. God had graciously saved two households in that city. The households of Lydia and the jailer formed the gospel church at Philippi. They had the responsibility now of continuing and propagating the faith of Christ. They must have assumed their responsibility with great zeal, because soon there was a strong, flourishing church there.

The missionary trio (Paul, Silas and Timothy) walked through Amphipolis and Apollonia to Thessalonica, one of Macedonia's most populous and important cities. In all they walked about 100 miles to get to Thessalonica, apparently spending two nights on the road (17:1). When they got to Thessalonica they engaged in intensive evangelism, preaching in the Jewish synagogue there for three weeks in a row, every sabbath day (17:2). Traditionally, travelling rabbis were invited to speak at local synagogues as a matter of courtesy when visiting an area. Apparently Paul was asked to speak for that reason. He was obviously well received.

1. Paul's method of preaching (17:2, 3)

Paul was wise enough to adapt himself to his circumstances and to the needs of the hour. Sometimes he stood before an assembly and preached lengthy discourses (13:16-41). But there are other methods of preaching. At Thessalonica we are told that his preaching included three things: 'He reasoned with them out of the Scriptures, opening,' or explaining the message of the Scriptures, 'and alleging' that Christ had to suffer and rise from the dead.

Paul's first technique in preaching was reasoning. The word translated 'reason' here is the one from which we get the English word 'dialogue'. It has the idea of give-and-take conversation. The sense of Luke's words is that, using the Old Testament, with which the Jews were thoroughly familiar, Paul reasoned with them. He listened to their arguments and patiently refuted them by the Word of God.

His second tactic was opening, or explaining the Word of God. The word that is translated 'opening' is very strong. It means 'to expand' or 'to force open'. When the Scriptures were read, Paul opened up and explained their meaning. That is what preaching is. It is opening the Scriptures, and thus opening the understanding of one's hearers to see that all the Scriptures speak of Christ's sufferings, death and resurrection glory (Luke 24:27, 44-47).

Thirdly, the apostle's method in preaching was alleging. He alleged, or proved from the Old Testament Scriptures, the necessity of Christ's sin-atoning death and triumphant resurrection. This word, 'allege', means 'to put alongside'. In preaching at Thessalonica Paul compared spiritual things with spiritual (1 Corinthians 2:13). He took a text from Isaiah and compared it with one from Daniel and put alongside them some passages from the Psalms or one of the other prophets — thus alleging, or proving from the Word of God, the necessity of Christ's redemptive work.

2. Some believed and some did not believe (17:4-9)

Wherever Christ comes and wherever he is faithfully preached, there is a division because of him (John 7:43). The preaching of the gospel humbles some and brings them to repentance while it hardens others (2 Corinthians 2:14-16). The difference between those who believe and those who do not is the distinguishing grace of God (1 Corinthians 4:7). Some of the Jews, many of the Gentiles and several women, being chosen, redeemed and called by the grace of God, were persuaded by Paul's doctrine and identified themselves with Christ and his servants (17:4). However, those who did not believe were by no means indifferent. Not only did they not believe the gospel, they set themselves in opposition to it. How often this is repeated! Unbelief hardens into resentment, and resentment breaks out in malicious abuse. The unbelieving Jews apparently had connections with the criminal element in the city. They hired some street thugs to stir up trouble and assault the house of Jason, where Paul, Silas and Timothy were staying (17:5). This stirring of violence and slander was caused by religious, churchgoing people. When they could not refute the doctrine of Christ and would not give up their false religion, their hearts, filled with hatred for God and his gospel, erupted in cruel and vicious attacks upon God's messengers. Any preacher who has preached free grace to a congregation of those who believe a free-will religion of works knows exactly what happened at Thessalonica!

The malicious mob did not find the preachers at home, so they arrested Jason and some of the brethren because of their association with God's servants. Deliberately twisting Paul's words and his doctrines, they accused the saints of God of insurrection and riotousness, as promoters of evil things (17:6-8). This has always been the common tactic of religious men against Christ and the gospel of his grace (Luke 23:2; John 19:12; Romans 3:8). Jason and the brethren were released on bail (17:9). To avoid further trouble for Jason and the young believers at Thessalonica, Paul, Silas and Timothy slipped out of town under cover of darkness and went to Berea (17:10).

3. The charge against God's church by her enemies greatly honoured her

The mob cried out against Paul, Silas, Timothy and the believing men and women at Thessalonica, 'These ... have turned the world upside down' (17:6). Would to God the church today had a reputation for turning the world upside down! Instead, the church today has made peace with the world, walks hand in hand and has married the world. Fire and zeal for the glory of God have been drowned in the flood of compromise and conciliation. Instead of setting the world on fire with the truth of God, the church today warms itself at the fires of the world, fires fuelled by burning God's truth! The church has betrayed Christ, the souls of men and the gospel of the grace of God. All has been sold for the silver of praise, popularity and worldly recognition!

4. The church needs men who will, with the reason, force and persuasion of Holy Scripture, preach as Paul did in the synagogue at Thessalonica

The basis of Paul's appeal to men was the Word of God alone. He reasoned with his hearers out of the Scriptures (17:2). The Bible is the only source of divine truth in this world. God's preachers appeal to no other authority (Isaiah 8:20; 2 Timothy 3:16, 17). The message Paul preached was Jesus Christ and him crucified (17:3; 1 Corinthians 2:2). He showed from the Word of God the necessity of Christ's substitutionary death. According to the Word of God four things necessitated Christ's death on the cross: God's decree (1 Peter 1:18-20; Acts 2:23); Christ's voluntary engagements to become a surety for his people (Isaiah 50:5-7; John 10:16-18; 12:27, 28); the Old Testament prophets (Mark 14:49; Luke 24:44); and the justice of God (Romans 3:24-26; Galatians 3:21). Paul boldly pressed upon his hearers the claims of Christ the King, demanding immediate and total surrender to him as Lord. Blessed are the people to whom God sends such a preacher!

Acts 17:10 And the brethren immediately sent away Paul and Silas by night unto Berea: who coming thither went into the synagogue of the Jews.

Acts 17:11 These were more noble than those in Thessalonica, in that they received the word with all readiness of mind, and searched the scriptures daily, whether those things were so.

Acts 17:12 Therefore many of them believed; also of honourable women which were Greeks, and of men, not a few.

Acts 17:13 But when the Jews of Thessalonica had knowledge that the word of God was preached of Paul at Berea, they came thither also, and stirred up the people.

Acts 17:14 And then immediately the brethren sent away Paul to go as it were to the sea: but Silas and Timotheus abode there still.

Acts 17:15 And they that conducted Paul brought him unto Athens: and receiving a commandment unto Silas and Timotheus for to come to him with all speed, they departed.

Chapter 50

Those Noble Bereans

Acts 17:10-15

Unlike so many at Thessalonica, when the people at Berea heard Paul preach the gospel they profited from the Word. The Bereans did not go to church half asleep, or with their minds wandering in a thousand directions. When they went to the house of worship, they went seeking a word from God for their souls. They listened attentively, turned to the passages cited, compared scripture with scripture and received what was taught from the Word of God with readiness of mind. The Bereans were determined to know the truth of God. As Paul preached they took down notes to fix his doctrine in their minds. When they went home, they searched the Scriptures. The Holy Spirit holds these Bereans before us as examples to follow. If you would receive spiritual good for your soul by the preaching of the gospel, you would be wise to hear the Word attentively, as did the Bereans.

1. Paul and Silas were sent by God to Berea with a message (17:10)

By one means or another God always brings the messenger of mercy and the object of mercy together at the appointed time. Paul was sent to Philippi by a supernatural vision because the time had come for the Lord to open Lydia's heart. The apostle was beaten and imprisoned at Philippi because the time had come for the jailer and his household to be saved. The officials at Philippi pleaded with Paul and Silas to leave their town because the time had come when God would save some elect Thessalonians. Paul was driven from Thessalonica to Berea by persecution because there were many at Berea to whom God was determined to be gracious. The eye of faith sees the overruling hand of divine providence using the wicked deeds of men to move God's servant to the place where God wanted him (Psalm 76:10). 'The devil was outshot in his own bow,' Matthew Henry wrote. 'He thought by persecuting the apostles to stop the progress of the gospel, but it was so overruled as to be made to further it.'

Paul and Silas came to Berea as messengers commissioned by God. Knowing that God had sent him to preach the gospel at Berea, as soon as he arrived in the town Paul found the local synagogue and began preaching! He was God's ambassador and he knew it (Matthew 10:40; 2 Corinthians 5:18-20). As such, he had a message from God and boldly delivered it (2 Corinthians 5:21; 1 Corinthians 2:2). God's ambassadors all faithfully deliver the message God has given them, the message of free and gracious salvation through the obedience and death of the sinner's substitute, the Lord Jesus Christ. He will not alter or trim his message for any reason. God sent Paul and Silas to Berea at the appointed time of mercy for the calling of chosen sinners. As we shall see in verse 11, grace had gone before them and had prepared the way for grace, for there were some chosen sinners at Berea seeking the Lord. These three things are certain: wherever there is a sinner seeking the Saviour, there is the Saviour seeking a sinner; wherever there is a sinner seeking light, there will be a gospel preacher bringing light; and wherever there is a sinner seeking grace, grace has begun its work. No sinner will ever seek the Lord until grace causes him or her to do so (Romans 3:11).

2. The Bereans received the Word of God with readiness of mind (17:11)

There is nothing more delightful to a preacher than the privilege of preaching the gospel of Christ to people who are ready and anxious to hear it (Acts 10:33). Like Cornelius and his household, the Bereans were prepared by God to receive his Word. Luke was inspired to tell us three things about them.

First, the Bereans were more noble than the Jews of Thessalonica. This was not a reference to their social status! Luke's reference is to their attitude towards the Word of God and the preaching of the gospel. The Bereans reverenced the Old Testament Scriptures as the Word of God and as the only source of divine truth (Isaiah 8:20). Their minds were not hardened against the Word by their religious customs, doctrinal traditions, or philosophical opinions. They were open to anything taught in the Scriptures. Our minds must always be open to 'Thus saith the Lord,' and completely closed to all else. When the Bereans came to church, they came with the hope of hearing from God. They reverenced the worship of God and the ministry of the Word as God's ordained means of doing their souls eternal good (Ecclesiastes 5:1, 2; 1 Corinthians 1:21; Ephesians 4:11-14; James 1:17-19).

Secondly, the Bereans received the Word of God with all readiness of mind. 'This more noble disposition of mind and conduct was owing to the grace of God bestowed upon them,' commented John Gill. Blessed is the soul God causes to hunger, for he will be filled. Blessed are those God causes to thirst, for they will be satisfied. Blessed is the sinner God causes to seek, for he will find. Notice, 'They received the Word!' They did not ignore the Word. They did not find fault with the preacher. They did not argue with the Word. 'They received the Word!'

Thirdly, they searched the Scriptures. As Paul reasoned with them out of the Scriptures the Bereans followed along, taking notes. When they got home, they searched the Scriptures daily, to see if Paul's doctrine was according to the Word of God. All who care for their souls should do the same (John 5:39; 1 John 4:1). The gospel of Christ will bear scrutiny and examination. God's servants want their hearers to examine what they preach and teach by the Scriptures.

4. 'Therefore many of them believed' (17:12)

The word 'therefore' is important. It refers back to verse 11. As a direct result of the diligent use of the means at their disposal, God gave the Bereans faith and salvation in Christ. It is written, 'Seek and ye shall find!' God promises to be found by all who seek him (Jeremiah 29:13; Lamentations 3:25). No one ever yet sought the Lord in vain! Many of the Jews believed. Many of the Gentile women believed. And they, as faithful witnesses, persuaded their husbands to believe (1 Corinthians 7:16). Grace prepared the way, grace brought the Word and grace gave faith.

5. The offence of the cross has not ceased, or even diminished (17:13-15)

Though many believed (those who were chosen, redeemed and called by the grace of God), many were offended. Persecution again broke out, forcing Paul to leave Berea, too. We learn four things from this brief history of the gospel at Berea.

1. To those who are called, to God's elect, the gospel is the power of God unto salvation (Romans 1:15, 16; 1 Corinthians1:21-23). There is no need for compromise. The message we preach is God's means of grace to his people. To compromise the message is to destroy the means.

2. To the unbeliever the gospel of Christ is a stone of stumbling and a rock of offence (1 Peter 2:7, 8). It is not possible to make divine truth palatable to natural men. The only way God's ambassador can deal with his enemies is to confront them and demand surrender on God's terms.

3. Any preacher, or church, who faithfully preaches the gospel of God's free and sovereign grace in Christ will suffer for it (Matthew 10:16-34). The world will never embrace those who faithfully declare the truth of God.

4. However, our God, the God we trust and serve, is still on his throne. Nothing should deter us from serving our God. He will arrange even the persecutions of our most implacable foes to do us good, to further his cause and to increase his kingdom (Romans 8:28).

Acts 17:16 Now while Paul waited for them at Athens, his spirit was stirred in him, when he saw the city wholly given to idolatry.

Acts 17:17 Therefore disputed he in the synagogue with the Jews, and with the devout persons, and in the market daily with them that met with him.

Acts 17:18 Then certain philosophers of the Epicureans, and of the Stoicks, encountered him. And some said, What will this babbler say? other some, He seemeth to be a setter forth of strange gods: because he preached unto them Jesus, and the resurrection.

Acts 17:19 And they took him, and brought him unto Areopagus, saying, May we know what this new doctrine, whereof thou speakest, is?

Acts 17:20 For thou bringest certain strange things to our ears: we would know therefore what these things mean.

Acts 17:21 (For all the Athenians and strangers which were there spent their time in nothing else, but either to tell, or to hear some new thing.)

Acts 17:22 Then Paul stood in the midst of Mars' hill, and said, Ye men of Athens, I perceive that in all things ye are too superstitious.

Acts 17:23 For as I passed by, and beheld your devotions, I found an altar with this inscription, TO THE UNKNOWN GOD. Whom therefore ye ignorantly worship, him declare I unto you.

Acts 17:24 God that made the world and all things therein, seeing that he is Lord of heaven and earth, dwelleth not in temples made with hands;

Acts 17:25 Neither is worshipped with men's hands, as though he needed any thing, seeing he giveth to all life, and breath, and all things;

Acts 17:26 And hath made of one blood all nations of men for to dwell on all the face of the earth, and hath determined the times before appointed, and the bounds of their habitation;

Acts 17:27 That they should seek the Lord, if haply they might feel after him, and find him, though he be not far from every one of us:

Acts 17:28 For in him we live, and move, and have our being; as certain also of your own poets have said, For we are also his offspring.

Acts 17:29 Forasmuch then as we are the offspring of God, we ought not to think that the Godhead is like unto gold, or silver, or stone, graven by art and man's device.

Acts 17:30 And the times of this ignorance God winked at; but now commandeth all men every where to repent:

Acts 17:31 Because he hath appointed a day, in the which he will judge the world in righteousness by that man whom he hath ordained; whereof he hath given assurance unto all men, in that he hath raised him from the dead.

Acts 17:32 And when they heard of the resurrection of the dead, some mocked: and others said, We will hear thee again of this matter.

Acts 17:33 So Paul departed from among them.

Acts 17:34 Howbeit certain men clave unto him, and believed: among the which was Dionysius the Areopagite, and a woman named Damaris, and others with them.

Chapter 51

'THE UNKNOWN GOD'

Acts 17:16-34

Because of the uproar in Berea and the threat of persecution there, certain of the Berean brethren escorted Paul safely to Athens. Luke was left behind in Philippi, Timothy in Thessalonica, to minister to the new converts there, and Silas stayed in Berea, where he was later joined by Timothy. They were all to meet in Athens and from there continue their missionary travels. In verse 16 we find Paul waiting for his fellow-workers.

The apostle of Christ was alone in the city of Athens, the cultural, educational, philosophical centre of the Gentile world. As he walked through the streets of the city, his spirit was stirred with both anger and compassion, 'when he saw the city wholly given to idolatry' (17:16). In the city of Athens it was easier to find a god than a man! Everywhere, down every street, in every corner, wherever a nook was found, there was a statue of some pagan god or goddess. Someone estimated that there were more than 30,000 gods in Athens! With his soul on fire and his heart bursting with the message of free salvation by the grace of God in Christ, Paul went into the synagogue, into the streets and into the market-place preaching 'Jesus, and the resurrection'. He preached that Jesus Christ is the one true and living God, incarnate, crucified, resurrected and exalted (Colossians 1:12-20; 2:9, 10; Hebrews 1:1-3), the only God and Saviour of men. He preached the resurrection of the dead as a matter of certainty (1 Thessalonians 4:13-18; 1 Corinthians 15:50-58), declaring that there is a day appointed when all people must meet the Lord Jesus Christ in judgment (2 Corinthians 5:10, 11), to be rewarded by him with eternal life or eternal death upon the grounds of strict justice (Revelation 20:11, 12).

Paul spoke plainly and distinctly. Soon the whole city was talking about this strange preacher, his strange message and the 'strange gods' he preached. The controversy grew so hot that Paul was brought to the Areopagus, Mars' Hill, for trial (17:7-23). Mars' Hill was the highest court of the Athenians. This was the place where Socrates had been condemned for turning the people against their gods. Like a bold gladiator in an arena of lions, Paul stepped forward in the name of God, for the glory of Christ, to do battle with the powers of darkness. His only weapon was the Word of God, but that was

243

enough! The man of God boldly declared the Lord Jesus Christ, 'the unknown God', to the assembled pagans at Mars' Hill, without thought of cost or consequence. May God raise up such men to speak for him today!

We may note that the apostle took the Athenians' idolatrous inscription 'To THE UNKNOWN GOD', and applied it to the true and living God with good reason. Though the Lord God has plainly revealed himself in his Word and in the person and work of his Son, the Lord Jesus Christ, the one true and living God is still unknown to most people.

1. A stern condemnation (17:22, 23)

Most of the commentators in recent times have tried to tone down the language Paul used, to make it less condemning, suggesting, 'It would not be in order for an invited speaker to insult such an august body.' But there is no way to honestly translate Paul's language into conciliatory words. It was Paul's intention to condemn the idolatry of the men. When he stood before this august body, the apostle sternly condemned the learned, philosophical religious customs of the Athenians as foolish idolatry.

Human religion takes on many forms. It is always very tolerant and compromising, so that almost anything is acceptable as a religious practice or doctrine. The only thing that is always offensive to religious men and women is the plain declaration of the fact that salvation is by the free and sovereign grace of God alone, through the merits of the Lord Jesus Christ, the only sin-atoning substitute for sinners. This is the doctrine of the Bible (Psalm 37:39; Isaiah 53:1-12; Jonah 2:9; Romans 3:24-28; Ephesians 2:8, 9; 2 Timothy 1:9). Any doctrine that is contrary to this message is a false gospel, damning to the souls of men and idolatrous (Galatians 1:6-9). But this gospel, the message of salvation by grace through the merits of the crucified substitute, is offensive to men (Galatians 5:11).

Paul spoke plainly. He did not come to Mars' Hill to play games. He came to lay the axe to the root of the tree. His first words were an unflinching criticism of idolatry: 'I perceive that in all things ye are too superstitious,' literally, 'too religious'! Though the Athenians had over 30,000 gods to whom they gave homage, only three religious groups are mentioned. Those three groups essentially embrace the tenets of all false religion.

The Jews worshipped Jehovah, the one true and living God. They kept the religious practices of the Mosaic law. They lived by the rule of the Ten Commandments. Their religion required them to be morally upright. They refused to worship graven images. But their religion was a vain pretence and an idolatrous substitute for divine worship. They rejected the revelation of God concerning his Son, refused to be saved by the merits of the crucified, risen, exalted Son of God, refused to bow to Christ the Lord and refused to be saved by grace alone. Christ is the door. He is the way (John 10:9; 14:6). There is no other. To reject him is to choose idolatry!

The Epicureans were philosophical liberals. They admitted the existence of God, or of some sort of a god. But they thought God was somewhat like themselves, good but not great, gracious but not glorious. They denied creation and the resurrection. The Epicureans lived for pleasure.

The Stoics were philosophical conservatives. They believed in creation by God, some god. They believed in the resurrection of the body, taught moral virtue, believed in the power of the human will and, of course, denied God's sovereign rule of the world. The people of Athens, all three groups, were very religious and very lost. Though they called him a 'babbler', a nit-picker, for doing so, Paul told them their religion was a dark, damning delusion.

2. A stubborn confrontation (17:24-29)

The apostle confronted the men of Athens with the claims of God's character at the very points where they were most rebellious. He declared four things about the character of God that are essential to true worship. First, God is the Creator and original source of all (17:24; Romans 11:36). Second, God is absolutely sovereign over all (17:24; Daniel 4:35-37). Third, God is Spirit (17:25). He requires that we worship him in spirit and in truth. He has no regard for imaginary, idolatrous, 'holy things' or 'holy places' (John 4:23, 24; Isaiah 1:10-14). Fourth, God sovereignly rules and disposes of all men according to his own purpose in predestination (17:26-29).

3. A straightforward command (17:30, 31)

When Paul says, 'The times of this ignorance God winked at,' his meaning is, 'In ages past God passed over the Gentiles in judgment, but now, in this gospel age, he commands all men everywhere to trust his Son,' before whom all men must soon stand in judgment.

4. A solemn conclusion (17:32-34)

When the message was finished and the day was over, 'Some mocked.' Some hesitated; wavering in indecision and unbelief, they lost the opportunity they had. They never heard God's servant again! But there were some who believed the gospel (17:34). When Paul's work at Athens was done, he left and went to Corinth, confident of God's blessing upon the message he preached (2 Corinthians 2:14-17).

Acts 17:24 God that made the world and all things therein, seeing that he is Lord of heaven and earth, dwelleth not in temples made with hands;

Acts 17:25 Neither is worshipped with men's hands, as though he needed any thing, seeing he giveth to all life, and breath, and all things;

Acts 17:26 And hath made of one blood all nations of men for to dwell on all the face of the earth, and hath determined the times before appointed, and the bounds of their habitation;

Acts 17:27 That they should seek the Lord, if haply they might feel after him, and find him, though he be not far from every one of us:

Acts 17:28 For in him we live, and move, and have our being; as certain also of your own poets have said, For we are also his offspring.

Acts 17:29 Forasmuch then as we are the offspring of God, we ought not to think that the Godhead is like unto gold, or silver, or stone, graven by art and man's device.

Acts 17:30 And the times of this ignorance God winked at; but now commandeth all men every where to repent:

Acts 17:31 Because he hath appointed a day, in the which he will judge the world in righteousness by that man whom he hath ordained; whereof he hath given assurance unto all men, in that he hath raised him from the dead.

Chapter 52

God, Man And The Day Of Judgment

Acts 17:24-31

Paul here describes the character of the only true and living God and the responsibility of men before him. Obviously, he does not tell us everything about God's character. The infinite God can never be fully known by finite man. But the apostle's purpose in this passage is to distinguish God from all the false gods worshipped by men. He does this by declaring seven things.

1. The Lord our God is the sovereign Creator and Ruler of all (17:24)

He who created all things owns all things, rules all things and disposes of all things as he will (Matthew 20:15; Psalm 115:3; 135:6; Daniel 4:34, 35; Romans 11:36). The universe is absolutely governed by God for the accomplishment of his will (Ephesians 1:11; Isaiah 45:7; Proverbs 16:4).

2. The holy Lord God cannot be enshrined in temples or worshipped by physical acts or objects (17:24, 25)

God is Spirit. All who worship him must worship him in spirit and in truth (John 4:24; Philippians 3:3). It is true, in the Old Testament, God did establish his worship in the tabernacle and later in the temple at Jerusalem. However, like the sacrifices, the priesthood and the laws of Israel, temple worship was a temporary, physical ordinance designed to portray what Christ would do for the redemption and salvation of his people. Now that he has finished his work, the physical ordinances have been forever abolished (Colossians 2:8-23; Hebrews 10:1-14). Any worship of God in 'holy places', the use of images, icons, or crosses is nothing less than idolatry (17:29). All true worship is spiritual worship.

3. God Almighty, from eternity, determined all things regarding the lives of all people upon the earth (17:26)

Before the world was made he determined that all men would spring from one man, our father Adam. He 'hath made of one blood all nations of men'.

247

All the races of men in the world have their origin in one man. In reality we are not many races, but one race with many distinguishing traits. This verse also declares that God determined the time and place of every person's birth, the length of his or her life, the space each would occupy upon the earth and the time and means of their death (Job 7:1). While full acknowledgement is given to the responsibility of all men to take proper care of their health, it must be understood that the most careful will not extend his life beyond the appointed time and the most careless will not shorten his allotted span by so much as a fraction of a second. Our times are in God's hands!

4. It is our responsibility to seek the Lord in the time allotted us (17:27)

Every person has one life to live, one death to die, one judgment to face and one eternity to spend. If we hope to spend eternity in the bliss of God's eternal glory, we must seek him now, while we have both the opportunity and the ability to do so. 'Seek ye the Lord while he may be found, call ye upon him while he is near' (Isaiah 5:6). 'The Lord is good ... to the soul that seeketh him' (Lamentations 3:25).

5. The Lord God is near every one of us (17:27, 28)

The Lord God is omnipresent, everywhere present at one time, in all the fulness of his glorious, triune being! God is the infinite Spirit. He has no limitations. He is near us all, believers and unbelievers, so near us that 'In him we live, and move, and have our being' (see Psalm 139:7-12). Augustine wrote, 'God is an infinite circle whose centre is everywhere and whose circumference is nowhere!' Nothing is more serious and sobering than the realization that we are always in the presence of God! When our father Adam rebelled against God and died spiritually, we died in him, because we sinned in him (Romans 5:12). This spiritual death is the separation of our souls from God. Because man is far off from God, he imagines that God is far off from him; but it is not so. The living God is 'not far from every one of us: for in him we live, and move, and have our being'. God is as much with you as if there were no other persons in the universe but you and God! Yet his being near you does not make him far off from anyone else. God perceives the inmost, secret thoughts and intents of every heart. He feels for us. He thinks of us. He is near us in all the power of omnipotence, ready to intervene and help us. He is near us in all places and at all times. By day and by night he surrounds us. Let us take Paul's words to heart and apply them to our own lives. The contemplation of them should fill us with awe: 'He is not far from every one of us: for in him we live, and move, and have our being.'

This is a matter of great assurance and peace to the believer. 'The Lord is at hand' (Philippians 4:5). He is near to preserve us in trial, to protect us from danger and to provide for our every need. He is near to hear and answer our prayers, to commune with us, make himself known to us, and renew and revive us with his grace. If the Lord is near, all is well (2 Timothy 4:9-18).

This is a matter of great encouragement to those who know their need of Christ and seek him. Paul's argument is that the Lord is near every one of us so that all who seek him may find him (17:27, 28). If the Lord is near and you seek him, you will surely find him (Romans 10:6-10; Jeremiah 29:13). If you seek him, you may be assured of the fact that he is seeking you. Otherwise, you would never seek him. When the sinner seeks God and God seeks the sinner, the two will soon come together! The Lord is near to save, to pardon and to justify all who seek him.

This is a warning to every rebel: ' ... he be not far from every one of us'. All sin, rebellion, unbelief is committed in the presence of the holy Lord God! No sinner will escape the wrath of God, who is near to every one of us, except by taking refuge in Christ, who is himself the omnipresent God.

6. God commands all men everywhere to repent (17:30)

When Paul says that God 'winked at' the ignorance, idolatry and unbelief of the Gentiles in ages past, he does not mean that God ignored it, or did not notice it, or excused it. He means that in those days God passed by the Gentile nations in judgment and revealed himself only to the children of Israel. But now, in this gospel age, God 'commandeth all men everywhere to repent'. Because it is the commandment of God, it is also the duty of all men to repent of their sins and trust the Lord Jesus Christ (1 John 3:23; Ezekiel 36:31). All who obey the command of the gospel will be saved. All who refuse to obey will be damned (Proverbs 1:22-33).

7. God will judge all men in righteousness by the God-man Jesus Christ (John 5:28; 2 Corinthians 5:10, 11; Revelation 20:11-15)

The Day of Judgment will be the day of settling. In that great day everyone will receive exactly what justice demands, exactly what he or she lawfully deserves. When the books are opened and each person is examined by the omniscient eye of strict justice, the unbelieving, standing before God without a substitute, will be rewarded with everlasting wrath, in exact proportion to their measure of wickedness. The redeemed, being totally free from sin and perfectly righteous in Christ their substitute, will inherit all the fulness of heaven's glory, because justice declares they are worthy!

Acts 18:1 After these things Paul departed from Athens, and came to Corinth;

Acts 18:2 And found a certain Jew named Aquila, born in Pontus, lately come from Italy, with his wife Priscilla; (because that Claudius had commanded all Jews to depart from Rome:) and came unto them.

Acts 18:3 And because he was of the same craft, he abode with them, and wrought: for by their occupation they were tentmakers.

Acts 18:4 And he reasoned in the synagogue every sabbath, and persuaded the Jews and the Greeks.

Acts 18:5 And when Silas and Timotheus were come from Macedonia, Paul was pressed in the spirit, and testified to the Jews that Jesus was Christ.

Acts 18:6 And when they opposed themselves, and blasphemed, he shook his raiment, and said unto them, Your blood be upon your own heads; I am clean: from henceforth I will go unto the Gentiles.

Acts 18:7 And he departed thence, and entered into a certain man's house, named Justus, one that worshipped God, whose house joined hard to the synagogue.

Acts 18:8 And Crispus, the chief ruler of the synagogue, believed on the Lord with all his house; and many of the Corinthians hearing believed, and were baptized.

Acts 18:9 Then spake the Lord to Paul in the night by a vision, Be not afraid, but speak, and hold not thy peace:

Acts 18:10 For I am with thee, and no man shall set on thee to hurt thee: for I have much people in this city.

Acts 18:11 And he continued there a year and six months, teaching the word of God among them.

Chapter 53

Paul's Ministry At Corinth

Acts 18:1-11

Corinth was a large seaport city. It was the commercial meeting place of the East and the West. On one side of the city there was a port to the Ionian Sea, on the other side one to the Aegean Sea. As Athens was the intellectual centre of the ancient Greek world, so Corinth was the economic centre. It was famous for its spectacular bronze and infamous for its sensuality. In the temple of Venus at Corinth there were over a thousand prostitutes to be hired by the many travellers who passed through the city. It was to this materialistic, idolatrous, perverse city that Paul came preaching the gospel of Christ. Timothy and Silas were still in Macedonia. Paul came to Corinth alone. He had no companion but his heavenly Companion. He had no friend with him but the Friend of sinners whom he had come to proclaim. In these eleven verses the Spirit of God teaches us six very important lessons.

1. God's servants' are not hirelings (18:1-4)

Though trained as a scholar at the feet of Gamaliel and though he was an apostle of the Lord Jesus Christ, when Paul came to Corinth to preach the gospel he earned his living by making tents. Aquila and Priscilla were Jewish believers who were also tentmakers. They received Paul into their home and into their business. Tent making at the time was a common trade. Yet it was a noble trade. As Matthew Henry wrote, 'An honest trade, by which a man may get his bread, is not to be looked upon by any with contempt.'

Why did Paul work as a tentmaker? Many point to Paul as an excuse for being stingy with God's servants, suggesting that those who preach the gospel should not live by the gospel. Such an attitude is contrary to the plain teachings of the New Testament. God has ordained that every man who faithfully labours in the work of the gospel ministry should live by the gospel (1 Corinthians 9:6-14; Galatians 6:6; 1 Timothy 5:17). Individual believers, deacons and local churches should make it their business to see to it that those men who faithfully preach the gospel (pastors, missionaries, evangelists) lack for nothing materially. Those who give themselves to the work of the ministry are worthy of financial support. They should never have to ask for anything. In a local church deacons should make certain that the pastor has no earthly, material concern, so that he may give himself entirely to study, prayer and preaching (Acts 6:2-4).

Paul made tents at Corinth because there was no church established among the Corinthians to maintain him. The churches at Jerusalem and Antioch should have assumed that responsibility, but for some reason did not, and Paul refused to ask for help. Being the servant of God, he would not stoop to begging for the help of men! And rather than give the appearance of greed, the apostle chose to work with his hands while he preached the gospel to the unbelieving (2 Corinthians 11:7, 8; 2 Thessalonians 3:8, 9). However, once converted, Paul taught the Corinthian believers to support generously those who preached the gospel (1 Corinthians 9; 2 Corinthians 8; 9).

Though he worked with his hands through the week, Paul preached the gospel freely to the Jews every sabbath day. He reasoned with them from the Old Testament Scriptures, showing that Jesus of Nazareth is the Christ (18:4, 5; Genesis 49:10; Deuteronomy 18:15; Psalm 132:11; Isaiah 7:14; 9:6; 53:1-12; Jeremiah 23:5, 6).

2. Faithful men need the fellowship and support of other faithful men

Paul seems to have become somewhat discouraged, but when Timothy and Silas finally arrived at Corinth (18:5), they apparently gave him the boost he needed. The fact is, we all need other people. Pastors need one another's encouragement. Believers need one another's encouragement. We should always strengthen one another's arms in the service of Christ.

3. The greatest curse God can ever bring upon any people in this world is to remove from them the light of the gospel

That is what is described in verse 6. Because the Jews wilfully rejected the counsel of God against themselves, God took his Word from them and sent it to the Gentiles (Matthew 22:8, 9; 23:37, 38; Romans 11:22). What a warning is given here! Those who trifle with and oppose the gospel of Christ court divine reprobation (Proverbs 1:22-33). Those who oppose God's messengers oppose God (Matthew 10:40). All who despise and reject the gospel of Christ bring ruin upon themselves. Their damnation will be their own fault. Their blood will be upon their own heads (Acts 20:26; Ezekiel 33:8, 9).

4. God's great blessing

The greatest blessing God can bestow upon any people in this world is to send them a man to faithfully preach the gospel of Christ to them (18:7, 8).

The Jews despised Paul's message and despised him for preaching it. But there was a man named Justus who opened his house to Paul and turned it into a preaching centre. The fact is, all who love the gospel love those who preach it and do what they can to accommodate it. Paul had seen little response to his message at Athens and had met with great opposition at Corinth, but he was faithful. God always honours faithfulness (1 Samuel 2:30). At the time appointed, God began calling out his elect at Corinth: first Justus; then Crispus, the chief ruler of the synagogue; then his household; then many of the Corinthians.

Notice the order of events in verse 8. It is important. This is God's method of grace. First, the gospel was preached. Then, many who heard believed. Finally, those who believed were baptized.

According to the pattern and the precept of the New Testament, baptism is for believers only (Acts 8:37). No infants were ever baptized because their parents were believers, only believers themselves. Believers follow Christ in baptism because he commands it (Mark 16:15, 16). By baptism we identify ourselves with Christ and his people, confess our faith in him and renounce our former religion as darkness and idolatry (Acts 2:38; Romans 6:4-6).

5. God has a great multitude of chosen sinners in this world whom he will save by the preaching of the gospel (18:9, 10)

The fear of man must never stop the mouths of God's servants (Jeremiah 1:8-10). The Lord appeared to Paul in a vision and encouraged him to continue faithfully to preach the gospel at Corinth, assuring him of three things. The presence of God — 'I am with thee'. The protection of God — 'No man shall set on thee to hurt thee'. The purpose of God — 'I have much people in this city.' The inspiration God gave Paul for evangelism at Corinth was the certain salvation of his elect. All who were chosen in eternity and redeemed at Calvary must be called at God's appointed time, and he will call them through the voice of a gospel preacher (Romans 10:17; 1 Peter 1:23-25).

6. God's servants seek and follow his direction (18:11)

Having his orders from God, Paul stayed in Corinth for a year and six months. He remained there seeking the Lord's sheep (John 10:16) and establishing the church in the doctrine of Christ (Ephesians 4:11-16). Though he was a resident preacher at Corinth, the apostle continued to serve the church of God at large. Both 1 and 2 Thessalonians were written while Paul was at Corinth. Let all who worship God pray for, support and obey their faithful, God-ordained pastors (1 Thessalonians 5:12, 13; Hebrews 13:7, 17).

Acts 18:12 And when Gallio was the deputy of Achaia, the Jews made insurrection with one accord against Paul, and brought him to the judgment seat,

Acts 18:13 Saying, This fellow persuadeth men to worship God contrary to the law.

Acts 18:14 And when Paul was now about to open his mouth, Gallio said unto the Jews, If it were a matter of wrong or wicked lewdness, O ye Jews, reason would that I should bear with you:

Acts 18:15 But if it be a question of words and names, and of your law, look ye to it; for I will be no judge of such matters.

Acts 18:16 And he drave them from the judgment seat.

Acts 18:17 Then all the Greeks took Sosthenes, the chief ruler of the synagogue, and beat him before the judgment seat. And Gallio cared for none of those things.

Acts 18:18 And Paul after this tarried there yet a good while, and then took his leave of the brethren, and sailed thence into Syria, and with him Priscilla and Aquila; having shorn his head in Cenchrea: for he had a vow.

Acts 18:19 And he came to Ephesus, and left them there: but he himself entered into the synagogue, and reasoned with the Jews.

Acts 18:20 When they desired him to tarry longer time with them, he consented not;

Acts 18:21 But bade them farewell, saying, I must by all means keep this feast that cometh in Jerusalem: but I will return again unto you, if God will. And he sailed from Ephesus.

Acts 18:22 And when he had landed at Caesarea, and gone up, and saluted the church, he went down to Antioch.

Acts 18:23 And after he had spent some time there, he departed, and went over all the country of Galatia and Phrygia in order, strengthening all the disciples.

Acts 18:24 And a certain Jew named Apollos, born at Alexandria, an eloquent man, and mighty in the scriptures, came to Ephesus.

Acts 18:25 This man was instructed in the way of the Lord; and being fervent in the spirit, he spake and taught diligently the things of the Lord, knowing only the baptism of John.

Acts 18:26 And he began to speak boldly in the synagogue: whom when Aquila and Priscilla had heard, they took him unto them, and expounded unto him the way of God more perfectly.

Acts 18:27 And when he was disposed to pass into Achaia, the brethren wrote, exhorting the disciples to receive him: who, when he was come, helped them much which had believed through grace:

Acts 18:28 For he mightily convinced the Jews, and that publickly, shewing by the scriptures that Jesus was Christ.

Chapter 54

Apollos: The Alexandrian Orator

Acts 18:12-28

In the passage before us we have a hurried account of the last part of Paul's second missionary journey and the beginning of his third. We follow the apostle from Corinth to Ephesus, from Ephesus to Jerusalem and from Jerusalem back to Antioch. After spending some time in Antioch, he visited the churches of Galatia and Phrygia. Then he went back to Ephesus, where chapter 19 begins. That is a lot of territory to cover in nineteen verses! We want to say, 'Wait, Luke! Tell us more. What happened at Cenchrea? How did Phoebe, that lady in the Cenchrean church, win the praise Paul bestowed upon her in Romans 16:1, 2? What happened while Paul was at Jerusalem, Antioch, Galatia and Phrygia?' But Luke chose to omit all the details. He appears to have been anxious to introduce the next scene in the history of the early church and a man who impressed him greatly, Apollos, the Alexandrian orator. Luke was moved by the Holy Spirit to introduce this man to us with deeper respect and admiration than he used to present any other man in the book of Acts (18:24, 25). Apollos is set before us as an example of Christian character, whose faith and faithfulness should be followed (Hebrews 13:7, 17). However, before Apollos is introduced, Luke was directed to give some account of Paul's journey from Corinth to Antioch for our instruction.

1. The typical persecution (18:12-17)

God restrained the malice of his enemies at Corinth for a while, but in time he allowed the venom of the old serpent, Satan, to spew out against his servant. 'The Jews made insurrection with one accord against Paul' (18:12, 13). The Authorized Version reads, 'This fellow ... ', but the Jews did not say 'fellow', that was added by the translators. The Jews said, 'This ... !' They had no word disgusting enough to describe God's messenger!

Gallio should not have allowed the Gentiles to beat Sosthenes. As a civil magistrate it was his duty to protect all. However, he is to be commended in that he refused to hear the charges brought against Paul. It is not the business of civil courts to make rules or judgments in matters regarding the free exercise of religion.

255

Crispus, who was the ruler of the synagogue, had been converted by the grace of God (18:8) and Sosthenes had been elected to take his place. Sosthenes, who had come to Gallio to have Paul beaten, was himself beaten with the lashes he had hoped to inflict upon Paul. Many a Haman has been hanged on the gallows he built for the hanging of God's faithful Mordecais.

By these events at Corinth the Holy Spirit teaches two forceful lessons.

First, the gospel of Christ is offensive to lost men. The plain declaration of redemption by Christ and salvation by grace alone through faith in him is foolishness, a stone of stumbling and a rock of offence, to those who are perishing. Natural man is tolerant of, and even likes, natural religion. Any religion that bases salvation upon man's free will, good works, or religious ceremonies is acceptable to him. But he will not tolerate the gospel of God's free and sovereign grace in Christ (Galatians 5:11). All who faithfully confess Christ to men will have to endure the wrath of men (Matthew 10:16-39). All who preach the gospel in purity, without compromise, will pay a price for doing so (Galatians 1:10-12).

The second lesson is equally obvious: God's providential rule of this world works all things together for the good of his elect (Romans 8:28). The Jews' persecution was as much the work of God's providence for Paul as the benevolence of Aquila and Priscilla. It became evident to Paul that his work at Corinth was done. He did not flee for fear of the Jews, but he saw their persecution as an indication that God would have him move to another place. God thwarted the Jews' plans, and confirmed his promise to Paul (18:10).

This beating of Sosthenes was one of the things God used to bring him to Christ (1 Corinthians 1:1).

2. The travelling preacher (18:18-23)

It is highly improbable that Paul took a Jewish vow and shaved his head (18:18). The one Luke refers to as having taken a vow must have been Aquila. Paul, above all men, cast aside all Jewish laws, ceremonies and rituals (Colossians 2:16-23). He might for expediency have Timothy circumcised, but he would never have taken a vow and shaved his head in pledge of it — not Paul!

When he came to Ephesus, where he left Aquila and Priscilla, Paul went again into the synagogue to reason with the Jews (18:19). So great was his compassion for his kinsmen that he could not let them perish without preaching Christ to them (Romans 10:1, 2).

The apostle was determined to go up to Jerusalem, not to keep the Jewish feast, but to be there during the Passover because there he would have opportunity to preach the gospel to many. Recognizing and submitting to

God's providence, he made all his plans and commitments with one condition: 'if God will' (James 4:13-15).

Young believers, like young plants, need much care. Paul tenderly cared for and ministered to the needs of these young churches and young saints (18:22, 23). He travelled alone for hundreds of miles, at his own expense, to preach the gospel to the unbelieving Jews and Gentiles and for the comfort and edification of God's saints (Ephesians 4:11-16).

3. The talented pulpiteer (18:24-28)

While Paul was away Apollos came to Ephesus, preaching the gospel of Christ (18:24). Born in Alexandria in Egypt, he was a man of exceptional gifts. He was 'an eloquent man', rational, prudent, well-educated and influential in speech. He was 'mighty in the scriptures'. That is to say, he was greatly gifted of God in understanding and explaining the Old Testament Scripture in the light of Christ's person and work.

Apollos was taught in the way of the Lord Jesus Christ (18:25), who is the way, the truth and the life (John 14:6). He zealously promoted the glory of God and sought the salvation of his people (Romans 12:11). Yet he knew only the message and doctrine of John the Baptist: repentance towards God and the remission of sins by Christ, the Lamb of God (Matthew 3:1, 2; John 1:29). He knew nothing of the outpouring of the Holy Spirit and the mighty works of God through the apostles. His doctrine was true gospel doctrine, but Apollos had not been instructed in those things which had been revealed since the time of John the Baptist.

Aquila and Priscilla invited Apollos to their house and privately instructed him more fully in the gospel (18:26). Priscilla assisted her husband in the teaching of Apollos privately in her own house, not publicly in the church. As a godly woman, she behaved with meekness (1 Peter 3:1, 2). It is contrary to both Scripture and modesty for a woman to publicly reprove or instruct a man (1 Timothy 2:11, 12; 1 Corinthians 14:34).

The believers at Ephesus sent a letter to the church at Corinth, recommending Apollos to them as an able gospel preacher (18:27). When he arrived there, he was an instrument in the hands of God for much spiritual good to the brethren who 'had believed through grace'. Faith in Christ is not the work of man's free will, but of God's free grace (Ephesians 2:8; Colossians 2:12; Philippians 1:29).

Being taught by God, Apollos was a mighty and convincing teacher (18:28). He proved by the Old Testament Scriptures 'that Jesus [is the] Christ', the sent one of God, the Saviour of the world (1 John 4:1-4).

Acts 19:1 And it came to pass, that, while Apollos was at Corinth, Paul having passed through the upper coasts came to Ephesus: and finding certain disciples,

Acts 19:2 He said unto them, Have ye received the Holy Ghost since ye believed? And they said unto him, We have not so much as heard whether there be any Holy Ghost.

Acts 19:3 And he said unto them, Unto what then were ye baptized? And they said, Unto John's baptism.

Acts 19:4 Then said Paul, John verily baptized with the baptism of repentance, saying unto the people, that they should believe on him which should come after him, that is, on Christ Jesus.

Acts 19:5 When they heard this, they were baptized in the name of the Lord Jesus.

Acts 19:6 And when Paul had laid his hands upon them, the Holy Ghost came on them; and they spake with tongues, and prophesied.

Acts 19:7 And all the men were about twelve.

Acts 19:8 And he went into the synagogue, and spake boldly for the space of three months, disputing and persuading the things concerning the kingdom of God.

Acts 19:9 But when divers were hardened, and believed not, but spake evil of that way before the multitude, he departed from them, and separated the disciples, disputing daily in the school of one Tyrannus.

Acts 19:10 And this continued by the space of two years; so that all they which dwelt in Asia heard the word of the Lord Jesus, both Jews and Greeks.

Acts 19:11 And God wrought special miracles by the hands of Paul:

Acts 19:12 So that from his body were brought unto the sick handkerchiefs or aprons, and the diseases departed from them, and the evil spirits went out of them.

Chapter 55

'Come out from among them'

Acts 19:1-12

We follow Paul back to Ephesus, where he had left Aquila and Priscilla (18:19-21). While he was away Apollos had come and spent some time there preaching 'the baptism of John' in the synagogue (18:24, 25). Aquila and Priscilla befriended him and instructed him more fully in the gospel of the grace of God (18:26). Apollos then went to Corinth to preach to the church Paul had established there. When the apostle Paul came back to Ephesus he found 'certain disciples' there who, like Apollos, were disciples of John the Baptist. These disciples of the Baptist had come in among and identified themselves with the brethren who were still worshipping with the Jews in the synagogue. Acts 19 opens with Paul meeting these brethren.

1. A time of transition

If we are to interpret any portion of the book of Acts properly, we must remember that the history of the church recorded in Acts was a period of transitional development, much as we find in the four Gospels. During those early years Christianity was still looked upon as a sect of Judaism. Believers worshiped with the Jews in their synagogues. At Jerusalem they continued to worship in the Jewish temple. Many genuine believers remained ignorant of important gospel truths until God sent them a gospel preacher to instruct them in the faith of Christ. We have already seen two examples.

Cornelius (10:1, 2) was a true believer. That cannot be disputed. The Word of God describes him as a just and devout man who feared and worshipped God (10:2, 4, 22). But he worshipped God only in the light of the Old Testament Scriptures until Peter came and told him that the Saviour for whom he looked had already come, redeemed his people and ascended back into heaven. What he believed before was true. He trusted the Son of God as he was revealed in the types, promises and prophecies of the Old Testament, walking in the light God had given him.

Apollos had more light than Cornelius (18:24-28), but he too was greatly lacking. He was not misinformed, but uninformed. He knew only the teachings of John the Baptist until Aquila and Priscilla explained the doctrine of Christ to him more fully.

Neither Cornelius nor Apollos were heretics. They did not embrace a false gospel. They believed the truth as fully as they knew it. They trusted Christ according to the light they had. When God gave them more light they gladly received it, submitted to it and obeyed it. In the opening verses of Acts 19 Paul met another group of twelve men like Apollos. They were true believers who knew only the baptism of John.

2. The question Paul asked (19:1-3)

These men were disciples of Christ. They followed the teachings of his servant John the Baptist. They trusted the Lord Jesus, professed faith in his name and were baptized in his name, either by John or his disciples. After some discussion with them, Paul asked, 'Have ye received the Holy Ghost' (according to the Authorized Version) 'since ye believed?' The question is more accurately translated: 'Did you receive the Holy Spirit when you believed?'. Their response, 'We have not so much as heard whether there be any Holy Ghost,' really amounts to: 'Do you mean the Holy Spirit has come?' Certainly, being John's disciples, they knew that the Holy Spirit existed and knew the promise of his descent (Matthew 3:11; Mark 1:8; Luke 3:16). John's disciples were well instructed in the Old Testament prophecies relating to the coming of Christ, the outpouring of, and baptism in, the Spirit by him and the extraordinary signs that would accompany it (Ezekiel 36:21-28; Joel 2:28-32; Zechariah 12:10; John 7:39). But these men were totally ignorant of the fact that the Holy Spirit had been given. They knew he had been promised, but did not know that he had come. It is a mistake to make more out of the text than this — a mistake that leads to serious error. 'Unto what then were ye baptized?' Paul assumed that since they claimed to be believers they had been baptized (Mark 16:16; Romans 6:3-6). His question to these men was: 'If you were not baptized in the name of the Father, the Son and the Holy Spirit, in what name were you baptized?' They answered, 'Unto John's baptism.' Believing the message of John concerning the coming of Christ, they were baptized.

Two things need to be clearly understood. First, all who truly believe on the Lord Jesus Christ have received the Holy Spirit. This is the glaring difference between the true believer and the one who makes a profession of faith but is not truly born of God (John 3:3-8; Romans 8:9-14; Galatians 5:22, 23). Second, it is the responsibility of every believer to follow the command and example of Christ in believer's baptism (Romans 6:3-6). By baptism, being immersed in the watery grave and rising up out of it, we publicly confess our faith in Christ and identify ourselves with him.

3. John's baptism (19:4, 5)

Many teach that John's baptism was not Christian baptism. Dividing verses 4 and 5, they insist that Paul rebaptized these disciples. But the text teaches exactly the opposite. Read the two verses together. Put the whole passage in quotation marks. Both verses are to be understood as Paul's explanation of John's baptism. He is stating that John's baptism is exactly the same as we practise today, the immersion of professed believers in the name of the Lord Jesus. In support of this interpretation, it should be observed that there is no indication anywhere in the New Testament that any of John's disciples were rebaptized by our Lord or his apostles, though the opportunity clearly presented itself (John 3:22-36), and there is no indication that Apollos was rebaptized after being instructed in the way of God more perfectly (18:26). Moreover, if verse 5 contained Luke's words describing what Paul had done, it seems most reasonable that he would have specified that Paul baptized them, as he specified that Paul laid hands upon them in verse 6. In verses 4 and 5 Luke tells us what Paul said. In verse 6 he tells us what Paul did.

4. The communication of the Holy Spirit (19:6, 7)

Just as Peter and John laid their hands on the believing Samaritans who had been baptized by Philip (8:14-17), Paul laid his hands upon these twelve men who had been baptized by John the Baptist and they received the extraordinary gifts of the Spirit. Once more Paul was evidently confirmed as an apostle of Christ (Hebrews 2:3, 4). In the apostolic era many received those gifts, but only an apostle could communicate them to others. Remember Philip, who possessed the gifts, could not communicate them to the Samaritans, but had to wait for the apostles to do so. Therefore, these extraordinary, outward signs necessarily ceased when the apostles were gone, not because God has changed, but because they are no longer needed. We now have the perfect, complete revelation of God in Holy Scripture (1 Corinthians 13:10; 2 Peter 1:16-21).

5. The separation of the believers (19:8-12)

The saints of God at this time met with the Jews in their synagogues. They sought the salvation of the Jewish people. But there comes a time when those who follow Christ must separate themselves from those who despise him. Light and darkness cannot abide together. So after three months of faithful instruction, Paul led the saints of God to separate themselves from those who hated the gospel of Christ (2 Corinthians 6:14-7:1; Revelation 18:4).

Acts 19:13 Then certain of the vagabond Jews, exorcists, took upon them to call over them which had evil spirits the name of the Lord Jesus, saying, We adjure you by Jesus whom Paul preacheth.

Acts 19:14 And there were seven sons of one Sceva, a Jew, and chief of the priests, which did so.

Acts 19:15 And the evil spirit answered and said, Jesus I know, and Paul I know; but who are ye?

Acts 19:16 And the man in whom the evil spirit was leaped on them, and overcame them, and prevailed against them, so that they fled out of that house naked and wounded.

Acts 19:17 And this was known to all the Jews and Greeks also dwelling at Ephesus; and fear fell on them all, and the name of the Lord Jesus was magnified.

Acts 19:18 And many that believed came, and confessed, and shewed their deeds.

Acts 19:19 Many of them also which used curious arts brought their books together, and burned them before all men: and they counted the price of them, and found it fifty thousand pieces of silver.

Acts 19:20 So mightily grew the word of God and prevailed.

Chapter 56

'So mightily grew the word of God'

Acts 19:13-20

Sometimes it appears that the cause of Christ is failing, that Satan and the powers of darkness are triumphant; but that is never the case (Matthew 16:18; Isaiah 55:11; 1 Corinthians 15:58). In the end all things will show forth the praise of our God and Saviour, all of God's elect will be saved, every purpose of God will be accomplished and the kingdoms of this world will become the kingdoms of our God. Things are not as they seem. Our great Saviour is sovereignly ruling this world from his heavenly throne, accomplishing his will by his omnipotent power and grace. The instrument by which Christ prevails over the hearts of men is the gospel of his free grace. The church of God is a conquering army and the weapon, the only weapon, of her warfare is the sword of the Spirit, the Word of God, the gospel of Christ.

Nowhere is this fact so vividly displayed as in the book of Acts. In Acts 19, when Paul came to the city of Ephesus, he found twelve men who believed God. They began meeting together in a little room in a schoolhouse to worship God and preach the gospel. From the beginning they met with opposition. The Jewish zealots, the idolatrous worshippers of Diana, the businessmen and even the Jewish gypsies who passed through town were all united in their opposition to the band of God's saints who met at the school of Tyrannus. Satan did everything he could to stop the spread of the gospel in Ephesus. But Paul and his little band went right on preaching Jesus Christ and him crucified. They had no regard for the religions of the people, the opinions of the people, or the power of the people. Their only concern was for the glory of God and the truth of God. God honours people like that (1 Samuel 2:30). In less than three years that little band of believers had become a large, influential congregation, well grounded in the doctrine of Christ. By the end of three years of faithful preaching the church at Ephesus was so large it required several elders to oversee its ministry (Acts 20:17).

This phenomenal growth came about without the use of puppet shows, musical recitals, Sunday school contests, sports teams, or the testimonials of famous film stars, athletes or politicians. Without gimmickry or political influence, the naked truth of God, preached in the power of the Holy Spirit, in the simplicity of everyday language, had done its work. 'So mightily grew the word of God and prevailed' (19:20). Four things in verses 13-20 are set before us by God the Holy Spirit for our learning and admonition.

1. An example of men who make merchandise of the gospel (19:13-16)

The sons of Sceva were vagabond Jews, gypsies who travelled from city to city practising witchcraft in the name of God! They claimed to tell men's fortunes by astrological signs, cast evil or good spells on people, conjure up the spirits of the dead and cast out demons. To give some credibility to their work they claimed that their magic was passed on from one generation to another since the days of Solomon. These demonic people were active in our Lord's day (Matthew 12:27). They were active in Paul's day. And their successors are active today. Beware of the occult. Do not toy with witchcraft, astrology, etc.. God commands us to have nothing to do with such people (Leviticus 19:31; 20:6; Deuteronomy 18:10, 11).

These men did whatever they had to do to make money and to gain influence. When they saw the power Paul possessed by the name of Christ (19:11, 12), they decided to imitate his power and tried to cast out demons by the name of 'Jesus whom Paul preacheth' (19:13). They had no regard for the honour of Christ, his Word, or the souls of men. But if it could get them gain, they were willing to prostitute anything, even the things of God. We have many like these sons of Sceva today in pulpits, on radio and on television. Like the wilfully ignorant multitudes in Ephesus, multitudes today follow them, send them money and keep them in business. Those charlatans are money-grubbing, self-serving false prophets who willingly sell the gospel of Christ and the glory of God for their own interests (Jeremiah 5:30, 31; 6:13, 14; Isaiah 56:10, 11). Like self-serving politicians, the preachers of this age keep their ears to the ground and say exactly what people want to hear (2 Timothy 4:3, 4; 2 Corinthians 11:14, 15). They will do or say whatever they have to in order to get a name for themselves, a crowd to follow them and money in their coffers. Have nothing to do with the religious hullabaloo of this age. God is not in it (2 John 10, 11). As the sons of Sceva were exposed, even by the demons of hell, God will expose the modem sons of Sceva, if not in this world, in the world to come (Matthew 7:21-23).

2. An example of God's overruling providence (19:17)

When these sons of Sceva went running out of the house, beaten and naked, everyone in Ephesus heard about it. The demon in that man, being forced by the Son of God to do so, confessed his subjection to Christ and to his servant Paul by the power of Christ's name (19:15). Thus the evil the sons of Sceva thought to do was overruled by our sovereign Lord for the glory of his own great name. We worship a God who is sovereign (Psalm 76:10). No creature in heaven, earth, or hell can wiggle a finger without his decree and direction. 'The Most High ruleth!' (Daniel 4:32; Psalm 115:3; 135:6; Isaiah 46:9-11; Lamentations 3:37). Even the evil that men do, he turns to good!

3. An example of true repentance (19:18-20)

As a result of what happened to the sons of Sceva the curiosity of many was aroused, and they came to hear Paul preach the gospel of Christ. When they heard the gospel, God saved many and gave them faith in Christ (Romans 10:17). Three marks of true repentance were displayed in these people.

First, they believed on the Lord Jesus Christ (19:18). They trusted his righteousness, his redemption and his rule. They trusted Christ alone for all their salvation (1 Corinthians 1:30).

Secondly, they confessed faith in Christ (19:18). This was not a confession of sin in Paul's ear, as if he were a priest, but a public confession of faith in Christ by believer's baptism (Matthew 3:6; Romans 6:3-6).

Thirdly, they publicly denounced their former religion of works, superstition and will-worship (19:19). Being saved by God's free grace in Christ, they denounced the religion that had held them in bondage for so long. They did so by making a bonfire to burn their books of false religion and witchcraft.

Why did they go to such extreme measures?

1. To show their indignation and contempt for their former religion.
2. To show their determination never to return to it.
3. To put as great a distance as they could between themselves and those who continued in the ways of darkness.
4. To prevent others from being led astray.
5. To show their complete allegiance to Christ and his gospel.

4. An example of Christ's conquest by the gospel (19:20)

I cannot help thinking that above all else, this incident at Ephesus is recorded here by inspiration to encourage God's church and his servants to go on preaching the gospel. Luke is saying, 'Carry the gospel of Christ into the field of battle and make war against the gates of hell. As you preach the grace of God, the Son of God rides forth on his white stallion, conquering and to conquer. Thus the mighty Word of God will prevail!'

Acts 19:21 After these things were ended, Paul purposed in the spirit, when he had passed through Macedonia and Achaia, to go to Jerusalem, saying, After I have been there, I must also see Rome.

Acts 19:22 So he sent into Macedonia two of them that ministered unto him, Timotheus and Erastus; but he himself stayed in Asia for a season.

Acts 19:23 And the same time there arose no small stir about that way.

Acts 19:24 For a certain man named Demetrius, a silversmith, which made silver shrines for Diana, brought no small gain unto the craftsmen;

Acts 19:25 Whom he called together with the workmen of like occupation, and said, Sirs, ye know that by this craft we have our wealth.

Acts 19:26 Moreover ye see and hear, that not alone at Ephesus, but almost throughout all Asia, this Paul hath persuaded and turned away much people, saying that they be no gods, which are made with hands:

Acts 19:27 So that not only this our craft is in danger to be set at nought; but also that the temple of the great goddess Diana should be despised, and her magnificence should be destroyed, whom all Asia and the world worshippeth.

Acts 19:28 And when they heard these sayings, they were full of wrath, and cried out, saying, Great is Diana of the Ephesians.

Acts 19:29 And the whole city was filled with confusion: and having caught Gaius and Aristarchus, men of Macedonia, Paul's companions in travel, they rushed with one accord into the theatre.

Acts 19:30 And when Paul would have entered in unto the people, the disciples suffered him not.

Acts 19:31 And certain of the chief of Asia, which were his friends, sent unto him, desiring him that he would not adventure himself into the theatre.

Acts 19:32 Some therefore cried one thing, and some another: for the assembly was confused; and the more part knew not wherefore they were come together.

Acts 19:33 And they drew Alexander out of the multitude, the Jews putting him forward. And Alexander beckoned with the hand, and would have made his defence unto the people.

Acts 19:34 But when they knew that he was a Jew, all with one voice about the space of two hours cried out, Great is Diana of the Ephesians.

Acts 19:35 And when the townclerk had appeased the people, he said, Ye men of Ephesus, what man is there that knoweth not how that the city of the Ephesians is a worshipper of the great goddess Diana, and of the image which fell down from Jupiter?

Acts 19:36 Seeing then that these things cannot be spoken against, ye ought to be quiet, and to do nothing rashly.

Acts 19:37 For ye have brought hither these men, which are neither robbers of churches, nor yet blasphemers of your goddess.

Acts 19:38 Wherefore if Demetrius, and the craftsmen which are with him, have a matter against any man, the law is open, and there are deputies: let them implead one another.

Acts 19:39 But if ye enquire any thing concerning other matters, it shall be determined in a lawful assembly.

Acts 19:40 For we are in danger to be called in question for this day's uproar, there being no cause whereby we may give an account of this concourse.

Acts 19:41 And when he had thus spoken, he dismissed the assembly.

Chapter 57

Ephesus: A Lesson In Divine Providence

Acts 19:21-41

The uproar of the multitudes against the saints of God at Ephesus was no accident. It was not the result of men being beyond God's control. Rather, it was one event among many by which the Lord our God sovereignly accomplished, and is accomplishing, his purpose of grace. The uproar came to pass because wicked men, with wicked hearts, for wicked purposes, set themselves in opposition to the preaching of the gospel of God's free grace in Christ. God overruled their wickedness for the accomplishment of his good designs. Here are four basic, foundation truths of Holy Scripture by which believing hearts are sustained with peace in the midst of earthly troubles.

1. The Lord our God is totally sovereign

He has the right and the power to do what he will with all things, and he always exercises his right of sovereignty (Job 42:2; Isaiah 14:24, 27; 46:9-11; 55:11; Psalm 115:3; 135:6; Jeremiah 32:17; Daniel 4:35-37; Matthew 20:15; Romans 9:11-23; Ephesians 1:11, 22). In creation, in providence and in grace, the Lord our God always has his way.

2. Our God's purpose of grace and predestination is the rule of all things

His plan is eternal (2 Timothy 1:9; 2 Thessalonians 2:13; Matthew 25:34), unalterable (Numbers 23:19; Malachi 3:6; James 1:17), and all-inclusive. Nothing happens in time except that which God purposed in eternity (Genesis 50:20; Isaiah 45:7, Proverbs 16:1-4, 9, 33; 21:1; Amos 3:6).

3. God rules all things in heaven, earth and hell to accomplish his eternal purpose of predestination (Romans 8:28-30; 11:36; Ephesians 1:11)

God is not a mere spectator standing on the sidelines, rooting and cheering for the accomplishment of his goals. He is everywhere, sustaining all things, ruling all things and bringing all things to their predestined end. The tiny sparrow appears to us as an insignificant thing. Its flight looks giddy and

267

haphazard. But the sparrow does not light upon any branch or fall to the ground without God's direction. 'God's all-wise providence hath before appointed what bough the sparrow shall perch upon, what grains it shall pick up, where it shall lodge and where it shall build, on what it shall live, and where it shall die,' said Augustus Toplady. God's providence rules everywhere and everything absolutely: the physical world (Isaiah 40:12; Nahum 1:3); the animal world (Daniel 6:22; Matthew 10:29); the nations of the world (Psalm 33:9-11; Isaiah 40:15; Daniel 2:21; 4:17); all the people of the world (Proverbs 16:9; 21:1; Acts 18:9, 10; Exodus 12:36; 2 Samuel 16:10, 11; Psalm 76:10; Exodus 14:17; Acts 4:27, 28); and even Satan and the demons of hell (Job 1:6-12; 2:1-6). Everything in the universe is under the rule of God — everything!

4. God rules everything in providence to accomplish the salvation of his elect and the glory of his own great name (Romans 8:28; 11:36)

Nothing in creation is left to chance, luck, fate, or the will of man. Everything is directed by God so that in the end all his people will be with Christ and like Christ (Romans 8:29, 30), and everything that has ever been will praise him (Revelation 5:13). It was no accident that brought Rebecca to the well to meet Abraham's servant. It was not a streak of luck that brought Joseph to Egypt 'to save much people alive'. It was not by chance that Pharaoh's daughter found Moses in the ark and preserved him alive. It was not blind fate that directed the millstone which crushed Abimelech's head. Every event in history is directed by the hand of God. He even gives the lightning the charge to strike its mark (Job 28:26; 37:3; 38:25, 35).

We shall now study the events recorded in Acts 19:21-41 seeking to see how that the hand of God sovereignly ruled, even in the uproar at Ephesus; and understand that the unseen hand of divine providence rules all things today for the good of God's elect and the glory of his name. Here, God the Holy Spirit teaches us four things.

First, all who are born of God are led by the Spirit of God (19:21, 22). As it was the Spirit of God who led Simeon to the temple to see Christ (Luke 2:27), so it was the Spirit of God who led Paul from place to place preaching the gospel of Christ (20:22) and so it is to this day. The steps of God's people are ordered by the Holy Spirit (Psalm 37:23; Romans 8:14).

We should note that Timothy and Erastus ministered to Paul and to God's saints under Paul's direction (19:22). They subjected themselves to the Lord's apostle, being themselves filled with the Spirit (Ephesians 5:18, 21; Hebrews 13:7, 17). Those who are led by the Spirit submit themselves to those whom God has placed in authority over them.

Secondly, the gospel of Christ always stirs up the wrath of men (19:23-28). Men are never indifferent to the message or the messengers of God's free grace. Whenever the gospel of Christ is preached in the power of the Holy Spirit, those who hear it will either bow to the claims of Christ or rise up in opposition against his ambassador (Matthew 10:22, 34). 'There arose no small stir about that way.' The gospel of Christ is distinct from the religions of men. The way of grace, the way of Christ, is not one way among many, but the way, 'that way', altogether different from the ways of men. All the religions of men make the way to God and salvation dependent in some way upon man. But the ways of free-will, works religion are the ways of death (Proverbs 14:12; 16:25). The gospel of Christ makes the way to God and salvation to be Christ alone (John 10:9; 14:6). We notice two things:

1. The business of religion has always been, as it is today, a popular, profitable business (19:24, 25). These men made and sold religious trinkets, such as icons, images, etc., just as many today sell crosses, images, religious pictures, etc..
2. The gods which men make and cherish are puny, helpless things, worthy of contempt rather than praise (19:26-28; Isaiah 46:5-7; 1 Kings 18:27-29).

Thirdly, trials and persecutions are for the good of God's people (19:29-34). Yes, even the wrath of wicked men is used by God for the good of his elect (Psalm 76:10). By means of this uproar and persecution, God's church was refined. The chaff was separated from the wheat. In the midst of the trial, Gaius and Aristarchus stood firm, while Alexander the coppersmith withered before the fire (1 Timothy 1:19, 20; 2 Timothy 4:15, 16). Yet God stopped his mouth (19:33, 34).

Fourthly, the Lord knows how to deliver his people out of their troubles (19:35-41; Psalm 18:1-7, 43-50). The Lord God used the priests of the temple of Diana (19:31) and a frightened town clerk to preserve his people from a raging mob. Matthew Poole comments, 'Thus God, one way or other, sometimes by friends, and sometimes by foes, kept his church and people from being ruined; and his hand is not shortened now.' If God will give us grace to understand that all things are under his absolute control and to trust his wisdom, love and grace towards us in Christ, we will worship and trust him at all times and give thanks to him at all times, in all things and for all things (1 Thessalonians 5:16-18).

Acts 20:1 And after the uproar was ceased, Paul called unto him the disciples, and embraced them, and departed for to go into Macedonia.

Acts 20:2 And when he had gone over those parts, and had given them much exhortation, he came into Greece,

Acts 20:3 And there abode three months. And when the Jews laid wait for him, as he was about to sail into Syria, he purposed to return through Macedonia.

Acts 20:4 And there accompanied him into Asia Sopater of Berea; and of the Thessalonians, Aristarchus and Secundus; and Gaius of Derbe, and Timotheus; and of Asia, Tychicus and Trophimus.

Acts 20:5 These going before tarried for us at Troas.

Acts 20:6 And we sailed away from Philippi after the days of unleavened bread, and came unto them to Troas in five days; where we abode seven days.

Acts 20:7 And upon the first day of the week, when the disciples came together to break bread, Paul preached unto them, ready to depart on the morrow; and continued his speech until midnight.

Acts 20:8 And there were many lights in the upper chamber, where they were gathered together.

Acts 20:9 And there sat in a window a certain young man named Eutychus, being fallen into a deep sleep: and as Paul was long preaching, he sunk down with sleep, and fell down from the third loft, and was taken up dead.

Acts 20:10 And Paul went down, and fell on him, and embracing him said, Trouble not yourselves; for his life is in him.

Acts 20:11 When he therefore was come up again, and had broken bread, and eaten, and talked a long while, even till break of day, so he departed.

Acts 20:12 And they brought the young man alive, and were not a little comforted.

Acts 20:13 And we went before to ship, and sailed unto Assos, there intending to take in Paul: for so had he appointed, minding himself to go afoot.

Acts 20:14 And when he met with us at Assos, we took him in, and came to Mitylene.

Acts 20:15 And we sailed thence, and came the next day over against Chios; and the next day we arrived at Samos, and tarried at Trogyllium; and the next day we came to Miletus.

Acts 20:16 For Paul had determined to sail by Ephesus, because he would not spend the time in Asia: for he hasted, if it were possible for him, to be at Jerusalem the day of Pentecost.

Chapter 58

Hurrying To Jerusalem With The Gospel

Acts 20:1-16

In the previous chapter we read about the uproar at Ephesus. The angry mob stood for more than two hours crying out, 'Great is Diana of the Ephesians.' Finally, 'The town clerk ... appeased the people' and 'dismissed the assembly.' We pick up the story in the opening verses of chapter 20.

1. Paul's determination to go to Jerusalem (20:1-16)

Here we have another of Luke's rapid descriptions of Paul's ministry. He is leading up to the apostle's farewell message to the Ephesian elders at Miletus, but in these verses Luke very quickly tells us that after the uproar at Ephesus, Paul went right on doing what God had called him to do. He spent the next few months travelling, by land and sea, through Asia, Macedonia and Greece, visiting the churches which had been established during his earlier ministry. Everywhere he went he did the same thing. In the synagogues, in the streets, in the churches and in the market-places, Paul preached Christ to the people. But all the while he was hurrying to Jerusalem (20:16).

Why did Paul have this preoccupation with Jerusalem? God distinctly appointed him to be the apostle to the Gentiles. Yet, in reading through the book of Acts, we see him repeatedly determined to return to Jerusalem on the feast days. Was this, as some have suggested, because he had a hard time breaking with the past and shaking off the grave-clothes of dead Judaism? Not at all! The apostle Paul was forthright and constant in his declaration of the believer's freedom from legal, ceremonial, earthly ordinances (Romans 6:14, 15; 7:1; 10:4; Galatians 5:2, 4; Colossians 2:8-23). Rather, Paul was determined, if at all possible, to be in Jerusalem on the feast days, not to observe those feasts, but because he knew that on those days he would be able to preach the gospel to more of his kinsmen than at any other time. And he was determined to do everything in his power to see them saved by the grace of God (Romans 9:1-3; 10:1-4).

2. The message of the Bible

Wherever he went, the message Paul preached was Jesus Christ and him crucified (1 Corinthians 2:2). Sometimes he preached to Jews; sometimes to Gentiles. He preached to large crowds of lost people and to small bands of believers. He preached to learned philosophers and a small band of women. But his message was always the same. He preached Christ, the whole of Christ, and only Christ to all people. Sometimes he was a little long-winded, preaching until midnight. Sometimes people grew tired while he was preaching and fell asleep (20:9). Often he was persecuted for his message. But Paul never changed it. It was always Jesus Christ and him crucified.

3. The Bible, the Word of God, is entirely about the Lord Jesus Christ

The Bible is not a book about science, history, politics, morality, or even religious dogma. It is a book about Christ (Luke 24:27, 44-47). Christ is the living Word of whom the written Word speaks. It is the business and responsibility of every gospel preacher to preach and teach nothing else but Jesus Christ and him crucified. To do so is to faithfully preach and teach 'all the counsel of God' (20:27; 1 Corinthians 2:2). All the prophecies of the Old Testament are predictions of Christ. All the sacrifices and ceremonies of the law were pictures of Christ. All the temporal deliverances of individual believers and the nation of Israel were illustrations of the redemption of God's elect by Christ. The law was given by Moses to show man his need of Christ. The four Gospels record the history of Christ and his teachings, and the epistles explain the meaning of our Lord's teachings. Every book of the Bible, every chapter, every verse, every line, every word in Holy Scripture is designed by God the Holy Spirit to reveal Christ to his people. Stop studying the Bible to find out facts and buttress doctrine. Study the Word of God with the desire to know him of whom the Scriptures speak (John 5:39). If you find any text in God's book that does not immediately cause your heart to look to Christ, you do not yet understand that text. The doctrine of the Bible is Christ. The law of the Bible is Christ. The gospel of the Bible is Christ. Do you see that? Any doctrine divorced from Christ is heresy, a mere show of intellectualism. Any precept divorced from Christ is self-righteousness. Paul went everywhere preaching Christ. And any sermon that does not point men to Christ ought never to have been preached. Any doctrine that does not have Christ for its essence must not be believed. Any precept that is not motivated by love for, and faith in, Christ must not be obeyed. From Genesis 1:1 to Revelation 22:21, 'Christ is all, and in all!'

272

4. A plot discovered (20:1-6)

Wherever Paul went preaching the gospel of Christ he met with opposition. Proud flesh cannot tolerate the message of salvation by grace alone through the merits of Christ alone. Paul again discovered a plot against his life. While in Greece the enemies of the cross 'laid wait for him' (20:2, 3). 'Over the centuries of the Christian church the lives of God's servants often have been in danger,' wrote Donald Grey Barnhouse. 'Many have been martyred for their faith in Jesus Christ. Others have suffered intensely. God has never promised a bed of roses. Remember what Paul himself wrote to the Philippians: "For unto you it is given in the behalf of Christ, not only to believe on him, but also to suffer for his sake" (1:29) ... As a matter of fact, the church has always been at its purest when it has had to face suffering and martyrdom for Jesus Christ.'

Paul left Greece after three months. As he prepared to sail to Syria, he learned about the plot against him. So he took Sopater and Luke, his travelling companions, and went by land through Macedonia to Philippi, and sailed from Philippi to Troas. There they met up with their other co-workers and stayed for seven days.

5. A communion service on the Lord's day (20:7-12)

Notice that the disciples came together for worship on 'the first day of the week' rather than the seventh. Like many things in this transitional period, sabbath observance was terminated gradually. The new day of worship, the Lord's day (Revelation 1:10), was established by the resurrection of our Lord (Matthew 28:1). Sunday is not the 'Christian sabbath'. We are expressly forbidden to observe a legalistic sabbath day (Colossians 2:16) in this day of grace. Christ is our Sabbath. We cease from our own works and rest in him by faith (Hebrews 4:9, 10). Yet it is clear that the established day of worship in the New Testament was Sunday (Acts 20:7; 1 Corinthians 16:2). On this day the church gathered to observe the Lord's Supper and listen to the preaching of the gospel. The communion service was a very simple part of public worship, not an elaborate ceremony. When the saints of God met for worship on the Lord's day, they passed around a loaf of unleavened bread and a cup of wine and every believer took a portion for him or herself.

There was no restricted or closed communion in the New Testament! Here disciples from many different places observed the Lord's Table together because in Christ all true believers are truly one. They did not examine one another to see who was worthy to participate in the ordinance, but each believer examined him or herself before the Lord (1 Corinthians 11:28).

Acts 20:17 And from Miletus he sent to Ephesus, and called the elders of the church.

Acts 20:18 And when they were come to him, he said unto them, Ye know, from the first day that I came into Asia, after what manner I have been with you at all seasons,

Acts 20:19 Serving the Lord with all humility of mind, and with many tears, and temptations, which befell me by the lying in wait of the Jews:

Acts 20:20 And how I kept back nothing that was profitable unto you, but have shewed you, and have taught you publickly, and from house to house,

Acts 20:21 Testifying both to the Jews, and also to the Greeks, repentance toward God, and faith toward our Lord Jesus Christ.

Acts 20:22 And now, behold, I go bound in the spirit unto Jerusalem, not knowing the things that shall befall me there:

Acts 20:23 Save that the Holy Ghost witnesseth in every city, saying that bonds and afflictions abide me.

Acts 20:24 But none of these things move me, neither count I my life dear unto myself, so that I might finish my course with joy, and the ministry, which I have received of the Lord Jesus, to testify the gospel of the grace of God.

Acts 20:25 And now, behold, I know that ye all, among whom I have gone preaching the kingdom of God, shall see my face no more.

Acts 20:26 Wherefore I take you to record this day, that I am pure from the blood of all men.

Acts 20:27 For I have not shunned to declare unto you all the counsel of God.

Acts 20:28 Take heed therefore unto yourselves, and to all the flock, over the which the Holy Ghost hath made you overseers, to feed the church of God, which he hath purchased with his own blood.

Acts 20:29 For I know this, that after my departing shall grievous wolves enter in among you, not sparing the flock.

Acts 20:30 Also of your own selves shall men arise, speaking perverse things, to draw away disciples after them.

Acts 20:31 Therefore watch, and remember, that by the space of three years I ceased not to warn every one night and day with tears.

Acts 20:32 And now, brethren, I commend you to God, and to the word of his grace, which is able to build you up, and to give you an inheritance among all them which are sanctified.

Acts 20:33 I have coveted no man's silver, or gold, or apparel.

Acts 20:34 Yea, ye yourselves know, that these hands have ministered unto my necessities, and to them that were with me.

Acts 20:35 I have shewed you all things, how that so labouring ye ought to support the weak, and to remember the words of the Lord Jesus, how he said, It is more blessed to give than to receive.

Acts 20:36 And when he had thus spoken, he kneeled down, and prayed with them all.

Acts 20:37 And they all wept sore, and fell on Paul's neck, and kissed him,

Acts 20:38 Sorrowing most of all for the words which he spake, that they should see his face no more. And they accompanied him unto the ship.

Chapter 59

Farewell To The Ephesian Elders

Acts 20:17-38

Sometimes God places a man in a field of service for life to preach the gospel and rule the church of God in a given place permanently. The man who is truly the servant of God will be faithful in the place of his calling. He cannot be driven away by hardships, trials, or opposition, and he cannot be drawn away by the allurements of personal gain, worldly comfort, or greater recognition. Preachers who use churches as stepping-stones on the road to ministerial success are not God's servants. They are hirelings who sell their services to the highest bidder.

However, the Lord sometimes sends a man to a place to do a specific work. When his work has been accomplished, the Lord sends him to another place to accomplish other things. Faithful men move from place to place to preach the gospel as they are led by the Spirit of God. Their place of service is not determined by anything except their desire to serve the interests of Christ's kingdom according to the will of God. Every preacher who is sent by God is a spokesman for God, and is to be received and honoured as such (1 Thessalonians 5:12, 13; Hebrews 13:7, 17). However, he is only a temporary spokesman, a voice crying in the wilderness (John 1:23). No matter how useful, influential, or beneficial a man's ministry is in a given place, it is only temporary. It will come to an end, either by death or by the direction of God the Holy Spirit. Yet the cause of Christ, the church of God and the gospel of God's free grace in Christ continue. Thus it becomes the duty of God's servants to prepare the people they serve for a continued, uninterrupted, vibrant ministry when they are removed.

That is what Paul is doing in Acts 20:17-38. He had preached the gospel of Christ at Ephesus for three years. The Lord had blessed his labours to the conversion of many. But the time had come for him to move elsewhere. His work at Ephesus was done. The Spirit of God led him to Jerusalem. Paul was leaving behind a large congregation that required the labours of several preachers (elders). Probably, the church at Ephesus met in several groups throughout the city, with each congregation having its own pastor/teacher. The apostle Paul called for all the elders at Ephesus to meet him at Miletus, where he gave them his solemn farewell message.

1. Paul was an exemplary gospel preacher (20:17-27)

Here Paul sets himself before the elders at Ephesus as an example of what every gospel preacher ought to be, both in life and in doctrine. He did not speak with arrogance, but with honest confidence (2 Timothy 4:6-8). He had conscientiously done what God sent him to do. He had been an example to these men of what he expected from them, and they all knew it. They knew him to be a gracious, sober-minded, faithful man. He was not a self-seeking, self-promoting, self-serving religious charlatan (1 Corinthians 4:1-5). Both the tenor of his life and the doctrine of his lips demonstrated his devotion to the gospel and the glory of Christ (Philippians 4:9).

First, in his daily life, as in the pulpit, Paul was the servant of the Lord Jesus Christ (20:18, 19). He made no pretence of perfection, but he did live blamelessly before men, as one whose manner of life was above reproach. That simply means that in the tenor of his life Paul was evidently a man consecrated to Christ. That is what God requires of every gospel preacher (1 Timothy 3:2-7). Paul served the Lord with humility, knowing his own insufficiency in the flesh (2 Corinthians 2:16) and the sufficiency of God's grace (2 Corinthians 3:5; 12:9). He served the people of God with sincerity. He was faithful to God and men in the midst of many trials and temptations (2 Corinthians 4:7-14). He was consistent in his devotion to Christ, not spasmodic. For three years the men to whom he was speaking had watched him day and night. They found him to be stedfast, never wavering. He was a preacher whose doctrine was demonstrated in a life of devotion.

Secondly, Paul's preaching, like his life, exemplified what the servant of God must be and do (20:20-27). He came to Ephesus to preach the gospel of Christ to the people of that city; and he had been faithful to his calling. His message was constant. In public and in private, he preached Jesus Christ crucified, teaching 'repentance toward God, and faith toward our Lord Jesus Christ' (20:20, 21). Paul never deviated from his message (1 Corinthians 2:1, 2; 9:16). His motive was pure (20:22-25). Knowing by divine revelation the troubles that awaited him, Paul would not be deterred from the work to which he was called (21:4, 11). Pray for the grace and commitment to the gospel that Paul demonstrated! (v. 24). His hands were clean (20:26, 27). As God's appointed watch man he had faithfully proclaimed the word of life and grace God gave him (Ezekiel 3:15-21; 33:1-16). No one perished because Paul kept back the Word of God! Every gospel preacher must live by the gospel. The man who preaches the gospel must live by gospel principles as one who is dedicated to the glory of God. He must preach the gospel. He must, with honesty, plainness and boldness, preach the gospel to all who will hear him, never hedging, never trimming his message.

2. Paul lays a great burden of responsibility upon all who are ordained by God to preach the gospel (20:28-31)

This charge is specifically addressed to pastors, but its implications extend to all who are in positions of leadership in local churches (elders, teachers, deacons, missionaries and evangelists).

It is the responsibility of every pastor to be an overseer, a spiritual shepherd and ruler in the church of God (20:28). The church belongs to Christ. He bought it with his precious, sin-atoning blood. It does not belong to the pastor or the people. It belongs to Christ, and must ever be regarded as his peculiar possession. Pastors are under shepherds to Christ, placed in the church by the gifts and graces of God (Ephesians 4:8-16). God raises up chosen men, gives them the gifts necessary for the work he has for them to do and places them where he wants them in his vineyard (Jeremiah 3:15). Yet the work of the gospel ministry is a laborious responsibility that demands the preacher be diligent in prayer, study and preaching and watchful over his own soul (1 Timothy 4:12-16; 2 Timothy 4:1-5). As Christ's under-shepherd, it is the pastor's task to watch over, protect, feed and rule the church of God. He must watch over men's souls, protect them from danger, feed them with knowledge and understanding by the gospel and rule the house of God by the preaching of the gospel and personal walk (Hebrews 13:7, 17; 1 Peter 5:1-3).

The pastor's work is necessary because the people of God in this world, like sheep in the wilderness, face many dangers (20:29-31). Many wolves rise up within the walls of professed Christianity that would devour the flock (free-willism, legalism, ritualism, etc.). It is the pastor's responsibility, by sound instruction in gospel doctrine, to protect Christ's sheep from the wolves of false religion.

3. Only God himself can preserve his church in the gospel (20:32-38)

Though he had faithfully laboured among the Ephesians, preaching the gospel for three years to them, though he left the church in the hands of capable men, Paul knew that only God himself and the gospel of his grace could effectually preserve the church in the faith of Christ. So he commended the church to God and to the word of his grace. He told them to look to God and to the word of his grace (his gospel) for direction (20:32). He taught them to measure all who claimed to be gospel preachers by his own example of faithfulness and generosity (20:33-35). As he left Ephesus, he prayed with his brethren and for them (20:36-38; Ephesians 1:15-23; 3:14-21).

Acts 20:17 And from Miletus he sent to Ephesus, and called the elders of the church.

Acts 20:18 And when they were come to him, he said unto them, Ye know, from the first day that I came into Asia, after what manner I have been with you at all seasons,

Acts 20:19 Serving the Lord with all humility of mind, and with many tears, and temptations, which befell me by the lying in wait of the Jews:

Acts 20:20 And how I kept back nothing that was profitable unto you, but have shewed you, and have taught you publickly, and from house to house,

Acts 20:21 Testifying both to the Jews, and also to the Greeks, repentance toward God, and faith toward our Lord Jesus Christ.

Acts 20:22 And now, behold, I go bound in the spirit unto Jerusalem, not knowing the things that shall befall me there:

Acts 20:23 Save that the Holy Ghost witnesseth in every city, saying that bonds and afflictions abide me.

Acts 20:24 But none of these things move me, neither count I my life dear unto myself, so that I might finish my course with joy, and the ministry, which I have received of the Lord Jesus, to testify the gospel of the grace of God.

Acts 20:25 And now, behold, I know that ye all, among whom I have gone preaching the kingdom of God, shall see my face no more.

Acts 20:26 Wherefore I take you to record this day, that I am pure from the blood of all men.

Acts 20:27 For I have not shunned to declare unto you all the counsel of God.

Acts 20:28 Take heed therefore unto yourselves, and to all the flock, over the which the Holy Ghost hath made you overseers, to feed the church of God, which he hath purchased with his own blood.

Acts 20:29 For I know this, that after my departing shall grievous wolves enter in among you, not sparing the flock.

Acts 20:30 Also of your own selves shall men arise, speaking perverse things, to draw away disciples after them.

Acts 20:31 Therefore watch, and remember, that by the space of three years I ceased not to warn every one night and day with tears.

Acts 20:32 And now, brethren, I commend you to God, and to the word of his grace, which is able to build you up, and to give you an inheritance among all them which are sanctified.

Acts 20:33 I have coveted no man's silver, or gold, or apparel.

Acts 20:34 Yea, ye yourselves know, that these hands have ministered unto my necessities, and to them that were with me.

Acts 20:35 I have shewed you all things, how that so labouring ye ought to support the weak, and to remember the words of the Lord Jesus, how he said, It is more blessed to give than to receive.

Acts 20:36 And when he had thus spoken, he kneeled down, and prayed with them all.

Acts 20:37 And they all wept sore, and fell on Paul's neck, and kissed him,

Acts 20:38 Sorrowing most of all for the words which he spake, that they should see his face no more. And they accompanied him unto the ship.

Chapter 60

Five Christian Graces

Acts 20:17-38

Grace makes people gracious. Grace experienced in the heart causes grace to flow from the heart. Our Lord teaches us plainly that all who know the love of God in reality love one another (1 John 3:10, 16-18; 4:8; 5:1), and that all who have experienced God's forgiveness are forgiving of others (Matthew 6:14, 15). All who are born of God are new creatures in Christ (2 Corinthians 5:17). All true believers have been given by the Holy Spirit a new nature which is gracious (Galatians 5:22, 23). Believers are not perfect. The child of God has a nature of flesh and sin, with which he has a continual warfare (Romans 7:14-25). However, in the tenor of his life, a believer is a person who walks not after the flesh but after the Spirit.

Here are five graces, five God-given spiritual qualities, which are characteristics of all true believers.

1. Humility (20:19)

Paul, speaking by the inspiration of God, says he served the Lord 'with all humility of mind'. Without humility there is no salvation (Psalm 34:18; 51:17; Isaiah 66:2; Matthew 5:3-5; 18:3, 4; Philippians 3:3). And no man can serve God or the cause of his glory in this world without this God-given 'humbleness of mind' (Colossians 3:12). Anything done for Christ must be done with humility (Matthew 6:3, 5, 16, 33). Most people seem to think that humility is demonstrated by a timid, weak, cowardly spirit, or that it is to be seen in an unwillingness to be bold, decisive and uncompromising. Nothing could be further from the truth. Moses was none of those things, though he was the meekest, humblest man on the face of the earth (Numbers 12:3). Humility is not an act. It is an attitude of the heart. Humility is brokenness of heart before God by reason of sin and in gratitude for his love, mercy and grace to sinners in Christ. Here are six things revealed in the Word of God as characteristics of humility.

279

1. Humility is a realization of personal unworthiness by reason of one's own sin before God (Job 42:1, 2; Psalm 51:4, 5). It is not a show of words which sound humble, but are really designed to gain praise. Rather, it is a heartfelt unworthiness before the holy Lord God (Luke 18:13; Isaiah 6:5).

2. Humility is a renunciation of all merit and personal righteousness in the sight of God (Philippians 3:9). No man's heart is humbled before God who imagines he may merit God's favour above another, or his righteousnesses are better than filthy rags in God's sight (Isaiah 64:6).

3. Humility is an inexpressible gratitude of heart to God for his abundant, amazing grace to sinners in Christ (Psalm 116:12, 16). It causes a person to live with a sense of delightful obligation to the Lord (2 Corinthians 9:15).

4. Humility is a willing submission and devotion of one's heart to the Lord Jesus Christ that cries, 'Lord, what wilt thou have me to do?' (9:6). It is devotion to Christ as Lord, submission to his providential rule of all things and a determination of heart to obey him and honour him regardless of cost.

5. Humility gladly ascribes the whole work of salvation to God's free and sovereign grace through Christ (1 Corinthians 15:10).

6. Humility is the mind of Christ in a person which causes him to love his brethren, esteem them more highly than himself, prefer their honour to his own and gladly give himself to serve their interests (Philippians 2:3-8).

2. Repentance (20:21)

'Repentance toward God and faith toward our Lord Jesus Christ' always go hand in hand. You cannot have one without the other. It is only through 'repentance toward God and faith toward our Lord Jesus Christ' that sinners obtain eternal salvation. Both are necessary. Both are vital. Both are gifts of God's grace. True repentance is towards God. Paul did not say, 'I preached repentance.' He said, 'I preached repentance towards God,' because there is a repentance that is not towards God. There is a legal repentance that is no more than a sense of guilt, a dread of God's wrath and a fear of hell. But repentance towards God is produced by the goodness of God (Romans 2:4), not the wrath of God. It comes from the revelation of redemption by Christ (Zechariah 12:10), not from the fear of judgment. Repentance, in essence, is a change of heart towards God, as illustrated in the prodigal son (Luke 15:14-20), the tax collector (Luke 18:13) and David (Psalm 51:4). Repentance is the honest acknowledgement and confession of sin to God (1 John 1:9). It is an acknowledgement by a person that he has offended God by his sin, his very heart is enmity against God and it is right for God to punish his sin (Psalm 51:4; Romans 8:7). Repentance is sitting in judgment with God against yourself, abhorring yourself by reason of your sin and pleading for mercy on the basis of pure grace by the merits of Christ alone. Only God can cause a person thus to repent (Acts 5:31; Jeremiah 31:18; Lamentations 5:21).

3. Faith (20:21)

'Faith toward our Lord Jesus Christ' is the gift, work and operation of God the Holy Spirit within saved sinners (Ephesians 1:19; 2:8; Colossians 2:12). Faith towards Christ is the believer's confidence in Christ as Saviour and Lord. It involves knowledge of the person and work of Christ, for you cannot trust a Saviour you do not know. The knowledge at the heart of saving faith comes by hearing the Word of God preached (Romans 10:17) in the power of the Holy Spirit (1 Thessalonians 1:5). Faith is the agreement of a person's heart with the gospel, which causes him to trust the blood and righteousness of Christ alone as the grounds of his acceptance with God. Both repentance and faith are continual, progressive, growing and persevering graces. They are not isolated acts or events in life. They are characteristic attitudes of every believer's life. The believer continually looks to God with repentance and continually looks to God through Christ in faith, trusting his propitiatory sacrifice, providential rule, heavenly intercession and Word of promise.

4. Commitment (20:24)

Believers are men and women who are consecrated to Christ and his gospel. They are committed to him. As men and women who love one another commit themselves to one another in marriage, so believers, loving Christ, commit themselves to him. Paul was convinced that the gospel of God's grace and the cause of Christ's glory in this world are worthy of the ultimate sacrifice of life itself. Ultimately, he made that sacrifice (2 Timothy 4:6-8). Let every sinner saved by the grace of God follow his example. The experience of God's mercy, love and grace in Christ demands the commitment of our lives to him (Romans 12:1, 2).

5. Generosity (20:35)

God's saints are a generous, giving people. Grace makes people generous. Find a person who has the grace of God in his heart, and you will find a person who serves the cause of God and the people of God with open heart and open hand. Find a person who is tight fisted with his money, miserly with his possessions and ever seeking to increase his riches, and you will find a person who does not know God. Search the Scriptures for yourself and see if grace and generosity do not go together (James 2:14-17; 1 John 3:16-18).

Acts 20:26 Wherefore I take you to record this day, that I am pure from the blood of all men.

Acts 20:27 For I have not shunned to declare unto you all the counsel of God.

Acts 20:28 Take heed therefore unto yourselves, and to all the flock, over the which the Holy Ghost hath made you overseers, to feed the church of God, which he hath purchased with his own blood.

Acts 20:29 For I know this, that after my departing shall grievous wolves enter in among you, not sparing the flock.

Acts 20:30 Also of your own selves shall men arise, speaking perverse things, to draw away disciples after them.

Acts 20:31 Therefore watch, and remember, that by the space of three years I ceased not to warn every one night and day with tears.

Acts 20:32 And now, brethren, I commend you to God, and to the word of his grace, which is able to build you up, and to give you an inheritance among all them which are sanctified.

Acts 20:33 I have coveted no man's silver, or gold, or apparel.

Acts 20:34 Yea, ye yourselves know, that these hands have ministered unto my necessities, and to them that were with me.

Acts 20:35 I have shewed you all things, how that so labouring ye ought to support the weak, and to remember the words of the Lord Jesus, how he said, It is more blessed to give than to receive.

Chapter 61

'Take heed'

Acts 20:26-35

When Paul called the Ephesian elders together at Miletus, his object was to impart to them some final words of instruction by which they might be enabled to serve God and his people in their generation. Paul's words on that momentous occasion have been preserved for us in this chapter so that we too might know how to serve our God and Saviour, his church and his interests in our generation. If we would do so, there are certain things to which we must 'take heed', knowing that Satan will constantly attempt to draw us away from Christ by drawing us away from our responsibilities in this world. In particular, the apostle, speaking by inspiration of God the Holy Spirit, tells us that there are three things to which we must 'take heed': the ministry of the gospel, the church of God and the words of the Lord Jesus.

1. The ministry of the gospel (20:26-31)

Paul's primary purpose is instruction of elders, pastors and teachers, as to their responsibilities as God's servants. Every preacher called by God must 'take heed to the ministry which [he has] received in the Lord' to fulfil it (Colossians 4:17; 1 Timothy 4:12-16). However, it is also the responsibility of God's people to know, follow and obey those who labour among them (1 Thessalonians 5:12, 13; Hebrews 13:7, 17). Paul tells us three things about every true gospel preacher, every true pastor in the church of God.

First, God's servants are watchmen over his church and over the souls of men (20:26, 27; Hebrews 13:17; Ezekiel 3:15-21; 33:1-16). The work of a watchman is not mysterious. He has just one thing to do.

He must watch over the camp. God says, 'Thou shalt hear the word at my mouth, and warn them from me' (Ezekiel 33:7). When Paul gave account of himself, he simply said, 'I have not shunned to declare unto you all the counsel of God.' The word he received from God, he faithfully declared. He kept back nothing. That is the whole work of the ministry. A faithful pastor is a man who seeks a word from God for his people and faithfully delivers that word. He seeks and finds his message in the Bible alone and faithfully declares the message of Holy Scripture. The phrase, 'all the counsel of God', means the gospel of the crucified Redeemer (1 Corinthians 2:7). God's watchmen proclaim to men and women bound for eternity the message of salvation by grace alone, through faith alone, in Christ alone.

Secondly, pastors are the spiritual rulers and overseers of God's house (20:28). It is every pastor's responsibility to take the oversight of the church he serves (1 Peter 5:1-3). The care of the house of God is his responsibility. He is to rule the church of God as a husband is to rule his house (1 Timothy 3:4, 5). A pastor must rule by example and in love. He must win the respect of men and women, so they are willing to be ruled by him. And he must rule by the Word of God. But rule he must! The church is not to be ruled by the voice of the people, but by the voice of God through his messenger. Read Numbers 16:1-35 and see how serious God makes this matter to be!

As the overseer of God's church, it is the pastor's responsibility to feed the church. Many fleece the church. God's servants feed it with knowledge and understanding (Jeremiah 3:15). He must feed God's people with the knowledge of pure gospel doctrine and an understanding of their peculiar needs. Such knowledge and understanding can be gained only by prayer and study. The pastor must give himself wholly to this work (1 Timothy 4:12-16).

Thirdly, God's preachers are set as pastors for the protection of his church (20:29-31; Ephesians 4:14; 2 Timothy 3:1-4:5). As shepherds watch over their sheep, pastors watch over the flock of Christ's sheep to protect them from the pernicious, subtle, cunning doctrines of wolves. These wolves (false prophets) come in many guises, but they always have four things in common: they deny God's total and absolute sovereignty; they deny the effectual accomplishment of redemption by the blood of Christ; they deny the efficacy of God's grace in salvation and they give sinners something to do to make the blood of Christ and the grace of God efficacious for them personally.

2. The church of God (20:28)

The church of God is a spiritual society, a family of believers. The only bond holding its members together is their relationship to the Lord Jesus Christ. The word 'church' is used in at least three ways in the New Testament.

It is used to describe all true believers of all ages, both those of the Old Testament and those of the New, on earth and in heaven. This is what we call 'the universal church'. It is the mystical, spiritual body of which Christ is the head (Ephesians 1:22; 5:25-27; Hebrews 12:23, 24). 'Church' is also used to describe local, visible assemblies of all professed believers in a given place. In a local church are both believers and unbelievers, those who truly possess faith and those who merely profess to have faith. Yet every assembly of professed believers is a local church; 'the church of God' (Romans 16:1-5).

Finally, 'church' is used for all local churches at any given time in the world (1 Corinthians 10:32; 12:28). Not that all religions, or all denominations together, make up the church of God. However, all true churches, that worship God in the pattern and doctrine of the New Testament, are one.

In Acts 20:28 Paul is addressing the elders of a particular local assembly at Ephesus, or perhaps, as noted before, these elders were preachers from several local assemblies in the Ephesus area. He calls this body of believers 'the church of God'. Two things are here revealed about the church of God.

1. It belongs to God. He chose it (2 Thessalonians 2:13). He bought it with his own blood (Ephesians 5:25-27; Titus 2:14). And he calls it out of the world in effectual grace (Colossians 1:12-14).

2. The church of God is a flock of sheep. Before we were converted, God's saints were lost sheep, straying from him. After conversion, believers are compared to sheep because they are meek, inoffensive, patient and entirely dependent upon their Shepherd, Christ Jesus.

3. The words of our Lord Jesus Christ (20:33-35)

In verse 35 Paul refers to one of the statements made by Christ that was commonly known to his disciples, though it was nowhere recorded in the four Gospels. But, read together, verses 33-35 teach us three facts that need to be recognized and remembered.

First, God's servants are not greedy, covetous men, and they are not beggars (20:33). Paul did not seek luxury, or even comfort. He would not grovel before men. He would either be maintained by the free, voluntary gifts of God's people, or he would work to provide for his necessities. But he refused to beg!

Secondly, every believing man ought to labour as one working not for himself, but for the glory of God and to help others (20:35). Every man is responsible to work and provide for himself and his family (1 Timothy 5:8; 2 Thessalonians 3:10). We should each labour with diligence, not to amass great wealth, but, like Paul, to have the means to support those who preach the gospel and those who are less fortunate. Believers should work with their hands so that they may have the means to give to those who are in need (Ephesians 4:28). This is love indeed (1 John 3:16-19).

Thirdly, we must ever remember that 'It is more blessed to give than to receive', because the person who gives generously, with a willing heart, gives evidence by his gifts that he is born of God, whereas the person who receives but does not give proves, by hoarding God's bounty for himself, that he does not know God (1 John 3:16-19).

Acts 21:1 And it came to pass, that after we were gotten from them, and had launched, we came with a straight course unto Coos, and the day following unto Rhodes, and from thence unto Patara:

Acts 21:2 And finding a ship sailing over unto Phenicia, we went aboard, and set forth.

Acts 21:3 Now when we had discovered Cyprus, we left it on the left hand, and sailed into Syria, and landed at Tyre: for there the ship was to unlade her burden.

Acts 21:4 And finding disciples, we tarried there seven days: who said to Paul through the Spirit, that he should not go up to Jerusalem.

Acts 21:5 And when we had accomplished those days, we departed and went our way; and they all brought us on our way, with wives and children, till we were out of the city: and we kneeled down on the shore, and prayed.

Acts 21:6 And when we had taken our leave one of another, we took ship; and they returned home again.

Acts 21:7 And when we had finished our course from Tyre, we came to Ptolemais, and saluted the brethren, and abode with them one day.

Acts 21:8 And the next day we that were of Paul's company departed, and came unto Caesarea: and we entered into the house of Philip the evangelist, which was one of the seven; and abode with him.

Acts 21:9 And the same man had four daughters, virgins, which did prophesy.

Acts 21:10 And as we tarried there many days, there came down from Judaea a certain prophet, named Agabus.

Acts 21:11 And when he was come unto us, he took Paul's girdle, and bound his own hands and feet, and said, Thus saith the Holy Ghost, So shall the Jews at Jerusalem bind the man that owneth this girdle, and shall deliver him into the hands of the Gentiles.

Acts 21:12 And when we heard these things, both we, and they of that place, besought him not to go up to Jerusalem.

Acts 21:13 Then Paul answered, What mean ye to weep and to break mine heart? for I am ready not to be bound only, but also to die at Jerusalem for the name of the Lord Jesus.

Acts 21:14 And when he would not be persuaded, we ceased, saying, The will of the Lord be done.

Acts 21:15 And after those days we took up our carriages, and went up to Jerusalem.

Acts 21:16 There went with us also certain of the disciples of Caesarea, and brought with them one Mnason of Cyprus, an old disciple, with whom we should lodge.

Acts 21:17 And when we were come to Jerusalem, the brethren received us gladly.

Acts 21:18 And the day following Paul went in with us unto James; and all the elders were present.

Acts 21:19 And when he had saluted them, he declared particularly what things God had wrought among the Gentiles by his ministry.

Acts 21:20 And when they heard it, they glorified the Lord, and said unto him, Thou seest, brother, how many thousands of Jews there are which believe; and they are all zealous of the law:

Acts 21:21 And they are informed of thee, that thou teachest all the Jews which are among the Gentiles to forsake Moses, saying that they ought not to circumcise their children, neither to walk after the customs.

Acts 21:22 What is it therefore? the multitude must needs come together: for they will hear that thou art come.

Acts 21:23 Do therefore this that we say to thee: We have four men which have a vow on them;

Acts 21:24 Them take, and purify thyself with them, and be at charges with them, that they may shave their heads: and all may know that those things, whereof they were informed concerning thee, are nothing; but that thou thyself also walkest orderly, and keepest the law.

Acts 21:25 As touching the Gentiles which believe, we have written and concluded that they observe no such thing, save only that they keep themselves from things offered to idols, and from blood, and from strangled, and from fornication.

Acts 21:26 Then Paul took the men, and the next day purifying himself with them entered into the temple, to signify the accomplishment of the days of purification, until that an offering should be offered for every one of them.

Acts 21:27 And when the seven days were almost ended, the Jews which were of Asia, when they saw him in the temple, stirred up all the people, and laid hands on him,

Acts 21:28 Crying out, Men of Israel, help: This is the man, that teacheth all men every where against the people, and the law, and this place: and further brought Greeks also into the temple, and hath polluted this holy place.

Acts 21:29 (For they had seen before with him in the city Trophimus an Ephesian, whom they supposed that Paul had brought into the temple.)

Acts 21:30 And all the city was moved, and the people ran together: and they took Paul, and drew him out of the temple: and forthwith the doors were shut.

Acts 21:31 And as they went about to kill him, tidings came unto the chief captain of the band, that all Jerusalem was in an uproar.

Acts 21:32 Who immediately took soldiers and centurions, and ran down unto them: and when they saw the chief captain and the soldiers, they left beating of Paul.

Acts 21:33 Then the chief captain came near, and took him, and commanded him to be bound with two chains; and demanded who he was, and what he had done.

Acts 21:34 And some cried one thing, some another, among the multitude: and when he could not know the certainty for the tumult, he commanded him to be carried into the castle.

Acts 21:35 And when he came upon the stairs, so it was, that he was borne of the soldiers for the violence of the people.

Acts 21:36 For the multitude of the people followed after, crying, Away with him.

Acts 21:37 And as Paul was to be led into the castle, he said unto the chief captain, May I speak unto thee? Who said, Canst thou speak Greek?

Acts 21:38 Art not thou that Egyptian, which before these days madest an uproar, and leddest out into the wilderness four thousand men that were murderers?

Acts 21:39 But Paul said, I am a man which am a Jew of Tarsus, a city in Cilicia, a citizen of no mean city: and, I beseech thee, suffer me to speak unto the people.

Acts 21:40 And when he had given him licence, Paul stood on the stairs, and beckoned with the hand unto the people. And when there was made a great silence, he spake unto them in the Hebrew tongue, saying,

Chapter 62

'The will of the Lord be done'

Acts 21:1-40

Paul was en route to Jerusalem, knowing full well that upon his arrival there he would meet with vehement opposition because of the gospel he preached (20:22-24). But he would allow nothing to keep him from doing what he knew God had called him to do. After his brief stop at Miletus (20:17-38), he sailed down the west coast of Asia Minor, stopping at Coos, Rhodes and Patara. Then he sailed around the island of Cyprus to Tyre in Syria. Finding disciples there, he and his companions stayed at Tyre for seven days (21:1-4).

1. At Tyre, the disciples warned Paul not to go up to Jerusalem (21:4, 5)

Without question, they gave this warning 'to Paul through the Spirit'. Neither can it be doubted that Paul was 'bound in the Spirit' to go to Jerusalem (20:22). There is only one way to understand this apparent contradiction: the warnings given to Paul by the Holy Spirit were meant to test and prove his faith and faithfulness so he might stand as an example to others. When Paul could not be dissuaded, the disciples at Tyre, with their families, prayed with Paul and bade him farewell, submitting to the will of the Lord.

2. After leaving Tyre, Paul and his friends came to Caesarea, where they were the guests of Philip the evangelist (21:7-9)

Philip was one of the original deacons (6:5). Later he became an evangelist. He is the one who was sent by God to preach the gospel to the Samaritans and the Ethiopian eunuch in Acts 8. The last we saw of him, he was settled in Caesarea (8:40). Now, some twenty years later, he was still there, serving the Lord with a family of four daughters who had the gift of prophecy.

This servant of God was a married man. Contrary to papal doctrine, which forbids the marriage of God's servants, almost all the pastors, deacons and evangelists of the New Testament were married men (1 Timothy 4:1-5). Philip, being given to hospitality, graciously opened his home to Paul and his travelling companions. Grace makes people gracious and generous. Philip counted it an honour and privilege to have God's servants and his saints as guests in his home. Happy is the home and household where the servants of God and the people of God are guests. Where God's servants and his people are lodged, blessings are lodged (Matthew 10:41, 42; Hebrews 13:1, 2).

Philip's virgin daughters prophesied. There is no indication that these girls had taken a vow of virginity! They were simply young women who were not yet married and were virgins, as all unmarried women should be. These young ladies had a gift of prophecy. That does not imply that they taught and explained the Scriptures, or preached in the public assemblies of the church. That would have been a direct violation of the Word of God (1 Corinthians 14:34, 35; 1 Timothy 2:11, 12). When Luke tells us they 'did prophesy', he simply means that they had the gift to foretell future events by the Spirit of God. This was one of the many extraordinary signs of the fulfilment of Joel's prophecy in apostolic times (Joel 2:28). We can only guess what the subject of their prophecy was, but the context helps us. Like the disciples at Tyre (21:4) and Agabus (21:11), Philip's daughters probably warned Paul of the danger awaiting him at Jerusalem. Over and over again the Holy Spirit plainly told Paul the things he would face at Jerusalem. He knew that certain death awaited him (20:25).

3. Agabus prophesies of Paul's imprisonment at Jerusalem (21:11-14)

Paul had met Agabus fifteen or sixteen years earlier at Antioch. It was Agabus who had prophesied of the famine that came in the days of Claudius Caesar (11:28). Paul was familiar with this man and aware of his divine commission and gifts. Agabus publicly prophesied that Paul would be bound by the Jews and delivered up to the Romans. The disciples were heartbroken for Paul's sake. They tenderly and urgently begged him not to proceed with his plans, but Paul would not be dissuaded. He was committed to Christ and determined to obey what he knew to be the will of God, even if it cost him his life (21:13; 20:22-24). Seeing Paul's determination, all the disciples submitted to the will of the Lord. They would not be found in rebellion to God. This is the spirit of faith. It is the spirit of Christ (Matthew 26:42). All who believe God submit to the will of God, preferring his will to their own because his will is best.

4. At last Paul went up to Jerusalem, where he was compelled by James to give approval to the observance of the Mosaic law (21:15-40)

Acts 21:17-26 is one of the saddest paragraphs in the Bible. A terrible, tragic thing is about to take place. No man was a greater, or more consistent exponent of the believer's freedom from the law than Paul. Yet here he is about to go back under the yoke of bondage!

James and the elders at Jerusalem persuaded Paul that, in order to conciliate the Jews and put an end to the scandalous reports they had heard about him, he should give public approval to the observance of the ceremonial law of Moses. They compelled him to go into the temple with four men who had taken a Nazarite vow (Numbers 6:2, 13) and offer a sacrifice of purification — and Paul did it!

Without question, this action was contrary to everything Paul taught (Galatians 2:3, 11; 3:1-3; 5:1; Colossians 2:16). By example and association, Paul gave approval to legalism. His action could only encourage others to retain the spirit of legalism and both confuse and dishearten the Gentile believers. To this day, legalists point to this passage as an argument why we should live under the yoke of the law.

Why did Paul submit to this legal ceremony? The believing Jews had not yet seen the destruction of the temple. During this time of transition, most Jewish believers continued to observe the customs of the law. God had virtually to break their hands to make them let go of Moses and the earthly ceremonies of the law. Why did Paul, who knew better, do this awful thing?

No doubt, he was trying to be appease the believing Jews who were yet weak in the faith (1 Corinthians 9:19-23). That is commendable. Those who are weak in the faith are to be borne with in patience. We must do nothing to offend them. But we must not, even for the sake of nurturing the weak, do what is contrary to the gospel of Christ or in violation of our own conscience. We can do without wine or meat to keep a brother from stumbling, but we cannot, and must not, pretend to live by legal principles to keep from offending a legalist! If we join others in committing evil and compromise the gospel of grace in the name of Christian love, we shall not help them, and are likely to hinder many others. Perhaps Paul was weary of fighting with his brethren over the law. He finally gave in, but he regretted it. His strongest instructions about the believer's total freedom from the law in Christ were written after this incident.

Besides, the compromise did not work (21:27-40). It never does! The Jews were not conciliated. It is a vain thing to imagine that men can be pleased and that their approval of the gospel can be won by compromise. However, it must not be forgotten that God graciously overruled even this sad blemish in Paul's life to accomplish his purpose. This too proved to be good for Paul, good for God's elect and for the glory of God. Had he not gone into the temple that day, he would not have been arrested, not have gone to Rome, not have written his prison epistles, not have been martyred for Christ. God brought good out of evil — and he still does!

Acts 21:13 Then Paul answered, What mean ye to weep and to break mine heart? for I am ready not to be bound only, but also to die at Jerusalem for the name of the Lord Jesus.

Acts 21:14 And when he would not be persuaded, we ceased, saying, The will of the Lord be done.

Acts 21:15 And after those days we took up our carriages, and went up to Jerusalem.

Acts 21:16 There went with us also certain of the disciples of Caesarea, and brought with them one Mnason of Cyprus, an old disciple, with whom we should lodge.

Chapter 63

Surrender

Acts 21:13-16

Faith in Christ is nothing less than the surrender of one's life to the rule and dominion of Jesus Christ as Lord. It is implicit confidence in him that causes a person to trust Christ to control all the affairs of his life. Faith is losing your life to Christ. Anything short of the surrender of heart and life to Jesus Christ as Lord is not faith (Matthew 10:37, 38; Mark 8:34-38; Luke 9:23, 24; 14:25-33; John 12:25). In Acts 21:13-16, Luke gives us several examples of that surrender of life that always accompanies true faith.

Paul, being 'bound in the Spirit' to go (20:22), was, as we have already seen, on his way to Jerusalem. He did not know exactly what awaited him there. But the Holy Spirit assured him that 'bonds and afflictions' (20:23) would certainly be waiting for him. Still this faithful servant of God was determined to finish his course with the joyful awareness that he had been obedient to Christ, no matter what difficulties and dangers awaited him.

All along the way the Lord tested his resolve and proved his faith. First, the disciples at Tyre pleaded with Paul, urging him not to go up to Jerusalem because the Holy Spirit had shown them the danger awaiting him (21:4). Then Agabus came down to Caesarea and made a very bold and vivid prophecy of the bonds awaiting Paul at Jerusalem (21:10, 11). After that all the disciples began to weep and begged Paul not to go up to Jerusalem (21:12). The disciples at Tyre, Agabus and these disciples at Caesarea were all spiritual men. They all had Paul's best interests at heart. They all spoke to him by the Spirit of God. But Paul knew what the will of God was, and he was determined to do God's will, regardless of cost or consequence. What an example he sets before us! When God has shown us his will, when the path of our responsibility is clear, we must be obedient and walk in it, no matter what it may cost us to do so. Nothing will justify the neglect of disobedience to the known will of God (1 Kings 13:26).

1. True faith involves loving commitment and surrender of life to the Lord Jesus Christ

When Paul called upon the saints at Rome to present their bodies as living sacrifices to the Lord (Romans 12:1, 2), he himself had already done so. His life was one of self-sacrificing devotion to Christ, as verse 13 indicates: 'Then Paul answered, What mean ye to weep and to break mine heart? For I am ready not to be bound only, but also to die at Jerusalem for the name of the Lord Jesus.'

The Lord Jesus Christ is worthy of all that we might be called upon to do or suffer for him, and infinitely more. This is an obvious fact to all who know him. It is not something that has to be proved. He who is worthy of heaven's highest praise is worthy of our hearts' highest love, esteem and devotion. He is worthy of our full surrender to his claims and total commitment to his glory. He is worthy because of:

1. Who he is: God over all and blessed forever, our incarnate mediator and substitute (Isaiah 9:6, 7; John 1:1-3, 14; Philippians 2:6-8; Colossians 2:9; 1 Timothy 3:16; Hebrews 1:1-3).

2. All that he has done for us: his engagements to be our surety (Hebrews 10:5-14), his assumption of our nature (2 Corinthians 8:9; Galatians 4:4, 5), his representative obedience (Romans 5:19) and his substitutionary, sin-atoning, sacrificial death (Romans 5:6-8; 2 Corinthians 5:21; 1 Peter 2:24; Galatians 3:13).

3. All that he is doing and will yet do for us: his advocacy (1 John 2:1, 2), his providential rule (John 17:2), his preparation of heaven for us (John 14:1-3), the resurrection of the saints (1 Thessalonians 4:13-18) and the perfection of glorification (Ephesians 5:25-27).

When we think of who Christ is, what he has done and what he has promised, we are compelled to shout with the saints in heaven, 'Thou art worthy!'

2. True faith loves and esteems the Son of God above all things, even above life itself

To those who believe, 'He is precious' (1 Peter 2:7). Faith perceives the infinite worth of Christ and the comparative worthlessness of all but Christ (Philippians 3:4-11). I realise that there are varying degrees of consecration to Christ and that believers grow in grace, but wherever grace is experienced, indebtedness is felt (Luke 7:36-50). The believer is never satisfied with anything done for, or given to, Christ. Love yearns to give more, do more, surrender more and be more for Christ. Faith can never be satisfied with anything less than total commitment to Christ, total communion with Christ and total conformity to Christ. Faith counts that kind of devotion to be a very reasonable thing (Romans 12:1, 2; 14:7, 8; 2 Corinthians 5:15).

3. True faith surrenders to the will of God

When the disciples realised that Paul could not be persuaded to follow the course of personal safety, they committed their friend, the cause of Christ and their own lives to the will of God, saying, 'The will of the Lord be done' (21:14). In the same way, it is our responsibility and in our best interests to submit all things to the will of God. It is an act of faith to submit all our plans to his will (James 4:15). And it is an act of patience to humbly endure personal trials, troubles and heartaches, realizing all we suffer, we suffer by the will of God (1 Samuel 3:18). As we seek to walk in obedience to the will of God, three things need to be understood:

1. The secret will of God is his eternal purpose and decree of predestination. God is the first cause of all things (Romans 11:36; 2 Corinthians 5:18; Ephesians 1:11). Some things are permitted by God, and some things are directly caused by God, but all things were decreed by God in his eternal purpose (Isaiah 46:9-11).

2. The revealed will of God is what we are called to obey. Our duty is determined not by the decree of God, but by the revelation of God. We are responsible to do what we know God has commanded us to do in his Word (John 2:5). For example, all men are responsible to repent (Acts 17:30); all believers are responsible to be baptized, confessing and identifying with Christ in the watery grave (Acts 2:38); and all who know Christ are responsible to be his witnesses (Acts 1:8). Once we know God's will in any area of life, we must obey, without consideration of cost or consequence.

3. The providential will of God is whatever comes to pass in time. All that comes to pass is brought to pass by the will of God (Romans 8:28; 1 Thessalonians 5:16-18). It is our responsibility to trust God's will of purpose, obey God's will of revelation and submit to God's will of providence, saying, 'The will of the Lord be done.'

4. True faith perseveres to the end

Verse 16 speaks of 'one Mnason of Cyprus, an old disciple, with whom' Paul lodged at Jerusalem. What charming words! If I should live to be an old man,

295

let me live to be 'an old disciple'! I want no more. 'Mnason' means 'one who remembers'. He had seen, heard, learned and experienced much of Christ, of redemption and of grace. What precious memories he must have enjoyed! He came from the little island of Cyprus, the home of Barnabas. And he was 'an old disciple'. Those words imply that he was a man advanced in years, but literally they mean he was 'a disciple from the beginning'. Mnason was one of the original group of believers. Thirty years had passed since the death of Christ. Mnason was one of the very few left who had seen, heard and believed Christ in the flesh. Most of his friends from the early days had gone already to heaven. But Mnason was still a disciple. He was still learning from his Master, following his Master and growing in grace. He was still given to hospitality and a man so highly esteemed in the church that his acceptance of Paul carried such weight that the Jewish brethren received him gladly (21:17). Thank God for old disciples!

Acts 22:1 Men, brethren, and fathers, hear ye my defence which I make now unto you.

Acts 22:2 (And when they heard that he spake in the Hebrew tongue to them, they kept the more silence: and he saith,)

Acts 22:3 I am verily a man which am a Jew, born in Tarsus, a city in Cilicia, yet brought up in this city at the feet of Gamaliel, and taught according to the perfect manner of the law of the fathers, and was zealous toward God, as ye all are this day.

Acts 22:4 And I persecuted this way unto the death, binding and delivering into prisons both men and women.

Acts 22:5 As also the high priest doth bear me witness, and all the estate of the elders: from whom also I received letters unto the brethren, and went to Damascus, to bring them which were there bound unto Jerusalem, for to be punished.

Acts 22:6 And it came to pass, that, as I made my journey, and was come nigh unto Damascus about noon, suddenly there shone from heaven a great light round about me.

Acts 22:7 And I fell unto the ground, and heard a voice saying unto me, Saul, Saul, why persecutest thou me?

Acts 22:8 And I answered, Who art thou, Lord? And he said unto me, I am Jesus of Nazareth, whom thou persecutest.

Acts 22:9 And they that were with me saw indeed the light, and were afraid; but they heard not the voice of him that spake to me.

Acts 22:10 And I said, What shall I do, Lord? And the Lord said unto me, Arise, and go into Damascus; and there it shall be told thee of all things which are appointed for thee to do.

Acts 22:11 And when I could not see for the glory of that light, being led by the hand of them that were with me, I came into Damascus.

Acts 22:12 And one Ananias, a devout man according to the law, having a good report of all the Jews which dwelt there,

Acts 22:13 Came unto me, and stood, and said unto me, Brother Saul, receive thy sight. And the same hour I looked up upon him.

Acts 22:14 And he said, The God of our fathers hath chosen thee, that thou shouldest know his will, and see that Just One, and shouldest hear the voice of his mouth.

Acts 22:15 For thou shalt be his witness unto all men of what thou hast seen and heard.

Acts 22:16 And now why tarriest thou? arise, and be baptized, and wash away thy sins, calling on the name of the Lord.

Acts 22:17 And it came to pass, that, when I was come again to Jerusalem, even while I prayed in the temple, I was in a trance;

Acts 22:18 And saw him saying unto me, Make haste, and get thee quickly out of Jerusalem: for they will not receive thy testimony concerning me.

Acts 22:19 And I said, Lord, they know that I imprisoned and beat in every synagogue them that believed on thee:

Acts 22:20 And when the blood of thy martyr Stephen was shed, I also was standing by, and consenting unto his death, and kept the raiment of them that slew him.

Acts 22:21 And he said unto me, Depart: for I will send thee far hence unto the Gentiles.

Acts 22:22 And they gave him audience unto this word, and then lifted up their voices, and said, Away with such a fellow from the earth: for it is not fit that he should live.

Acts 22:23 And as they cried out, and cast off their clothes, and threw dust into the air,

Acts 22:24 The chief captain commanded him to be brought into the castle, and bade that he should be examined by scourging; that he might know wherefore they cried so against him.

Acts 22:25 And as they bound him with thongs, Paul said unto the centurion that stood by, Is it lawful for you to scourge a man that is a Roman, and uncondemned?

Acts 22:26 When the centurion heard that, he went and told the chief captain, saying, Take heed what thou doest: for this man is a Roman.

Acts 22:27 Then the chief captain came, and said unto him, Tell me, art thou a Roman? He said, Yea.

Acts 22:28 And the chief captain answered, With a great sum obtained I this freedom. And Paul said, But I was free born.

Acts 22:29 Then straightway they departed from him which should have examined him: and the chief captain also was afraid, after he knew that he was a Roman, and because he had bound him.

Acts 22:30 On the morrow, because he would have known the certainty wherefore he was accused of the Jews, he loosed him from his bands, and commanded the chief priests and all their council to appear, and brought Paul down, and set him before them.

Chapter 64

Paul's Defence Of The Faith

Acts 22:1-30

Acts 22 opens with Paul standing before an angry, religious mob. Bound with chains like a dangerous criminal, he beckoned to the people with his hand and got their attention (21:40). Then he gave a solemn and powerful defence of the faith. Speaking in calm, conciliatory terms in the Hebrew language, Paul addressed these angry Jews as brethren. Though they were not his brethren in any spiritual sense, they were in a natural sense. Paul spoke to them as he did because he wanted to calm their tempers and incline them to listen to what he had to say. In that, he was successful (22:1, 2).

We should take special notice of the simplicity of Paul's language as we read this chapter. Though he was a very well-trained intellectual, capable of fetching arguments and illustrations from history, tradition, philosophy, literature, logic and theological orthodoxy, though he was capable of using poetic imagery, oratorical eloquence and stunning imagination, he carefully avoided doing so (1 Corinthians 2:4, 5). In this dramatic moment, the great apostle to the Gentiles simply told the story of his conversion. He told his hearers, in the simplest language possible, what God had done for him by his almighty, free grace in the Lord Jesus Christ. That is the way the gospel ought always to be preached. It is the way we ought to witness to men. The very best defence of the faith is the testimony of men and women who have experienced the transforming power of God's saving grace in Christ, and know it. To be a good preacher, a man must simply tell what he knows. To be a good witness for Christ, saved sinners must simply tell other sinners what they know (John 9:25). Three spiritual lessons are given to us in this chapter.

1. A person may be very religious and yet be lost (22:1-5)

It is entirely possible for a person to be well learned in the letter of Holy Scripture, consecrated and devoted to the point of self-denial, and very zealous towards God — all without knowing God. The angry mob that Paul was addressing was a mob of people who were very zealous for their religion, but who did not know God. In verses 3-5, Paul told them that before God saved him he was just like them, 'as ye all are this day'.

He was born and reared in a strict orthodox Jewish family: 'I am verily a man which am a Jew, born in Tarsus, a city in Cilicia.' He had a religious pedigree that was unrivalled (Philippians 3:4-6). His mother and father were respected, loyal members of the synagogue. He had been religious all his life. But grace does not run in blood or come by natural descent (John 1:11-13).

Paul was very well trained in the letter of the law too: ' ... brought up in this city (Jerusalem] at the feet of Gamaliel, and taught according to the perfect manner of the law'. He knew the Scriptures. His life was an example of moral and religious purity. He was a Pharisee who lived such a good life that he even made other Pharisees look impure! Paul was raised in religion and raised to be religious. But he did not know God, though he was sure he did. Faith cannot be learned. It must be given (Philippians 1:29). Salvation is not the result of training, but of revelation (2 Corinthians 4:5, 6).

More, Paul was devoted, consecrated and zealous in his religious works. He was 'zealous toward God'. He was not someone whose profession of religion was a sham. He did not take the things of God lightly. He gave himself sincerely to the pursuit of his religious profession (22:4, 5). But grace cannot be earned by religious works (Romans 3:20; 11:6; Ephesians 2:8, 9).

Paul was a religious man from his youth; but he was without God, without Christ, without life, lost in the world (Ephesians 2:12). In spite of his religion, Paul obtained mercy and never lost a sense of amazement at the mercy he had obtained (1 Timothy 1:12-17). It may be that as you read these lines you are made to realise that you are like Paul — religious but lost! If you would be saved, you must have something more than religion. You must have Christ (John 17:3; Colossians 1:27; 1 John 5:11, 12).

2. Salvation is of the Lord (22:6-21)

In verses 3-5, Paul tells us what he was before God saved him. In verses 6-21, he tells us what God did for him and in him by his grace in Christ. From start to finish, the apostle ascribes the whole of his salvation to the grace of God. The essence of all he says in these verses is: 'By the grace of God I am what I am' (1 Corinthians 15:10). Paul tells us four things in which he stands as 'a pattern to them which should hereafter believe' (1 Timothy 1:16).

First, Paul was confronted in his path of rebellion by the sovereign Christ, the living Lord (22:6-11). Sooner or later, God will cross the path of every sinner whom he has chosen. Notice the words at the beginning of verse 6: 'And it came to pass ... ' What came to pass? God's eternal purpose of grace towards Paul. How did it come to pass? By God's gracious hand of providence. Here again we see a marvellous display of God's providence overruling evil for good. Paul went to Damascus full of hatred for Christ. But

Christ brought him down the Damascus road because the time of love had come when Saul of Tarsus must be saved (Ezekiel 16:8). He was not seeking the Lord. The Lord was seeking him. At the time appointed, and in the place appointed, the Lord Jesus revealed himself to this chosen, redeemed sinner in grace and saving power. Overwhelmed by Christ's glory, confronted with the claims of Christ's lordship, called by the personal, particular and effectual call of the Saviour, Saul of Tarsus was broken in repentance.

Secondly, by the instruction of a faithful, gospel preacher, Paul was granted spiritual illumination and given understanding in the gospel (22:12-15). Even in Paul's case the rule of grace was not broken. 'Faith cometh by hearing, and hearing by the word of God' (Romans 10:17). He had heard the gospel from the lips of Stephen (7:1-59). But now he heard it from Ananias. Though he learned the letter of the Word at the feet of Gamaliel, Saul was as devoid of spiritual truth as any barbarian. Spiritual truth must be spiritually revealed and spiritually learned (1 Corinthians 2:11-16). God's means to teach spiritual truth is the ministry of the gospel (Ephesians 4:11-14).

The very first thing Ananias taught Paul was God's electing grace: 'The God of our fathers hath chosen thee.' Then he told him that the object of election is salvation: ' ... that thou shouldest know his will' — that is, his revealed will, the gospel, how through Christ's blood atonement God can be just and the justifier of all who trust his Son (Romans 3:24-26). Next, Ananias told Paul that salvation comes by knowing Christ, the sinner's substitute, the only mediator between God and men, by seeing 'that Just One' (John 17:3). He talked of an effectual call: 'and shouldest hear the voice of his mouth'. If any sinner will ever know Christ it is by the call of his Spirit (1 Thessalonians 1:4, 5; 2 Thessalonians 2:13, 14; Psalm 65:4). Finally, Ananias told Paul that God had chosen him to be 'his witness'. That is the lifelong business of every saved sinner (Isaiah 44:8; John 20:21).

Thirdly, Paul then confessed Christ in public, believer's baptism (22:16). Baptism has no saving, redeeming efficacy; but it is symbolic of the washing away of the believer's sins by the death, burial and resurrection of Christ.

Fourthly, as a believer, Paul was led by, and walked in, the Spirit (22:17-21). Believers are men and women whose lives are ruled by Jesus Christ by the indwelling power and grace of God the Holy Spirit (Romans 8:9-16).

3. The gospel of grace is an offence to unregenerate men (22:22-30)

The message of grace Paul preached to these religious people, his testimony of the grace he had experienced in Christ, enraged them. Salvation by grace alone, through faith alone, in Christ alone always infuriates lost, religious people, but the saints of God rejoice in it (1 Corinthians 1:22-24).

Acts 22:22 And they gave him audience unto this word, and then lifted up their voices, and said, Away with such a fellow from the earth: for it is not fit that he should live.

Acts 22:23 And as they cried out, and cast off their clothes, and threw dust into the air,

Acts 22:24 The chief captain commanded him to be brought into the castle, and bade that he should be examined by scourging; that he might know wherefore they cried so against him.

Acts 22:25 And as they bound him with thongs, Paul said unto the centurion that stood by, Is it lawful for you to scourge a man that is a Roman, and uncondemned?

Acts 22:26 When the centurion heard that, he went and told the chief captain, saying, Take heed what thou doest: for this man is a Roman.

Acts 22:27 Then the chief captain came, and said unto him, Tell me, art thou a Roman? He said, Yea.

Acts 22:28 And the chief captain answered, With a great sum obtained I this freedom. And Paul said, But I was free born.

Acts 22:29 Then straightway they departed from him which should have examined him: and the chief captain also was afraid, after he knew that he was a Roman, and because he had bound him.

Acts 22:30 On the morrow, because he would have known the certainty wherefore he was accused of the Jews, he loosed him from his bands, and commanded the chief priests and all their council to appear, and brought Paul down, and set him before them.

Chapter 65

'I was free born'

Acts 22:22-28

'And they gave him audience unto this word.' Paul had been telling the Jews how God had saved him by his free grace and sovereign mercy in Christ. They listened with relative patience until he told them how God, in his glorious sovereignty, had rejected Israel as a nation and sent the gospel to his elect among the Gentiles (22:17-21). When they heard that God has mercy on whom he will, without regard to human merit, religious rearing, family descent, or racial heritage, they were enraged. Fallen men are always angered by the declaration of God's sovereignty in the exercise of his grace (Luke 4:25-29). Hearing that God had rejected them and had chosen to save worthless Gentiles, these self-righteous Jews were filled with rage. They began to act like wild beasts. They cried out, 'Away with such a fellow from the earth: for it is not fit that he should live.' As they screamed for Paul's blood, they tore off their clothes, preparing to stone him to death, and threw dust into the air. Their hatred of God's sovereign character nearly drove them insane. They could not get their hands around God's throat, so they tried to kill Paul.

Then the chief captain commanded one of his soldiers to bring Paul into the castle to beat a confession out of him (22:24). As they were preparing to do so, Paul asked, 'Is it lawful for you to scourge a man that is a Roman, and uncondemned?' (22:25). Of course it was not. The thought of beating a Roman citizen was horrifying to the soldier. He ran to tell his commanding officer, 'You ordered us to beat a Roman citizen.' That scared the chief captain. He came to Paul and asked, 'Art thou a Roman? He said, Yea. And the chief captain answered, With a great sum obtained I this freedom. And Paul said, But I was free born' (22:27, 28). He was born in Tarsus, a free city, which had been declared free by Mark Antony, long before Paul was born.

For the purpose of our study of this passage, I take these words as coming, not from the mouth of Saul of Tarsus, a citizen of Rome, but from the mouth of Paul the believer, a citizen of the heavenly Jerusalem. What Paul here says of himself, every true believer may joyfully declare concerning him or herself: 'I was free born.' We are citizens of the heavenly Jerusalem. The Lord Jesus Christ, the King of Heaven, has declared that city to be free by the power of his blood. And he did it long before we were born. Being free-born citizens of the kingdom of heaven, we shall never be brought into bondage (Galatians 5:1). Four things are clearly revealed in the New Testament about this spiritual freedom that need to be understood by every child of God.

1. All men and women by nature are in bondage

Man loves to boast of freedom, independence and liberty. But all men are, in a spiritual sense, abject slaves by nature. All are in bondage to sin (Romans 6:20), the servants of 'the lusts of the flesh' (Ephesians 2:3). Those who serve their own passions are slaves to the worst possible despot. Yet, by nature, we are all ruled by the evil passions of our own depraved hearts. Having broken God's law, all are in bondage to the law and under the curse of the law (Galatians 3:10), under the sentence of death (Romans 6:23). To one degree or another, all of us are natural slaves to other men, craving their approval, acceptance and applause. And all men and women are by nature slaves to religious tradition, custom and superstition. The maxim of the humanist is true: 'Man believes what he is raised to believe.' Religion is a cultural thing. It is passed on from father to son, generation after generation. This natural, cultural, environmental religion brings people into terrible bondage. The Lord Jesus Christ came into this world to set the captive free, to open the doors of the prison, break the iron chains and steel fetters and bring his people into freedom and liberty, even 'the glorious liberty of the children of God' (Isaiah 61:1; Luke 4:16-20; Romans 8:21).

2. Christ alone makes sinners free

No one ever comes to enjoy true liberty before God and in his own conscience, except by the blood, righteousness and grace of the Lord Jesus Christ. But we must beware of false liberty. Every good thing is imitated by Satan, and he has deceived many with a false liberty. Some are so naive that they imagine a mere profession of faith is liberty. Others presume they have found liberty when they have mended their lives by self-righteous reformation, ceasing from certain evil habits of outward behaviour. Some even substitute a spirit of licentiousness in the name of grace for spiritual freedom. But neither legalism nor antinomianism nor empty religious profession can bring true liberty. Only Christ, the Son of God, can make sinners free (John 8:36). He purchased liberty for God's elect by his sin-atoning death as our substitute (Galatians 3:13). He proclaims liberty to sinners through the preaching of the gospel (Isaiah 61:1-3). And he sets his people free by the power of his sovereign grace through the regenerating work of the Holy Spirit, who causes awakened sinners to know him who is the truth (John 8:32).

3. All who are born of God are born free, born into freedom (Galatians 4:1-7)

The moment a person is born again he, or she, is a child of God, and is free in Christ. The moment a sinner believes on the Lord Jesus Christ he begins to enjoy a real and lasting freedom in his soul. As the believer grows and matures he enjoys his liberty more freely and appreciates it better. But the liberty is his as soon as he trusts Christ.

In Christ, we are free from sin, Satan and the law. Christ has freed us from the guilt, condemnation and dominion of sin (Hebrews 9:14; Romans 8:1; Ephesians 2:1-5; Romans 6:11-18). Our Saviour has delivered us from the power and tyranny of Satan, too. By nature, Satan holds a usurped dominion over all men, blinding them, deceiving them and leading them into captivity at his will. In salvation, Christ dethrones the devil by the power of his Spirit. He enters the hearts of his elect, binds the strong man and takes possession of his house (Luke 11:21, 22). And the Son of God has freed his people from the Mosaic law (Romans 5:20, 21; 6:15; 7:4; 8:1, 2; 10:4). The New Testament never addresses God's saints as people under the law, but always as people free from the law: free from the statutes of Old Testament judicial law, free from the ceremonies of the law, free from the bondage of the moral law. Believers in Christ have no covenant with the law, no condemnation by the law, no constraint from the law and no obligation to the law. Christ satisfied all things in the law for us. The lives of God's saints are not governed by the rules and regulations of the law, but by love and faith in Christ and the glory of God (1 John 3:23; 2 Corinthians 5:14; 1 Corinthians 10:31).

However, according to the New Testament, our freedom in Christ extends far beyond these matters of doctrine, and reaches to the common affairs of everyday life. Faith in Christ gives us freedom from all the customs, traditions and superstitions of human religion. We are not to be the servants of self-righteous, religious traditions and customs. We are duty-bound to repudiate them (Matthew 15:1-9; Colossians 2:6-8, 16, 17, 20-23). Neither the church of God nor gospel preachers have any right to develop laws and rules of conduct for God's people. To do so is to add to the Word of God.

In Christ we are free to use every creature of God for food, happiness, satisfaction and comfort as we seek to serve him in this world. Old Testament Levitical law made the use of some things unlawful, but in this gospel age, for the believer, there is nothing common or unclean (Acts 10:14, 15; Romans 14:14; 1 Timothy 4:1-4). Use all things in moderation. Carefully avoid offending a weaker brother. Make your use of all things subservient to the glory of God and the welfare of his church. But understand that you are free to use God's creation as his child (Romans 14:2, 3, 13-15, 20-23; 1 Corinthians 8:9-13).

Christ has given us freedom to worship God (Ephesians 2:18; Hebrews 4:16): freedom to call upon God in prayer, freedom to observe the ordinances of his house and freedom to serve him.

Furthermore, being born of God, in Christ, believers are made free from the fear of death (Hebrews 2:14, 15). Since they are justified by his grace, redeemed by his blood, robed in his righteousness and born of his Spirit, the second death has no power over God's elect (Revelation 20:6; John 5:25).

4. There is a glorious liberty yet to be revealed (Romans 8:21-23)

In heaven we shall be totally free from sin and everything sinful. But when Christ comes and makes all things new, in our resurrected, glorified bodies, in immortality and glory, we shall be completely freed from all the consequences of sin. That will be 'the glorious liberty of the sons of God'!

Acts 23:1 And Paul, earnestly beholding the council, said, Men and brethren, I have lived in all good conscience before God until this day.

Acts 23:2 And the high priest Ananias commanded them that stood by him to smite him on the mouth.

Acts 23:3 Then said Paul unto him, God shall smite thee, thou whited wall: for sittest thou to judge me after the law, and commandest me to be smitten contrary to the law?

Acts 23:4 And they that stood by said, Revilest thou God's high priest?

Acts 23:5 Then said Paul, I wist not, brethren, that he was the high priest: for it is written, Thou shalt not speak evil of the ruler of thy people.

Acts 23:6 But when Paul perceived that the one part were Sadducees, and the other Pharisees, he cried out in the council, Men and brethren, I am a Pharisee, the son of a Pharisee: of the hope and resurrection of the dead I am called in question.

Acts 23:7 And when he had so said, there arose a dissension between the Pharisees and the Sadducees: and the multitude was divided.

Acts 23:8 For the Sadducees say that there is no resurrection, neither angel, nor spirit: but the Pharisees confess both.

Acts 23:9 And there arose a great cry: and the scribes that were of the Pharisees' part arose, and strove, saying, We find no evil in this man: but if a spirit or an angel hath spoken to him, let us not fight against God.

Acts 23:10 And when there arose a great dissension, the chief captain, fearing lest Paul should have been pulled in pieces of them, commanded the soldiers to go down, and to take him by force from among them, and to bring him into the castle.

Acts 23:11 And the night following the Lord stood by him, and said, Be of good cheer, Paul: for as thou hast testified of me in Jerusalem, so must thou bear witness also at Rome.

Acts 23:12 And when it was day, certain of the Jews banded together, and bound themselves under a curse, saying that they would neither eat nor drink till they had killed Paul.

Acts 23:13 And they were more than forty which had made this conspiracy.

Acts 23:14 And they came to the chief priests and elders, and said, We have bound ourselves under a great curse, that we will eat nothing until we have slain Paul.

Acts 23:15 Now therefore ye with the council signify to the chief captain that he bring him down unto you to morrow, as though ye would enquire something more perfectly concerning him: and we, or ever he come near, are ready to kill him.

Acts 23:16 And when Paul's sister's son heard of their lying in wait, he went and entered into the castle, and told Paul.

Acts 23:17 Then Paul called one of the centurions unto him, and said, Bring this young man unto the chief captain: for he hath a certain thing to tell him.

Acts 23:18 So he took him, and brought him to the chief captain, and said, Paul the prisoner called me unto him, and prayed me to bring this young man unto thee, who hath something to say unto thee.

Acts 23:19 Then the chief captain took him by the hand, and went with him aside privately, and asked him, What is that thou hast to tell me?

Acts 23:20 And he said, The Jews have agreed to desire thee that thou wouldest bring down Paul to morrow into the council, as though they would enquire somewhat of him more perfectly.

Acts 23:21 But do not thou yield unto them: for there lie in wait for him of them more than forty men, which have bound themselves with an oath, that they will neither eat nor drink till they have killed him: and now are they ready, looking for a promise from thee.

Acts 23:22 So the chief captain then let the young man depart, and charged him, See thou tell no man that thou hast shewed these things to me.

Acts 23:23 And he called unto him two centurions, saying, Make ready two hundred soldiers to go to Caesarea, and horsemen threescore and ten, and spearmen two hundred, at the third hour of the night;

Acts 23:24 And provide them beasts, that they may set Paul on, and bring him safe unto Felix the governor.

Acts 23:25 And he wrote a letter after this manner:

Acts 23:26 Claudius Lysias unto the most excellent governor Felix sendeth greeting.

Acts 23:27 This man was taken of the Jews, and should have been killed of them: then came I with an army, and rescued him, having understood that he was a Roman.

Acts 23:28 And when I would have known the cause wherefore they accused him, I brought him forth into their council:

Acts 23:29 Whom I perceived to be accused of questions of their law, but to have nothing laid to his charge worthy of death or of bonds.

Acts 23:30 And when it was told me how that the Jews laid wait for the man, I sent straightway to thee, and gave commandment to his accusers also to say before thee what they had against him. Farewell.

Acts 23:31 Then the soldiers, as it was commanded them, took Paul, and brought him by night to Antipatris.

Acts 23:32 On the morrow they left the horsemen to go with him, and returned to the castle:

Acts 23:33 Who, when they came to Caesarea, and delivered the epistle to the governor, presented Paul also before him.

Acts 23:34 And when the governor had read the letter, he asked of what province he was. And when he understood that he was of Cilicia;

Acts 23:35 I will hear thee, said he, when thine accusers are also come. And he commanded him to be kept in Herod's judgment hall.

Chapter 66

Paul And His Enemies

Acts 23:1-35

It is faith in God's sovereign providence that enables believers to live in this world of woe with peaceful hearts. 'We know', beyond the least shadow of a doubt, 'that all things', without exception, 'work together for good', eternal, spiritual good, 'to them that love God, to them who are the called according to his purpose' (Romans 8:28). God is on his throne! Though we cannot always see immediate good in what he does, we know that he is doing good. Therefore our hearts are kept in peace, even in the midst of troubles, trials and temptations. One marked feature of the book of Acts is its evident display of God's sovereign providence constantly bringing good out of evil for the accomplishment of his own purposes. Acts 23 gives us an instructive example of this fact. Four things in these thirty-five verses of the inspired record need to be clearly understood and constantly remembered.

1. The gospel of Christ is offensive to men (23:1-10)

We must always avoid offensive attitudes, actions and words, but we must never expect natural men and women to receive, embrace, or even be tolerant of the gospel of Christ. Natural men are tolerant of every opinion and every religion of man's making. But the gospel of Christ, the truth of God, the religion of the Bible, the message of free salvation by grace alone, through faith alone, in Christ alone, the message of salvation by blood atonement, imputed righteousness and divine regeneration is offensive to all unregenerate men (1 Corinthians 1:18-25). It is offensive because men, by nature, hate God (Romans 8:7). The gospel of Christ exposes man's depravity, sin and spiritual impotence (Matthew 15:19; Romans 3:9-19; Ephesians 2:1-4). It nullifies man's goodness, reveals the evil of man's righteousness and denounces man's religion as a worthless thing (Isaiah 1:2-15; Amos 5:21-23). The gospel proclaims that salvation is by grace alone, without works (Romans 11:5, 6; Ephesians 2:8, 9; 2 Timothy 1:9). These things the natural man will not tolerate. The terrible uproar at Jerusalem was caused by one thing. Paul had preached God's sovereign, electing, distinguishing, saving grace, and the Jews hated it. Enraged, they cried,

'Away with such a fellow from the earth: for it is not fit that he should live' (22:20-22; cf. Luke 4:25-29). With that as the background, read again Paul's speech before the Jewish Sanhedrin and its results (23:1-10).

Admire the boldness of God's servant (23:1-5). The Roman commander brought Paul in and set him before this bloodthirsty mob to be examined by them. But Paul was not intimidated. Even in bonds, he was bold for Christ. He told these men that his life had always been one of integrity, which they all knew to be true (23:1). Throughout his life, Paul was a man of principle. He was saying, 'I have always done what I thought was right for the glory of God.' Even before he was converted, he did what he did with zeal for God, though his zeal lacked knowledge (Philippians 3:6).

As soon as Paul said that, Ananias commanded him to be hit in the mouth (23:2). Paul responded in a blaze of anger and indignation: 'God shall smite thee, thou whited wall' (23:3). He called Ananias a hypocrite (cf. Matthew 23:27) because he pretended to judge according to the law, but commanded him to be smitten contrary to the law. Self-righteous men who pretend to live by the law and judge others according to the law are hypocrites, for none of them obeys the law (1 Timothy 1:6, 7; Galatians 6:12, 13).

This word from Paul was obviously an inspired word of prophecy. Five years later, this man, Ananias, was stabbed to death. In the same way, there is a day coming when God will avenge his elect by smiting their enemies with the rod of his wrath. When Paul was challenged for making this statement about Ananias (23:4), he responded, 'I wist not, brethren, that he was the high priest: for it is written, Thou shalt not speak evil of the ruler of thy people' (23:5; Exodus 22:28). No doubt, Paul knew that the Jews regarded Ananias as the high priest. He was not an ignorant man. But he also knew that the Jewish priesthood had degenerated into nothing but a pretentious show, that the typical priesthood of the Old Testament had been fulfilled and thus nullified by Christ and that there is no high priest before God but Jesus Christ, the sinner's substitute (Hebrews 7:24, 25; 10:1-14; 1 John 2:1, 2). Paul's words in verse 5 have a tone of sarcasm in them. It is as though he were saying, 'Him — a high priest! If that man was God's high priest, I would not speak evil of him.'

Then the apostle outwitted his enemies (23:6-10). He knew the Pharisees and Sadducees were enemies. The Pharisees were self-righteous legalists, but they did believe the letter of the Scriptures and tenaciously defended the doctrines of immortality and the resurrection of the dead. The Sadducees were liberals. The only time the two ever got together was to crucify Christ or persecute his people. Knowing their hatred of one another, Paul said, 'I am a Pharisee,' and got the two groups fighting one another. He made no compromise. In all points of doctrine wherein the Pharisees differed from the

310

Sadducees, Paul was still a Pharisee. He hoped for and believed in the resurrection of the dead. Once the two groups started fighting, the chief captain sent his soldiers to bring Paul back into the castle, lest he be pulled to pieces by them.

2. The Lord Jesus Christ is always faithful to his own (23:11)

After two days of constant harassment, the Lord made himself known to his afflicted servant. Christ never leaves nor forsakes his own (Matthew 28:20; Hebrews 13:5). We are never alone, but we do not always sense our Lord's presence. So in our darkest hours he appears and causes us to know that he is with us (Daniel 3:25). Perhaps Paul had become despondent. Perhaps he feared he had made a mistake in ignoring the warnings of his friends about coming to Jerusalem (20:16; 21:13). Perhaps he feared he might never reach Rome. So, 'The Lord stood by him, and said, Be of good cheer, Paul: for as thou hast testified of me in Jerusalem, so must thou bear witness also at Rome' (Psalm 42:11; Isaiah 41:10; 43:1-5; 46:4).

3. Our God wisely rules all the events of providence for good (23:12-35)

God rules all things absolutely for the eternal good of his elect and the accomplishment of his eternal purpose, for the glory of his own great name (Psalm 76:10; 115:3; 135:6; Romans 8:28-30; 11:36). It was the wrath of wicked men that carried Paul to Caesarea and ultimately to Rome. God took the evil conspiracy of a band of Jewish zealots (terrorists) and brought good out of it. Because they plotted to kill Paul, God moved a pagan Roman commander to send Paul on his way under the protection of 470 soldiers! When he arrived at Caesarea and was brought before Felix, the governor, the latter said, 'I will hear thee ... when thine accusers are also come. And he commanded him to be kept in Herod's judgment hall' (23:35).

4. The saints of God are a harmless and blameless people (23:29)

The Jews sought every way imaginable to bring an accusation against Paul, but they found none. They hated him. They wanted to kill him, but he was a man of blameless reputation. His life adorned his doctrine. May the same be true of us (Titus 2:10; Philippians 2:14-16). If we faithfully confess Christ before men, we shall meet with opposition, as Paul did. When men oppose us, the Lord will stand by us, as he stood by Paul. Let us confidently trust our heavenly Father's wise and good providence and seek, for the glory of his name, to live blamelessly before men.

311

Acts 24:1 And after five days Ananias the high priest descended with the elders, and with a certain orator named Tertullus, who informed the governor against Paul.

Acts 24:2 And when he was called forth, Tertullus began to accuse him, saying, Seeing that by thee we enjoy great quietness, and that very worthy deeds are done unto this nation by thy providence,

Acts 24:3 We accept it always, and in all places, most noble Felix, with all thankfulness.

Acts 24:4 Notwithstanding, that I be not further tedious unto thee, I pray thee that thou wouldest hear us of thy clemency a few words.

Acts 24:5 For we have found this man a pestilent fellow, and a mover of sedition among all the Jews throughout the world, and a ringleader of the sect of the Nazarenes:

Acts 24:6 Who also hath gone about to profane the temple: whom we took, and would have judged according to our law.

Acts 24:7 But the chief captain Lysias came upon us, and with great violence took him away out of our hands,

Acts 24:8 Commanding his accusers to come unto thee: by examining of whom thyself mayest take knowledge of all these things, whereof we accuse him.

Acts 24:9 And the Jews also assented, saying that these things were so.

Acts 24:10 Then Paul, after that the governor had beckoned unto him to speak, answered, Forasmuch as I know that thou hast been of many years a judge unto this nation, I do the more cheerfully answer for myself:

Acts 24:11 Because that thou mayest understand, that there are yet but twelve days since I went up to Jerusalem for to worship.

Acts 24:12 And they neither found me in the temple disputing with any man, neither raising up the people, neither in the synagogues, nor in the city:

Acts 24:13 Neither can they prove the things whereof they now accuse me.

Acts 24:14 But this I confess unto thee, that after the way which they call heresy, so worship I the God of my fathers, believing all things which are written in the law and in the prophets:

Acts 24:15 And have hope toward God, which they themselves also allow, that there shall be a resurrection of the dead, both of the just and unjust.

Acts 24:16 And herein do I exercise myself, to have always a conscience void of offence toward God, and toward men.

Acts 24:17 Now after many years I came to bring alms to my nation, and offerings.

Acts 24:18 Whereupon certain Jews from Asia found me purified in the temple, neither with multitude, nor with tumult.

Acts 24:19 Who ought to have been here before thee, and object, if they had ought against me.

Acts 24:20 Or else let these same here say, if they have found any evil doing in me, while I stood before the council,

Acts 24:21 Except it be for this one voice, that I cried standing among them, Touching the resurrection of the dead I am called in question by you this day.

Acts 24:22 And when Felix heard these things, having more perfect knowledge of that way, he deferred them, and said, When Lysias the chief captain shall come down, I will know the uttermost of your matter.

Acts 24:23 And he commanded a centurion to keep Paul, and to let him have liberty, and that he should forbid none of his acquaintance to minister or come unto him.

Acts 24:24 And after certain days, when Felix came with his wife Drusilla, which was a Jewess, he sent for Paul, and heard him concerning the faith in Christ.

Acts 24:25 And as he reasoned of righteousness, temperance, and judgment to come, Felix trembled, and answered, Go thy way for this time; when I have a convenient season, I will call for thee.

Acts 24:26 He hoped also that money should have been given him of Paul, that he might loose him: wherefore he sent for him the oftener, and communed with him.

Acts 24:27 But after two years Porcius Festus came into Felix' room: and Felix, willing to shew the Jews a pleasure, left Paul bound.

Chapter 67

'The way which they call heresy'

Acts 24:1-27

Acts 23 closed with Paul at Caesarea under arrest in Herod's judgment hall. He had been brought there under cover of night and under the protection of 470 Roman soldiers by order of Claudius Lysias. Claudius Lysias wrote a letter to Felix, the Roman governor, explaining the unusual circumstances of Paul's case and the reason for his actions (23:25-30). When Paul arrived at Caesarea, Felix told him that he would hear his case once his accusers had arrived from Jerusalem. This historical narrative of what transpired at Caesarea is intended by the Holy Spirit to teach us specific spiritual truths which the wise will lay to heart.

1. The Jews' accusations against Paul show us it is easy, though base, to slander and falsely accuse upright, honest people of wicked deeds and sinister motives (24:1-9)

Paul was an upright, honest man. He had done nothing wrong, certainly nothing criminal. He had done nothing, except faithfully preach the gospel of Christ to lost followers of religion. For that he was arrested and treated as a common criminal (2 Timothy 1:8, 9).

When his accusers arrived; 'Ananias the high priest,' a delegation of the Sanhedrin ('the elders') and a slick, polished lawyer named Tertullus — Paul was brought to trial before Felix. Tertullus began with flowery accolades designed to bias Felix's sentiments towards the Jews, knowing that proud men love the praises of men (Job 32:21, 22; Psalm 12:2, 3; Proverbs 26:28). The accusations against Paul were narrowed down to three.

'We have found this man a pestilent fellow.' This charge was intended to identify Paul as a troublemaker, one who constantly stirred up social unrest. Palestine was filled with such men, and the governor would naturally be disposed against them.

'A mover of sedition among all the Jews throughout the world, and a ringleader of the sect of the Nazarenes.' Here Tertullus brings to Felix's attention the fact that Paul was connected with the followers of Jesus, the Nazarene. They were considered both by the Jews and the Romans to be a heretical sect. In those days, the preaching of the gospel met with such unusual success that the political and ecclesiastical worlds feared ultimately being dominated by the church of God, though none of God's servants sought to influence the world by political power. Then, as now, God's true people sought not moral, political and social reform, but the conquest of men's hearts and lives by the power of the gospel (2 Corinthians 10:3-5).

'Who also hath gone about to profane the temple.' This indictment seems to be the most serious. Yet it states no specific charge. It is not charged Paul had profaned the temple, but he went about to do so. In an attempt to implicate the chief captain, Lysias, and put their own case in a more favourable light Tertullus said, 'You would not have been bothered with this matter if Lysias had left us alone.' Then he said, 'We are certain that your own examination of this man will prove our charges.' And all the elders said, 'Amen'.

These charges were made against Paul by religious men who knew they were not true. Their hatred for God, the gospel of his grace and the man who stood on the front lines, leading the church of God against the gates of hell, allowed them to justify violating their own consciences, their own religious codes and the law of God — all in the name of God and righteousness!

2. Paul acknowledged that true religion, the gospel of God's free, sovereign, saving grace in Jesus Christ, is always regarded by mainstream, human religious opinion as the way of heresy (24:10-21)

Paul boldly declared to Felix, 'This I confess unto thee, that after the way which they call heresy, so worship I the God of my fathers!'

Paul's response was much more specific than Tertullus' general charges. After briefly addressing the bench, giving honour to whom honour is due, but without flattery, Paul said to his accusers, 'Prove it!' He knew they had no basis for their charges. He had been away from Jerusalem for a long time (24:17). He had returned simply to worship God, bringing alms and offerings from the Gentile churches to their Jewish brethren (24:17; 11:29, 30; Romans 15:25; 2 Corinthians 8:4; Galatians 2:10). He came in a quiet, lawful manner. He made no disturbance. The real culprits were the troublemakers who followed him from Asia Minor and spread slanderous rumours about him (24:18, 19). Mainstream religion has always been opposed to the gospel of God. The message of salvation by grace alone, through faith alone, in Christ alone offends man's pride because it exposes his sin; it offends his intelligence because it can only be known by revelation; it offends his self-righteousness because it declares his own righteousness to be filthy rags and reveals the necessity of a substitutionary atonement for sin and the imputed righteousness of an infinitely meritorious representative, the Lord Jesus Christ. Though all the world (academic, political and religious), may say otherwise, there is only one religion and one message that fully satisfies all that is written in the law and the prophets, honouring the justice and truth of God, while holding forth the hope of resurrection and eternal life to sinners who deserve the wrath of God. That message, the gospel of Christ, declares seven facts, seven spiritual truths, about which there can be no compromise, though all the world should denounce them as heresy.

1. The Bible alone is the Word of God and as such must be our only rule of faith and practice (2 Timothy 3:16, 17; 2 Peter 1:19-21; Isaiah 8:20).
2. God Almighty; Father, Son and Holy Spirit, is absolutely sovereign over all things and constantly exercises sovereignty in creation, providence and grace (Psalm 115:3; 135:6; Romans 11:36).
3. All men and women by nature by the fall of Adam are totally depraved, spiritually dead sinners (Psalm 51:5; Romans 5:12; Ephesians 2:1-4).
4. By eternal, unconditional election, the Lord God chose a people before the world began, who must and will be saved (Ephesians 1:3-6; 2 Thessalonians 2:13).
5. The Lord Jesus Christ effectually redeemed all God's elect, putting away their sins by the sacrifice of himself, and obtained eternal redemption for them (Isaiah 53:1-12; 2 Corinthians 5:21; Galatians 3:13; Hebrews 9:12; 1 Peter 2:24).
6. The grace of God is irresistible, always effecting the salvation of chosen, redeemed sinners at the time appointed (Psalm 65:4; 110:3).
7. Every true believer will persevere in grace and faith, being kept by the power and grace of God unto eternal salvation (John 10:28; Philippians 1:6; 1 Peter 1:5).

3. Felix stands before us to warn us that all who put off the claims of Christ to 'a more convenient season' court divine reprobation (24:22-27)

Paul spoke plainly to the Roman governor and his wife about 'the faith in Christ', about 'that way', of which they had heard so much (24:24, 25). He pressed home both the necessity of Christ's imputed righteousness and the moral implications of the gospel. Felix was obviously moved, but not humbled. Confronted with the claims of Christ, he postponed commitment to him to 'a [more] convenient season'. But 'a more convenient season' never came. Today Felix is in hell because, having heard the gospel, he refused the claims of Christ in the gospel. Let all who are wise be warned!

315

Acts 24:10 Then Paul, after that the governor had beckoned unto him to speak, answered, Forasmuch as I know that thou hast been of many years a judge unto this nation, I do the more cheerfully answer for myself:

Acts 24:11 Because that thou mayest understand, that there are yet but twelve days since I went up to Jerusalem for to worship.

Acts 24:12 And they neither found me in the temple disputing with any man, neither raising up the people, neither in the synagogues, nor in the city:

Acts 24:13 Neither can they prove the things whereof they now accuse me.

Acts 24:14 But this I confess unto thee, that after the way which they call heresy, so worship I the God of my fathers, believing all things which are written in the law and in the prophets:

Acts 24:15 And have hope toward God, which they themselves also allow, that there shall be a resurrection of the dead, both of the just and unjust.

Acts 24:16 And herein do I exercise myself, to have always a conscience void of offence toward God, and toward men.

Acts 24:17 Now after many years I came to bring alms to my nation, and offerings.

Acts 24:18 Whereupon certain Jews from Asia found me purified in the temple, neither with multitude, nor with tumult.

Acts 24:19 Who ought to have been here before thee, and object, if they had ought against me.

Acts 24:20 Or else let these same here say, if they have found any evil doing in me, while I stood before the council,

Acts 24:21 Except it be for this one voice, that I cried standing among them, Touching the resurrection of the dead I am called in question by you this day.

Chapter 68

'The resurrection of the dead'

Acts 24:10-21

Throughout the book of Acts, the apostles constantly emphasized the resurrection of Christ and the consequent resurrection of the dead by his power. When Matthias was chosen to replace the apostate Judas, Peter said one must be 'ordained to be a witness with us of the resurrection' (1:22). A primary function of an apostle was being a witness of the Lord's resurrection. On the Day of Pentecost, the apostle showed the multitude how that David by the Spirit 'spake of the resurrection of Christ' (2:31). When Peter and John were arrested and brought before the council, the reason given for their arrest was that 'They taught the people and preached through Jesus the resurrection from the dead' (4:2). When they were set free, we are told, 'And with great power gave the apostles witness of the resurrection of the Lord Jesus: and great grace was upon them all' (4:33). It was the preaching of the resurrection that aroused the curiosity of the Athenians. They said Paul seemed 'to be a setter forth of strange gods: because he preached unto them Jesus, and the resurrection' (17:18). And when Paul answered the Jewish council which accused him before Felix he said, 'I ... have hope toward God ... that there shall be a resurrection of the dead, both of the just and unjust' (24:15).

The resurrection of the dead is a blessed gospel doctrine believed by, and full of comfort for, all God's saints. We believe, according to the Word of God, that every person who ever lived will live forever, not only in the immortality of their souls, but also that their bodies will be raised from the dead at the last day. The very flesh in which you now live will be raised to life again and you will live forever, either in the bliss of heaven, in the presence of God, the holy angels and 'just men made perfect', or in the torments of hell, in the company of Satan, demons and ungodly sinners, enduring the fires of the wrath of God which cannot be quenched!

1. There will be a resurrection of the just

The light of nature tells all men that the soul is immortal. Even the heathen acknowledge that the soul of man is something so wonderful and mysterious that it must endure forever. But the resurrection of the body is another matter.

This is not something that can be discovered and proved by science and nature. It is something that can be known only by divine revelation and faith in the Lord Jesus Christ. When the Word of God speaks of the resurrection of the just, it is referring to the resurrection of those people who have been justified and made righteous by the imputation of Christ's righteousness to them. When Christ comes again, all who trust him, who have been redeemed by his blood and saved by his grace, will be raised to eternal life and joy.

The saints of God in all ages have lived in hope of the resurrection. The faith of God's elect regarding the resurrection has been a matter of constant, unwavering confidence from the beginning. Job, Abraham, Joseph, Moses, Hannah, David, Isaiah, Ezekiel and Daniel all spoke of it with confidence and joy (Job 14:12, 14, 15; 19:25-27; Hebrews 11:19, 22; Deuteronomy 32:39; 1 Samuel 2:6; Psalm 16:8-11; 17:15; Isaiah 26:19; Ezekiel 37:11-14; Daniel 12:2). In the New Testament, references to the resurrection are so numerous that they simply cannot be listed here. But two passages from the lips of our Saviour will suffice to declare his doctrine: John 5:25-29; 11:23-26. The first resurrection, spoken of in John 5:25 and Revelation 20:6, is a spiritual resurrection. It is the new birth, the regeneration of chosen, redeemed sinners from spiritual death to spiritual life by the irresistible power and grace of God the Holy Spirit (Ephesians 2:1-4). But there will also be the literal resurrection of the body at Christ's second coming (John 5:28, 29; 11:23-26).

The translation of Enoch and that of Elijah stand as pledges of every believer's resurrection (Genesis 5:24; 2 Kings 2:11). As those two men were translated from earth to heaven, so all believers living on the earth when Christ comes again will be taken up to glory, but only after the dead in Christ have been raised (1 Thessalonians 4:13-18).

'The resurrection of the dead' is a frequent subject in Scripture. The angels of God watching over the bodies of God's saints assures us of the resurrection (Jude 9). Though our bodies must sleep for a while beneath the sod, God's angels watch over them to protect them until the trump of God sounds. The many instances of the resurrection of the dead recorded in the Scriptures are visible, documented assurances of the resurrection to come. Our God has given us proof over and over again that he is able to raise the dead to life again (1 Kings 17:21, 22; 2 Kings 13:21; Matthew 27:50-54; Luke 7:14; 8:54, 55; John 11:43, 44; Acts 9:40; 20:9, 10).

Our bodies as well as our souls belong to Christ and must be with him in glory (1 Corinthians 6:13). Christ does not save only the souls of his elect, but their bodies too. His work of redemption will not be complete until he has raised the bodies of all for whom he made atonement at Calvary (Romans 8:23; Ephesians 1:14). The body is for the Lord, and he shall have it. 'Your bodies are the members of Christ' (1 Corinthians 6:15). Not only are our souls vitally joined to him, but our bodies as well (Ephesians 5:30-32). The believer's body is the temple of the Holy Spirit (1 Corinthians 6:19, 20). The fact that the Holy Spirit dwells in the body of a saint not only sanctifies it, but also renders it immortal. Though this temple must go to the dust, it will be rebuilt in 'the resurrection of the just'!

Above all else, our hope of the resurrection is built upon the fact that the Lord Jesus Christ, our Saviour, arose from the dead (1 Corinthians 15:1-23, 49). If Christ arose from the dead as our head and representative, then all his people must also be raised. And if there is no resurrection, then Christ did not rise and we are still in our sins. If there is no resurrection, then there is: no atonement for sin, for justice is not satisfied; no righteousness to impute to us; no acceptance with God; and no salvation! But since Christ did die for us and did rise from the dead, we are assured that: our sins which were imputed to him are gone, washed away by his blood; justice is satisfied; his righteousness is of infinite merit for all who trust him; and all his people, all who are one with him, must be raised from the dead. Christ is the first-fruits of the resurrection, and the first-fruits are the pledge of more to come. There will be a resurrection of the just. This is the faith of the gospel. If you do not believe it, you have not been taught of God.

2. There will also be a resurrection of the unjust

At the Lord's second coming, both the righteous and the wicked, the believing and the unbelieving, the living and the dead, the sheep and the goats will be raised. Those who stand before God in the spotless garments of Christ's imputed righteousness, whose sins have been put away by his substitutionary sacrifice, will enter into and forever enjoy the glory of heavenly bliss in their bodies. But all who stand before God naked, polluted in their sins, without a substitute, will be cast body and soul into hell to endure eternally the torments of God's holy and just wrath. This is the second death. By some means, known only to himself, the Lord God will sustain the bodies and souls of the damned eternally, so that, though his unmitigated wrath is poured out upon them, they will not die (Matthew 5:27-30; 10:28).

Paul wrote, 'Knowing therefore the terror of the Lord, we persuade men' (2 Corinthians 5:11). There will be a resurrection of the dead, both the righteous and the wicked. You will be damned forever, body and soul, if you are not washed in the blood of Christ and robed in his righteousness. I urge you therefore, if you are yet without Christ, even as you read these lines, to be reconciled to God. Trust his Son, the Lord Jesus Christ, and live forever.

Let all who are wise live daily in the immediate prospect of death, the resurrection, judgment and eternity (Mark 8:35-37; 2 Corinthians 4:18-5:21).

319

Chapter 69

Deadly Procrastination

Acts 24:22-27

The closing verses of Acts 24 stand as a warning of the evil and danger of procrastination. 'After certain days, when Felix came with his wife Drusilla, which was a Jewess, he sent for Paul, and heard him concerning the faith in Christ. And as he reasoned of righteousness, temperance, and judgment to come, Felix trembled, and answered, Go thy way for this time; when I have a convenient season, I will call for thee.' But he never did. For two years, 'Felix, willing to show the Jews a pleasure, left Paul bound.' Some time later, this same Felix committed suicide. Felix warns us all that anyone who trifles with the things of God courts eternal damnation. Procrastination is always evil, but procrastination regarding the claims of Christ in the gospel is deadly. If a person will not repent when he is confronted with the claims of Christ, delivered to him by the power of the Holy Spirit, he cannot repent later. Such procrastination is blasphemy against the Holy Spirit (Matthew 12:31; Proverbs 1:23-33).

Paul reasoned with Felix concerning 'the faith in Christ'. Felix was a notoriously wicked man. He rose from slavery to be the Roman governor of Judea by cunning and treachery. His wife, Drusilla, was of the same character. Having the power of Rome behind him, Felix could do whatever he desired with Paul: kill him, leave him in prison, or set him free. Paul was fully aware of these things. Felix called Paul before him because he was curious about 'the faith in Christ'. He imagined that Paul's philosophical and religious opinions might be stimulating and entertaining. He certainly did not expect his prisoner to expose his sin and demand that he repent. But that is exactly what happened. God's faithful servant, being full of the Holy Spirit, powerfully preached the gospel of Christ to his captor. Without question, Paul boldly exposed Felix's sin, both the corruption of his heart and the evil of his deeds. But do not imagine that the apostle spent his time lecturing this pagan governor about the immorality of his behaviour and tried to persuade him to become a morally reformed man. Paul was aiming at the governor's heart. His subject was not morality, but 'the faith in Christ'. He was endeavouring to persuade this proud, wicked man to bow before the throne of God in repentance and faith, 'the faith in Christ'. His sermon had three points.

1. Paul reasoned with Felix about righteousness

No one will ever be saved until he or she is made to see what the Word of God teaches about righteousness. When the Spirit of God deals with sinners in grace, he reproves them of righteousness (John 16:8, 10).

In essence Paul said, 'Felix, God is holy, righteous, just and true. Because he is holy, he requires you to be perfectly holy, or else he will consume you in his wrath. You know that you are a sinful man before the holy Lord God, you have no righteousness and, being a sinful man, you cannot produce righteousness. That is why the Lord Jesus Christ, the Son of God, came into this world. He came to establish righteousness before God as a man, to make sinners righteous by his obedience to God as a man and his satisfaction of divine justice by his death as the sinner's substitute. He is "the Lord our Righteousness". Felix, the only way sinners like you and me can ever be made righteous is by the doing and dying of Jesus Christ, the sinner's substitute. Trust him. Believe on the Lord Jesus Christ. If you do but trust him, he is your righteousness. Your faith in him is evidence of the fact that he put away your sins by the shedding of his blood, that God has imputed to you his righteousness, and you are born of God.'

This is what the Word of God teaches about righteousness. We need to be certain that we understand these things:

1. The Lord God is perfect, righteous and holy (Psalm 7:9-11; Daniel 9:14).

2. The holy Lord God demands perfect righteousness in all his moral creatures, in all who are accepted by him (Leviticus 11:44, 45; 22:21; Matthew 5:20; Hebrews 12:14).

3. No man is capable of producing righteousness before God (Isaiah 64:6; Romans 3:9-20).

4. The only way a sinner can obtain righteousness before God is by faith in the Lord Jesus Christ (Romans 3:19-26; 10:1-4).

2. Paul reasoned with Felix about temperance

The word 'temperance' means 'self-control'. It is yielding to Christ the rule of one's life. That is the essence of faith (Mark 8:34-36; Luke 14:26-33). It is ever the tendency of sinful man to abuse the powers God has bestowed upon him, to allow the passions of his flesh to rule his life, and to give in to the persuasive allurements of the world and of Satan. But when a person is born of God, the Holy Spirit graciously subdues him, brings him under the rule of Christ and of righteousness, so that Christ as King rules over his life and the affairs of it, inspiring obedience to the will of God, for the glory of God (Galatians 5:23; Romans 6:11-18; Revelation 1:6). As the believer grows in the grace and knowledge of Christ, he grows in the exercise of temperance (2 Peter 1:6). Yet this temperance is something that requires watchfulness and diligence (1 Corinthians 9:27).

Felix was a proud and powerful man. Paul told him that the only way he could ever obtain righteousness with God and eternal salvation was to bow to Christ as a needy sinner, submitting to his dominion and trusting the merits of his obedience as Lord and Saviour. Then he pressed home the claims of Christ.

3. Paul warned Felix and reasoned with him concerning eternity and judgment to come

He pressed the governor to make a decision. I suspect he said something like this: 'Felix, I have reasoned with you from the Word of God. I have told you the truth. You know that I have done so. Here are your options. You must either repent or perish. You must either turn or burn. You must either trust Christ and be saved by him, or you must meet him in judgment and be damned by him. Which will it be?' Knowing the terror of the Lord, Paul pressed and persuaded Felix, urging him to repent and believe on the Lord Jesus Christ (2 Corinthians 5:10, 11).

When he heard the gospel, Felix trembled with conviction. I know that the grace and power of God the Holy Spirit is effectual and irresistible. If God the Holy Spirit goes after a sinner, he always fetches him home (Psalm 65:4). But I also know that everyone is responsible to believe the gospel and that every sinner who obeys the gospel is saved by Christ (Proverbs 1:23-33; Romans 10:21; John 3:36). If at this point Felix had repented and trusted Christ he would have been saved, but he chose not to do so. His conviction passed. He chose death rather than life, because he refused to give himself up to the rule and dominion of Christ. Conviction is not conversion. Emotion is not salvation. Trembling is not believing. But why did Felix tremble at the message Paul preached? He trembled because he was convinced of all that Paul said; but he was still a rebel at heart. His heart was not broken. His will was not subdued. He would not bow to the rule of Christ as his Lord.

Because of his heart's rebellion against the sovereign Christ, Felix wilfully rejected the claims of Christ in the gospel. He said to Paul, 'Go thy way for this time; when I have a convenient season, I will call for thee.' He said, 'Not today; perhaps tomorrow. I have some things to take care of first. I will call you tomorrow.' But tomorrow never came. God never promised to save anyone tomorrow (2 Corinthians 6:1, 2; Hebrews 3:15; Psalm 95:6-8).

Here is a solemn warning. Felix was damned by his procrastination! He could have been saved, but he stopped his ears. He wilfully rejected the counsel of God, and God never spoke to him again. What a warning Felix is to all who would trifle with the things of God! There is such a thing as judicial reprobation. There are people living upon the earth who are as sure of being in hell as if they were already there. There is no hope for them. God will not show them mercy. Though still alive, like Felix, they are damned for ever (Jeremiah 7:15, 16; Hosea 4:17; Romans 11:20, 21). Many were still alive in Noah's day when God shut the door of the ark. The five foolish virgins were still alive when God shut them out of his kingdom. Esau was still alive when he tried to repent, but found no place of repentance. Whenever God speaks and those who hear his voice refuse to obey it immediately, they are courting reprobation (2 Corinthians 2:14-16). If a sinner does not respond to the call of God in the gospel, the day will come when he will want to respond but will not be able to do so. Once more, I direct your attention to God's warning in Proverbs 1:23-33. Read it and be warned. Felix stands as a beacon to warn sinners of the danger of procrastination.

Acts 25:1 Now when Festus was come into the province, after three days he ascended from Caesarea to Jerusalem.

Acts 25:2 Then the high priest and the chief of the Jews informed him against Paul, and besought him,

Acts 25:3 And desired favour against him, that he would send for him to Jerusalem, laying wait in the way to kill him.

Acts 25:4 But Festus answered, that Paul should be kept at Caesarea, and that he himself would depart shortly thither.

Acts 25:5 Let them therefore, said he, which among you are able, go down with me, and accuse this man, if there be any wickedness in him.

Acts 25:6 And when he had tarried among them more than ten days, he went down unto Caesarea; and the next day sitting on the judgment seat commanded Paul to be brought.

Acts 25:7 And when he was come, the Jews which came down from Jerusalem stood round about, and laid many and grievous complaints against Paul, which they could not prove.

Acts 25:8 While he answered for himself, Neither against the law of the Jews, neither against the temple, nor yet against Caesar, have I offended any thing at all.

Acts 25:9 But Festus, willing to do the Jews a pleasure, answered Paul, and said, Wilt thou go up to Jerusalem, and there be judged of these things before me?

Acts 25:10 Then said Paul, I stand at Caesar's judgment seat, where I ought to be judged: to the Jews have I done no wrong, as thou very well knowest.

Acts 25:11 For if I be an offender, or have committed any thing worthy of death, I refuse not to die: but if there be none of these things whereof these accuse me, no man may deliver me unto them. I appeal unto Caesar.

Acts 25:12 Then Festus, when he had conferred with the council, answered, Hast thou appealed unto Caesar? unto Caesar shalt thou go.

Acts 25:13 And after certain days king Agrippa and Bernice came unto Caesarea to salute Festus.

Acts 25:14 And when they had been there many days, Festus declared Paul's cause unto the king, saying, There is a certain man left in bonds by Felix:

Acts 25:15 About whom, when I was at Jerusalem, the chief priests and the elders of the Jews informed me, desiring to have judgment against him.

Acts 25:16 To whom I answered, It is not the manner of the Romans to deliver any man to die, before that he which is accused have the accusers face to face, and have licence to answer for himself concerning the crime laid against him.

Acts 25:17 Therefore, when they were come hither, without any delay on the morrow I sat on the judgment seat, and commanded the man to be brought forth.

Acts 25:18 Against whom when the accusers stood up, they brought none accusation of such things as I supposed:

Acts 25:19 But had certain questions against him of their own superstition, and of one Jesus, which was dead, whom Paul affirmed to be alive.

Acts 25:20 And because I doubted of such manner of questions, I asked him whether he would go to Jerusalem, and there be judged of these matters.

Acts 25:21 But when Paul had appealed to be reserved unto the hearing of Augustus, I commanded him to be kept till I might send him to Caesar.

Acts 25:22 Then Agrippa said unto Festus, I would also hear the man myself. To morrow, said he, thou shalt hear him.

Acts 25:23 And on the morrow, when Agrippa was come, and Bernice, with great pomp, and was entered into the place of hearing, with the chief captains, and principal men of the city, at Festus' commandment Paul was brought forth.

Acts 25:24 And Festus said, King Agrippa, and all men which are here present with us, ye see this man, about whom all the multitude of the Jews have dealt with me, both at Jerusalem, and also here, crying that he ought not to live any longer.

Acts 25:25 But when I found that he had committed nothing worthy of death, and that he himself hath appealed to Augustus, I have determined to send him.

Acts 25:26 Of whom I have no certain thing to write unto my lord. Wherefore I have brought him forth before you, and specially before thee, O king Agrippa, that, after examination had, I might have somewhat to write.

Acts 25:27 For it seemeth to me unreasonable to send a prisoner, and not withal to signify the crimes laid against him.

Chapter 70

Jesus Affirmed To Be Alive

Acts 25:1-27

The Jews were not at all happy about the way Felix had handled Paul. So, shortly after Festus took the governor's seat at Caesarea, they tried to get him to bring Paul to Jerusalem for trial, or so they intimated. Actually, they intended to assassinate him along the way (25:1-12). The respected religious leaders of the day were so savage in their hatred towards Paul, the gospel he preached and the God he represented, that in the name of God they were determined to murder him (cf. John 16:2). But Paul, being a Roman citizen, took advantage of his legal rights. Refusing to be tried by a lower court at Jerusalem he said, 'I appeal unto Caesar' (25:11). Festus had no choice under Roman law. He said, 'Unto Caesar shalt thou go' (25:12).

When Agrippa, who was reputed to be a specialist in Jewish matters, came to Caesarea, Festus welcomed the opportunity to discuss Paul's case with him (25:13-21). Agrippa expressed a desire to hear Paul for himself (25:32). Arrangements were made. Agrippa and his sister Bernice came to 'the place of hearing' in great pomp (25:23). And Festus displayed the customary flattery and false adulation of one politician to another (25:24-27). The fact of the matter was that Festus was fearful of sending Paul to Rome with no legitimate charges against him (25:19, 27). By involving Agrippa in the matter he had something to fall back on, were his actions questioned by his superiors at Rome.

1. What distinguished Paul from his enemies

Two things were apparent to Festus. Remember, he was a pagan politician. He had no regard for Paul, or for the Jews. He did not even know what the controversy was about. Yet he quickly perceived two things that distinguished Paul from his enemies.

First, the Jews, the religious sceptics, the unbelieving followers of religion, raised 'certain questions', but Paul made bold affirmations (25:18, 19). That is ever the case. Those who oppose the gospel and take offence at the preaching of the cross of Christ assert nothing, but question everything. Where they cannot prove evil, they hope to cast a shadow of doubt by raising questions. In doctrinal matters, their questions are almost always foolish carping about meaningless things. It is pointless and futile to answer such questions. We are repeatedly warned not to do so (1 Timothy 1:4; 6:4; 2 Timothy 2:23; Titus 3:9). We do not need to defend the truth, but simply declare it. That was Paul's method. He boldly, dogmatically affirmed the truth as God revealed it.

Believing men and women are God's witnesses (Isaiah 44:8; Acts 1:8). A witness is one who simply tells what he knows. He cares nothing for the questions, speculations, or objections of others. So we simply affirm certain, definite, revealed facts, facts plainly laid down in the Word of God and experienced in our own hearts. Here we stand, oblivious to the science, wisdom and reason of educated fools. The basis of our faith is the Word of God alone (Isaiah 8:20; 2 Timothy 3:16). The Jews were full of questions. But Paul affirmed that Jesus, who was dead, is alive. He made no attempt to answer their questions or prove his doctrine. He simply affirmed that it was so upon the basis of Holy Scripture and his own experience. He had seen, spoken to, heard from, and felt the power of the risen, exalted, living Christ. He affirmed what he knew to be the truth. That is what we must do as God's witnesses in this world today.

Secondly, Festus observed that the Jews were concerned about their own religion, 'their own superstition', but Paul was concerned with a living person (25:19). Paul's religion was not a religion of books and creeds. His religion was a person. He found all his treasure in the person and work of the Lord Jesus Christ. He knew, trusted, loved, worshipped, served, walked with and preached a person. Christ is more than the author and finisher of our faith. He is the sum and substance of it. We glory not in our creed or denomination, but in the Lord Jesus Christ himself (1 Corinthians 1:30, 31; Galatians 6:14; Philippians 3:3). Christianity is a living union with a living person. It is Christ in you and you in Christ.

2. Paul preached Christ

Preaching, according to the pattern and precept of the New Testament, is the declaration and description of the Lord Jesus Christ. The thing that so greatly disturbed the Jews was not that Paul did any of the things they accused him of doing. They knew he was innocent of their charges. But he went everywhere preaching that Christ, whom they had crucified, was alive. This was such an obvious thing that Festus himself declared it (25:19). Paul spoke so much of the risen, exalted, reigning, saving Christ that even this pagan magistrate knew that his message was 'Jesus Christ, and him crucified' (1 Corinthians 2:2).

In those early days of Christianity, God's preachers, as often as they could get anyone to listen, preached Christ to men. Indeed, to this day, God's preachers go everywhere preaching the Lord Jesus Christ. Any sermon that is not full of Christ, does not point sinners to Christ and cause men to think upon him, or that does not send men away with Christ on their minds, ought never to have been preached (1 Corinthians 2:2; 9:16). A Christless sermon is a useless sermon! 'Jesus Christ and him crucified' is the message of Holy Scripture (Luke 24:27, 44, 45). The only hope of perishing sinners (John 12:32) and the believer's motive, inspiration and guide in all things (2 Corinthians 8:9; 1 Peter 2:21-24) is the Lord Jesus Christ.

Paul laid great stress upon and particularly emphasized Christ's death upon the cross as the sinner's substitute. He preached, as Festus said, 'one Jesus, which was dead'. That which was thought to be the most obnoxious, offensive and ridiculous point of his theology was the very thing which Paul preached most (1 Corinthians 1:17-23). That which the Jews most despised and the Gentiles most ridiculed, Paul most constantly affirmed (Galatians 6:14). He preached life by Christ's death, salvation by the crucified substitute, blood atonement and justification by the penal death of Christ in the place of God's elect as their all-sufficient and effectual Redeemer (Romans 3:24-26). Because of his faithful dogmatism in preaching Christ to men, Paul was hounded to death by lost religious men who, being ignorant of God's righteousness in Christ, went about to establish their own righteousness (24:5; Romans 10:1-4). And you may be assured of this fact: that man who faithfully preaches the gospel of Christ as Paul did, and the congregation which hears and follows him, will have to bear the scandalous reproach and bitter wrath of lost religious people today. The offence of the cross has not ceased (Galatians 5:11).

In preaching the gospel, Paul affirmed that Jesus Christ, who died at Calvary, is alive! He had seen the risen Saviour, heard his voice and experienced the transforming power of his grace. Every believer has affirmed this fact in his or her own soul. Jesus is alive! He lives to claim heaven for his redeemed ones (Psalm 68:18, 19); to bestow his Spirit upon God's elect in regenerating grace (Zechariah 12:9, 10; Galatians 3:13, 14); to prepare heaven for the homecoming of his saints (John 14:1-3); to make intercession for his people (Hebrews 7:25; 1 John 2:1, 2); to rule all things on behalf of chosen, redeemed sinners (John 17:2); and to come again in power and great glory to consummate his great work of saving his people from their sins (Matthew 1:21; 1 Thessalonians 4:13-18).

Acts 25:19 But had certain questions against him of their own superstition, and of one Jesus, which was dead, whom Paul affirmed to be alive.

Chapter 71

The Resurrection Of Christ

Acts 25:19

Festus summed up the dispute between the apostle Paul and his Jewish accusers in one issue. The whole controversy was about 'one Jesus, which was dead, whom Paul affirmed to be alive'. The object of this chapter is just that: to affirm that Christ Jesus is alive. The incarnation of Christ is a source of great comfort and joy to every believer. How blessed it is for us to know that God assumed our nature! God in human flesh is able to redeem us, understands and sympathizes with us and is touched with the feeling of our infirmities (Matthew 1:21, 23; Hebrews 2:17, 18; 4:15).

The righteous life of Christ as a man is the righteousness he wrought out for his people. His life of obedience is a moral example of faith, love, holiness and devotion which every believer strives to follow (John 13:15; Ephesians 4:32-5:1; 1 Peter 2:21). But it is much more than a moral example! Christ's righteous obedience to God as our representative and substitute is that 'holiness without which no man shall see the Lord' (Hebrews 12:14). His righteous obedience is the robe of pure white, the garment of salvation in which every believer is clothed. It is the righteousness performed by Christ which God imputes to his elect in justification, by which we are made righteous, perfectly holy and accepted with the holy Lord God (Jeremiah 23:6; Romans 5:18-21; 10:1-4; 2 Corinthians 5:21).

The blood of Christ is our redemption. His death as our vicarious, sin-atoning, substitutionary sacrifice is the basis of our hope before God. He paid our debt, satisfied divine justice and put away the sins of God's elect. He obtained eternal redemption for us! 'Christ hath redeemed us from the curse of the law' (Galatians 3:13). He did not try to redeem us; he redeemed us! He died; therefore we shall never die (Romans 3:24-26; 8:1, 33-39; 2 Corinthians 5:21; Hebrews 9:12; 1 Peter 1:18-20; 2:24; 3:18).

We rejoice in, and give thanks to God for the accomplishments of our dear Saviour. He came into the world as a man for us. He lived in righteousness for us. He died on the cursed tree for us. But had he not risen from the grave, ascended into heaven and sat down on the right hand of the majesty on high, his obedience, life and death would have been as meaningless and useless to us as that of any other man. The fact is, the whole

Acts 24:22 And when Felix heard these things, having more perfect knowledge of that way, he deferred them, and said, When Lysias the chief captain shall come down, I will know the uttermost of your matter.

Acts 24:23 And he commanded a centurion to keep Paul, and to let him have liberty, and that he should forbid none of his acquaintance to minister or come unto him.

Acts 24:24 And after certain days, when Felix came with his wife Drusilla, which was a Jewess, he sent for Paul, and heard him concerning the faith in Christ.

Acts 24:25 And as he reasoned of righteousness, temperance, and judgment to come, Felix trembled, and answered, Go thy way for this time; when I have a convenient season, I will call for thee.

Acts 24:26 He hoped also that money should have been given him of Paul, that he might loose him: wherefore he sent for him the oftener, and communed with him.

Acts 24:27 But after two years Porcius Festus came into Felix' room: and Felix, willing to shew the Jews a pleasure, left Paul bound.

truth of God, the whole gospel, the whole of our faith, the whole of our salvation and the whole glory of the triune God stands or falls with the resurrection of Christ (1 Corinthians 15:14-18). Therefore it is needful that the fact of it be established clearly in every believer's heart and mind.

1. The fact stated

The Lord Jesus Christ, our Saviour, died upon a Roman cross 2,000 years ago. He died at the hands of wicked men by the will of God as a substitute for sinners (Isaiah 53:9-12; Acts 2:23). Having died, he was taken down from the cross, wrapped in grave-clothes and buried in a borrowed tomb. That tomb was covered with a large rock, sealed by the Roman government and guarded by soldiers (Matthew 27:57-66). But on the third day, he arose from the dead.

Christ really did die upon the cross. When the soldiers came to break his legs, to finish him off, they saw he was already dead and did not bother. Yet with malicious spite, one of them thrust a spear into his side (John 19:31-37).

That very same Jesus who died arose from the dead (1 Corinthians 15:3, 4; Romans 14:9). Yes, our Lord's resurrection was literal, physical, bodily. It was not the resurrection of his divine nature. His divine nature could not, and did not die! It was not the resurrection of his human soul. The soul of man is immortal! His soul, like that of every believer, departed immediately to paradise upon the death of his body (Luke 23:43; 2 Corinthians 5:1-9). It was his physical body that was raised from the dead (John 2:19-21; Luke 24:39, 40; John 20:25, 27). Though now immortal and glorified, our Lord's human body in heaven is the same in appearance, size, form and substance as it was when he walked upon the earth. He is a real man, even today!

2. The fact affirmed

Our Lord's resurrection is so clearly affirmed that it cannot be denied by any honest person. Those who are determined in their obstinate rebellion against God may suppress the truth and loudly denounce it; but they know in their hearts that it is so, even as the heathen know in their hearts that the wrath of God is upon them (Romans 1:18). But the clear affirmations of Christ's resurrection are given for the comfort and edification of God's saints.

First, the Old Testament prophets declared that Messiah would be one who would arise from the dead (Isaiah 53:10-12). It was clearly revealed in the Old Testament that Christ would both die to redeem and rise again to rule over all things to save his elect. Compare scripture with scripture and you will see that the New Testament is the fulfilment and explanation of the Old (Psalm 2:7 with Hebrews 1:5; Psalm 16:10 with Acts 2:27-31; Psalm 68:18

with Ephesians 4:8; Psalm 110:1 with Hebrews 1:13; Psalm 110:4 with Hebrews 7:17; Isaiah 26:19 with Matthew 27:52, 53; Hosea 6:2 with Ephesians 2:6 and Colossians 3:1).

Secondly, in addition to the many direct prophecies, there were many types and pictures of our Lord's resurrection in the Old Testament: Adam awakening out of a deep sleep to behold and receive the bride formed from his side (Genesis 2:21-23); Isaac's resurrection from the sacrificial altar three days after the sentence of death was passed upon him (Genesis 22:4; Hebrews 11:17-19); the bush that was burned with fire but was not consumed, out of which God spoke to Moses (Exodus 3:2-6); Aaron's rod that budded and blossomed with life (Numbers 17:5-9); the living bird that was set free after it was dipped in the blood of the bird that was slain for the purification of the leper (Leviticus 14:6); the scapegoat that was set free after the other goat was slain for atonement (Leviticus 16:8-10, 15-17, 20-22); the deliverance of Jonah from the belly of the whale after three days (Matthew 12:40).

Thirdly, the witnesses of our Lord's resurrection are of such number and credibility that no court in the world could deny their testimony. He was seen by angels (Matthew 28:2, 5, 6; Luke 24:5, 6; John 20:12). Holy women saw the risen Christ and declared it (Matthew 28:9; Mark 16:4, 9; Luke 24:2-9; John 20:11-18). The soldiers who guarded the tomb themselves testified of the resurrection (Matthew 28:4, 11-15). More than 500 disciples saw the risen Christ at one time (1 Corinthians 15:6). The risen Saviour was seen by Peter, then by the rest of the apostles and last of all by Paul, both before and after he was converted (1 Corinthians 15:5-8; Acts 22:17, 18; 26:16, 19). These men were witnesses chosen by God for the purpose of declaring the resurrection to men (Acts 10:34-43). All who reject their testimony wilfully shut their eyes to the best-attested fact in history.

Fourthly, the Holy Spirit is himself the witness of Christ's resurrection (Acts 5:30-32; Hebrews 2:4). God the Holy Spirit was poured out on the Day of Pentecost and wrought miracles in the apostolic age as a confirmation of the fact that Christ, having accomplished the redemption of his people, is risen and exalted.

3. The fact explained

The fact of our Lord's resurrection is vital. Without it there is no salvation for any sinner. But because Christ is risen from the dead, exalted to the throne of God and makes intercession for his people, three things are guaranteed for God's elect:

1. Their redemption: Justice being satisfied, our sins have been purged from the record of heaven, and sin can never be imputed to a believer (Hebrews 9:12; Romans 4:8; 1 John 2:2).

2. Their regeneration: All for whom atonement was made and who were raised with Christ representatively will be raised by his Spirit from death to life in the new birth (Ephesians 2:5, 6; 1 Peter 1:3).

3. Their resurrection: Every believer, every chosen, redeemed, regenerate soul, will be completely conformed to the image of Christ, body, soul and spirit, in resurrection glory (Romans 8:28-30; 1 Corinthians 15:20, 23; 1 Thessalonians 4:13-18).

Acts 26:1 Then Agrippa said unto Paul, Thou art permitted to speak for thyself. Then Paul stretched forth the hand, and answered for himself:

Acts 26:2 I think myself happy, king Agrippa, because I shall answer for myself this day before thee touching all the things whereof I am accused of the Jews:

Acts 26:3 Especially because I know thee to be expert in all customs and questions which are among the Jews: wherefore I beseech thee to hear me patiently.

Acts 26:4 My manner of life from my youth, which was at the first among mine own nation at Jerusalem, know all the Jews;

Acts 26:5 Which knew me from the beginning, if they would testify, that after the most straitest sect of our religion I lived a Pharisee.

Acts 26:6 And now I stand and am judged for the hope of the promise made of God unto our fathers:

Acts 26:7 Unto which promise our twelve tribes, instantly serving God day and night, hope to come. For which hope's sake, king Agrippa, I am accused of the Jews.

Acts 26:8 Why should it be thought a thing incredible with you, that God should raise the dead?

Acts 26:9 I verily thought with myself, that I ought to do many things contrary to the name of Jesus of Nazareth.

Acts 26:10 Which thing I also did in Jerusalem: and many of the saints did I shut up in prison, having received authority from the chief priests; and when they were put to death, I gave my voice against them.

Acts 26:11 And I punished them oft in every synagogue, and compelled them to blaspheme; and being exceedingly mad against them, I persecuted them even unto strange cities.

Acts 26:12 Whereupon as I went to Damascus with authority and commission from the chief priests,

Acts 26:13 At midday, O king, I saw in the way a light from heaven, above the brightness of the sun, shining round about me and them which journeyed with me.

Acts 26:14 And when we were all fallen to the earth, I heard a voice speaking unto me, and saying in the Hebrew tongue, Saul, Saul, why persecutest thou me? it is hard for thee to kick against the pricks.

Acts 26:15 And I said, Who art thou, Lord? And he said, I am Jesus whom thou persecutest.

Acts 26:16 But rise, and stand upon thy feet: for I have appeared unto thee for this purpose, to make thee a minister and a witness both of these things which thou hast seen, and of those things in the which I will appear unto thee;

Acts 26:17 Delivering thee from the people, and from the Gentiles, unto whom now I send thee,

Acts 26:18 To open their eyes, and to turn them from darkness to light, and from the power of Satan unto God, that they may receive forgiveness of sins, and inheritance among them which are sanctified by faith that is in me.

Acts 26:19 Whereupon, O king Agrippa, I was not disobedient unto the heavenly vision:

Acts 26:20 But shewed first unto them of Damascus, and at Jerusalem, and throughout all the coasts of Judaea, and then to the Gentiles, that they should repent and turn to God, and do works meet for repentance.

Acts 26:21 For these causes the Jews caught me in the temple, and went about to kill me.

Acts 26:22 Having therefore obtained help of God, I continue unto this day, witnessing both to small and great, saying none other things than those which the prophets and Moses did say should come:

Acts 26:23 That Christ should suffer, and that he should be the first that should rise from the dead, and should shew light unto the people, and to the Gentiles.

Acts 26:24 And as he thus spake for himself, Festus said with a loud voice, Paul, thou art beside thyself; much learning doth make thee mad.

Acts 26:25 But he said, I am not mad, most noble Festus; but speak forth the words of truth and soberness.

Acts 26:26 For the king knoweth of these things, before whom also I speak freely: for I am persuaded that none of these things are hidden from him; for this thing was not done in a corner.

Acts 26:27 King Agrippa, believest thou the prophets? I know that thou believest.

Acts 26:28 Then Agrippa said unto Paul, Almost thou persuadest me to be a Christian.

Acts 26:29 And Paul said, I would to God, that not only thou, but also all that hear me this day, were both almost, and altogether such as I am, except these bonds.

Acts 26:30 And when he had thus spoken, the king rose up, and the governor, and Bernice, and they that sat with them:

Acts 26:31 And when they were gone aside, they talked between themselves, saying, This man doeth nothing worthy of death or of bonds.

Acts 26:32 Then said Agrippa unto Festus, This man might have been set at liberty, if he had not appealed unto Caesar.

Chapter 72

Paul's Testimony Before Agrippa

Acts 26:1-32

Though Paul stood before a Roman tribunal in defence of his life, he seized the opportunity to tell both the court and his accusers what God had done for him and in him by his free and sovereign grace in Christ. In the thirty-two verses of this chapter, Paul describes himself, his life, his conversion and his ministry. In doing so, he faithfully fulfilled his responsibility as the Lord's servant (Isaiah 44:8; Acts 1:8), preaching Jesus Christ and him crucified even to his captors. The preaching of the gospel always calls for sinners to become followers of Christ, trusting him as Lord and Saviour. Agrippa understood that and said, after Paul had finished speaking, 'Almost thou persuadest me to be a Christian.' What did Paul tell Agrippa that so moved him?

1. He had been a lost religious zealot (26:1-11)

Paul said, 'After the most straitest sect of our religion I lived a Pharisee' (26:5). Saul of Tarsus never was a profligate, immoral person. He was from his youth an upright, religious man; a man of principle and integrity. Like the rich young ruler, he kept the law from his youth up. Insofar as the letter of the law and its outward requirements were concerned, he was blameless (Philippians 3:4-6). Yet he was lost!

Unlike most religious people, Saul was a very zealous man. He was devoted. He studied the Scriptures with diligence. He talked about the things of God with zeal. He was wholehearted, earnest and thoroughly committed. Saul of Tarsus never neglected the hour of prayer, the study of God's Word, or the house of God. So zealous was he in religion that, in accordance with Old Testament law, he relentlessly persecuted those who followed Jesus of Nazareth, believing them to be blasphemers. Saul was so zealous that most who truly worship God must blush with shame when comparing themselves to him. Yet he was lost!

Moreover, Saul of Tarsus was thoroughly orthodox in his doctrine. This man was no scoffer, sceptic, or liberal, and he certainly was not an Arminian! Even before he was converted, he knew and embraced doctrinal truth (26:4-8). I do not mean to suggest that he had spiritual understanding, but his doctrine was orthodox. Saul was a Pharisee. He believed in divine election, divine sovereignty, absolute predestination, total depravity, the inspiration of Scripture, the resurrection of the dead and even particular redemption. No Pharisee, or anyone else who understands the Old Testament sacrifices, ever dreamed of a universal atonement! Saul even looked for the Christ, believing all the Old Testament prophecies relating to him. His doctrine was right. Yet he was lost! Saul believed in Christ as a matter of doctrine, but he did not know Christ. He believed all that the Bible said about Christ; but he did not know him (John 17:3). He was a lost religious zealot.

2. At God's appointment he was confronted, conquered and converted by the grace and power of the Lord Jesus Christ (26:12-15)

There is a time of love appointed by God for the saving of each of his elect (Ezekiel 16:8; Psalm 65:4; 110:3; Galatians 4:4-6). For Saul, the appointed time and place of mercy was when he was on his way to Damascus to persecute the saints of God. Suddenly, the Son of God stepped into his life. He was not seeking the Lord, but the Lord sought him. He was not looking for grace, but grace looked for him. He did not find the Saviour, but the Saviour found him (Isaiah 65:1; Acts 9:1-20; 22:6-21).

He was 'in the way'. Though he did not know it, Saul was in the way that would lead him to Christ, following a pre-arranged path, walking in a pre-ordained way. Each of his steps was ordered by the Lord, predestinated and marked out before the world began (Proverbs 16:9; Romans 8:28).

Saul of Tarsus was an object of God's electing love. There were many travelling the Damascus road that day, but only one was called by God's effectual power and grace because only one had been chosen and redeemed. The irresistible grace and call came only to the chosen (Romans 8:29, 30; 2 Thessalonians 2:13, 14).

The proud Pharisee was conquered and subdued by the revelation of Christ. The Lord Jesus met him in the way, revealed himself in him and called him with a call he could not resist. He saw the Lord (26:13), heard his voice (26:14) and surrendered to his will (26:15). All who are saved by God's grace are saved by the same sovereign intervention of God into their lives (Ephesians 2:1-6; Galatians 1:15, 16).

3. The Lord Jesus Christ himself put Paul into the ministry (26:16-18)

God's preachers do not decide to go into the ministry and begin looking for somewhere to preach. Any man who goes looking for a place to preach will compromise to get it and compromise to keep it. God's preachers are made by God and put into the work of the ministry by him. Paul said, 'I was made a minister' (Ephesians 3:7-11). God's preachers are sent by God with a message to proclaim to men. As it was with Paul, so it is with all who are called by God to preach the gospel. Their message and their method are determined by God. Paul was required to preach what he had experienced, no more and no less (26:16). It was his privilege and responsibility to carry the light of the gospel into a world of darkness and superstition (26:18). The message he was sent to preach was clear and simple (26:18). The Lord Jesus sent Paul to preach to sinners the forgiveness of sin by his blood (Ephesians 1:7), the hope of eternal life by his grace (2 Thessalonians 2:16), and sanctification (holiness) by faith in him (1 Corinthians 1:30).

4. Paul was obedient to his Master (26:19-23)

Wherever Paul went, he preached the gospel to all; Jews and Gentiles. His message was always the same (1 Corinthians 2:2). He constantly preached repentance towards God (26:20), redemption by Christ (26:23) and the resurrection of the dead (26:23). He preached the first resurrection, which is spiritual regeneration by the power and grace of God the Holy Spirit (John 3:3-8; 5:25; Revelation 20:6), and the resurrection of the body at the last day (John 5:28; 1 Thessalonians 4:13-18).

5. Being called by God, Paul was far more concerned about the souls of men and the glory of God than his own comfort and welfare (26:24-32)

Paul stood as a prisoner in chains before Festus and Agrippa. Yet he was not seeking freedom, or even to prove his innocence. Paul's obvious intent in this defence of himself was to make Christ known to his captors. Read the chapter carefully. Throughout these verses, Paul was pointing Festus, Agrippa, Bernice and his accusers to Christ as the hope of Israel (26:6), the crucified Saviour (26:9), the light from heaven (26:13), the exalted Lord (26:13-15), the head of the church (26:15) and the sovereign God (26:16-23). He told them that forgiveness, eternal life, repentance, redemption, sanctification, resurrection and faith are all the gifts of God's free, saving grace in Christ. Festus considered him nothing but a madman (26:24, 25). But Paul (26:26-32), sensing that he had caught Agrippa's attention, pressed the claims of Christ upon him personally and urgently. Agrippa was, according to his own words, 'almost persuaded' to become a worshipper and follower of Christ — 'almost persuaded' but lost at last! Being reproved and instructed, Agrippa deliberately hardened his heart. Therefore he perished. All who follow his example should tremble with fear (Proverbs 29:1).

Acts 26:13 At midday, O king, I saw in the way a light from heaven, above the brightness of the sun, shining round about me and them which journeyed with me.

Acts 26:14 And when we were all fallen to the earth, I heard a voice speaking unto me, and saying in the Hebrew tongue, Saul, Saul, why persecutest thou me? it is hard for thee to kick against the pricks.

Acts 26:15 And I said, Who art thou, Lord? And he said, I am Jesus whom thou persecutest.

Acts 26:16 But rise, and stand upon thy feet: for I have appeared unto thee for this purpose, to make thee a minister and a witness both of these things which thou hast seen, and of those things in the which I will appear unto thee;

Acts 26:17 Delivering thee from the people, and from the Gentiles, unto whom now I send thee,

Acts 26:18 To open their eyes, and to turn them from darkness to light, and from the power of Satan unto God, that they may receive forgiveness of sins, and inheritance among them which are sanctified by faith that is in me.

Acts 26:19 Whereupon, O king Agrippa, I was not disobedient unto the heavenly vision:

Acts 26:20 But shewed first unto them of Damascus, and at Jerusalem, and throughout all the coasts of Judaea, and then to the Gentiles, that they should repent and turn to God, and do works meet for repentance.

Chapter 73

'For this purpose'

Acts 26:13-20

Salvation is not determined by what man does for God, but by what God does for man! 'Salvation is of the Lord' (Jonah 2:9). For a sinner to be saved, three things are essential. If you, who read these lines, are saved it is because God has done three things for you that you would not and could not do for yourself, three things which he has not done for any who perish under his wrath. God Almighty has chosen you, redeemed you and saved you!

1. Election

Salvation begins with divine election (Psalm 65:4; Romans 8:28-30; 11:5-8; Ephesians 1:3-6; 2 Thessalonians 2:13). No sinner could ever have been saved apart from God's sovereign, eternal, electing love. Pardon is not the decision of the criminal, but the prerogative of the judge. Salvation comes to sinners in time according to the purpose of God in election from eternity (2 Timothy 1:9; John 15:16). But election alone could save no one.

2. Redemption

The second essential to salvation is redemption by the blood of Christ. Justice would never allow sin to be put away without satisfaction (Romans 3:24-26; Hebrews 9:22). And justice can never allow one sinner for whom atonement has been made to suffer the wrath of God (Romans 5:11; Galatians 3:13; Hebrews 9:12; 10:10-14). Christ laid down his life for his sheep (John 10:11, 15). He died in the place of his people (Isaiah 53:8). He made atonement for God's elect, the people he came to save (Matthew 1:21; John 17:9, 20).

3. Regeneration

Election and redemption are essential to salvation, but something else is essential: 'Ye must be born again!' In order for a sinner to see and enter into the kingdom of God, he must be regenerated, born again, by the irresistible power and grace of God the Holy Spirit (John 3:3-7). Election opens the door of mercy. Redemption removes sin, the obstacle to grace. And regeneration gives life to the dead. Regeneration is a resurrection from the dead. It is the creation of life. All who have been chosen by God the Father from eternity and redeemed by God the Son at Calvary, will be given new life and called by God the Holy Spirit at the appointed time of love (Psalm 65:4; 110:3).

The fruit of regeneration is repentance, faith and conversion. Sinners are not born again because they repent. Rather, we repent, trust Christ and are converted because we have been born of God. If, as the Scriptures say, man is spiritually dead, salvation must be the result of what God does and in no way dependent upon what the sinner does (Ephesians 2:1-8; Romans 9:16-18).

The means God uses

All whom the Father chose, the Son redeemed and the Spirit calls must be saved. Yet God always accomplishes his purpose of grace through the use of specific means. God speaks to men through men. Sovereign grace always operates through the use of human instrumentality. In Acts 26:13-20, Paul tells Agrippa how and why the Lord appeared to him and made him a preacher of the gospel. The Lord said to Paul, 'I have appeared unto thee for this purpose' — for the purpose of saving chosen, redeemed sinners.

To save his elect God prepares chosen men to preach the gospel (26:13-17; Romans 10:14, 15). Salvation is not a haphazard affair. It is accomplished by the all-wise plan and eternal purpose of God. One part of that plan and purpose is the preparation of preachers by whom he will call his elect. This is a wonderful thing: God calls, prepares, equips and commissions specific men to preach the gospel to specific sinners in specific circumstances (Jeremiah 3:15), just as he prepared Paul to preach to the Gentiles! This business of making a preacher is God's work (Galatians 1:1; Ephesians 3:7-11; 4:8-16).

In verse 18, the apostle declares that God graciously saves sinners through the preaching of the gospel. God has not sent his servants into the world for nothing. 'It pleased God by the foolishness of preaching to save them that believe' (1 Corinthians 1:21). 'Faith cometh by hearing and hearing by the word of God' (Romans 10:17). The gospel ministry must never be viewed as a light thing. Preaching the gospel must ever be a matter of highest importance in the church of God. It must never become secondary. God does not save sinners apart from the preaching of the gospel. The issue is not whether he can do so, but whether he has chosen to do so. Let the Word of God alone settle the matter: read Romans 1:15, 16; James 1:18 and 1 Peter 1:23-25. Gospel preaching is God's ordained means of saving sinners. God sent Philip to preach Christ to the Ethiopian eunuch precisely because that eunuch could not understand Isaiah 53 until some man sent by God showed him of whom the prophet spoke (Acts 8:26-35). This is the reason for placing such high importance upon the public ministry of the Word. Nothing is so important as the preaching of the gospel. If you care for your soul let nothing keep you from hearing God's servant preach his gospel. If you care for the souls of others do all within your power to bring them under the sound of the gospel. If you care for the souls of men and women around the world, give generously for the furtherance of the gospel through missionary endeavours.

God will save his elect by the preaching of the gospel. Read verse 18 again carefully. God's servants are not beating the air. God has sent them to open the eyes of chosen sinners and turn their hearts to the Lord. Gospel preachers are men on the trail of Christ's sheep. They seek the salvation of God's elect. And they will not fail! They preach with the confident expectation of success. God has promised to honour his Word (Isaiah 55:11; Romans 1:16, 17; Hebrews 4:12). Our labour is not in vain in the Lord (1 Corinthians 15:58). God will save his elect by the means he has ordained.

The sinner's response to God's call

One more lesson to be learned from this passage is that all who are called by God repent and turn to him in faith willingly (26:19, 20). Divine sovereignty does not nullify human responsibility any more than it nullifies human instrumentality. In election, redemption and regeneration, the sinner is totally passive. But as soon as a person is called by God he or she is fully active.

No sinner is saved without repentance (Luke 13:3, 5; Acts 5:30, 31; Romans 2:4). Without question, repentance is the gift of God. But God does not repent for us. We must repent. Indeed, repentance is a voluntary act of a renewed heart. It is a change of mind, a change of manners, a change of motives and a change of masters. In Psalms 32 and 51 we learn from the man after God's own heart what true repentance is.

No one can be saved who does not turn to God by faith in Christ. No sinner will turn to God until God turns him. No sinner will trust Christ until God gives him faith. Yet we must believe on Christ (Acts 16:31; Mark 16:15, 16). Conversion is a heart work. It is believing on the Lord Jesus Christ with all your heart, trusting him alone as Lord and Saviour (Romans 10:9-13; 1 Corinthians 1:30, 31; Philippians 3:3). All who repent and turn to God in faith will do works which give evidence of grace. Salvation is not dependent upon our works. But all saved people, in the tenor of their lives, walk in good works (Romans 6:11-18; Ephesians 2:8-10; Titus 3:8; James 2:14-26). Good works are works of obedience to the Word of God, works of love to Christ and his people and works of faith. Good works are the fruit of faith in Christ.

343

Acts 26:16 But rise, and stand upon thy feet: for I have appeared unto thee for this purpose, to make thee a minister and a witness both of these things which thou hast seen, and of those things in the which I will appear unto thee;

Acts 26:17 Delivering thee from the people, and from the Gentiles, unto whom now I send thee,

Acts 26:18 To open their eyes, and to turn them from darkness to light, and from the power of Satan unto God, that they may receive forgiveness of sins, and inheritance among them which are sanctified by faith that is in me.

Acts 26:19 Whereupon, O king Agrippa, I was not disobedient unto the heavenly vision:

Acts 26:20 But shewed first unto them of Damascus, and at Jerusalem, and throughout all the coasts of Judaea, and then to the Gentiles, that they should repent and turn to God, and do works meet for repentance.

Acts 26:21 For these causes the Jews caught me in the temple, and went about to kill me.

Acts 26:22 Having therefore obtained help of God, I continue unto this day, witnessing both to small and great, saying none other things than those which the prophets and Moses did say should come:

Acts 26:23 That Christ should suffer, and that he should be the first that should rise from the dead, and should shew light unto the people, and to the Gentiles.

Chapter 74

Gospel Preachers And God's Salvation

Acts 26:16-23

The apostle Paul told Agrippa the Lord Jesus Christ had appeared to him and made him a minister of the gospel, an instrument in the hands of God for the salvation of chosen sinners (26:16-18). We know, of course, that salvation is not caused or accomplished by preachers. Salvation is God's work, the gift of God (Romans 6:23). It is the work of his grace (Ephesians 2:8, 9). Yet, 'it pleased God by the foolishness of preaching to save them that believe' (1 Corinthians 1:21). Gospel preachers are the means God uses to save his people (Romans 10:13-17; James 1:18; 1 Peter 1:23-25). God, who ordained the salvation of an elect multitude, ordained their salvation through gospel preaching (2 Thessalonians 2:13, 14). Though the Ethiopian eunuch was chosen by God and redeemed by the blood of Christ, he did not understand the Scriptures or obtain salvation by faith in Christ until he came into contact with a God-sent preacher who 'preached unto him Jesus' (Acts 8:26-39).

Preachers must never be exalted to a priestly role. We have no priest but Christ. There is no power in any preacher to illuminate, convert, forgive, or sanctify anyone. No preacher can give sinners life and faith in Christ. That is the work of God the Holy Spirit. Yet God's method of grace and his chosen instruments must not be despised. No sinner will ever obtain divine illumination, conversion to God, the forgiveness of sins, sanctification and faith in Christ apart from the preaching of the gospel. Therefore those men who faithfully preach the gospel of God's free grace in Christ are to be loved and highly esteemed for their work's sake (1 Thessalonians 5:12, 13; Isaiah 52:7). Salvation comes to sinners by faith in Christ, and faith in Christ comes by the preaching of the gospel. In the verses under consideration, the Holy Spirit records seven things God does for sinners when he saves them by his almighty grace through the preaching of the gospel.

1. He opens the eyes of the blind

All are spiritually blind by nature, totally ignorant of the things of God. But when God saves sinners, he sends a man to preach the gospel to them in the power of the Holy Spirit, 'to open their eyes'. The preacher cannot do the

345

work. Only the Holy Spirit can open spiritually blind eyes (John 3:3; 1 Corinthians 2:9-14; 2 Corinthians 4:6; Ephesians 1:17, 18). The preacher is merely the instrument of illumination. He holds forth the light of the knowledge of the glory of God in Christ. God opens a sinner's eyes to see himself as a sinner, justly condemned (Psalm 51:4; Job 42:5, 6; Isaiah 6:1-5; Romans 3:19; 7:9), and utterly incapable of justifying himself (Job 9:20, 30-33). God shows men their need of a substitute. Then he shows them the glory of Christ as the sinner's substitute (Romans 3:24-26).

2. He turns 'from darkness to light and from the power of Satan to God'

Conversion is evidence of election, redemption, regeneration and effectual calling. It is the work of God. Believers turn to God with willing hearts, but only as they have been turned by God (Psalm 80:3, 7, 17; 85:4; Lamentations 5:21). Conversion is more than reformation of life. It is a turning of the heart to God. 'Conversion', wrote Joseph Alleine, 'is a deep work, a heart work. It goes throughout the man, throughout the mind, throughout the members, throughout the entire life.' Conversion is a lifelong work. It begins a lifelong devotion to God. Believers are described by Peter as those who are always 'coming' to Christ until, at last, they come to him in heaven (1 Peter 2:4).

3. He grants 'the forgiveness of sins'

Convicted sinners want and need forgiveness. It is the first thing they desire from God. The first prayer of every saved sinner is the prayer of the tax collector: 'God, be merciful to me, a sinner.' The sweetest words ever heard on earth are the words of Christ, spoken to repenting sinners: 'Thy sins be forgiven thee!' Guilt is terrible; forgiveness is glorious! God's forgiveness of the believer's sins is a faithful forgiveness promised in the covenant (1 John 1:9; Jeremiah 31:34); a just forgiveness, purchased, secured and demanded by the blood of Christ (Ephesians 1:6); a full forgiveness, including all sin, past, present and future (Isaiah 43:25; 44:22); and an everlasting, irrevocable forgiveness (Romans 4:8; Jeremiah 50:20). Once bestowed, it can never be denied or taken away. This forgiveness cannot be purchased with money, or earned by the merits of good works. It is the free grace gift of God, received by the hand of faith. Trusting Christ, sinners obtain 'forgiveness of sins'.

4. He gives an eternal inheritance in Christ

In salvation, God bestows an eternal inheritance of grace and glory in Christ upon forgiven sinners, an 'inheritance among them which are sanctified'.

This inheritance is something we enjoy now, for Christ is our portion now, and in him we now possess all the blessings of grace (Ephesians 1:3). But Paul's reference is obviously to the believer's eternal, heavenly inheritance. All who believe on the Lord Jesus are 'heirs of God, and joint-heirs with Christ' (Romans 8:17). It is an inheritance of grace. It belongs to every child of God equally and completely. There are no degrees of reward in heaven! How can anyone who believes in salvation by grace alone imagine that some part of heaven's glorious inheritance is earned or lost by works, or the lack of them? Heavenly glory is simply the climax and completion of saving grace.

5. He completely sanctifies by his grace

The Lord Jesus declared to Paul that, just as we are saved and forgiven by faith, we are 'sanctified by faith that is in' him. Most people imagine that sanctification (holiness) is a matter of progressive effort and work. It is not! Sanctification is altogether the gift and work of grace, received by faith in Christ. We were separated unto God in holy election (Jude 1), declared to be holy by the blood of Christ in justification (Hebrews 10:10-14) and given a holy nature by God the Holy Spirit in regeneration (2 Peter 1:4; 1 John 3:9). We grow in grace, love, faith, etc.. Every living thing grows. But we do not grow in holiness, righteousness and sanctification. Our standing before God never varies. We are perfect and complete in Christ (Colossians 2:10).

6. He gives faith in Christ

The Lord Jesus declares that all these blessings of grace are 'by faith that is in' him. This faith is the gift of God, the operation of his grace (Ephesians 1:19; 2:8; Colossians 2:12; Philippians 1:29). Faith is not the cause of grace, but the gift of grace and the evidence of grace (Hebrews 11:1). And this faith is created in sinners by the power of God the Holy Spirit through the preaching of the gospel (Romans 10:17).

7. He makes his servants willing

When God saves a rebel, he makes him a willingly obedient servant, as he did Saul of Tarsus (26:19). Grace conquers the heart, subdues the will and makes those who naturally hate God (Romans 8:7) willing servants of God. Believers bow to Christ and gladly take his yoke upon them (Matthew 11:28-30). Where there is no surrender to the rule of Christ as Lord there is no faith in Christ as Saviour (Luke 14:25-33).

347

Acts 26:24 And as he thus spake for himself, Festus said with a loud voice, Paul, thou art beside thyself; much learning doth make thee mad.

Acts 26:25 But he said, I am not mad, most noble Festus; but speak forth the words of truth and soberness.

Acts 26:26 For the king knoweth of these things, before whom also I speak freely: for I am persuaded that none of these things are hidden from him; for this thing was not done in a corner.

Acts 26:27 King Agrippa, believest thou the prophets? I know that thou believest.

Acts 26:28 Then Agrippa said unto Paul, Almost thou persuadest me to be a Christian.

Acts 26:29 And Paul said, I would to God, that not only thou, but also all that hear me this day, were both almost, and altogether such as I am, except these bonds.

Acts 26:30 And when he had thus spoken, the king rose up, and the governor, and Bernice, and they that sat with them:

Acts 26:31 And when they were gone aside, they talked between themselves, saying, This man doeth nothing worthy of death or of bonds.

Acts 26:32 Then said Agrippa unto Festus, This man might have been set at liberty, if he had not appealed unto Caesar.

Chapter 75

Almost Persuaded, But Altogether Lost

Acts 26:24-32

Agrippa was a man of wealth, power and respectability. He was king over Judea. Unlike his predecessors or his peers, he was a thoughtful, religious man. He had embraced the tenets of the Jews' religion, avowed his faith in the Old Testament Scriptures and enjoyed a rare privilege and opportunity. Agrippa heard the man of God deliver a message from God in the power of God! He not only heard Paul preach, he was fully convinced of the truthfulness of Paul's message. The way of life and salvation was set before him. Before his very eyes, Jesus Christ crucified was evidently set forth. The door of mercy was opened to him. He had opportunity to enter it. But this man wilfully disobeyed the command of the gospel. When God spoke, he stopped his ears. He was, according to his own words, 'almost persuaded' to be a Christian, but was altogether lost. In these verses, the Holy Spirit holds Agrippa before the eyes of souls facing the prospect of eternity to warn them that God will not trifle with those who trifle with the gospel!

Are you, like the Jews of Elijah's day, halting between two opinions? convinced that the gospel of God's grace in Christ is true, yet continuing in the path of unbelief and rebellion? You may compliment yourself that you are 'almost persuaded'. You may think it is commendable to be like the rich young ruler who was near the kingdom of God (Mark 12:34). Other people may praise you for your interest in the things of God. Be warned: to be near the kingdom is to be outside the kingdom! To be almost persuaded is to be lost! If you continue halting between two opinions, you will soon be confirmed in reprobate unbelief. If you continue to trifle with God, you will soon be destroyed by God (Proverbs 1:23-33; 29:1). You must enter the door of mercy while it is open. God's ambassador warns you, 'Receive not the grace of God in vain ... Behold, now is the accepted time; behold, now is the day of salvation' (2 Corinthians 6:1, 2).

1. What is a Christian?

A Christian is one who is anointed by God, a follower of Christ, one who is like Christ. That is what the word 'Christian' means. Nothing in this world can properly be called 'Christian' except the church and people of our God. Paul tells us what a Christian is in verse 18. A Christian is a person who is taught by God, one whose eyes God has opened to see and know the truth (John 6:44, 45). Being taught by God, all true believers 'have the mind of Christ' (1 Corinthians 2:16) to understand spiritual things. A Christian is a person who has been taught by God to acknowledge and confess his sin (1 John 1:9), to trust the God-man, Jesus Christ, as his only sin-atoning substitute and Saviour (1 Corinthians 1:30), and to gratefully confess, 'By the grace of God I am what I am' (1 Corinthians 15:10).

Christians are sinners who have been transformed by the grace and power of God, turned 'from darkness to light, and from the power of Satan unto God' (26:18; 2 Corinthians 5:17). Christians have received the forgiveness of sins by the blood of Christ (Ephesians 1:7). All sins, past, present and future, are forgiven us through our Saviour's blood. Blessed are they to whom God will not impute sin! (Psalm 32:1, 2; Romans 4:8). A Christian is a person whose treasure is in heaven. We have an inheritance among the saints to which we were predestinated in eternity (Ephesians 1:11), which was earned, purchased and claimed for us by Christ our forerunner (Hebrews 6:20), and which we shall fully possess at last (John 14:1-3).

All true Christians are sanctified by the grace of God. That is to say, God has made them holy by his grace in Christ, so that all who are Christians are saints, made holy by the imputed righteousness of Christ in justification (Romans 3:24-26; 5:19) and the imparted righteousness of Christ in regeneration (1 John 3:9). In short, a Christian is a person who trusts the Lord Jesus Christ. We are saved by 'faith that is in' him. We have been effectually taught by God to trust the Lord Jesus Christ.

2. How did Paul persuade Agrippa to trust Christ and be a Christian?

He was not indifferent to this man's soul. Knowing the terror of the Lord, he persuaded him to come to Christ (2 Corinthians 5:11) with four strong arguments. First, he appealed to the Word of God (26:22). His only argument was: 'Thus saith the Lord ... '. This is the only weapon of our warfare. We do not appeal to science, history, or logic as a buttress for faith. Rather, we demand that all men bow to the Word of God. Believing God's Word as a revelation from him is the only way anyone can be saved (1 John 4:10-14).

Secondly, Paul testified to Agrippa of what he had personally experienced of the grace of God (26:6-19). He told the king what the Lord had done for him. That is good witnessing! Everyone can tell what he or she has experienced, and there is no better way to persuade sinners than telling them what God has done for you as a sinner.

350

Thirdly, the apostle gave Agrippa a clear statement of the historic facts of the gospel (26:23). God became incarnate (John 1:14). The incarnate Christ bore the sins of his people upon the cross as the sinner's substitute, satisfying divine justice for all his people by his vicarious death (2 Corinthians 5:21; Hebrews 9:26; 1 Peter 3:18). He rose from the dead on the third day (Romans 4:25), ascended into heaven and makes intercession there as an advocate and High Priest for his people (1 John 2:1, 2). This risen, exalted Christ is able to save to the uttermost all who trust him (Hebrews 7:25; John 17:2).

Then Paul laid the axe to the root of the tree, demanding that Agrippa openly acknowledge the claims of Christ in the gospel (26:27-29). Though he was wearing Roman chains, Paul was still the servant of Christ, and he boldly behaved as the servant of Christ, even to the point of laying his life on the line! Agrippa must have been shocked! Yet he could not deny the truthfulness of Paul's message. So the question must be raised:

3. If he was convinced of the message Paul preached, why was this man only 'almost persuaded'?

Why will men and women who know that the gospel is true persist in wilful rebellion against its claims? For the same reasons Agrippa did. There was one sitting by his side he was unwilling to give up. Bernice was his sister, a beautiful, but shameless woman. She and Agrippa were living together in an incestuous relationship. If he laid hold on Christ, he must let Bernice go, but he would not do so. This was his point of rebellion. That is where God always meets a sinner.

There was another sitting beside Agrippa whose disapproval he did not want. Festus was lower in rank than Agrippa, but if he wanted to, he could cause the king much trouble with Caesar. It was, at least in part, the fear of man that kept Agrippa from Christ.

Paul was probably an obstacle to his faith as well. He saw the bonds, imprisonment, shame, sorrow and reproach that Paul had to endure for Christ, and was unwilling to pay that price. He counted the cost (Matthew 13:44-46; Luke 14:28) and said, 'Christ is not worth that to me!'

But, primarily, the problem was in his own heart. Agrippa loved the world; the pomp, the pleasures, the fame, the riches, the sin, the power and the comfort of the world. He was almost persuaded, but he could not, and would not, forsake the world and follow Christ. Will you?

The warning the Holy Spirit gives us by this man Agrippa is written in clear letters: to be almost persuaded is to be altogether lost! If you meet God almost persuaded, you will be altogether lost forever!

Acts 27:1 And when it was determined that we should sail into Italy, they delivered Paul and certain other prisoners unto one named Julius, a centurion of Augustus' band.

Acts 27:2 And entering into a ship of Adramyttium, we launched, meaning to sail by the coasts of Asia; one Aristarchus, a Macedonian of Thessalonica, being with us.

Acts 27:3 And the next day we touched at Sidon. And Julius courteously entreated Paul, and gave him liberty to go unto his friends to refresh himself.

Acts 27:4 And when we had launched from thence, we sailed under Cyprus, because the winds were contrary.

Acts 27:5 And when we had sailed over the sea of Cilicia and Pamphylia, we came to Myra, a city of Lycia.

Acts 27:6 And there the centurion found a ship of Alexandria sailing into Italy; and he put us therein.

Acts 27:7 And when we had sailed slowly many days, and scarce were come over against Cnidus, the wind not suffering us, we sailed under Crete, over against Salmone;

Acts 27:8 And, hardly passing it, came unto a place which is called The fair havens; nigh whereunto was the city of Lasea.

Acts 27:9 Now when much time was spent, and when sailing was now dangerous, because the fast was now already past, Paul admonished them,

Acts 27:10 And said unto them, Sirs, I perceive that this voyage will be with hurt and much damage, not only of the lading and ship, but also of our lives.

Acts 27:11 Nevertheless the centurion believed the master and the owner of the ship, more than those things which were spoken by Paul.

Acts 27:12 And because the haven was not commodious to winter in, the more part advised to depart thence also, if by any means they might attain to Phenice, and there to winter; which is an haven of Crete, and lieth toward the south west and north west.

Acts 27:13 And when the south wind blew softly, supposing that they had obtained their purpose, loosing thence, they sailed close by Crete.

Acts 27:14 But not long after there arose against it a tempestuous wind, called Euroclydon.

Acts 27:15 And when the ship was caught, and could not bear up into the wind, we let her drive.

Acts 27:16 And running under a certain island which is called Clauda, we had much work to come by the boat:

Acts 27:17 Which when they had taken up, they used helps, undergirding the ship; and, fearing lest they should fall into the quicksands, strake sail, and so were driven.

Acts 27:18 And we being exceedingly tossed with a tempest, the next day they lightened the ship;

Acts 27:19 And the third day we cast out with our own hands the tackling of the ship.

Acts 27:20 And when neither sun nor stars in many days appeared, and no small tempest lay on us, all hope that we should be saved was then taken away.

Acts 27:21 But after long abstinence Paul stood forth in the midst of them, and said, Sirs, ye should have hearkened unto me, and not have loosed from Crete, and to have gained this harm and loss.

Acts 27:22 And now I exhort you to be of good cheer: for there shall be no loss of any man's life among you, but of the ship.

Acts 27:23 For there stood by me this night the angel of God, whose I am, and whom I serve,

Acts 27:24 Saying, Fear not, Paul; thou must be brought before Caesar: and, lo, God hath given thee all them that sail with thee.

Acts 27:25 Wherefore, sirs, be of good cheer: for I believe God, that it shall be even as it was told me.

Acts 27:26 Howbeit we must be cast upon a certain island.

Acts 27:27 But when the fourteenth night was come, as we were driven up and down in Adria, about midnight the shipmen deemed that they drew near to some country;

Acts 27:28 And sounded, and found it twenty fathoms: and when they had gone a little further, they sounded again, and found it fifteen fathoms.

Acts 27:29 Then fearing lest we should have fallen upon rocks, they cast four anchors out of the stern, and wished for the day.

Acts 27:30 And as the shipmen were about to flee out of the ship, when they had let down the boat into the sea, under colour as though they would have cast anchors out of the foreship,

Acts 27:31 Paul said to the centurion and to the soldiers, Except these abide in the ship, ye cannot be saved.

Acts 27:32 Then the soldiers cut off the ropes of the boat, and let her fall off.

Acts 27:33 And while the day was coming on, Paul besought them all to take meat, saying, This day is the fourteenth day that ye have tarried and continued fasting, having taken nothing.

Acts 27:34 Wherefore I pray you to take some meat: for this is for your health: for there shall not an hair fall from the head of any of you.

Acts 27:35 And when he had thus spoken, he took bread, and gave thanks to God in presence of them all: and when he had broken it, he began to eat.

Acts 27:36 Then were they all of good cheer, and they also took some meat.

Acts 27:37 And we were in all in the ship two hundred threescore and sixteen souls.

Acts 27:38 And when they had eaten enough, they lightened the ship, and cast out the wheat into the sea.

Acts 27:39 And when it was day, they knew not the land: but they discovered a certain creek with a shore, into the which they were minded, if it were possible, to thrust in the ship.

Acts 27:40 And when they had taken up the anchors, they committed themselves unto the sea, and loosed the rudder bands, and hoised up the mainsail to the wind, and made toward shore.

Acts 27:41 And falling into a place where two seas met, they ran the ship aground; and the forepart stuck fast, and remained unmoveable, but the hinder part was broken with the violence of the waves.

Acts 27:42 And the soldiers' counsel was to kill the prisoners, lest any of them should swim out, and escape.

Acts 27:43 But the centurion, willing to save Paul, kept them from their purpose; and commanded that they which could swim should cast themselves first into the sea, and get to land:

Acts 27:44 And the rest, some on boards, and some on broken pieces of the ship. And so it came to pass, that they escaped all safe to land.

Chapter 76

Preparation For The Storm

Acts 27:1-44

After being a prisoner at Caesarea for more than two years, Paul was sent to Rome. There he would make his personal appeal to Caesar. While he was en route for Rome, travelling by sea, a terrible storm arose from the north-east which placed the whole company in great danger. Acts 27 is a detailed account of the storm. We need no more than an atlas and common sense to understand the literal, historical events recorded in this chapter. But the chapter is recorded to give us more than historical data. It is recorded in the Scriptures to give us practical, spiritual, gospel instruction (2 Timothy 3:16).

In Paul's day the sea could be a terrible thing. The sailor had no compass, so when the sun and the stars were blotted out, he had no idea where he was, or where he was going. He had no engine to propel his ship through the mighty winds and raging waters. His sails and oars were helpless before the force of a hurricane. The imagery of the sea's terror is used throughout the Word of God. Jonah was thrown into the sea to appease its wrath (Jonah 1:12-15). The disciples were terribly frightened on the Sea of Galilee and cried out to the Master to save them (Mark 4:38). In 2 Corinthians 11:25 Paul tells us he was shipwrecked three times and spent a night and a day in the deep. Jude compares the influence of false religion to the 'raging waves of the sea' (Jude 13). John saw the 'beast rise up out of the sea' (Revelation 13:1). In Revelation 21:1 he says in the new creation there will be 'no more sea', as if to indicate that the sea is a symbol of terrible calamity and evil.

Life in this world is compared to a voyage across a vast sea (Job 9:26). As we sail across the vast sea of life in this world we must all pass through many storms. God's book shows us how to prepare for and survive those storms. 'He that hath ears to hear, let him hear' the spiritual lessons of this chapter.

1. Things seldom happen as we desire, plan or expect (27:1-8)

The band of soldiers took their prisoners on board the ship and 'launched, meaning to sail by the coasts of Asia' (27:2). They mapped out their course, prepared for their voyage and hoped to have smooth sailing to Rome by the Asian coasts. But divine providence interfered with their well-laid plans. A storm arose and 'The winds were contrary' (27:4). That is contrary to their plans! When we are making our plans, we will be wise to consider the storms ahead and submit our will to God's will, even in our plans (James 4:13-15). Life is full of storms and contrary winds (Job 5:7; 14:1). They usually arise suddenly and without warning.

The greatest storm anyone will ever face is that of his own sin. When a person comes face to face with his sin, the mighty wind of conviction and judgment is overwhelming. He feels the storm of God's wrath in his soul (Nahum 1:2, 3). But, blessed be God, in Christ Jesus there is a refuge for sinners and a hiding-place for the guilty (Isaiah 4:6; 32:2).

2. Storms are often the fruit of disobedience to the will of God (27:9-14)

I do not mean to suggest that all trials are the result of some particular sin. But many of our trials and sorrows could be avoided by simple obedience to our God. If these men had just given heed to the Word of God, they would not have suffered the terrible shipwreck recorded in this chapter. Read these verses carefully and learn their obvious lessons. The will of God is usually contrary to the opinion of the majority (27:11) and always contrary to the pleasures and accommodations of the flesh (27:12). The path of least resistance is most appealing to the flesh, but it is the path to destruction (27:13, 14). No matter how unreasonable, unpleasant, or costly it seems to be to obey God, 'Whatsoever he saith unto you, do it' (John 2:5). Obedience may be costly; but disobedience is always more costly. Faith in Christ evidences itself by obedience to Christ (Proverbs 3:5, 6).

3. When the storm comes, the course to safety is surrender (27:15-20)

Luke says, 'When the ship was caught, and could not bear up into [against] the wind, we let her drive' (27:15). That is all we can do, just hold on and 'let her drive'. This was not an act of fatalism. They had done all they could. They worked hard. They used all the help they could get. They lightened their load. They even threw all the tacklings overboard. But all hope of deliverance by their hands was gone. So they hoisted their sails and 'let her drive'.

The men in command of the ship had no fear of God. But for Luke, Paul and Aristarchus, this was an act of faith. Luke says, 'We let her drive.' They knew who was really in command of the ship! They realised who had sent the storm (Psalm 107:25; Isaiah 45:7; Amos 3:6; Jonah 1:4; Nahum 1:3). Like Eli of old, they humbled themselves under the hand of God, saying, 'It is the Lord: let him do what seemeth him good' (1 Samuel 3:18; James 4:7, 10). Turning to the Lord in submission and faith, they found peace (Isaiah 26:3, 4;

Psalm 42:11). Bow to the will of Christ. Slip your neck into his yoke, and you will find peace (Matthew 11:29). Trust the wisdom, grace and promise of God. Hoist the sails of your little ship into the wind of divine providence and 'let her drive' (Romans 8:28).

4. In the storm, God will comfort, instruct and direct (27:21-25)

If you would find comfort in trouble, bury yourself in the book of consolation (Romans 15:4). Paul found a word from God, believed it and faithfully delivered it, even in the midst of the storm. It was a word of stern reproof (27:21) and of cheering assurance (27:22-24).

5. No matter how severe the storm is, stay in the ship (27:26-38)

Some sailors considered forsaking the ship. They let down the lifeboat and were about to leave when Paul said, 'Except these abide in the ship, ye cannot be saved.' Immediately, the soldiers cut the ropes and let the boat fall. They did not stand around arguing about divine predestination and human responsibility. They cut the ropes! They cut off every other source of hope and cast themselves upon the Word of God. They took only what they needed and threw everything else overboard (27:19, 38). Storms have a way of changing values and making all the things of this world appear to be what they really are — vanity!

They stayed in the ship and were saved (27:37). When storms arise, cling to Christ. Stay in the good ship grace. Those who endure the trials and storms of life, who persevere in faith, are saved (Matthew 10:22; John 8:31; 15:9; Acts 13:43; 14:22; Colossians 1:23; Hebrews 3:6, 14; James 1:12).

6. Set your heart upon Christ alone (27:39, 40)

Seek him and nothing else. Throw everything else to the wind. Ask for nothing, care for nothing and pursue nothing but Christ, and make 'toward shore' (Colossians 3:1-3). If Christ is all your desire, you will have all your desire and the storms of life will do you no harm.

7. Our God will bring us to our desired haven of rest (27:41-44)

Some swam to safety or floated on boards or rode on broken pieces of the ship. But when they came to that place where two seas met, they all came to shore safely. 'And so it came to pass, that they escaped all safe to land.' So it will be with all God's elect (1 Peter 5:10, 11; Jude 24, 25; Romans 8:35-39).

Acts 27:21 But after long abstinence Paul stood forth in the midst of them, and said, Sirs, ye should have hearkened unto me, and not have loosed from Crete, and to have gained this harm and loss.

Acts 27:22 And now I exhort you to be of good cheer: for there shall be no loss of any man's life among you, but of the ship.

Acts 27:23 For there stood by me this night the angel of God, whose I am, and whom I serve,

Acts 27:24 Saying, Fear not, Paul; thou must be brought before Caesar: and, lo, God hath given thee all them that sail with thee.

Acts 27:25 Wherefore, sirs, be of good cheer: for I believe God, that it shall be even as it was told me.

Acts 27:26 Howbeit we must be cast upon a certain island.

Acts 27:27 But when the fourteenth night was come, as we were driven up and down in Adria, about midnight the shipmen deemed that they drew near to some country;

Acts 27:28 And sounded, and found it twenty fathoms: and when they had gone a little further, they sounded again, and found it fifteen fathoms.

Acts 27:29 Then fearing lest we should have fallen upon rocks, they cast four anchors out of the stern, and wished for the day.

Acts 27:30 And as the shipmen were about to flee out of the ship, when they had let down the boat into the sea, under colour as though they would have cast anchors out of the foreship,

Acts 27:31 Paul said to the centurion and to the soldiers, Except these abide in the ship, ye cannot be saved.

Acts 27:32 Then the soldiers cut off the ropes of the boat, and let her fall off.

Acts 27:33 And while the day was coming on, Paul besought them all to take meat, saying, This day is the fourteenth day that ye have tarried and continued fasting, having taken nothing.

Acts 27:34 Wherefore I pray you to take some meat: for this is for your health: for there shall not an hair fall from the head of any of you.

Acts 27:35 And when he had thus spoken, he took bread, and gave thanks to God in presence of them all: and when he had broken it, he began to eat.

Acts 27:36 Then were they all of good cheer, and they also took some meat.

Acts 27:37 And we were in all in the ship two hundred threescore and sixteen souls.

Acts 27:38 And when they had eaten enough, they lightened the ship, and cast out the wheat into the sea.

Acts 27:39 And when it was day, they knew not the land: but they discovered a certain creek with a shore, into the which they were minded, if it were possible, to thrust in the ship.

Acts 27:40 And when they had taken up the anchors, they committed themselves unto the sea, and loosed the rudder bands, and hoised up the mainsail to the wind, and made toward shore.

Acts 27:41 And falling into a place where two seas met, they ran the ship aground; and the forepart stuck fast, and remained unmoveable, but the hinder part was broken with the violence of the waves.

Acts 27:42 And the soldiers' counsel was to kill the prisoners, lest any of them should swim out, and escape.

Acts 27:43 But the centurion, willing to save Paul, kept them from their purpose; and commanded that they which could swim should cast themselves first into the sea, and get to land:

Acts 27:44 And the rest, some on boards, and some on broken pieces of the ship. And so it came to pass, that they escaped all safe to land.

Chapter 77

God's Sovereignty And Man's Responsibility

Acts 27:21-44

God is totally sovereign and man is totally responsible. Both of these truths are plainly revealed in Holy Scripture and must be believed by all who acknowledge the authority of the Word of God. God's sovereignty does not relieve man of responsibility. And man's responsibility does not negate God's sovereignty. Both of these blessed gospel truths are illustrated in the passage before us.

In verse 24, the angel of the Lord spoke to Paul, 'saying, Fear not, Paul; thou must be brought before Caesar: and, lo, God hath given thee all them that sail with thee.' Paul, believing God, said, 'There shall be no loss of any man's life among you, but of the ship' (27:22). That is God's sovereign decree, immutable, unalterable and certain. God purposed it, and it must come to pass. Not all the power of hell could prevent it. God says, 'I have spoken it, I will also bring it to pass; I have purposed it, I will also do it' (Isaiah 46:11). Did that sovereign decree relieve the men on board the ship of all responsibility? Did God's decree mean that they would be saved no matter what they might do? Did God's sure and certain purpose mean that these 276 men were no longer obliged to obey him? Not on your life! In verse 31, Paul shows us the place of human responsibility. Some of the sailors panicked in the storm and were about to abandon the ship. Paul said, 'Except these abide in the ship, ye cannot be saved.' God had ordained their safety and deliverance from the storm. So their safety and deliverance were matters of absolute certainty. Yet they could only be saved if they remained in the ship, and they were responsible to do so. If they abandoned the ship, they would all have been lost. If they stayed in the ship, they would all be saved. The burden of responsibility lay squarely upon their shoulders. If they were saved, it would be God's work, and God's work alone. If they were lost, it would be their work, and their work alone.

In the end, God's purpose was accomplished. The ship was lost and the cargo was lost, but every man on board the ship was saved, according to God's unalterable purpose. When the ship was wrecked, 'The soldiers' counsel was to kill the prisoners, lest any of them should swim out, and escape. But God graciously intervened and the centurion, willing to save Paul, kept them from their purpose, and commanded that they which could swim should cast themselves first into the sea, and get to land: and the rest, some on boards, and some on broken pieces of the ship. And so it came to pass' (exactly as God had ordained!) 'that they escaped all safe to land' (27:42-44).

The events recorded in Acts 27:21-44 clearly illustrate God's absolute sovereignty and man's complete responsibility in the matter of salvation. Salvation is accomplished entirely by the sovereign, eternal purpose and work of the triune God (Ephesians 1:3-14). Yet every sinner is responsible to repent and believe the gospel, to trust the Lord Jesus Christ (Acts 17:30; 1 John 3:23). All who do so will be saved, and all who refuse to do so will justly be damned for ever (Mark 16:16). Here are eight irrefutable facts, plainly revealed in the Word of God. Study them carefully and ask God the Holy Spirit to give you an understanding of them.

1. God the Father has a people in this world whom he has sovereignly chosen and determined to save in eternal, electing love (Ephesians 1:3-6; 2 Thessalonians 2:13, 14; Romans 9:11-18).

2. The Lord God eternally predestinated all things that come to pass in time to secure the salvation of his elect, for the glory of his own great name (Romans 8:28-30; Ephesians 1:5, 11).

3. The Lord Jesus Christ, the Son of God, died for and effectually redeemed all whom God the Father chose and purposed to save in eternity (Isaiah 53:8; Matthew 1:21; Galatians 3:13; Hebrews 9:12).

4. God the Holy Spirit regenerates all who were chosen in eternity and redeemed at Calvary, by the power of his irresistible grace, and causes them to trust Christ (Ephesians 2:1-6; John 3:3-8; Psalm 65:4; 110:3).

5. God sovereignly rules all things in providence with the absolute power of omnipotence and the total wisdom of omniscience, according to his eternal purpose of grace, for the salvation of his elect (Romans 8:28; John 17:2).

6. All God's elect, all true believers, are eternally and infallibly secure in Christ, preserved and kept in him by the power and grace of God (John 10:27-30; Philippians 1:6; 1 Peter 1:5; Jude 24, 25).

7. Every sinner who trusts the Lord Jesus Christ will be saved (John 3:14-16; Acts 16:31; Romans 10:9-13).

8. All who despise God's free grace in Christ and refuse to trust him will justly be damned for ever (Proverbs 1:23-33).

These are matters of divine revelation. They are things clearly stated in the Word of God. All who are saved are saved by God's work alone. All who are damned are damned by their own work alone. Read Acts 27:21-44 again and see how it illustrates these truths of Holy Scripture.

1. It was the purpose of God to save every person in the ship (27:21-25)

God said he would save them. Therefore, he was honour-bound to do so. If even one were to be lost, God's word would be broken, his honour would be lost and the Almighty would be found to be a liar! So it is with his elect!

2. In order for those whom God purposed to save actually to be saved, they had to obey his word (27:29-34)

God required them to stay in the ship. Had they not done so, they would have perished. But once they committed themselves to the Lord God, they were given the cheering assurance of his saving purpose (27:34, 35). In the same way, God requires us to trust Christ alone for salvation. All who trust him are assured of God's grace (1 John 5:10-13). All who refuse to obey the gospel will perish by their unbelief (John 3:18).

3. God graciously overrules all obstacles to accomplish his purpose of grace towards his elect (27:41-44).

Carefully read Psalm 76:10 and Proverbs 16:1, 4, 9, 33, and understand that nothing is a hindrance to God. All things are his servants, sovereignly used by him to accomplish his purpose of grace towards his elect.

4. All whom God purposed to save were saved (27:44)

God said, 'There shall be no loss of any man's life among you ... So it came to pass, that they escaped all safe to land' (27:22, 44). So also in the end all God's elect will be saved (Romans 11:26, 33-36). Believe God, and be of good cheer. His purpose is sure (Romans 8:28-39).

Acts 27:18 And we being exceedingly tossed with a tempest, the next day they lightened the ship;

Acts 27:19 And the third day we cast out with our own hands the tackling of the ship.

Acts 27:20 And when neither sun nor stars in many days appeared, and no small tempest lay on us, all hope that we should be saved was then taken away.

Acts 27:21 But after long abstinence Paul stood forth in the midst of them, and said, Sirs, ye should have hearkened unto me, and not have loosed from Crete, and to have gained this harm and loss.

Acts 27:22 And now I exhort you to be of good cheer: for there shall be no loss of any man's life among you, but of the ship.

Acts 27:23 For there stood by me this night the angel of God, whose I am, and whom I serve,

Acts 27:24 Saying, Fear not, Paul; thou must be brought before Caesar: and, lo, God hath given thee all them that sail with thee.

Acts 27:25 Wherefore, sirs, be of good cheer: for I believe God, that it shall be even as it was told me.

Chapter 78

'I believe God'

Acts 27:18-25

Here is a tried, tempest-tossed believer full of comfort and comforting others. He describes the source and cause of his comfort in three words: 'I believe God.' Because he believed God, Paul was confident that God would do what he said. He was full of comfort regarding his own life and destiny. And he had a word of comfort for those who were in the tempest-tossed ship with him. What an example of faith the Holy Spirit holds before us here!

It is astonishing we should need examples of faith and encouragements to believe God, but we do. Faith in our God should be, to regenerate men and women, a matter of fact. But often our hearts blush with shame because of unbelief. One of the most glaring evidences of human depravity is the fact that even men and women who are born of God struggle with unbelief. We are so fallen, so depraved, even in our regenerate state, that we dare question and doubt the living God! Some little trial comes our way, some slight ruffle, and we are out of sorts. We begin to worry, murmur, complain and feel sorry for ourselves. How easily our hearts are troubled! We ought to trust our God completely. In all things he is true and faithful. His covenant is sure. His oath stands fast. His word cannot be broken. His promises are all yea and amen in Christ Jesus. God cannot lie. It is impossible for him to deny himself. We ought to trust him unreservedly. That which God has promised, we have every reason to believe.

1. Paul's faith was based upon God's revelation

He said, 'I believe God, that it shall be even as it was told me' (27:25). God had told him something, and he believed it. His faith was based upon the Word of God. Granted, it was a special revelation. An angel of God told him what God would do. But we do not need to envy the source of Paul's revelation. We have the written, complete Word of God, which is a more sure word of prophecy than anything else could be (2 Peter 1:16-21). It is far better to have God's written Word than to have a vision, a mountain top experience, or even an angelic visitation (Hebrews 1:1-3).

2. Paul's faith was his absolute certainty God would do all he said

'It shall be even as it was told me.' He did not say, 'It may be,' or 'I hope it will be,' or 'God wants it to be.' He said, 'It shall be!' What God has spoken will be. What God has caused to be written in his Word will certainly come to pass. When the book of history is complete and God stamps 'The End' upon it, it will in all things tally with what God has said in his Word (1 Peter 1:24, 25; Isaiah 40:8; Luke 16:17).

3. Paul's faith gave him hope when all hope was gone

He said, 'I believe God,' when, to all outward appearance, 'All hope that they should be saved was ... taken away' (27:20). It is one thing to believe God when everything is going in the direction of God's promise, but it is another to believe God in a sinking ship when everything appears to contradict God's promise. That requires faith. Faith does not trust God because providence is smooth, and faith does not distrust God because providence is contrary. Faith trusts God's revelation, God's Word, even when everything appears to contradict it. Paul had nothing upon which to hang his faith but the Word of God, and the same is true of us. God hung the world upon nothing but his Word. Shall we not hang our faith upon that which God has hung the world?

4. He believed God and plainly and boldly confessed his faith before men

Paul was in a ship full of convicted felons, guarded by Roman soldiers and seasoned seamen. These were not respectable, church-going, religious people, but rugged men of notoriously vile character. Yet Paul spoke out plainly for the glory of God and confessed his faith in him. Indeed, all who believe God confess their faith in him. They do so by believer's baptism (Romans 6:4-6), by being his witnesses to the world around them (1:8) and in the teeth of opposition (Acts 4:10-12). We should make everyone around us conscious of our conviction that God is true and that he is to be trusted.

5. Paul acted like a man who believed God

When others were hysterical, Paul was calm. Why? He believed God. His faith was real. For most people religion is nothing but pious fiction. They look upon the promises of God as pretty, sentimental things to talk about. They view divine providence as a nice theological idea. Not Paul! He acted like a man who believed God. Trusting God, he rested himself upon the purpose, promise and providence of his heavenly Father.

6. The promises of God

'I believe God,' applies to all matters of doctrine, all areas of a believer's life and experience, and to all that concerns our hope regarding the world to come. It is qualified and limited only by the Word of God (2 Corinthians 1:20). Take out your Bible and search out its promises.

1. Promises to sinners (Isaiah 55:6, 7; Matthew 11:28-30; Mark 16:16; John 3:14-18; 1 John 1:9);
2. Promises to sinning saints (1 John 2:1, 2; 1 Corinthians 10:13; Psalm 89:19-36; 2 Chronicles 7:14);
3. Promises to his afflicted children (Isaiah 41:10, 11; 43:1-5; Acts 18:10; Romans 8:28; 2 Corinthians 12:9; Hebrews 13:5);
4. Promises to his church (1 Corinthians 15:58; Isaiah 55:11; Ecclesiastes 11:1; Psalm 126:5, 6);
5. Promises to his needy people (Philippians 4:19; Matthew 6:25-34);
6. Promises to them that honour him (1 Samuel 2:30; Malachi 3:10; Matthew 6:33; Luke 6:38);
7. Promises to them that look for Christ's coming (James 1:12; 1 Thessalonians 4:13-18; 2 Timothy 1:12).

The triune God, Father, Son and Holy Spirit, made certain promises to one another in the everlasting covenant of grace, which must, and will, be fulfilled (2 Samuel 23:5; Jeremiah 31:31-34; 32:38-40). The Son of God promised to redeem, justify and save all God's elect (Hebrews 10:5-10; John 10:16). God the Father promised his Son all his elect as the reward of the travail of his soul (Isaiah 53:9-12; Psalm 2:8; 22:30). God the Holy Spirit promised to regenerate, call, seal and preserve every chosen, redeemed sinner by almighty, irresistible grace (Ephesians 1:13, 14; 2 Thessalonians 2:13, 14). God has made certain promises in his Word regarding the future. With regard to the future, every believer ought to say with Paul, 'I believe God, that it shall be even as it was told me.' He will yet hear and answer the prayers of his people (1 John 5:14, 15). God will yet preserve every believer unto his heavenly kingdom (Philippians 1:6). God will yet send his Son to this earth in his glorious second advent to make all things new and bring his elect into everlasting glory (Revelation 21:1-5; John 14:1-3).

Happy is that person who can speak with honesty and say, 'I believe God.' Blessed are they who believe the doctrine of his Word, the rule of his providence and the promises of his grace. For ever blessed are those sinners upon the earth who believe the record God has given concerning his Son, the Lord Jesus Christ (1 John 5:10-13). Do you believe God?

Acts 27:20 And when neither sun nor stars in many days appeared, and no small tempest lay on us, all hope that we should be saved was then taken away.

Acts 27:21 But after long abstinence Paul stood forth in the midst of them, and said, Sirs, ye should have hearkened unto me, and not have loosed from Crete, and to have gained this harm and loss.

Acts 27:22 And now I exhort you to be of good cheer: for there shall be no loss of any man's life among you, but of the ship.

Acts 27:23 For there stood by me this night the angel of God, whose I am, and whom I serve,

Acts 27:24 Saying, Fear not, Paul; thou must be brought before Caesar: and, lo, God hath given thee all them that sail with thee.

Acts 27:25 Wherefore, sirs, be of good cheer: for I believe God, that it shall be even as it was told me.

Chapter 79

'Be of good cheer'

Acts 27:20-25

'When neither sun nor stars in many days appeared, and no small tempest lay on us, all hope that we should be saved was taken away' (27:20). In those circumstances, Paul stood up and said, 'I exhort you to be of good cheer' (20:22). When all hope was gone, Paul said, 'Be of good cheer.' You can imagine the response: 'Come on now, Paul. What do you mean, "Be of good cheer"? Are you out of your mind? We are going to be wrecked, and there is nothing we can do!' 'Nevertheless,' Paul says, 'I exhort you to be of good cheer.' Remember, he had advised them not to set sail in the first place, warning them of imminent danger (27:10). And, though he reminded them that they should have listened to him and their present trouble was their own fault (27:21), yet he says, 'Be of good cheer.' Assuring them by the Word of God that not one of them would be lost, 'Sirs, be of good cheer' (27:25).

If Paul could speak those words to unbelieving men regarding deliverance from a storm at sea, surely every believer is justified in saying to himself with regard to all the affairs of his life, 'Be of good cheer.' It does not matter what your circumstances in this world are, if you belong to God, if you are born of his Spirit, you have every reason to 'be of good cheer'. There is nothing holy or sanctifying about gloominess, despondency and morbid pessimism. In fact, these things are the exact opposites of holiness and sanctification. God the Holy Spirit is our Comforter, not our tormentor! He comes to bring comfort and cheer, not despair and gloom. Our heavenly Father delights to see his children rejoicing. And those who honour God most are those saints who walk before him with cheerful, believing hearts.

Search the Scriptures and see if the Lord God does not constantly say to his people in this world, 'Be of good cheer' (Psalm 16:5, 6; Proverbs 15:13, 15:30; 17:22; Ecclesiastes 2:24; 9:8-10; Philippians 4:4). Among the first things named as the fruit of the Spirit is 'joy' (Galatians 5:22). Believers should be people of perpetual joy and good cheer!

When all hope was gone, insofar as outward evidence was concerned, in the midst of terrible darkness and a raging storm, Paul found five reasons to 'be of good cheer'.

1. Paul was conscious of the presence of God

In verse 23 Paul says, 'There stood by me this night the angel of God, whose I am, and whom I serve.' God was there with him in the midst of the storm! The angel of God stood by him and spoke to him. We, too, may be sure that when trouble comes to us, 'The Lord is at hand' (Philippians 4:5). When all outward evidence of hope is gone, the Lord God will speak to you and say, 'Be of good cheer.' No, he will not speak to you by an audible voice. But he will speak to you by his Spirit, through his Word, assuring you of his presence to protect you (Isaiah 43:1-7), provide for you (2 Corinthians 12:9) and preserve you (Jude 24, 25). Then, like Paul, you can say to others, 'Be of good cheer, the Lord God is still on his throne. He is still in charge. He is still running things. The Lord knows what he is doing. He has not made a mistake. So, "Be of good cheer."'

This episode on the sea was just one of many times when the Lord Jesus manifestly fulfilled his promise to Paul in which he said, 'Lo, I am with you alway, even unto the end of the world' (Matthew 28:20). The same thing happened to him at Corinth (18:9, 10), at Jerusalem (23:11) and at Rome (2 Timothy 4:16, 17). Child of God, the Lord Jesus is with you, too. In your times of great trouble and need, your God is with you. When the doctor says, 'I'm very sorry, but I have to tell you, you have cancer,' the Lord is with you. He will not forsake you. When the telephone rings and the sombre voice on the line says, 'I'm sorry to ring, but there has been an accident. Your loved one has been killed,' the Lord will be with you. So long as we live in this world, we must go through the deep waters of trouble and the fiery furnace of adversity. In the midst of problems, pains and perplexities, let every believer be convinced of the presence of God, hear him say, 'I will never leave thee, nor forsake thee' (Hebrews 13:5) and 'be of good cheer'.

2. Paul was conscious of the fact that he belonged to God

He said, 'There stood by me this night the angel of God, whose I am, and whom I serve.' If we can in the midst of our trials realise this great fact, that we belong to God, we shall find reason to 'be of good cheer', even in the midst of trouble. We sing, 'Now I belong to Jesus.' Is that a fact? Then be of good cheer! We who believe belong to Christ by divine predestination (Ephesians 1:4-6), divine purchase (Ephesians 1:7-12) and divine power

368

(Ephesians 1:13, 14). We belong to Christ as a bride belongs to her husband. In the Old Testament and in the New, the relationship of Christ and his people is constantly compared to the intimate, loving union of a husband and wife (Ephesians 5:25-30; Song of Solomon 6:3).

We belong to our God as a child belongs to his father. Donald Grey Barnhouse once suggested that as soon as the doctor cuts the umbilical cord that binds a baby to its mother, 'God creates a sort of invisible cord that binds the baby to the father. It immediately transforms the man's nature and he begins to understand, "That's my boy!"' When that happens, there is a blessed picture of our relationship to God. He loves us infinitely more than any earthly father ever loved his son (1 John 3:1).

Again, we belong to our Lord as sheep belong to the shepherd. The Lord calls us his sheep. David said, 'The Lord is my Shepherd.' The life and welfare of sheep are the responsibility of the shepherd charged with watching over them. And the Lord Jesus has promised to protect and keep his sheep (Isaiah 40:11; John 10:27-30). Someone once asked an old believer, 'What do you do when you are in trouble?' He replied, 'I look to heaven and say, "Lord, your property is in danger."' That is how Paul felt. He belonged to God. He knew God would take care of him.

3. Paul was conscious of the fact that he was God's servant

He was on business for God. He spoke plainly of God as him 'whom I serve'. The law of the land is clear. If you are working for a company, that company is responsible for you. If you are injured while working for the company, the company must take care of you. The Lord God will do no less! If you are God's servant, doing God's business, he will take care of you. His honour is at stake. He promised, 'Them that honour me I will honour' (1 Samuel 2:30). 'My God shall supply all your need according to his riches in glory by Christ Jesus' (Philippians 4:19). 'He shall give his angels charge over thee, to keep thee in all thy ways' (Psalm 91:11).

4. Paul was conscious of God's total sovereignty

He knew that the Lord God, to whom he belonged, whom he served, his heavenly Father, was as much in control of the storm as he is of the calm. Therefore, being confident that his God would and could do all that he had said, he was of good cheer. Nothing, child of God, will sustain your soul in trouble and give you peace and joy like the conscious realization of his absolute sovereignty over all things (Romans 8:28-30; 11:36).

5. Paul was fully convinced of God's faithfulness

God had made an absolute promise of deliverance and safety to Paul. Because he knew God to be faithful, he said, 'I believe God' and exhorted all who were with him to 'be of good cheer'. Do not ever imagine that anything takes God by surprise, or is beyond his control. He upholds all things by the word of his power, and he upholds you in his great faithfulness. Therefore, 'No weapon that is formed against thee shall prosper; and every tongue that shall rise against thee in judgment thou shalt condemn. This is the heritage of the servants of the Lord, and their righteousness is of me, saith the Lord' (Isaiah 54:17). Civilla D. Martin wrote,

> Be not dismayed, whate'er betide,
> God will take care of you.
> Beneath his wings of love abide;
> God will take care of you,
> Through every day, o'er all the way,
> He will take care of you.
> God will take care of you!

I exhort you, therefore, 'to be of good cheer'!

'Be of good cheer'

Acts 28:1 And when they were escaped, then they knew that the island was called Melita.

Acts 28:2 And the barbarous people shewed us no little kindness: for they kindled a fire, and received us every one, because of the present rain, and because of the cold.

Acts 28:3 And when Paul had gathered a bundle of sticks, and laid them on the fire, there came a viper out of the heat, and fastened on his hand.

Acts 28:4 And when the barbarians saw the venomous beast hang on his hand, they said among themselves, No doubt this man is a murderer, whom, though he hath escaped the sea, yet vengeance suffereth not to live.

Acts 28:5 And he shook off the beast into the fire, and felt no harm.

Acts 28:6 Howbeit they looked when he should have swollen, or fallen down dead suddenly: but after they had looked a great while, and saw no harm come to him, they changed their minds, and said that he was a god.

Acts 28:7 In the same quarters were possessions of the chief man of the island, whose name was Publius; who received us, and lodged us three days courteously.

Acts 28:8 And it came to pass, that the father of Publius lay sick of a fever and of a bloody flux: to whom Paul entered in, and prayed, and laid his hands on him, and healed him.

Acts 28:9 So when this was done, others also, which had diseases in the island, came, and were healed:

Acts 28:10 Who also honoured us with many honours; and when we departed, they laded us with such things as were necessary.

Chapter 80

The Religion Of The Natural Man

Acts 28:1-10

In Acts 28 we find Paul and those who had been sailing with him on the island of Melita. That island today is called Malta. It is found between Sicily and Africa, about sixty miles off the coast of Sicily. As we have already seen, the ship in which they were sailing had been torn to pieces in a furious storm, but according to the promise of God, all 276 men, passengers and crew, were safe on land. The survivors of the storm were drenched, weary and cold, but they were alive! Divine providence had brought them to the island of Malta because God was determined to be gracious to the Maltese people. Some of his elect were on the island who must be called by the preaching of the gospel. Therefore God, who has his way in the whirlwind, directed the path of this hurricane to bring Paul to Malta. Here is another incidental, but marvellous illustration of the fact 'All things work together for good to them who love God', even before they come to love him, 'to them who are the called, according to his purpose' even before they are called (Romans 8:28).

The Maltese people are described by Luke as 'barbarians'. That does not necessarily mean that they were uncivilized, though that might also have been true. The word simply means that they were not Greeks, Romans, or Jews. They did not conform to the customs of these three dominant societies and did not speak their language.

It does not appear that God had ever before sent these barbarians a gospel preacher. Yet they were naturally religious people. Their religion, as we see in this passage, made them both moral and charitable. It had a good effect upon them. They had nothing but the light of nature, but they walked in the light they had. Yet they were lost, perishing men and women without the light of the gospel and the knowledge of Christ. Their religion restrained and, in measure, outwardly corrected the natural depravity of their hearts, but it could not save them. Natural religion, that which is learned and acquired by conscience and nature, cannot save. In order for lost men and women to be saved they must be brought to faith in the Lord Jesus Christ by the power of the Holy Spirit through the preaching of the gospel. As we look at Paul's encounter with the men of Malta, we are taught six very important lessons.

1. When God saves sinners, he always sends a gospel preacher (28:1)

There is an elect multitude in this world who must be saved. Not only has God ordained the salvation of his people, he has also ordained the means by which it is to be accomplished, and God's appointed means of grace is the preaching of the gospel. Sinners are saved by hearing and believing the gospel of Christ (John 6:40; Romans 10:17; 1 Corinthians 1:21; James 1:18; 1 Peter 1:23-25). God never bypasses his ordained means of grace. If he intends to save a sinner, by one means or another, he will cause that sinner to hear the gospel. There are many illustrations of this fact in the book of Acts (8:26, 27; 9:10-18; 10:1-48; 16:9-15, 19-34).

In Acts 28, we see God's hand of providence graciously arranging all things to bring Paul to Malta that he might preach the gospel to the elect among the barbarians there. Though the inhabitants of Malta were unaware of it, they were highly favoured of God. By sending the hurricane that must have terrified them, God had blessed them above all people. He used that hurricane to plant a gospel preacher in their midst (Isaiah 52:7).

Knowing that God has ordained salvation by the preaching of the gospel, we ought to make it our business (by personal witness, distributing tracts, tapes, books, etc. and by the support of faithful ministries) to preach the gospel to all and seize every opportunity to hear the gospel preached.

2. All men by nature are religious (16:2-6)

God has by creation given all men a consciousness of his being, which they cannot escape (Romans 1:18-20). These men of Malta, though they were unlearned barbarians, displayed a certain natural religious creed. They knew there is a God who governs the world. Their language displayed an awareness of the Creator's dominion of the universe. They did not know God. But they knew that God exists! They also knew that God is holy, righteous and just. When they saw the snake hanging on Paul's hand, they concluded instinctively that God had judged him. These Maltese barbarians knew that God punishes sin. Though they had never heard of, or read, the Bible, the law of God was inscribed on their hearts (Romans 2:13-15). They knew that murder was a horrible crime and that no man can escape the justice of God.

3. The religion of natural men is always perverted

No matter how sincere a man is, without the revelation of Christ in the gospel, he gropes about in the blindness of his own depraved heart and the darkness of religious superstition, idolatry and will-worship. The men of

Malta ignorantly supposed that those who suffer evil things are evil people. They presumed that a person's acceptance with God is determined by his own personal goodness. Free-will, works religion is the religion of all lost men. It is the religion of the depraved, fallen sons of Adam. It is always fickle because it is ruled, not by the Word of God, but by emotion and experience (28:5, 6).

4. Anyone who walks in the light God gives him will be given more light

These men had nothing but the light of nature. Yet they walked in that light God had given them. At his own appointed time, God gave them the light of life. Evangelist Rolfe Barnard used to say, 'God won't send honest people to hell.' He was right. If a person despises the light God gives him, the light he has will be turned into darkness (Matthew 6:23). But if he walks in and obeys the light God gives him, God will give him greater light (Isaiah 2:5; 1 John 1:7). No one will ever seek to know God and perish in ignorance of him!

5. Any man called by God to preach the gospel will be manifestly distinguished by God as his messenger

God's servants do not promote themselves, or call attention to themselves. Paul was not looking for snakes to handle. He was gathering firewood. If he could not serve the souls of men by preaching to them, he was glad to serve their bodies. By his condition as a prisoner, Paul was the most contemptible man in the crowd. But God providentially distinguished him from the others and caused men to pay attention to him. The Lord often uses two legged snakes, who are determined to destroy the influence of his servants, as the very means by which he increases their usefulness — just as he used the viper that bit Paul to open the door of utterance before him.

6. Those who honour God will be honoured by God (28:7-10)

After hearing Paul preach the gospel, a prominent man, Publius, believed on the Lord Jesus. He received Paul and his companions into his house and lodged them. Having received a prophet in the name of a prophet, he received a prophet's reward (Matthew 10:41). When his father came down with a deadly fever, there was a prophet in his house with the power of God to heal him and all others who had need of healing. Those who served Paul were served by Paul. But, those who honoured and served God's servant were honoured and served by God himself (1 Samuel 2:30). All who are wise will apply to themselves the exhortation Paul gave (1 Thessalonians 5:12, 13).

Acts 28:11 And after three months we departed in a ship of Alexandria, which had wintered in the isle, whose sign was Castor and Pollux.

Acts 28:12 And landing at Syracuse, we tarried there three days.

Acts 28:13 And from thence we fetched a compass, and came to Rhegium: and after one day the south wind blew, and we came the next day to Puteoli:

Acts 28:14 Where we found brethren, and were desired to tarry with them seven days: and so we went toward Rome.

Acts 28:15 And from thence, when the brethren heard of us, they came to meet us as far as Appii forum, and The three taverns: whom when Paul saw, he thanked God, and took courage.

Acts 28:16 And when we came to Rome, the centurion delivered the prisoners to the captain of the guard: but Paul was suffered to dwell by himself with a soldier that kept him.

Chapter 81

'We found brethren'

Acts 28:11-16

All God's saints in heaven and on earth are one church, one kingdom and one family. 'There is no doubt,' wrote A.A. Hodge, 'but that if there be but one God, there is but one church; if there be but one Christ, there is but one church; if there be but one cross, there is but one church; if there be but one Holy Ghost, there is but one church.' All the members of that one, universal church are brothers and sisters in Christ (Ephesians 3:15). In Christ, all true believers of all ages and all places are one (Ephesians 2:14; Colossians 3:11). All have the same Father. All have been adopted by the same eternal, electing love. All have been redeemed by the same precious blood. All are called by the same Holy Spirit. All have the same Elder Brother. All are saved by the same grace. All are heirs to the same inheritance. All are married to the same Husband, members of the same body and united to the same Head. Christ is not divided. And his body, the church, is not divided. All true believers are one in him. One of the greatest blessings God's saints possess on this earth, and one of the greatest joys of heaven, is the fellowship of brethren. As we follow Paul and his companions from Malta to Rome, let us observe how precious his brethren were to him and learn from him to love and esteem one another as brethren in Christ.

1. Paul was separated from his brethren in Malta (28:11)

On the island of Malta Paul's preaching was obviously blessed of God to the conversion of some, perhaps many. Those converted became very gracious and generous. They valued the man who was used of God to bring the gospel of Christ to them (Isaiah 52:7; Romans 10:15). All winter they lodged and fed Paul, Luke and Aristarchus, honouring them as the servants of God. Paul had ministered to their spiritual needs so they took care of his physical, material needs (1 Corinthians 9:9-11; Galatians 6:6). When the time came for Paul to leave the Maltese brethren supplied him and his friends with everything they needed for their journey to Rome. God supplied for his shipwrecked servants the refreshing consolation of newborn brethren among a barbarian people. What a tender parting their separation must have been!

The young converts of Malta stand as examples to all believers in their generosity and esteem for God's servants. All who are privileged to sit under the ministry of a faithful gospel preacher should highly esteem that man for his work's sake (1 Thessalonians 5:12, 13) and generously support him, supplying his material needs (Galatians 6:6). The Lord Jesus Christ considers that which is done to his servants as being done to him (Matthew 10:40, 41). God's servants are not hirelings. They do not preach for gain. But the labourer is worthy of his pay (Luke 10:7). No man going to war should entangle himself with the affairs of this world (2 Timothy 2:4). No servant of God seeks material wealth, but it is only reasonable for those for whom he labours to provide for his daily needs with sufficient generosity so that he has no earthly, material concern for himself and his family.

Verse 11 gives us yet another incidental lesson about divine providence. Luke tells us they sailed away from Malta on a ship from Alexandria. The ship which had been wrecked in the storm was also from Alexandria (27:6). Here were two ships, both from Alexandria, both going to Rome, both caught in a horrible storm. One of the ships sailed safely to Malta. The other was completely destroyed. The interesting point is this: the ship that sailed safely through the storm carried a crew of ungodly pagans who sailed under the sign of Castor and Pollux, gods of the sea! The ship that was wrecked, whose passengers and crew were cast out into the cold winter sea, carried some men who were beloved servants of God. It is no accident that Luke records this. The Holy Spirit intends us to be aware of the fact that favourable providence is no indication of God's favour and providential hardships are no indications of his displeasure. God wrecked Paul, whom he loved, so that he might open the door for him to preach to a band of chosen Maltese barbarians. He left the other ship, loaded with men for whom he had no gracious designs, without disturbance or harm. Pity the people whom God leaves alone! Read Psalms 73:1-18 and 92:1-15 and thank God for his special providence, even when it brings you through bitter storms and freezing winter waters!

2. New brethren at Puteoli (28:12-14)

On the way to Rome, their ship docked for three days at Syracuse in Sicily and at Rhegium. Then they came to Puteoli, a city near Naples. From there they would travel to Rome by land. But at Puteoli, Luke says, 'We found brethren.' Paul had found favour in the eyes of the centurion who guarded him. He treated Paul with kindness, allowing him a great deal of liberty.

The first thing Paul did when he came to Puteoli was to search out and find the people who worshipped God there, his brethren (28:14). How these people heard the gospel we are not told. But here, too, God had his elect.

Persecution had scattered God's saints all over the Roman world. And whenever believers were scattered, the leaven of the gospel was spread. Paul made it his business to find those who worshipped God wherever he went. It was as natural for him to do so as it would be for any man passing through a town to look up his relatives who live there. The saints of God are a family. The blood that unites us is the blood of Christ. Paul, Luke and Aristarchus had been sailing for five days among ungodly men with whom they had nothing in common. At Puteoli they found brethren and were refreshed they loved one another immediately. The brethren at Puteoli constrained Paul and his companions to stay with them for seven days. They wanted God's servants to stay over at least one Sunday so that all the church could meet them and hear them preach the gospel of God's free grace in Christ.

3. The brethren from Rome greatly encouraged Paul (28:15)

By one means or another the saints at Rome heard that Paul, who had written to them long before, was on his way to Rome and came out to meet him. They had never met before, yet, they showed great love for God's servant. They were of the same family. They all loved the same Saviour. So they loved each other. Paul thanked God for them and was encouraged by them. They seem to have cheered and inspired the old warrior for the battles he was to face. Someone said, 'A church should be a fellowship of encouragement.' That is what these Roman believers were to Paul. Here is an interesting sidelight: the word translated 'meet' in verse 15 is also found in 1 Thessalonians 4:17, where we are given a beautiful picture of the resurrection of God's saints. When Christ comes again, the dead in Christ will rise first and we who are alive shall be caught up with them to meet the Lord in the air so that we may return with him to his new creation!

4. At last, Paul was delivered as a prisoner to Rome (28:16)

He came to Rome as a prisoner because of his faithfulness to God. There, by God's providence, he was given great liberty to preach the gospel, dwelling in a rented house with a guard constantly at his side. At last Paul had come to Rome to preach the gospel. It seems to have mattered little to him that he came as the prisoner of Rome. As far as he was concerned, he had come there as the prisoner of Jesus Christ by the will of God. He seized the opportunity now set before him to preach the gospel and to write a good portion of the New Testament. Knowing that God had brought him there and that God would use him there, Paul was content, even in Rome (Philippians 4:12). Would you be?

Acts 28:17 And it came to pass, that after three days Paul called the chief of the Jews together: and when they were come together, he said unto them, Men and brethren, though I have committed nothing against the people, or customs of our fathers, yet was I delivered prisoner from Jerusalem into the hands of the Romans.

Acts 28:18 Who, when they had examined me, would have let me go, because there was no cause of death in me.

Acts 28:19 But when the Jews spake against it, I was constrained to appeal unto Caesar; not that I had ought to accuse my nation of.

Acts 28:20 For this cause therefore have I called for you, to see you, and to speak with you: because that for the hope of Israel I am bound with this chain.

Chapter 82

'The hope of Israel'

Acts 28:17-20

Three days after he was delivered to Rome as a prisoner, Paul called the Jews of Rome together. Though despised and abused by his countrymen, he never failed to demonstrate genuine compassion for them. It was ever his prayer and heart's desire for Israel that they might be saved (Romans 10:1). Such compassion for those nearest us is exemplary. It is not selfishness, but the most reasonable expression of love to seek salvation and eternal life in Christ for those God has placed in the nearest relationship to us. If a man does not use his influence to reach those who are most under his influence, he is not likely to earnestly seek the salvation of others. If God does not save those whom we naturally love, we must not murmur and complain. He is sovereign. It is his right to do what he will and to give salvation to whom he will. However, knowing full well that none deserve God's mercy, it would be barbaric for us to let any perish without seeking the salvation of their souls.

Once he had called these Jews together, Paul told them exactly why he had been brought to Rome as a prisoner. He had broken no law, cast no reproach upon the Jewish nation and done nothing in violation of the Holy Scriptures. Paul assured the Jews of his innocence, hoping that they might more readily receive his message. He wanted to remove from their minds anything that might keep them from hearing the gospel he preached.

Then he told them why he had been arrested and brought to Rome and why he had called them together to speak to them. Paul had been arrested and was now a prisoner in Rome for one reason, preaching the gospel of the Lord Jesus Christ. He had proclaimed to men 'the hope of Israel'. He had declared to men that the one of whom all the prophets spoke, in whom all the promises of God must be fulfilled, in whom Abraham, Isaac and Jacob and all the saints of the Old Testament hoped, and for whom they waited, the Messiah, the King, the Son of David, the seed of Abraham, the true Prophet, the true Priest, the true sacrifice, the true Redeemer of Israel, has come, and he is Jesus of Nazareth, the Son of God. For preaching this Christ, Paul stood before these men a prisoner in chains. He had called these Jews together so that he could preach Christ to them. In this passage, Paul identifies the Lord Jesus Christ as 'the hope of Israel'.

381

1. Who is Israel?

Though Paul was addressing men who were by physical birth the descendants of Abraham, they were not part of that Israel of whom Paul spoke. They had no faith in Christ. They were Jews outwardly, but not inwardly. They were a part of the physical nation of Israel, but they were not part of that 'holy nation' called 'the Israel of God'. The promises of God's covenant and the blessings of his grace were never intended for Abraham's natural seed. Grace does not come by natural descent. Mercy does not run in families, neither to Jews nor to Gentiles (John 1:11-13; Romans 9:16).

Many imagine that the Jews as a nation and race have a special claim upon God's promises and that God deals with them in a special way. That is a myth. It is contrary to the gospel of God's free and sovereign grace in Christ. It is written in Holy Scripture that there are no promises to natural Israel that God has not fulfilled. He fulfilled them all a long time ago (see Joshua 21:44, 45). God gave Israel the gospel in the Old Testament, under the types and shadows of the law. Then God sent his Son to preach to them. Even after they crucified the Lord of glory, our Saviour sent his apostles to the Jews first. But after that nation despised Christ and his gospel, in righteous judgment God destroyed them (Matthew 22:1-7). He sent his gospel to the Gentiles that he might gather his elect (his Israel) from the four corners of the earth. This has always been his purpose (28:26-28; Romans 11:25, 26). The physical seed of Abraham are not the special, chosen people of God. The Scriptures are crystal clear in this regard (Romans 2:28; 9:6-8; Galatians 4:22-28).

All who believe the gospel of Christ, Jews and Gentiles of every age, are 'the Israel of God' (Galatians 6:16). Every true believer is a child of Abraham, an Israelite indeed (Romans 2:29; Galatians 3:6, 7; Philippians 3:3). The blessing of Abraham comes to men by the redeeming blood of Christ and the saving power of the Holy Spirit (Galatians 3:13, 14). God's Israel is not physical, but spiritual. Being circumcised in their hearts, they worship God in the Spirit, trust Christ as Saviour and have no confidence in the flesh (Philippians 3:3; Colossians 2:11). Like Abraham, they believe God (John 8:39). All the promises and blessings of God's covenant and grace belong to all the Israel of God (2 Corinthians 1:20; Galatians 3:13-18, 26-29; Ephesians 1:3-6; 2:11-14; 2 Timothy 1:9).

2. Why is the Lord Jesus Christ called 'the hope of Israel'?

Paul called him by this title because the prophets referred to the Messiah by this title (Jeremiah 14:8; 17:13; Joel 3:16). And he is called by this title because all the Israel of God recognize that Christ alone is our hope of salvation (1 Timothy 1:1; Colossians 1:27). Every believer looks to Christ in faith, hoping for and expecting grace, salvation and eternal glory in him (Romans 8:24, 25). We understand, and rejoice in the fact that he is our salvation (Luke 2:30; Romans 8:33-39). The whole work of salvation was finished for us by Christ's sacrifice (John 17:4; 19:28-30). It is complete and perfect in him (Colossians 2:10). This salvation is the free gift of God upon every sinner who, like Abraham, trusts God (Romans 6:23; Ephesians 2:8, 9).

Every true Israelite, every true believer, lives by faith in Christ in the hope and expectation of eternal life. We have it now, but we do not yet enjoy the full perfection of it. We are not yet in heaven; we have not yet been glorified; but, believing Christ, we have confidence that we shall be (Titus 2:11-13; 1 Thessalonians 4:13-18; 1 John 3:1-3). When the Lord Jesus Christ comes again, the whole Israel of God will be raised in his likeness!

3. What does Israel hope to obtain from Christ?

Believing him, we hope to obtain all that Christ, our God-man mediator, is and all he has obtained from God as the reward of his obedience. I fully believe that there is nothing that Christ is, in his mediatorial capacity, and nothing that he has obtained, that we shall not be and have. We shall never share his divinity. We shall not become God! But all his glorious humanity is and has, we shall be and have by virtue of our union with him (John 17:5, 22). It is not yet seen, but this is what we hope for (Romans 8:17, 18, 24, 25). He is freed from all sin, perfectly righteous and holy, perfectly satisfied, completely at rest, in perfect harmony with the triune God, possessing all things! We shall be all of that when he makes all things new!

4. What is the basis of Israel's hope?

In Lamentations 3:21-26 the old prophet cries, 'This I recall to my mind, therefore have I hope.' Then he tells us what his hope is: 'It is of the Lord's mercies that we are not consumed, because his compassions fail not. They are new every morning: great is thy faithfulness. The Lord is my portion, saith my soul; therefore will I hope in him. The Lord is good unto them that wait for him, to the soul that seeketh him. It is good that a man should both hope and quietly wait for the salvation of the Lord.'

Here are two things we who have hope in God's mercies, compassions, faithfulness and goodness must do. We must live a while longer in hope. Hope can see heaven through the thickest clouds. Hope is the mother of patience. We live in hope, expecting God to do what he has promised. We quietly and patiently wait for the salvation of the Lord.

Acts 28:21 And they said unto him, We neither received letters out of Judaea concerning thee, neither any of the brethren that came shewed or spake any harm of thee.

Acts 28:22 But we desire to hear of thee what thou thinkest: for as concerning this sect, we know that every where it is spoken against.

Acts 28:23 And when they had appointed him a day, there came many to him into his lodging; to whom he expounded and testified the kingdom of God, persuading them concerning Jesus, both out of the law of Moses, and out of the prophets, from morning till evening.

Acts 28:24 And some believed the things which were spoken, and some believed not.

Chapter 83

'Some believed ... and some believed not'

Acts 28:21-24

Wherever Paul went, he had only one errand. He was a gospel preacher, an ambassador sent from God with a message to deliver to sinners heading for eternity. Being 'separated unto the gospel' (Romans 1:1), he allowed nothing to turn him aside from his great work, not even imprisonment! He was sent by God to deliver the message of redemption and grace in Christ to perishing souls. He considered nothing to be of equal importance to that. Being God's messenger, his message was always the same. He was determined to know nothing among men except Jesus Christ and him crucified (1 Corinthians 2:2). He considered it his solemn duty, whenever and wherever he preached, to preach the gospel (1 Corinthians 9:16). He was a man of one subject. He was radically, fanatically committed to that one subject. He preached Christ and him crucified (1 Corinthians 1:23). Whatever ability he possessed, whenever he had opportunity, this great exemplary preacher expounded to men and women the doctrine of the cross (Galatians 6:14). Here, Luke gives us an example of the great apostle's message and his method of preaching.

1. Paul preached expositively

'He expounded ... both out of the law of Moses, and out of the prophets.' All true preaching involves the faithful exposition of Holy Scripture. Preaching is not the exposition of a creed or confession of faith. That is denominational indoctrination. Preaching is declaring with simplicity and clarity what is written in Holy Scripture. 'Faith cometh by hearing, and hearing by the Word of God' (Romans 10:17). It is not possible for anyone to trust the Lord Jesus Christ until he is taught by God. And the method by which God teaches chosen sinners is the preaching of the gospel (1 Corinthians 1:21; 1 Peter 1:23-25). It is the responsibility of those who preach the gospel to unfold the wondrous mysteries of the gospel, faithfully expounding the message of the Bible. Many preachers and teachers like to dazzle their hearers with their knowledge and understanding of facts and times and their ability to answer foolish questions and unravel the knots of endless genealogies. God's servants studiously avoid getting caught up in that snare of the devil (2

Timothy 2:23; Titus 3:9). Those men who are faithful to God, faithful to the souls of men and faithful to the Word of God expound the message of Scripture. Essentially, the message of the Bible is threefold.

The first message of the Bible is a message of ruin, the total spiritual ruin of our race by the sin and fall of our father Adam (Romans 5:12). What happened in the garden? Let a man find the answer to that question and he will have little difficulty understanding anything else in the Bible. Adam was much more than the progenitor of our race. He was, by God's decree, the federal head and representative of all men. God made Adam in his own image, holy and righteous, and gave him dominion over all the works of his hands. Adam and his children might have lived for ever in that happy condition, had he simply lived in the acknowledgement of God's righteous dominion over him. God gave Adam everything except the tree of the knowledge of good and evil (Genesis 2:15-17). That one tree stood as a constant reminder to Adam of God's rightful, sovereign dominion.

You know what happened. Adam did not stand in his uprightness. In time his heart swelled with pride. He could not stand the thought of God being God. Because of his pride, he stole the fruit of God's tree. By that act, Adam attempted to usurp God's authority and dominion as God. Immediately, he died spiritually, came under the curse of legal death, began to die physically and became liable to eternal death in hell, and so did we! When Adam sinned, we sinned in him. When he died, we died. Now we all bear the image of our father Adam. All the sons of Adam are born sinners, rebels against God, going astray as soon as they are born, speaking lies (Psalm 51:5; 58:3; Romans 3:9-19; 8:7; Ephesians 2:1-3). This is the doctrine of total depravity. It simply means man is so sinful and so completely helpless in spiritual death that he is incapable of changing his condition, or even assisting in the change of his condition before God (Jeremiah 13:23; 17:9). As Augustus H. Strong said, 'Man is a double-dyed villain. He is originally corrupted by nature and afterwards by practice.'

The second message of the Bible is a message of redemption, redemption by the precious blood of Christ, the second Adam (2 Corinthians 5:18-21; Galatians 3:13; 1 Peter 1:18-20; 2:24). Thank God there is a second Adam, another representative man, another substitute! In exactly the same way that all men were made sinners by Adam's disobedience, all God's elect are made righteous by Christ's obedience unto death as their substitute (Romans 5:17-21; 1 Corinthians 15:21, 22). By his obedience as our representative, Christ brought in perfect righteousness, which is imputed to all who trust him. By that righteousness, we are completely justified in God's sight (Jeremiah 23:6; Romans 3:28-31; 4:21-25). Our works have nothing to do with our righteousness. We are justified by his work being imputed to us. By pouring out his life's blood unto death, our Saviour made a complete atonement for sin, satisfying the justice of God for all who believe on him (Romans 3:24-26). Now God forgives all who trust his Son, justly removing from us both the guilt of sin and the curse of the law (John 3:14-18; Romans 8:1, 33, 34).

The third message of the Bible is a message of regeneration by the irresistible grace and power of God the Holy Spirit (John 3:3-8; Ephesians 2:1-4). This is the new birth. It is not something God offers; it is something God does. Eternal life is the gift of God. The fruit and result of the new birth is faith in Christ. For dead sinners to live, they must be given life. When God creates life in us, he also creates faith (Ephesians 2:8, 9; Colossians 2:12).

2. Paul also preached experimentally

As he expounded the message of Holy Scripture, he 'testified the kingdom of God'. He told his hearers how he had experienced the transforming power and grace of God on the Damascus road. He told his conversion experience so often that I imagine Luke and anyone else who frequently heard him preach knew it as well as he did (9:1-22; 22:1-16; 26:9-19). He never tired of telling what God had done for him. Grace experienced in the heart is worth telling and worth hearing. Someone said, 'No man can really preach anything until he has experienced it.' A man who has experienced grace will preach it.

3. This expository, experimental preaching was persuasive

Paul was 'persuading them concerning Jesus'. He pressed upon his hearers the claims of Christ, urging them to trust him as Saviour (2 Corinthians 5:11). 'And some believed the things which were spoken, and some believed not.' It is ever thus (2 Corinthians 2:14-16). Three things stand out from this fact:

1. The salvation of sinners is not determined by the gifts, abilities or power of the preacher. Those who did not believe heard the same preacher.

2. Those who believe the gospel do so because God, who willed it from eternity, gives them faith in Christ by the power of the Holy Spirit. Faith is not the work of man's free will, but the gift of God's sovereign grace (John 1:12, 13; 3:8; Romans 9:16-18; Ephesians 1:19, 2:8; Colossians 2:12).

3. Those who do not believe choose not to come to Christ and be saved by free grace alone (John 5:40). If any sinner is saved, it is God's action and the result of God's work alone. If any sinner is damned, it is his fault and the result of his work alone. No one is saved because of what he or she does, and no one is lost because of what God does. Salvation is God's work. Destruction is man's work.

387

Acts 28:23 And when they had appointed him a day, there came many to him into his lodging; to whom he expounded and testified the kingdom of God, persuading them concerning Jesus, both out of the law of Moses, and out of the prophets, from morning till evening.

Acts 28:24 And some believed the things which were spoken, and some believed not.

Acts 28:25 And when they agreed not among themselves, they departed, after that Paul had spoken one word, Well spake the Holy Ghost by Esaias the prophet unto our fathers,

Acts 28:26 Saying, Go unto this people, and say, Hearing ye shall hear, and shall not understand; and seeing ye shall see, and not perceive:

Acts 28:27 For the heart of this people is waxed gross, and their ears are dull of hearing, and their eyes have they closed; lest they should see with their eyes, and hear with their ears, and understand with their heart, and should be converted, and I should heal them.

Acts 28:28 Be it known therefore unto you, that the salvation of God is sent unto the Gentiles, and that they will hear it.

Acts 28:29 And when he had said these words, the Jews departed, and had great reasoning among themselves.

Chapter 84

When People Reject The Gospel

Acts 28:23-29

'When they had appointed him a day, there came many to him into his lodging.' It is not at all uncommon for preachers to go to jails and prisons to preach the gospel of Christ to the inmates. But here are men, religious men and their leaders, who were summoned by a prisoner that he might preach the gospel to them! Paul explained to these men, from the Scriptures and his own heart's experience, the nature of God's kingdom. He showed them that, contrary to what they had always been taught, the kingdom of God is not an outward, physical, earthly empire in which Jews rule the world, but an inward, spiritual, heavenly dominion of hearts and lives by the Lord Jesus Christ. Entrance into the kingdom of God is not by birth, but by the new birth (John 3:3-7). The kingdom of God is not a kingdom of pomp and ceremony, but of purity and conversion.

Paul also persuaded these men that Jesus is the Christ. Appealing to the Scriptures, his own experience and reason, he gave irrefutable proof that the crucified man of Nazareth is indeed the Christ, the Son of God. He told them of the Saviour's eternal deity, his incarnation and life of obedience, his death as the sinner's substitute, and his resurrection, ascension and exaltation as Lord of all. He carefully explained to them the glorious gospel doctrine of salvation by grace through Christ, the sinner's substitute. He showed them how that the Son of God brought in everlasting righteousness by his obedience to God as a man and made atonement for chosen sinners by his death upon the cursed tree. He told them of Christ's dominion as a Priest upon the throne, his heavenly intercession and his glorious second advent.

Paul urged these men, his kinsmen, to repent, to trust Christ and be saved by his grace. But, as we saw in the previous chapter, when the sermon was over, 'Some believed the things which were spoken, and some believed not.' Christ is set for the fall of some and the rising again of others. To some he is a stone of stumbling and a rock of offence. To others he is the sure foundation stone and the rock of salvation. Our Lord Jesus came not to bring peace but a sword (Matthew 10:34). This is the sword of division that he brings. Some believe the gospel when they hear it and some blaspheme against the Holy Spirit. The light is set before them, but they shut their eyes.

389

'And when they agreed not among themselves, they departed after that Paul had spoken one word.' These men could not agree among themselves, but they had had enough of Paul's doctrine. As they were getting up to leave in disgust and anger, Paul seems to have said, 'Hold on, I have one more thing to tell you before you go. I must tell you what the result of your obstinate unbelief will be.' Then we read verses 25-28. Because these Jews despised the light of the gospel and rejected the claims of Christ, God withdrew the light of the gospel from them and fixed it so that they could not come to Christ and be saved. Though they were still alive, these men were eternally damned! The lessons in this passage are of immense importance.

1. Reprobation is the wilful rejection of revealed truth (28:25-27)

The gospel promises, 'He that believeth and is baptized shall be saved' (Mark 16:16); 'Whosoever shall call upon the name of the Lord shall be saved' (Romans 10:13). But whenever men and women hear the gospel preached in the power of the Holy Spirit and do not believe it, they are courting eternal reprobation (Luke 13:23-30). Reprobation is the judgment of God that falls upon men and women because of their wilful rejection of the gospel (Proverbs 1:23-33; 29:1; Hosea 4:17; Matthew 21:28-46; 23:37, 38).

Like Pharaoh of old, these Jews hardened their hearts against the gospel of Christ. Therefore God hardened their hearts in unbelief, as he said he would (Isaiah 6:9, 10; Romans 11:8). Prophet after prophet had been sent from one generation to another. At last, God sent one more apostle to preach Christ to them. But 'The heart of this people ... waxed gross!'

Hardening their hearts against the message of free-grace salvation through a crucified substitute, they refused to hear. 'Their ears' were 'dull of hearing.' Being convinced of the truthfulness of Paul's message, but full of enmity towards God, they refused to bow to the claims of Christ. Proud, self-righteous men who will not deny their own merits or seek salvation by trusting the merits of Christ, wilfully shut their eyes to the glory of God in the face of Christ. 'Their eyes have they closed' (28:27; Romans 9:31-33).

Because these men wilfully despised the gospel and rejected the claims of Christ in it, God left them alone. They would not believe. So God fixed it so that they could not believe. God will not trifle with those who trifle with his Son (Jeremiah 7:16). Man's condemnation is the result of wilful unbelief. Matthew Henry was exactly right when he warned, 'Let all that hear the gospel, and do not heed it, tremble at this doom; for, when once they are given up to hardness of heart, they are already in the suburbs of hell!' Judicial reprobation is the just response of God to man's wilful suppression and rejection of undeniable truth (Romans 1:18-28; 2 Thessalonians 2:10-12).

2. God's method of grace is always the same (28:27)

Even as Paul announced terrible judgment upon the reprobate, he tells us plainly what God's method of grace is. When God saves sinners, it is necessary that 'they should see with their eyes, and hear with their ears, and understand with their heart, and should be converted, and I should heal them'. God never deviates from his ordained means of grace.

1. The Lord God causes every sinner whom he intends to save to hear the gospel of Christ. Faith is not a leap in the dark. It is the response of the heart to the Word of God. By one means or another, God will cause the chosen to be instructed in the gospel. Yes, God could save his people without the use of human instrumentality. There is no question about that. But he has chosen not to do so (Romans 10:17; 1 Corinthians 1:23; James 1:18; 1 Peter 1:23-25).

2. Through the preaching of the Word, by the power of his Holy Spirit, God causes chosen sinners to 'see with their eyes,' the Lord Jesus Christ. Salvation comes by revelation (Galatians 1:15, 16). None will trust Christ until he is revealed in them by the power of God the Holy Spirit. And all who see him are irresistibly drawn to him (Zechariah 12:10; 13:1).

3. God saves sinners by giving them understanding hearts. He teaches his elect all things necessary to life and faith in Christ (John 6:44, 45; 1 John 2:20, 27).

4. When God saves a sinner by his grace, he converts him. The grace of God that brings salvation causes rebels to bow before his throne as willing servants. Grace conquers the will, subdues the passions and reconciles the heart to God (1 Thessalonians 1:4-10).

5. When God saves sinners, he heals them of the deadly plague of their hearts, he causes the dead to live, delivering them from bondage, dominion and death of sin (Ezekiel 16:8).

3. God's purpose of grace is immutable (28:28)

We grieve to see multitudes perish in wilful unbelief. But we rejoice to know that man's unbelief does not defeat the purpose of God (Romans 3:3, 4). 'The foundation of God standeth sure!' There is a people to whom the gospel must be sent. And they will believe on Christ (Isaiah 56:8; John 10:16). All the Israel of God must be saved (Romans 11:26). Frequently, the unbelief of some is the instrumental cause of faith in others by the wise arrangement of God's sovereign providence (Romans 11:11, 25, 26, 33-36). All who were chosen by God the Father in eternity were redeemed by God the Son at Calvary and will be called by God the Spirit at the appointed time of love.

Acts 28:30 And Paul dwelt two whole years in his own hired house, and received all that came in unto him,

Acts 28:31 Preaching the kingdom of God, and teaching those things which concern the Lord Jesus Christ, with all confidence, no man forbidding him.

Chapter 85

Paul's Last Two Years

Acts 28:30, 31

The Spirit of God inspired Luke to describe Paul's last two years in very simple, but instructive words. 'And Paul dwelt two whole years in his own hired house, and received all that came in unto him, preaching the kingdom of God, and teaching those things which concern the Lord Jesus Christ, with all confidence, no man forbidding him' (28:30, 31). There are many traditions about Paul and his ministry after he came to Rome, but the Lord has told us nothing more than is contained in those two verses. It is most likely that, at the end of these two years, Paul was executed at Rome by Nero, dying as a martyr for Christ. In this final chapter we shall summarize the message of the book of Acts, review Paul's last two years as a prisoner at Rome and draw some lessons from the things we have seen in Acts.

The book of Acts constantly focuses our attention on five things that must never be overlooked. Throughout these twenty-eight chapters, Luke draws our attention to these five things. Let us lay them to heart.

1. The providential rule of Christ

Luke opens this brief history of the early church by declaring the ascension and exaltation of Christ as Lord over all things. Then he proceeds to show us how that the Lord Jesus Christ, our Saviour, rules the universe to accomplish his will. The abuses, imprisonments, persecutions and hardships suffered by those early believers were constantly overruled by our Lord for the spiritual, eternal good of his church and for the salvation of his elect.

We have seen that all things worked together for good to those who loved God, to those who were the called according to his purpose. The providential rule of Christ over all things sustained God's children in confident hope through all they suffered and did for his name's sake. Let all who trust Christ ever trust and rejoice in his sovereign rule of the universe. If Christ, who is our head, rules all things, then all is well. No matter how things may appear for the moment, our Saviour is accomplishing his will, for his glory and our good in all things (John 17:2; Ephesians 1:20-23).

393

2. The mission of God's church in this world

The church of Christ has been given a definite commission from him. It is our responsibility to carry out that commission. Our Lord said, 'Ye shall be witnesses unto me ... unto the uttermost part of the earth' (1:8). Every believer is a missionary sent by God to confess Christ to men, to carry the message of his greatness, grace and glory to perishing sinners. Every local church is to be a preaching centre from which the gospel of Christ is proclaimed to dying men. Let us renew our commitment to this cause. As the early church went everywhere preaching that Jesus is Lord, let us give our lives to this cause. It is not the mission of God's church to entertain the world, educate the world, heal the world, reform the world, or govern the world. Our singular mission from Christ is to preach the gospel to the world.

3. The offence of the cross

From the very beginning, God's people have been persecuted by the world. As Cain persecuted Abel and Ishmael persecuted Isaac, the religious world persecuted the church of God in the earliest days of Christianity. The cause of persecution was the message the church declared — salvation by God's free grace through Jesus Christ the Lord! Things are no different today. We do not experience the physical violence that our brethren endured in those days, but the message we preach is just as hated and despised by religious people today as it was when Peter and John were imprisoned and Stephen was stoned to death. The doctrine of the cross is an offence to man. We must never expect unconverted men to love the truth of God. As the natural heart is enmity against God, the natural heart hates the gospel of God's free and sovereign grace in Christ. If we preach the gospel, we must not expect anything but wrath and persecution from those who despise the gospel. While the world stands, the offence of the cross will not cease (Galatians 5:11).

4. The vital ministry of the Holy Spirit

Our Lord said, 'Without me ye can do nothing.' What he said of himself is equally true of God the Holy Spirit. We must have the Spirit of God! If the Holy Spirit does not work in us and by us, we can do nothing for the glory of Christ and the eternal good of men. As we read the book of Acts, we are constantly reminded that the ministry of the early church was the ministry of God the Holy Spirit. Let us ever seek his gracious wisdom, power and grace upon us. If we would worship, pray, sing, or do anything for the glory of

God, we must be motivated, guided and governed by God the Holy Spirit. Without him, we can do nothing.

5. The immutability of God's purpose

Throughout this book, we see the purpose of God being accomplished exactly as he would have it. Though all hell resists it, our God performs his will. He is not even slightly hindered by the opposition of men or of Satan himself. 'The foundation of God standeth sure!' Child of God, rejoice! Let nothing discourage you. Let nothing hinder you from doing the will of God. God is faithful. Our God will graciously accomplish his purpose in us and in all things for the glory of his own great name. These are the things we see constantly set before us in the book of Acts. May God keep them always before us and use them to sustain our hearts as we seek to serve his cause in this world.

Lessons from Paul's imprisonment

Paul's two years of imprisonment at Rome are full of instruction. Remember, Paul had done nothing wrong. He was a prisoner at Rome only because he would not be turned aside from what he knew God would have him to do (Acts 20:22-24; 21:10-14). He was a prisoner for two years under Felix. His trip to Rome took at least a year. Then he was held prisoner at Rome for two more years. In all, this faithful man was under constant guard for the last five years of his life.

He looked upon his imprisonment as he did all other things, as an act of God's wise and good providence. He knew that God had brought him to Rome in bonds for the furtherance of the gospel (Philippians 1:12-14). During these two years of imprisonment, Paul did not mope around complaining about how bad things were for him, or talk glowingly of all he had done for Christ, or dream about what he would do in better circumstances. Instead, he used the time and abilities God gave him for the glory of Christ, the good of immortal souls and the furtherance of the gospel. While a prisoner at Rome, this servant of God wrote half the epistles of the New Testament, preached to and trained Onesimus in the faith of Christ and preached the gospel to some in Nero's house and to his guards. As a result of what Paul did during those last two years, untold millions have been converted.

God knew what he was doing when he brought Paul to Rome in chains, and Paul knew that God knew what he was doing (Romans 8:28-30). Therefore he was content (Philippians 4:1-13). Carefully read what Paul wrote during this time and what Luke says of his behaviour. You will not find a single word to indicate any dissatisfaction on his part. Trusting God's providence, he was submissive, thankful and patient to the end. When the time came for him to leave this world, he was ready (2 Timothy 4:6-8).

What should we learn from the things we have seen? Much time could be wisely spent drawing out numerous lessons from just the last two years of Paul's life and ministry. Many more might be found if one takes the time to review the twenty-eight chapters of this book. But, overall, three lessons seem to leap out of these pages of God's inspired Word.

1. Learn to trust God's providence (Genesis 50:20; Romans 8:28).

2. Learn to do what God gives you the ability and opportunity to do for the glory of Christ and the good of immortal souls (Ecclesiastes 9:10).

3. Learn that all who honour God will be honoured by God (1 Samuel 2:30).

Finis

Scripture Index

Scripture Index

Jeremiah cont'd

31:3	223
31:18	281
31:31-34	106, 365
31:34	346
32:17	267
32:37-40	114
32:38-40	365
50:20	346

Lamentations

3:21-26	383
3:24-26	79
3:37	265
3:25	241, 248
5:21	281

Ezekiel

3:15-21	276, 283
11:19	115
11:23	21
16:6-8	123, 224
16:8	118, 167, 223, 301, 338, 391
33:7, 8	144, 283
33:8, 9	194, 252
33:1-16	276, 283
36:21-28	260
36:26	115
36:31	249
37:1-14	123
37:11-14	318
37:9	26

Daniel

2:21	268
3:25	311
4:17	268
4:32	265
4:34, 35	71, 247
4:34, 37	178
4:35, 37	245, 267
6:22	268
7:13, 14	17
9:14	322
12:2	318

Hosea

1:10	184
4:17	192, 221, 324, 390
6:2	333

Joel

2:28	14
2:28-32	31, 260, 290
3:16	382

Amos

3:6	267, 356
5:21-23	309
8:11, 12	217
9:11-12	205

Obadiah

21	193, 220

Jonah

1:4	356
1:12-15	355
2:9	244, 341

Micah

7:18	160

Nahum

1:2, 3	356
1:3	268, 356

Zechariah

2:8	71
12:9, 10	329
12:10	42, 89, 260, 280, 391
13:1	391
14:4	21
14:4, 5	18
14:9	18

Malachi

3:5	227
3:6	79, 213, 267
3:10	365
3:16	138
4:2	138

New Testament

Matthew

1:21	61, 329, 331, 341, 360
1:23	331
2:16	178
3:1, 2	257
3:6	265
3:11	260
3:17	106
5:3-5	279
5:10-12	128
5:14	193
5:14-16	65
5:20	322
5:22	165
5:27-30	319
6:1-5	173
6:1-18	65
6:3	45, 279
6:5	279
6:9	208
6:10	74
6:14, 15	279
6:16	279
6:23	375
6:24	73
6:25-34	365
6:31-33	73
6:33	74, 279, 365
7:1-5	164
7:21-23	264
8:28-34	92
9:13	89
10:11-15	42
10:16	93
10:16-34	241

Scripture Index

Philippians

1:1-8	171
1:6	315, 360, 365
1:12-14	395
1:25	228
1:29	233, 257, 300, 347
2:1-5	96
2:1-8	74, 133
2:3-8	280
2:5-8	65, 198
2:5-11	17, 33, 54
2:6-8	294
2:9	61
2:9-11	37, 38, 50, 61, 198
2:10, 11	54
2:14-16	311
3:2	164
3:3	107, 109, 207, 247, 279, 328, 343, 382
3:4-6	300, 337
3:4-11	294
3:4-14	123
3:6	310
3:8	128
3:9	280
3:10	65
3:20	18
3:21	66
4:1-13	395
4:4	367
4:5	249, 368
4:9	276
4:12	379
4:18	173
4:19	174, 365, 369

Colossians

1:12	183
1:12-14	285
1:12-20	243
1:18-22	38
1:20, 21	159
1:22	38
1:23	357

1:27	64, 115, 300, 383
2:6-8	305
2:8-23	105, 204, 247, 271
2:9	294
2:9, 10	243
2:10	208, 347, 383
2:11	106, 207, 382
2:12	51, 233, 257, 281, 347, 387
2:12-15	54
2:14, 15	159
2:16	273, 291
2:16-23	208, 256
3:1	333
3:1-3	65, 209, 357
3:11	32, 137, 151, 208, 213, 377
3:12	279
3:12-17	149
4:17	283

1 Thessalonians

1:3-10	64
1:4	43
1:4, 5	193, 301
1:4-10	124, 391
1:5	27, 281
1:8	157
1:9	165
4:13-18	17, 60, 243, 294, 318, 329, 334, 339, 365, 383
4:16	18
4:17	379
5:1-6	18
5:12, 13	23, 50, 139, 143, 253, 275, 283, 345, 375, 378
5:16-18	228, 269, 295

5:17	138
5:25	23

2 Thessalonians

1:7-10	18
1:8-10	17
2:10-12	390
2:13	64, 118, 131, 152, 267, 285, 315, 341
2:13, 14	46, 121, 132, 187, 193, 220, 301, 338, 345, 360, 365
2:16	339
3:8, 9	252
3:10	285

1 Timothy

1:1	383
1:4	328
1:5-10	204
1:6, 7	310
1:12-16	121
1:12-17	111, 300
1:15	51
1:16	300
1:19, 20	269
2:11, 12	85, 257, 290
2:12	133
3:1-6	168
3:1-7	75, 118, 144, 198, 215
3:2-7	276
3:4, 5	284
3:7	216
3:8-12	97
3:13	97, 99
3:15	183, 184
3:15, 16	65
3:16	32, 88, 294
4:1-4	306
4:1-5	208, 289
4:12-16	96, 144,

412

Revelation

		5:9-13	134	20:6	306, 318,
1:6	323	5:9-14	61, 79		339
1:7	17, 18	5:11-14	106	20:11, 12	243
1:10	273	5:13	19, 268	20:11-15	249
2:5	89	12:1	22	21:1	355
2:10	101	13:1	355	21:1-5	365
4:11	63, 106	13:8	33	22:11	160
5:5	61	18:4	261	22:19	215
5:9	184	19:11-16	61	22:20	18
5:9, 10	38, 152	19:11-17	17	22:21	272
		20:1-3	54